New Perspectives
on the Irish Diaspora

New Perspectives on the Irish Diaspora

Edited by Charles Fanning

Southern Illinois University Press

Carbondale and Edwardsville

03 02 01 00   4 3 2 1

Library of Congress Cataloging-in-Publication Data

New perspectives on the Irish diaspora / edited by Charles
Fanning.
    p. cm.
Includes bibliographical references and index.
    1. Irish Americans—History. 2. Irish Americans—Social
conditions. 3. Irish—Migrations—History. 4. Ireland—
Emigration and immigration—History. 5. United States—
Emigration and immigration—History. 6. Irish Americans in
literature. 7. American literature—Irish American authors—
History and criticism. I. Fanning, Charles.

E184.I6 N48 2000
973'.049162—dc21   00-025054
ISBN 0-8093-2343-5 (cloth : alk. paper)
ISBN 0-8093-2344-3 (pbk. : alk. paper)

Whin I was a young man in th' ol' counthry, we heerd th' same story about all America. We used to set be th' tur-rf fire o' nights, kickin' our bare legs on th' flure an' wishin' we was in New York, where all ye had to do was to hold ye'er hat an' th' goold guineas 'd dhrop into it. An' whin I got to be a man, I come over here with a ham and a bag iv oatmeal, as sure that I'd return in a year with money enough to dhrive me own ca-ar as I was that me name was Martin Dooley. An' that was a cinch.

But, faith, whin I'd been here a week, I seen that there was nawthin' but mud undher th' pavement,—I larned that be means iv a pick-axe at tin shillin's th' day,—an' that, though there was plenty iv goold, thim that had it were froze to it; an' I come west, still lookin' f'r mines. Th' on'y mine I sthruck at Pittsburgh was a hole f'r sewer pipe. I made it. Siven shillin's th' day. Smaller thin New York, but th' livin' was cheaper, with Mon'gahela rye at five a throw, put ye'er hand around th' glass.

I was still dreamin' goold, an' I wint down to Saint Looey. Th' nearest I come to a fortune there was findin' a quarther on th' sthreet as I leaned over th' dashboord iv a car to whack th' off mule. Whin I got to Chicago, I looked around f'r the goold mine. They was Injuns here thin. But they wasn't anny mines I cud see. They was mud to be shovelled an' dhrays to be dhruv an' beats to be walked. I choose th' dhray; f'r I was niver cut out f'r a copper, an' I'd had me fill iv excavatin'. An' I dhruv th' dhray till I wint into business.

—Finley Peter Dunne ("Mr. Dooley"),
Chicago Evening Post, July 17, 1897

Contents

Acknowledgments   xi

Editor's Introduction   1

Part One
Imagining Irish America

1. Diaspora Comparisons and Irish-American Uniqueness
   Lawrence J. McCaffrey   15
2. Witnessing Two Worlds: Poems
   Eamonn Wall   28
3. That Special Place: Poems and Stories from Irish America
   Terence Winch   40
4. Joseph Mitchell's Irish Imagination
   James Silas Rogers   52
   Illustration on page 57

Part Two
New Perspectives on Pre-Famine Immigration

5. From Ulster to Delaware: Two Poems
   by James Orr about an Eighteenth-Century Emigrant Voyage
   Andrew Carpenter   65
6. "Scotch-Irish" Myths and "Irish" Identities
   in Eighteenth- and Nineteenth-Century America
   Kerby A. Miller   75
7. The "Second Colonization of New England" Revisited:
   Irish Immigration Before the Famine
   Edward J. O'Day   93

Part Three
New Sources for Diaspora Studies

8.   *Rites de Passage:* Rituals of Separation
     in Irish Oral Tradition
     Grace Neville   117
9.   The Reynolds Letters: Sources for Understanding
     the Irish Emigrant Experience in America
     and England, 1865–1934
     Lawrence W. McBride   131
10. Bridget and Biddy: Images of the Irish
     Servant Girl in *Puck* Cartoons, 1880–1890
     Maureen Murphy   152
     Illustrations following page 158
11. "Slide, Kelly, Slide":
     The Irish in American Baseball
     Richard F. Peterson   176

Part Four
New Perspectives on Irish Diasporic Communities

12. The Irish of Chicago's Hull-House Neighborhood
     Ellen Skerrett   189
     Illustrations following page 198
13. Epidemics, Influenza, and the Irish:
     Norwood, Massachusetts, in 1918
     Patricia J. Fanning   223
     Illustrations following page 229
14. The Last Word: Reflections on *Angela's Ashes*
     George O'Brien   236

Part Five
Looking at Fiction of the Diaspora

15. Yank Outsiders: Irish Americans in Gaelic Fiction
    and Drama of the Irish Free State, 1922–1939
    Philip O'Leary   253
16. Donn Byrne: Bard of Armagh
    Ron Ebest   266
17. Winds Blowing from a Million Directions:
    Colum McCann's *Songdogs*
    Eamonn Wall   281
18. Ireland as Source-Country in New Zealand Fiction:
    Dan Davin and Maurice Duggan
    Charles Fanning   289

Contributors   317

Index   321

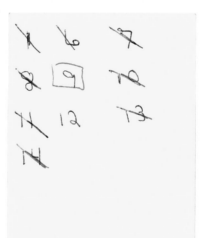

Acknowledgments

Everyone in this collection has contributed lectures, seminars, and readings to the program in Irish and Irish Immigration Studies at Southern Illinois University Carbondale. Many were participants in our Carbondale Symposium on the Irish Diaspora in April 1998. First, heartfelt thanks are due to these dedicated artists and scholars. I also much appreciate the many kindnesses provided by the accomplished, considerate SIUC administrators, faculty, and staff who have made these visits possible, among them Pat Eckert, Rich Falvo, Shari Garnett, Eileen Glass, John Jackson, Rob Jensen, Dick Peterson, and Virginia Williams. My colleagues in the SIUC Faculty Workshop in Irish Studies have been wonderfully supportive, and I thank them for the many insights that have come through our meetings. Over the past several years, our program has been blessed with students of remarkable intelligence and enthusiasm. For their many contributions to this project, I thank SIUC Irish Studies graduate assistants Matt Jockers, John Kavanaugh, Laura Halliday, Eva White, and Meghan Pontbriand, and I owe a special debt of gratitude to Elizabeth Brymer, whose work on this book has been diligent, painstaking, and invaluable.

The following are to be thanked for their kind permission to use materials in this book: Salmon Publishing Ltd., Cliffs of Moher, Ireland, for permission to reprint the following poems by Eamonn Wall—"New Words" and "Hart Crane's Bridge" from *Dyckman-200th Street* (1994), and "Father, Father," "Freewheeling by the Platte River," "The Westward Journey," and "Four Stern Faces/South Dakota," from *Iron Mountain Road* (1997); the Spencer Museum of Art at the University of Kansas-Lawrence for permission to reprint "McSorley's Back Room" by John Sloan; Sheila McGrath for permission to reprint extensive quotations from the work of Joseph Mitchell; and Coffee House Press, Minneapolis, Minnesota, for permission to reprint the following poems by Terence Winch— "Introduction to Dead Mothers" from *Total Strangers* (1982), and "A Remarkable Impression of Harry Truman" and "On the Fire Escape Naked" from *Irish Musicians/American Friends* (1985). These other poems by Terence Winch have also appeared previously: "What I Hear," in the *Journal of the New York Irish History Roundtable;* "On the Sad Height," in *Paris Review;* and "Custodian," in *SOLO.* A quotation from a legal document, *Laura D. Wilck v. Donn Byrne,* appears by courtesy of the Lilly Library, Indiana University, Bloomington, Indiana. Correspondence from the Donn Byrne manuscript collection dated between June 18, 1925, and May 31, 1928, appears by courtesy of the Trustees of the Boston Public Library.

New Perspectives
on the Irish Diaspora

Editor's Introduction

Irish and Irish diaspora studies have always involved multiple disciplinary perspectives. To begin at the beginning, we have John V. Kelleher's sound advice in his address to the inaugural meeting of the American Committee for Irish Studies at the MLA convention in Chicago in December 1961, later published as "Early Irish History and Pseudo-History." Asserting the openness and potential of Irish studies, "There is no corner of the field where you can dig and not strike paydirt," Kelleher went on to say that "compared with our colleagues in other fields we are still miserably poor."

> I would submit to you that our poverty is mostly our own fault. We have not gone about the task the right way. We have never visualized this field in its entirety. Our special areas of study are usually too small and are needlessly separated from one another, with the result that each of us is apt to depend upon too limited a body of information. Most of our historians know too little about Celtic and Anglo-Irish literature. Few of our students or critics of literature know much about Irish history. The celticists and linguists, though their scholarship is generally the most professional within the field, all too seldom have shown sufficient interest in the historical or literary content of what they so skillfully edit. As a rule we do not know enough about the areas that impinge, or should impinge, on our own to ask relevant information from them. How often do we know whom to ask? It is scarcely to our credit that these conditions which have existed for decades have not been remedied before now.[1]

He goes on to credit the newly formed ACIS as "a movement in the right direction," and "the most heartening and hopeful thing that has happened to us in years."

Certainly, Kelleher's own essays were founding exempla of the Irish studies approach: "*The Táin* and the Annals," "Matthew Arnold and the Celtic Revival," "History and Mythology in James Joyce's 'The Dead' "—and a dozen others.[2] These great pieces best illustrate what I believe to be the two governing principles and goals of all such studies work, both Irish studies and other studies: inclusiveness and communicability. For the former, Clifford Geertz's model of "thick description" still holds, with its aim: "to draw large conclusions from small, but very densely textured facts: to support broad assertions about the role of culture in the construction of collective life by engaging them exactly with complex specifics."[3] For the latter, I believe that the aim of scholarly discourse ought still to be what Richard Hoggart has defined as "the idea of a society talking within itself, as a whole." Abjuring the patronizing term *popularization,* Hoggart further declares that "to write in this way . . . is not a matter of writing-down, taking our complex truths, adding water and serving up with a few pally gestures. It is much more a matter of recognizing the extent to which many of our professional languages are unnecessary and defensive."[4] I hope that the essays and creative works collected in this book conform to these principles.

Consideration of the worldwide dispersal of emigrants from Ireland has become a significant emphasis among scholars and artists in the now flourishing field of Irish studies. This is an exciting time in the study of the Irish diaspora, with many new visions and revisions in the air. To put these in context, a brief backward look at the development of the field is in order. In the nineteenth century, as elsewhere in historical writing, an unwinnowed mix of Irish diaspora "history and pseudo-history" was generated in Irish studies. Credible attention to Irish emigration and immigration began during the 1920s, a decade that marked both the end of the greatest sustained exodus of people out of Ireland and the rise of academic scholarship as a profession.

Chicago School sociologist Edith Abbott was an early collector of immigration information, a focus that resulted in her *Immigration: Select Documents and Case Records* (Chicago: University of Chicago Press, 1924) and *Historical Aspects of the Immigration Problem* (Chicago: University of Chicago Press, 1926). The pioneering evenhanded study, in which immigration is not presented as a "problem," was George M. Stephenson's *A History of American Immigration, 1820–1924* (Boston: Ginn and Company, 1926). The first academic book to focus on Irish immigration was William Forbes Adams's *Ireland and Irish Emigration to the New World from 1815 to the Famine* (New Haven: Yale University Press, 1932). Although exhibiting an Anglophile and anti-Catholic slant, Adams did make the first systematic use of government documents and census figures. Further groundwork was laid by other pioneering historians of American immigration largely considered, among them Carl Wittke with *We Who Built America: The Saga of the Immigrant* (New York: Prentice Hall, 1939) and Marcus Lee Hansen with *The Atlantic Migration, 1607–1860* (Cambridge: Harvard University Press, 1940) and *The Immigrant in American History* (Cambridge: Harvard University Press, 1940).

The watershed volume in the scholarly study of urban Irish America was Oscar Handlin's Harvard dissertation, published in 1941 as *Boston's Immigrants, 1790–1865: A Study in Acculturation* (Cambridge: Harvard University Press). On the one hand, this book was a model of painstaking accretion of more detail about a single immigrant group and destination than had previously been seen; on the other, some distortion springs from Handlin's overemphasis on estrangement as the dominant effect of having been "uprooted." Also in the 1940s, John Kelleher began publishing the crystalline essays in which he defined terms and set problems for the study of the immigrant and ethnic cultures of Irish America. These essays included "Mr. Dooley and the Same Old World" (1946), "Irish-American Literature and Why There Isn't Any" (1947), "The Hero as an Irish-American" (1956), "A Long Way from Tipperary" (1960), and "Irishness in America" (1961).[5]

The next generation of scholars, made up primarily of historians and including several students of Oscar Handlin, began to dig deeper and to use more interdisciplinary resources. Two catalysts for their continuing interest in Irish America were, in practical terms, the G.I. Bill of Rights, which gave them the opportunity to attend college and graduate school, and, symbolically, the election to the presidency of Boston Irish American John F. Kennedy in 1960. Key authors and books included Arnold Schrier's *Ireland and the American Emigration, 1850–1900* (New York: Russell & Russell, 1958), which made early use of immigrant letters; George Potter's *To the Golden Door: The Story of the Irish in Ireland and America* (Boston: Little, Brown, 1960), a book densely packed with information but left undocumented by Potter's untimely death; James G. Leyburn's *The Scotch-Irish: A Social History* (Chapel Hill: University of North Carolina Press, 1962), which focused realistic attention on a much-romanticized subculture; William V. Shannon's *The American Irish: A Political and Social Portrait* (New York: Macmillan, 1963), the first book to meld the history, literature, politics, and popular culture of Irish America into an arresting overview; Stephan Thernstrom's *Poverty and Progress: Social Mobility in a Nineteenth-Century City* (Cambridge: Harvard University Press, 1964), which further honed the historian's statistical tools in a close look at Newburyport, Massachusetts; Edward M. Levine's *The Irish and Irish Politicians: A Study of Cultural and Social Alienation* (Notre Dame: University of Notre Dame Press, 1966), which examined ethnicity and urban political culture, especially in Chicago; and Thomas N. Brown's *Irish-American Nationalism, 1870–1890* (Philadelphia: Lippincott, 1966), which used sources both Irish and American, both literary and journalistic, to provide a profound revision of accepted views of the origins and nature of immigrant nationalist feeling for the old country.

During the 1970s, Irish-American scholarly research contributed to the heightened ethnic consciousness among descendants of European emigrants, who had been inspired by the example of African American self-awareness during the Civil Rights movement. For the Irish, a further catalyst was the increased attention that accompanied the renewal of sectarian violence in Northern Ireland. This decade marked the emergence of a new generation of American academics whose work built on the solid bibliography achieved in the 1960s. Continuing into the 1980s, much of the valuable new scholarship consisted of exploration of various immigrant destinations and subcultures, including studies of the Irish in Philadelphia,

Detroit, Chicago, New Orleans, San Francisco, Milwaukee, Lowell (Massachusetts), and Butte (Montana).[6]

Also in the 1970s, the field welcomed four scholars whose own work and encouragement of others have done a great deal to shape Irish diaspora studies over the past thirty years. Andrew M. Greeley published *That Most Distressful Nation: The Taming of the American Irish* (Chicago: Quadrangle Books, 1973), which brought the tools of sociology to bear on the evidence to date. Dennis Clark published *The Irish in Philadelphia: Ten Generations of Urban Experience* (Philadelphia: Temple University Press, 1973), the first of his many engagements with previously neglected Irish-American subcultures. Lawrence J. McCaffrey published *The Irish Diaspora in America* (Bloomington: Indiana University Press, 1976), an exhortative summary of scholarship up to that point. Finally, at the turn of the decade, in *Irish Historical Studies* for September 1980, came a provocative essay by Kerby Miller (with Bruce Boling and David N. Doyle) titled "Emigrants and Exiles: Irish Cultures and Irish Emigration to North America, 1790–1922."[7] This piece presented the thesis that a Catholic worldview of dependency, fatalism, and passivity caused emigrants from Ireland to see themselves as unwilling exiles, doomed to pervasive alienation in the New World. As fleshed out a few years later in Miller's book, *Emigrants and Exiles: Ireland and the Irish Exodus to North America* (New York: Oxford University Press, 1985), this thesis has been much challenged. (Indeed, the debate goes on in these pages as well.) Yet one thing is clear. Miller has served the field well, both by his creation of a benchmark of controversy that has provoked further work and by his exemplary use of detailed epistolary evidence.[8] It is also worth noting that measuring the degree of success and the psychological health of the Irish in America is part of the larger and probably unresolvable argument within immigration studies between those who emphasize the positive—adaptability, assimilation, "making it,"—and those who present the darker side of the story—racism, prejudice, discrimination. Since the late 1970s, the poles of this debate have been expressed in opposing historical syntheses, such as John Bodnar's *The Transplanted: A History of Immigrants in Urban America* (Bloomington: Indiana University Press, 1985) and Ronald Takaki's *Iron Cages: Race and Culture in Nineteenth-Century America* (New York: Knopf, 1979).

In the 1980s, two additional areas of Irish diaspora studies began to be explored: separate consideration of women, and significant forays into immigrant destinations other than the United States. Stimulated by increased academic attention to women's studies, Hasia Diner pioneered the former area in her *Erin's Daughters in America: Irish Immigrant Women in the Nineteenth Century* (Baltimore: Johns Hopkins University Press, 1983). The related study of the crucial role of religious orders in immigrant life began with Eileen M. Brewer's *Beyond Utility: The Role of the Nun in the Education of American Catholic Girls, 1860–*

1920 (Chicago: Loyola University Press, 1987), and much important work continues to be done.[9]

Scholarly investigation of the Irish diaspora worldwide also began in earnest during the 1980s. For the Antipodean Irish, the trailblazing scholar has been Patrick O'Farrell, whose *The Irish in Australia* (Kensington: New South Wales University Press, 1986) set the standard for all subsequent studies. This investigation has continued with O'Farrell's *Vanished Kingdoms: Irish in Australia and New Zealand* (Kensington: New South Wales University Press, 1990) and David Fitzpatrick's innovative epistolary study, *Oceans of Consolation: Personal Accounts of Irish Migration to Australia* (Ithaca: Cornell University Press, 1994).[10] For the Irish in Great Britain, the studies that began the new work were Lynn Hollen Lees's *Exiles of Erin: Irish Migrants in Victorian London* (Ithaca: Cornell University Press, 1979) and M. A. G. Ó Tuathaigh's 1981 essay "The Irish in Nineteenth-Century Britain: Problems of Integration."[11] Substantial subsequent research has been collected in two anthologies edited by Roger Swift and Sheridan Gilley, *The Irish in the Victorian City* (London: Croom Helm, 1985) and *The Irish in Britain, 1815–1939* (London: Pinter, 1989).[12] For the Irish in Canada, a valuable two-volume compendium, edited by Robert O'Driscoll and Lorna Reynolds, is *The Untold Story: The Irish in Canada* (Toronto: Celtic Arts, 1988), and the first modern survey of the territory was Cecil J. Houston and William J. Smyth's *Irish Emigration and Canadian Settlement: Patterns, Links, and Letters* (Toronto: University of Toronto Press, 1990).

In the widening gyre of Irish diaspora studies, a strong voice urging reevaluation has been that of Donald Harman Akenson. In *Being Had: Historians, Evidence, and the Irish in North America* (Toronto: P. D. Meany, 1985) and *Small Differences: Irish Catholics and Irish Protestants, 1815–1922: An International Perspective* (Kingston, Ont.: McGill-Queen's University Press, 1988), Akenson called into question the generally accepted idea that most Irish immigration to North America has been urban and Catholic. In *The Irish Diaspora: A Primer* (Toronto: P. D. Meany, 1993), he urged continuing comparative study of the Irish in North America, Australia, New Zealand, Great Britain, and South Africa.

My own scholarship has involved discovering, making available, and beginning discussion of the imaginative literature of Irish America. Two of my publications—*Mr. Dooley and the Chicago Irish: The Autobiography of an American Ethnic Group,* which is an anthology of Finley Peter Dunne's 1890s newspaper pieces, and *The Exiles of Erin: Nineteenth-Century Irish-American Fiction*—were compilations of one hundred years of mostly neglected but valuable fiction by Irish immigrant and ethnic writers. My synthesizing literary history has been *The Irish Voice in America: 250 Years of Irish-American Fiction.* Throughout, my argument has been that, as the most extended and continuous body of literature by members of a single American ethnic group available to us, Irish-American writing is a unique resource for understanding the human dimension of the Irish diaspora and its American aftermath.[13]

In recent years, diaspora studies have continued to expand, most notably into the area of popular culture. Useful books for understanding Irish America include Michael T. Isenberg's *John L. Sullivan and His America* (Urbana: University of Illinois Press, 1988), Joseph M. Curran's *Hibernian Green on the Silver Screen: The Irish and American Movies* (New York: Greenwood Press, 1989), William H. A. Williams's *'Twas Only an Irishman's Dream: The Image of Ireland and the Irish in American Popular Song Lyrics, 1800–1920* (Urbana: University of Illinois Press, 1996), and Kevin Kenny's *Making Sense of the Molly Maguires* (New York: Oxford University Press, 1998). An important stimulus of other recent work has been the commemoration of the 150th anniversary of the Great Hunger of the late 1840s. In addition to the many new perspectives on the Famine as a catastrophe centered in Ireland, there have been several essay collections and monographs that have focused attention on the consequent flood tide of emigration.[14]

It has been clear now for decades that the large size and complexity of Irish diaspora studies require concerted scholarly efforts. Happily, in the 1990s, these efforts have begun to appear. Patrick J. Blessing's indispensable bibliographical volume, *The Irish in America: A Guide to the Literature and the Manuscript Collections* (Washington, D.C.: Catholic University of America Press), came out in 1992. A much needed, one-thousand-page research tool edited by Michael Glazier, *The Encyclopedia of the Irish in America* (Notre Dame: University of Notre Dame Press), was published in 1999. Of great value have been the summary chapters on emigration in volume 5, *Ireland Under the Union I, 1801–70*, and volume 6, *Ireland Under the Union II, 1870–1921*, of *A New History of Ireland* (ed. W. E. Vaughan; Oxford: Clarendon Press, 1989 and 1996).[15]

Three recent studies on three different levels of inquiry illustrate the richness of the field and the efficacy of cooperative ventures. For the smallest urban ethnic unit, the neighborhood parish, we have the essays involving history, literature, politics, popular culture, art, and architecture collected by editor Ellen Skerrett in *At the Crossroads: Old St. Patrick's and the Chicago Irish* (Chicago: Loyola University Press, 1997). For a large city, we have *The New York Irish* (Baltimore: Johns Hopkins University Press, 1996), edited by Ronald H. Bayor and Timothy J. Meagher, in which twenty essays span more than two hundred years and engage aspects of social, political, religious, labor, and medical history as well as music, literature, and the Irish language. Finally, for the entire global dispersal, we have Patrick O'Sullivan's monumental series of edited volumes, *The Irish World-Wide,* of which half a dozen have appeared since *Volume One: Patterns of Migration* (Leicester, Eng.: Leicester University Press, 1992).[16]

The goal of this book is further illustration at the turn of the millenium of the creative, critical, and analytical energies of Irish immigrants, their descendants, and those who study the Irish diaspora. In this collection are eighteen new perspectives on Irish immigration during three centuries and around the world. The sources presented and examined include poems, creative essays and meditations, works of fiction, personal letters, cartoon representations, journalism, archived oral-history interviews, naturalization records, and the bricks and mortar of buildings, inside and out. Scholarly tools employed come from the disciplines of history, sociology, literary criticism, the visual arts and architecture, folklore, and popular culture studies.

Part one, "Imagining Irish America," begins with "Diaspora Comparisons and Irish-American Uniqueness" by Lawrence J. McCaffrey, a founder and guiding spirit of Irish immigration studies. Here the views of Kerby Miller and Donald Akenson, McCaffrey's fellow pioneers in defining the field, are engaged insightfully, and again our sense of the complexity of immigrant experience is expanded. This opening salvo is followed by the immediacy of recent creative work by two contemporary artists—poems by Eamonn Wall, an Irish immigrant to New York and Nebraska, and poems and stories by Terence Winch, the son of Irish immigrants to New York City. The fourth chapter is an exploration by James Rogers of the influence of urban Irishness on the imagination of legendary *New Yorker* writer Joseph Mitchell. The piece is a seminal reckoning of the subtle impact of an ethnic subculture beyond the pale of the Irish themselves.

Part two, "New Perspectives on Pre-Famine Immigration," contributes much new information to the least studied of the major diasporic periods—immigration during the eighteenth and early nineteenth centuries. Reclamation of forgotten writing is an essential thrust of new work in this field, and in chapter 5 Andrew Carpenter presents and glosses two poems of emigration "from Ulster to Delaware" by James Orr, one of many eighteenth-century Irish poets whose work Carpenter has resurrected. Following the labor of his major summary volume, *Emigrants and Exiles*, Kerby Miller has continued to scrutinize and sharpen our sense of the varieties of diasporic Irishness. In chapter 6 here, he clarifies the distinction of "Scotch-Irishness" in an essay that illustrates the importance of "thick description," including petitions and legal depositions as well as letters, in shaping our understanding of what such problematic labels actually meant. Similarly, in chapter 7, Edward J. O'Day demonstrates the usefulness of yet another early primary source. His analysis of five thousand naturalization records of pre-Famine immigrants shines the light of sharp, contextual detail on pioneering immigration historian Marcus Lee Hansen's early (1929) identification of "the second colonization of New England."

Part three, "New Sources for Diaspora Studies," focuses on new and exciting directions in current diaspora studies. In chapter 8, Grace Neville illustrates the great wealth of primary source material available to scholars who work in the

Irish language. Here she mines the wonderfully rich vein of the Irish Gaelic archives of the Irish Folklore Commission in Dublin to give us a vivid comprehension of the separation ritual of the "American wake" in late-nineteenth- and early-twentieth-century Ireland. Drawing once again from the great horn of plenty that is epistolary evidence, Lawrence W. McBride presents, annotates, and illustrates in chapter 9 the value of a trove of family letters that spans seventy years and two immigrant destinations, England and America. Maureen Murphy then presents in chapter 10 new material from the popular visual arts by charting and analyzing cartoon renderings of the Irish servant girls Bridget and Biddy in the American humor magazine *Puck* during the 1880s. Finally, combining his scholarly fields of Irish and American cultures, Richard F. Peterson strikes out into new territory in chapter 11 by examining perceptions of the Irish in the early history of baseball.

In part four, "New Perspectives on Irish Diasporic Communities," three very different places come to life through the application of three scholarly disciplines. Chapter 12 is a strongly revisionist essay in which historian Ellen Skerrett observes with fresh eyes one of America's most famous neighborhoods, the streets of Chicago's Near West Side, which has been known mostly as the site of Jane Addams's Hull-House. Skerrett's work emphasizes the primacy of "sacred space" in urban ethnic experience. In a community study with wide ramifications, sociologist Patricia Fanning looks in chapter 13 at the potent conjunction of illness and ethnicity in a New England town—Norwood, Massachusetts—during the great influenza epidemic of 1918. Then, in chapter 14, writer and critic George O'Brien provides a balanced assessment of the Irish-American publishing sensation of the late 1990s, Frank McCourt's amazingly popular *Angela's Ashes*. Himself an accomplished memoirist, O'Brien here examines relations between Ireland and Irish America and between fact and imagination in autobiography.

Imaginative literature constitutes the most accessible body of primary material available to us for discerning new perspectives on the Irish diaspora. Again, the words of Richard Hoggart are helpful. In an essay titled "Literature and Society," he states that literature has "documentary" value for illuminating a society and that it is first of all "a source of raw material from whatever period one is studying, a quarry to be raided for 'background.'" However, he then goes on to assert that literature provides the student of a society with something dramatically more valuable than mere illustration: "Works of literature give an insight into the life of an age, a kind and intensity of insight, which no other source can give." In particular, "good literature recreates the experiential wholeness of life—the life of the emotions, the life of the mind, the individual life and the social life, the object-laden world."[17]

The essays of part five, "Looking at Fiction," are meant to illustrate this precious, yet still underutilized, resource for immigration studies. In the first piece, chapter 15, Philip O'Leary opens another crucial, and for many scholars still closed, window into Irish-language sources by tracing the figure of the "returned Yank" in Irish Gaelic literature published in the 1920s and 1930s. In chapter 16, drawing on original manuscript and epistolary sources as well as fiction, Ron Ebest presents a portrait of a nearly forgotten but once culturally central Irish-American original: novelist Donn Byrne, the self-styled "Bard of Armagh." In chapter 17, poet Eamonn Wall places the fiction of his fellow Irish/American "nomad" Colum McCann in the burgeoning corpus of "New Irish" writing. As advocated by Patrick O'Farrell, Donald Akenson, and others, comparative study of different immigrant destinations is one of the great waves of the future for diaspora studies writ large. My own contribution in this book's final chapter is a discussion of two twentieth-century fictional chroniclers of Irish New Zealand, Dan Davin and Maurice Duggan. Born and raised as far away from Ireland as it is possible to get, these very different writers were nonetheless both drawn to their parents' homeland as a "source country" in ways that can help us to better understand immigration and ethnicity in our own and in other times.

Notes

1. John V. Kelleher, "Early Irish History and Pseudo-History," *Studia Hibernica* III (1963): 114.
2. "*The Táin* and the Annals," *Eriu* 22 (1971): 107–27; "Matthew Arnold and the Celtic Revival," in *Perspectives of Criticism*, ed. Harry Levin (Cambridge: Harvard University Press, 1950), 197–221; "History and Mythology in James Joyce's 'The Dead,'" *Review of Politics* 27, no. 3 (July 1965): 414–33.
3. Clifford Geertz, *Interpretation of Cultures* (New York: Basic Books, 1973), 28.
4. Richard Hoggart, *On Culture and Communication* (New York: Oxford University Press, 1972), 37, 36.
5. "Mr. Dooley and the Same Old World," *Atlantic Monthly*, June 1946, 119–25; "Irish-American Literature and Why There Isn't Any," *Irish Writing* (Cork, Ireland, November, 1947), 71–81; "The Hero as an Irish-American," *New York Times Book Review*, 5 February 1956, 1 [a review of Edwin O'Connor's *The Last Hurrah*]; "A Long Way from Tipperary," *Reporter* 22 (12 May 1960), 44–46; and "Irishness in America," *Atlantic Monthly*, July 1961, 38–40.
6. Dennis Clark, *The Irish in Philadelphia: Ten Generations of Urban Experience* (Philadelphia: Temple University Press, 1973); Jo Ellen Vinyard, *The Irish on the Urban Frontier: Nineteenth-Century Detroit, 1850–1880* (New York: Arno Press, 1976); Lawrence J. McCaffrey et al., eds., *The Irish in Chicago* (Urbana: University of Illinois Press, 1987); Earl F. Niehaus, *The Irish in New Orleans, 1800–1860* (Baton Rouge: Louisiana State University Press, 1965); R. A. Burchell, *San Francisco Irish, 1848–1880* (Berkeley and Los Angeles: University of California Press, 1980); Kathleen N. Conzen, *Immigrant Milwaukee, 1836–1860* (Cambridge: Harvard University Press, 1976); Brian C.

Mitchell, *The Paddy Camps: The Meaning of Community among the Irish in Lowell, Massachusetts, 1821–1861* (Urbana: University of Illinois Press, 1986); David M. Emmons, *The Butte Irish: Class and Ethnicity in an American Mining Town, 1875–1925* (Urbana: University of Illinois Press, 1989).

7. *Irish Historical Studies* 22, no. 86 (September 1980), 97–125.

8. Subsequent Irish-American research by these four scholars includes Andrew M. Greeley, *The Irish Americans: The Rise to Money and Power* (New York: Harper and Row, 1981); Dennis Clark, *Hibernia America: The Irish and Regional Cultures* (Westport: Greenwood Press, 1986) and *Erin's Heirs: Irish Bonds of Community* (Lexington: University Press of Kentucky, 1991); Lawrence J. McCaffrey, *Textures of Irish America* (Syracuse: Syracuse University Press, 1992) and *The Irish Catholic Diaspora in America* (Washington, D.C.: Catholic University of America Press, 1997); and Kerby Miller, *To Ye Land of Canaan, 1660–1814*, the first volume of his edition of Irish emigrant letters, forthcoming from Oxford University Press.

9. Other relevant studies include Suellen Hoy, "The Journey Out: The Recruitment and Emigration of Irish Religious Women to the United States, 1812–1914," *Journal of Women's History* 6 (winter-spring 1995): 64–98; Suellen Hoy, "Caring for Chicago's Women and Girls: The Sisters of the Good Shepherd, 1859–1911," *Journal of Urban History* 23 (March 1997): 260–94; Suellen Hoy, "Walking Nuns: Chicago's Irish Sisters of Mercy," in Ellen Skerrett, ed., *At the Crossroads: Old Saint Patrick's and the Chicago Irish* (Chicago: Loyola University Press, 1997), 39–51; Janet Nolan, *Ourselves Alone: Women's Emigration from Ireland 1885–1920* (Lexington: University Press of Kentucky, 1989); Joan Grant, ed., *Women, Migration and Empire* (Stoke-on-Trent, England: Trentham Books, 1996); Christiane Harzig, ed., *Peasant Maids, City Women: From the European Countryside to Urban America* (Ithaca: Cornell University Press, 1997); and Trevor McClaughlin, ed., *Irish Women in Colonial Australia* (St. Leonards, N.S.W., Australia: Allen & Unwin, 1998).

10. See also Patrick O'Farrell, ed., *Letters from Irish Australia 1825–1929* (Sydney: New South Wales University Press, 1984); Colm Kiernan, ed., *Australia and Ireland 1788–1988: Bicentenary Essays* (Dublin: Gill & Macmillan, 1986); Donald Harman Akenson *Half the World from Home: Perspectives on the Irish in New Zealand 1860–1950* (Wellington: Victoria University Press, 1990); Lyndon Fraser, *To Tara via Holyhead: Irish Catholic Immigrants in Nineteenth-Century Christchurch* (Auckland: Auckland University Press, 1997); and Thomas Keneally, *The Great Shame: A Story of the Irish in the Old World and the New* (London: Chatto & Windus, 1998).

11. *Transactions of the Royal Historical Society* 31 (1981): 149–73.

12. A useful summary of the field to date is Graham Davis's *The Irish in Britain, 1815–1914* (Dublin: Gill & Macmillan, 1991). See also T. M. Devine, ed., *Irish Immigrants and Scottish Society in the Nineteenth and Twentieth Centuries* (Edinburgh: University of Edinburgh Press, 1991), and Donald M. MacRaild, *Irish Migrants in Modern Britain, 1750–1922* (New York: St. Martin's Press, 1999).

13. See Charles Fanning, ed., *Mr. Dooley and the Chicago Irish: The Autobiography of an American Ethnic Group* (Washington, D.C.: Catholic University of America Press, 1987); *The Exiles of Erin: Nineteenth-Century Irish-American Fiction* (1987; Chester

Springs: Dufour Editions, 1997); and *The Irish Voice in America: 250 Years of Irish-American Fiction* (1990; Lexington, University Press of Kentucky, 1999).

14. See D. Hollett, *Passage to the New World: Packet Ships and Irish Famine Emigrants, 1845–1851* (Abergavenny, Gwent, Great Britain: P. M. Heaton, 1995); Edward Laxton, *The Famine Ships: The Irish Exodus to America, 1846–51* (London: Bloomsbury, 1996); E. Margaret Crawford, ed., *The Hungry Stream: Essays on Emigration and Famine* (Belfast: Institute of Irish Studies, 1997); Frank Neal, *Black '47: Britain and the Irish Famine* (New York: St. Martin's Press, 1998); and Arthur Gribben, ed., *The Great Famine and the Irish Diaspora in America* (Amherst: University of Massachusetts Press, 1999).

15. In volume 5 (1989), these are chapters 23, "Emigration, 1801–70," and 24, "'A Peculiar Tramping People': The Irish in Britain, 1801–70," by David Fitzpatrick (pp. 562–660); chapter 30, "The Irish in Australia and New Zealand, 1791–1870," by Patrick O'Farrell (pp. 661–81); and chapter 31, "The Irish in North America, 1776–1845," by David Noel Doyle (pp. 682–725). In volume 6 (1996), these are chapters 21, "Emigration, 1871–1921," and 22, "The Irish in Britain, 1871–1921," by David Fitzpatrick (pp. 606–702); chapter 23, "The Irish in Australia and New Zealand, 1870–1990," by Patrick O'Farrell (pp. 703–24); and chapter 24, "The Remaking of Irish America, 1845–80," by David Noel Doyle (pp. 725–63).

16. All edited by Patrick O'Sullivan for Leicester University Press; other volumes include *The Irish in the New Communities* (1992), *The Creative Migrant* (1994), *Irish Women and Irish Migration* (1995), *Religion and Identity* (1996), and *The Meaning of the Famine* (1997).

17. Richard Hoggart, "Literature and Society," in *Speaking to Each Other: Volume II, About Literature* (London: Chatto & Windus, 1970), 19–20.

Part One

Imagining Irish America

1

Diaspora Comparisons
and Irish-American Uniqueness

Lawrence J. McCaffrey

Frequently, Donald H. Akenson has chided some historians of Irish America for discussing our subject in isolation from other branches of the diaspora. He says that this has led to falsification, or the substitution of myth for reality. Akenson labels associations of the term *Irish* with the term *Catholic*, which are often made by others and by me, as racist. He insists that roots in a country rather than religious affiliation delineates nationality, and that those of Anglo-Irish Protestant and Ulster Presbyterian stock are just as Irish as are Catholics. To prove his point, Akenson refers to religious identification surveys by the National Opinion Research Center, Gallup Poll, and Graduate Center of the City University of New York that indicate that most of the forty million plus Americans claiming such a heritage are non-Catholics.

Citing relatively rapid economic and social mobility in Australia, Canada, New Zealand, South Africa, and the United States, Akenson disputes Kerby Miller's thesis that premodern Gaelic and religious facets of their cultural inheritance left Irish Catholic emigrants psychologically disabled for the competitive, Protestant, capitalist, urban-industrial, English-speaking world outside Ireland. Their successes indicate that most did not exist as unhappy, dysfunctional New World aliens lamenting their "exile" from the Old World. Akenson also dismisses experiences with and memories of British oppression in Ireland as the main source of Irish-American nationalism, suggesting that poverty and nativist prejudices in the United States have been more important.

Pointing to large Irish Catholic rural settlements in Canada and Australia, Akenson ridicules my explanation that inefficient agricultural skills and Catholic and Gaelic gregariousness and communalism directed Irish immigrants to American cities. He insists that Canadian and Australian examples prove that these immigrants were capable of efficient large-scale farming and of adapting to the isolation of rural life. Comparing the Canadian and American situations, and citing 1870 census figures that locate only 44.5 percent of Irish immigrants in cities with populations greater than twenty-five thousand, Akenson rejects the urban identity of Catholic Irish America, implying that the other 55.5 percent were rural dwellers. He charges that I and other historians of Irish America exaggerate its bleak, urban beginnings to manufacture a heroic ethnic journey from economic and social insignificance to significance. In doing so, he blames us for disrespecting the character and potential of the people we write about.[1]

Joined by Malcolm Campbell, a historian of the Australian Irish, Akenson urges scholars researching and writing about the Irish in the United States to pay attention to those who settled in other parts of the English-speaking world. Akenson and Campbell promise that such an effort would give these scholars' work a broader, richer, more cosmopolitan texture.[2]

Knowledge of and comparisons with other branches of the diaspora could provide fresh insights into Irish America. In addition to Great Britain and the Commonwealth countries, this is true for other places. For example, the situation in Argentina verifies Akenson's contention that Gaelic and religious features of their personalities did not prevent the economic and social advance of Irish Catholic immigrants and their descendants. In addition to chronicling success stories, there are other questions concerning the total diaspora worthy of attention. Did Catholicism play an essential role in the lives of the Irish wherever they went? If so, how? Throughout the British Commonwealth, did the Irish share space and compete for power and influence with Anglo Protestants similar to the way they did in the United States? Have the sources, character, objectives, and expressions of Irish nationalism been the same among the Irish in Argentina, Australia, Britain, Canada, New Zealand, and America? Does Irish politics throughout the diaspora exhibit a unique style, the same genius for mobilizing and organizing public opinion apparent in religion and the labor movement as well as in government?

Obviously, comparative analyses of the politics, nationalism, economic and social mobility, fascination with and skill in athletics, achievements in various aspects of show business and the theater, and religious and literary expressions of the Irish in various parts of the world can shed some light on the Irish-American personality. But examining adjustments to the United States and its various regions can be even more significant, interesting, and revealing.

While Irish Catholics throughout the diaspora have retained much of the cultural baggage carried from Ireland, this baggage has been transformed by adaptations to new environments. In the United States, Irish Catholics have become increasingly American. Even their religious perspective has been significantly modified by interaction with a pluralistic, Protestant-spirited, politically liberal environment. And, of course, similar Irish accommodations have occurred in other places. Since 1985, when Oxford University Press published Kerby Miller's impressively researched and presented *Emigrants and Exiles: Ireland and the Irish Exodus to North America,* many scholars, students, and general readers have accepted his interpretation of Irish Catholic immigrants as alienated exiles from a premodern world. In reality, these immigrants have been human chameleons quickly conforming to new situations, embracing and reflecting the virtues and vices, ambitions and prejudices, of adopted homelands.

While he has offered interesting and valuable information in his exploration of Irish diaspora history, Akenson also has presented distortions, especially on the subjects of religion and urban settlement. Today, among many of the Irish in the United States and elsewhere, including Ireland with the exception of the Six Counties in the North, Catholicism no longer reigns as the core of their nationality or cultural identity. Not so long ago it defined both. Stage, screen, and literary stereotypes of Irish clerics, politicians, athletes, teachers, domestic servants, policemen, firemen, soldiers, sailors, and marines were Catholics. Most Irish immigrants arrived in nineteenth-century American cities without a unique language and before Ireland began to develop a respected literary tradition. They resembled peasants in the "Proem" introducing the main text of *King of the Beggars,* Sean O'Faolain's brilliant and perceptive biography of Daniel O'Connell. O'Faolain described their Catholicism as "not an inconsiderable possession. . . . They had, in a word, with that one exception of their faith, nothing, neither a present, nor a past, nor a future."[3]

Given American opportunities, most of the Irish economically and socially advanced from proletarian pioneers of the American urban ghetto to prosperous, well-educated, influential, middle-class suburbanites, but prior to the 1970s, Catholicism continued as the intrinsic element and the symbol of who they were. It was, as Patrick O'Farrell described in *Ireland's English Question,* "a set of values, a culture, a historical tradition, a view on the world, a disposition of mind and heart, an emotion, a psychology—and a nationalism."[4] In the more recent work *The Lie of the Land: Irish Identities,* Fintan O'Toole has described "Irish Catholic" as words meaning something more than "a person of a specific faith born in a specific country. They have also come to stand for something born out of a fusion of the other two—a country, a culture, a politics. Catholicism in Ireland has been a matter of public identity more than of private faith. . . ."[5] The same could be said of Catholicism and the Irish in the United States and other lands as well. American as well as Irish experiences cemented ties between religion and nationality in grim urban settings in the United States. Catholicism persisted as culture, community, ethnicity, and a psychological as well as a spiritual comfort station. For former tenant farmers and agricultural laborers suffering, yet enduring, the traumatic shock of city life, it was a bridge of familiarity between the Old and New Worlds. Emotionally and socially, Catholic urban parishes took on the coloring and functions of rural Irish villages.

Wherever the Irish settled in the English-speaking world, they encountered Anglo-Protestant religious prejudice, but it was considerably more virulent in the United States than in Great Britain or Britain's colonies that became Dominions within the Commonwealth. The most zealous anti-Catholics left Britain for North America, often because they believed that the established Church of England was tainted with popery. In the New World they hoped to create pure Christian communities, free from Roman influences. Invading and polluting American cities, seizing the reins of political power, providing leadership for a labor movement that threatened unlimited capitalism, and creating a Catholicism large in number and strong in institutional foundations, Irish immigrant hordes nourished Anglo-American Protestant fears and fantasies. From the early nineteenth century through the 1960 presidential election, the Irish were the principal target of the passionate anti-Catholic dimension of American nativism.

For a time, Anglo-Irish Protestants and Ulster Presbyterians in the thirteen colonies and later the United States displayed some empathy for the plight of impoverished Irish Catholic immigrants. But increasing religious antagonisms in Ulster and the no-popery focus of American nativism encouraged them to reject Irish identities. Presbyterians from what is now Northern Ireland, their descendants, and even Protestants with non-Ulster roots began and continued to define themselves as Scotch Irish and joined the anti-Catholic crusade. Their attitude resembled that of John Taylor MP, the current vice-chair of the Ulster Unionist party, who in 1993 said: "Much as I enjoy the Irish and admire many of their cultural pursuits, I have to remind them that we in Northern Ireland are not Irish."[6]

Akenson has stressed many opinion and value similarities between Catholics and Protestants in both Ireland and the various branches of the diaspora. They do exist, but, as John Taylor insists, there also are significant differences, mainly a common sense of nationality. When the Duke of Wellington was quizzed concerning his birth in Ireland, he answered that it did not necessarily make him Irish any more than birth in a stable would have made him a horse. Daniel O'Connell allegedly responded that it could have made him an ass.

With favorable movie, television, stage, and literary portraits, as well as their successes in business, the professions, and politics, the Irish, as Joseph M. Curran describes them in *Hibernian Green on the Silver Screen: The Irish and American Movies*, have become America's favorite ethnics.[7] This new fashionable image, the retreat of religious prejudice, and the search for cultural identity in history, literature, and music rather than in Catholicism have encouraged and permitted non-Catholics to stake a claim on Irishness.

In reviewing Akenson's *Small Differences: Irish Catholics and Irish Protestants, 1815–1922* in the Canadian journal *Labour/Le Travail*, David W. Miller took issue with Akenson's use of the 1870 census. Miller cited figures indicating that at the time only 15 percent of Americans and 30.8 percent of non-Irish immigrants resided in cities with populations greater than twenty-five thousand, clearly revealing that the Irish were the most urbanized segment of the population. Miller also took issue with Akenson's assumption that the Irish not in urban areas with populations greater than twenty-five thousand were involved in farming, ignoring the probability that they were in smaller cities or towns working in mines or on railroads. Miller also emphasized that the Irish percentage of city dwellers continued to expand. From 1891 to 1900, it rose to 74.3 percent. Another 19.3 percent were in towns with populations of less than twenty-five thousand. Only 6.3 percent could be considered rural. Town Irish were more likely to be involved in the industrial, transportation, and commercial, rather than the agricultural, aspects of the economy.[8] According to historian Timothy W. Guinane, 45 percent of the Irish in 1910 were in the ten largest American cities and another 21 percent were in the next fifteen.[9]

Some Catholic bishops in Ireland feared that the materialism and social mores of urban America threatened the faith of peasant immigrants. Sharing these anxieties, Bishop John Timon of Buffalo and Archbishop John Ireland of St. Paul initiated efforts to settle the immigrants in farm country or small towns. But other prelates took exception to such a strategy. With considerable astuteness, they insisted that it was easier for the Church to preserve and serve the faith in metropolitan centers where Catholic human and financial resources and institutional structures were concentrated than in the vastness of essentially Protestant rural America.[10] The urban character and focus of Irish-American Catholicism strengthened the desire of its constituency to live in cities. And because the Irish dominated the Church in the United States, American Catholicism became urban in character.

Resemblances between the Irish in the United States and those in Britain, where they also flocked to metropolises, are more obvious than resemblances to those who emigrated to Australia, Canada, or New Zealand, where urban industrialism developed more slowly, offering fewer employment prospects. Perhaps, as Akenson asserts, Irish Catholics in those places made successful adjustments to agrarian economies and lifestyles, but that was not the case in the United States. Irish tenant farmers and agricultural laborers were used to spade, scythe, and hoe. They lacked confidence and skills for large-scale American agriculture, and their gregariousness did not easily fit with the isolation, reinforced by harsh winters, of rural America. Efforts to settle them in rural America met with more failure than success. In many sections of the rural Midwest, Irish settlers had reputations as charming, friendly neighbors but not as efficient farmers. Either Akenson's Australians, Canadians, and New Zealanders have had lower standards of agricultural expertise or else they have been more fortunate in the quality of their Irish Catholic fellow citizens. It is also important to note that the agrarian economy in Australia and New Zealand has had much to do with sheep raising, which is much less of a challenge than cultivating the spacious prairies of the United States.[11]

Support for and involvement in Irish nationalism has been far more pronounced in the United States than in Dominions attached to Britain through cultural heritage or loyalty to the Crown. In New Zealand, Canada, and Australia, involvement in Irish freedom movements, especially those advocating physical force against Britain, offended large portions of the community and hampered economic and social mobility, acceptability and respectability, and eventual assimilation. Irish emigrants to the United States entered a country that won her independence through revolution, went to war with Britain again in 1812, and throughout the nineteenth century confronted John Bull in numerous diplomatic skirmishes, sometimes approaching bloodshed. While Irish Catholicism and nationalism offended the Anglo-American Protestant establishment, particularly in the East, other ethnic groups, especially German Americans, were indifferent to or shared Irish Anglophobia.

The persistence of Irish-American nationalism and its perceived, perhaps exaggerated, impact on American foreign policy through political pressure was evident on St. Patrick's Day 1998. On that occasion representatives of the Irish and British governments and of Northern Ireland's Social Democratic and Labour, Sinn Fein, and Unionist parties assembled in Washington to discuss solutions to the seemingly unending crisis in the Six Counties with President Bill Clinton and other American leaders. They did not gather in Ottawa, Canada; Canberra, Australia; or Wellington, New Zealand.

As previously mentioned, Irish Catholics in the United States had to deal with a much more established and persistent Anglo-Protestant nativism than existed in Australia, Canada, or New Zealand. Consequently, responses to prejudice drew the bonds between religion and ethnicity tighter, and memories or tales of poverty and oppression in Ireland, often focusing on the bitter years of the Great Famine, did feed a bitter anti-British grudge. Most Famine refugees found shelter in the United States. The country also provided a home for victims of the agricultural depression of the late 1870s and early 1880s, which also fostered an intense Irish-American nationalism. But Akenson is correct when he characterizes much of the anger that Irish Catholic immigrants in the United States and their descendants expressed toward Britain as emotional reactions to unpleasant experiences with discrimination and hard times in their new homeland.

In Canada, particularly Ontario, and then later in the more western provinces, Irish Catholics also met with Protestant hostility, mostly from Orangemen, who, like their Ulster brethren, paraded to the sound of big, intimidating drums on July 12 and other celebration days of seventeenth-century Protestant triumphs and Catholic humiliations. But many of the Canadian Irish Catholics have lived in Quebec, where, until the recent emphasis on language rather than religion as a cultural bond, they shared with the French many values and hostility to things Anglo. In Australia and New Zealand, early Irish settlers did encounter anti-Catholic biases, but they matured with their countries and in time became respected, successful citizens, important in cultural, economic, and political spheres. Although they have preserved a loyalty to their religious faith, their Irishness is no longer as deeply felt, displayed, or exhibited as it is among Irish Americans.[12]

Throughout the nineteenth and much of the twentieth centuries, the United States featured a much more diversified population than the rest of the English-speaking world. Australia, New Zealand, and Anglophone Canada have been relatively homogeneous societies. The few nonwhites have been culturally and socially ostracized. Therefore, Irish Catholics interacted with only British and Irish Protestants. In the United States, they have had to relate to a variety of ethnic, racial, and religious groups as well as to Anglo and Irish Protestants. This pluralistic mosaic and interethnic, racial, and religious rivalries, as much as confrontations with American nativism, shaped and sharpened a distinct Irish-American identity. Despite melting-pot enthusiasts and critics of hyphenated Americanism, cultural differences persist in the United States. Since the 1950s, African American civil rights and black pride movements have encouraged white Americans to emphasize ethnic uniqueness.

Before embarking on comparative Irish diaspora explorations, scholars of Irish America should realize that their first priority should be sorting out the complexity of their own area of study. To date, there has been considerable research and publication on immigration and on Irish-American politics, religion, and nationalism, but not enough has been done in regard to regional varieties. There has been too much concentration on the East Coast and too little on the "urban frontier" Irish in Buffalo and points west.

In New England, the Irish settled in highly structured communities, preserves of a Yankee ruling class that viewed them as a social plague. This contempt and their own technological and cultural poverty and insecurities, which were manifested in crime, disease, and vice, ghettoized Irish Catholics psychologically as well as physically. When they managed to achieve political influence, economic power or social respectability did not match it.

In *Poverty and Progress,* Stephan Thernstrom discovered that in 1880s Newburyport, Massachusetts, Irish males were, like their fathers and grandfathers, still mostly unskilled laborers.[13] In *Irish-Americans, Native Rights and National Empire,* David Doyle concludes that by 1900 the Irish in other parts of the United States quickly exceeded the economic and social status of those of the third and fourth generation in New England.[14] He reveals how late-nineteenth-century Irish Americans, especially in midwestern cities, had climbed from the unskilled to the skilled, working with considerable representation in the lower middle class. Compared to New England, the Midwest was an open rather than a closed society, where nativism was not as deeply or widely entrenched and the economy was more dynamic and multidimensional with expansive potential. Factories, mills, stockyards, packing houses, and railroads begged for employees. Production and profit superseded prejudice. According to Jo Ellen McNergny Vinyard's *The Irish on the Urban Frontier: Detroit 1850–1880*, early Irish settlers in Detroit advanced economically as well as any group, and their success was typical of others who had moved away from the eastern seaboard.[15]

Location choices as well as arrival times were different for midwestern and eastern Irish. Often, if not always, emigration has been a selective process, involving vision, ambition, and courage. Many who left had little choice, but there were others who refused to accept the boredom and marginal existence of rural Ireland. They were enterprising and optimistic, determined to make a better life, if not for themselves at least for their children.

Before, during, and just after the Great Famine, Irish immigrants did not offer the United States much in the way of talent. But in the late nineteenth century, the quality of Irish immigrants vastly improved, reflecting significant changes in the land of their birth. They left an Ireland with a rising standard of living, fueled by increasing prices for agricultural products, stable rents, dollar gifts from children and siblings in the United States, more comfortable and sanitary domiciles, and an enriched and varied diet. Educated in national schools that emphasized a solid basic education, late-nineteenth-century immigrants were 95-percent literate. Still technologically impoverished, they had the intellectual skills to learn how to survive and prosper in an urban industrial society. Moreover, improved Irish immigration had moral as well as physical and mental dimensions. Emmet Larkin has described a post-Famine "Devotional Revolution," engineered by Paul Cardinal Cullen, that disciplined character and emphasized moral and respectable conduct.[16]

Opportunities in the Midwest and West appealed both to many of the eastern Irish, who were dissatisfied with life on the bottom of the social ladder, and to new immigrants seeking American economic success and social respectability. Both groups correctly understood that the American dream had a better chance of coming true farther west than in the static urban ghettos of the East.

In addition, Irish politics has been more liberal in the Midwest and West than along the East Coast. A more open environment and greater economic and social mobility have reduced defensiveness, encouraging the Irish to be more welcoming in their relationships with those neither Irish nor Catholic. The urban frontier Irish have been less physically and psychologically ghettoized, less introverted and fascinated with Irish issues, and more concerned with American issues than have their Eastern brethren. Irish America in general has less than a perfect record of generosity to other persecuted segments of the population, particularly African Americans. Westerners and Midwesterners, however, have been more willing to translate the implications of their historical experiences and the civil liberties principles of Irish nationalism into empathy for others who also have been victims of poverty and oppression.

Regional distinctions among the American Irish are perhaps more visible in religion than in politics. During the nineteenth and well into the twentieth centuries, Irish bishops in the East, mainly Boston and New York, distrusted the Protestant and secular facets of American life. Frequently they cooperated with members of the midwestern German American hierarchy, attempting to isolate Catholics from main currents of American thought, especially those that were liberal. Both eastern Irish-American and midwestern German American prelates agreed that ethnic and Catholic identities were so interwoven that to fertilize the former was to harvest the latter, and that American assimilation posed a serious danger to the faith.

The alliance between the midwestern German and the eastern Irish Catholic hierarchies was indifferent and often hostile to social movements that might have improved the material existence of the laity. They associated reformers and labor leaders, even Terence V. Powderly, Irish head of the Knights of Labor, with either Protestant proselytism or "Godless" and "materialistic" socialism. Blaming social injustices on original sin, they advised their flocks to suffer poverty with Christian forbearance, patiently awaiting God's justice in the next world. Quite a few of the Irish bishops in the East had difficulty approving one of the fundamental principles of the American constitutional system, the separation of church and state. Since Catholics were a minority, they pragmatically accepted religious pluralism. However, their Thomistic, medieval intellectualism; distrust of the liberal, Protestant, and secular facets of American life; and uncritical subservience to Rome and its reactionary political and intellectual perspectives led them into a theoretical ratification of church-state unity as the Christian ideal.

Things were quite different in midwestern and western Irish America. Economic and social success, along with familiarity and often friendship with non-Catholic fellow workers and neighbors, provided these Irish Americans with broader perspectives than were available to the eastern Irish. Reflecting the condition and the values of the laity, Irish bishops in the Midwest tended to cast a friendly eye on things American, praising the opportunities that the United States offered their people and their religion. They frequently disagreed with Rome-trained Archbishop Michael Corrigan (1839–1902) of New York and his friend, confidant, and adviser, Bishop Bernard McQuaid of Buffalo. Leader of the midwestern camp, Archbishop John Ireland (1838–1918) of St. Paul found an ally in James Cardinal Gibbons of Baltimore, where Irish progress exceeded that of other eastern cities. Ireland and Gibbons, and their supporters, insisted that the healthy condition of American Catholicism proved Daniel O'Connell's contention that religion prospered when free of state financing and meddling. Urging the cultural Americanization of the church in the United States, they adopted liberal positions on social issues, praising labor unions and collective bargaining and castigating the conservatism of Continental Catholicism for losing the loyalty of the European working class. They also praised and attempted to cooperate with public education.

Twisting their admiration for things American into a violation of essential Catholic dogma, conservative bishops in Canada, France, and the United States prodded Rome to censure Archbishop Ireland and those who agreed with him. In January 1899, Pope Leo XIII, in a letter to Cardinal Gibbons, branded the following opinions heretical: that action has priority over contemplation, that natural virtues take precedence over supernatural virtues, and that decisions of private consciences are more compelling than the teachings of the church guided by the Holy Spirit. Although Gibbons and Ireland and their friends in the American hierarchy correctly replied that what Rome had condemned was a distortion of their views, Rome had humiliated them, and the Corrigan-McQuaid faction was ecstatic and arrogant in victory. Pius X, Leo's successor, purged suspected modernists from the fold. His oppressive reign of terror introduced a long, bleak, conservative period for Catholic thought, one that lasted until Vatican II in the 1960s and that has resurfaced in the current papacy of Pope John Paul II.

While Roman oppression frustrated Catholic philosophical and theological efforts to bring the church into intellectual contact and harmony with the modern world, liberal American Catholic clerics and laymen addressed problems of social injustice. In their efforts, they employed two papal encyclicals, Leo XIII's *Rerum Novarum* (1891) and Pius XI's *Quadragesimo Anno* (1931), but they translated the encyclicals' irrelevant medieval distributist, corporate state messages into an instruction more appropriate, palatable, and relevant to contemporary urban industrial America. Social reform Catholicism was more pronounced in the Midwest than in the East, where many members of the hierarchy continued in the conservative camp. During the 1920s, Monsignor John A. Ryan of St. Paul, a protégé of John Ireland and head of the National Catholic Welfare Conference, authored a social justice agenda that anticipated the New Deal. In the 1930s he was a staunch champion of President Franklin D. Roosevelt's policies.

In addition to identifying the regional varieties of Irish America, today's scholars must devote more attention to its gender differences. *Erin's Daughters in America: Irish Immigrant Women in the Nineteenth Century* by Hasia R. Diner was a significant breakthrough in Irish-American women's studies by discussing domestic servants, mill workers, labor organizers, and wives and mothers.[17] Diner also gave special notice to nuns, America's premier professional women, who inspired many of their female students to follow them into nursing and teaching. Diner's Irish-American women rejected feminism and took little interest in the worlds of politics and nationalism so dear to their menfolk, but they were strong and sovereign, pillars of the church's parish communities, and the most important civilizing element in Irish America. Since the appearance of *Erin's*

Daughters in America, there have been a number of important contributions to the story of Irish-American women. Historians, social scientists, and literary scholars have discussed women's emigration from Ireland, their influence in the church, their place in the American economy, their contribution to the welfare of the urban poor, and their literary interpretations of the Irish-American experience.[18]

Despite the significant research and writing about women, religion, politics, and nationalism, there is still much work to be done in Irish-American studies. As previously indicated, regional differences have to be detailed. Surprisingly, prominent Irish segments of the population in many cities, large and small, have not received consideration. There are a number of good articles and books about Catholicism as religion, but too few on Catholicism as culture and ethnicity. There have been many studies dealing with Irish Catholic bishops and politicians, but too few that discuss working-class men and women, business executives, lawyers, doctors, teachers, labor leaders, firemen, policemen, athletes, nuns, priests, and that most humble group of religious: nursing and teaching brothers. It is also time to examine closely the impact of middle-class status and suburbanization on Irish-American values, which were originally shaped in rural Ireland and in the inner-cities of the United States.

While comparative diaspora studies offer tempting possibilities, they do not exceed the challenges of uncovering the many hidden facets of Irish America. At present, many young scholars spend their research time in Dublin's National Library of Ireland or Belfast's Public Records Office, working on topics relating to Ireland. They might find it more creative, interesting, and professionally profitable to search for Irish-American material in American city and state historical society libraries and in the columns of old American newspapers. In fact, the best future in Irish studies for Americans is right here at home.

Notes

1. Donald H. Akenson, *The Irish Diaspora: A Primer* (Toronto: Meany, 1993); *Being Had: Historians, Evidence and the Irish in North America* (Toronto: Meany, 1985); *Small Differences: Irish Catholics and Irish Protestants, 1815–1922* (Kingston, Ont.: McGill-Queen's University Press, 1988); and "Data: What Is Known about the Irish in North America," in *The Untold Story: The Irish in Canada,* vol. 1, ed. Robert O'Driscoll and Lorna Reynolds (Toronto: Celtic Arts, 1988), 15–25.

2. Malcolm Campbell, "The Other Immigrants: Comparing the Irish in Australia and the United States," *Journal of Ethnic History* 14 (Spring 1995): 3–22.

3. Sean O'Faolain, *King of the Beggars* (London: Nelson, 1938), 29.

4. Patrick O'Farrell, *Ireland's English Question* (New York: Schocken, 1972), 306.

5. Fintan O'Toole, *The Lie of the Land: Irish Identities* (London: Verso, 1997), 65.

6. *Irish Times,* 7 December 1993.

7. Joseph M. Curran, *Hibernian Green on the Silver Screen: The Irish and American Movies* (New York: Greenwood, 1989).

8. David W. Miller, review of *Small Differences: Irish Catholics and Irish Protestants, 1815–1922,* by Donald H. Akenson, *Labour/Le Travail* (1989): 366–67.

9. Timothy W. Guinane, *The Vanishing Irish: Households, Migration, and the Rural Economy in Ireland, 1850–1914* (Princeton: Princeton University Press, 1997), 224.

10. Leonard R. Riforgiato, "Bishop John Timon, Archbishop John Hughes and Irish Colonization: A Clash of Episcopal Views on the Future of the Irish and the Catholic Church in America," in *Immigration to New York,* ed. William Pencak, Selma Berrol, and Randall M. Miller (Philadelphia: Balch Institute, 1991), 7–26; and James Shannon, *Catholic Colonization on the Western Frontier* (New York: Arno, 1976).

11. My conversations with rural dwellers in Iowa and Wisconsin have confirmed my contention that the Irish in the American Midwest are not considered good farmers. A Jesuit priest of Czech ethnicity told me that his Wisconsin family on a Sunday afternoon visited neighboring Irish farms for a good laugh. When I mentioned to a German American farmer from the same state that the Irish in Ireland did not cultivate their land very well, he replied, "They do not do it very well here either."

12. A few years ago I had lunch with four members of the Australian Consulate in Chicago. Three came from Irish Catholic backgrounds. While they retained a strong loyalty to their religious heritage, their Irishness had faded into a strong sense of being Australian. They indicated that this was also true for other Irish Catholics in their country.

13. Stephan Thernstrom, *Poverty and Progress* (Cambridge: Harvard University Press, 1964).

14. David Doyle, *Irish-Americans, Native Rights and National Empires* (New York: Arno, 1976).

15. Jo Ellen McNergny Vinyard, *The Irish on the Urban Frontier: Detroit 1850–1880* (New York: Arno, 1976).

16. Larkin has discussed his thesis in a number of publications. He stated it first in "The Devotional Revolution in Ireland, 1850–1875," *American Historical Review* 77 (June 1972): 625–52. It has been reprinted with a new introduction in *The Historical Dimensions of Irish Catholicism* (Washington, D.C.: Catholic University of America Press, 1997).

17. Hasia R. Diner, *Erin's Daughters in America: Irish Immigrant Women in the Nineteenth Century* (Baltimore: Johns Hopkins University Press, 1983).

18. For some examples of the work mentioned in this paragraph, see Janet Nolan, *Ourselves Alone: Women's Emigration from Ireland, 1855–1920* (Lexington: University Press of Kentucky, 1989); Grace Neville, "'She Never Then after That Forgot Him': Irish Women and Emigration to the United States in Irish Folklore," *Mid-America* 74 (October 1992): 217–90; Rita Rhodes, *Women and the Family in Post-Famine Ireland: Status and Opportunity in a Patriarchal Society* (New York: Garland, 1992); Maureen Murphy, "The Fionnuala Factor: Irish Sibling Emigration at the Turn of the Century," in *Gender and Sexuality in Modern Ireland,* ed. Anthony Bradley and Maryann Gialanella Valiulis (Amherst: University of Massachusetts Press, 1997) and "Charlotte Grace O'Brien and the Mission of Our Lady of the Rosary for the Protection of Irish Immigrant Girls," *Mid-*

America 74 (October 1992): 253–70; Eileen Brewer, *Beyond Utility: The Role of Nuns in the Education of American Catholic Girls, 1860–1920* (Chicago: Loyola University Press, 1987); Maureen Fitzgerald, "Charity, Poverty, and Child Welfare," *Harvard Divinity Bulletin* 25, no. 4 (1996), 12–17; Sue Ellen Hoy, "Walking Nuns: Chicago's Sisters of Mercy," in *At the Crossroads: Old Saint Patrick's and the Chicago Irish,* ed. Ellen Skerrett (Chicago: Loyola University Press, 1997); and Colleen McDannell, "Going to the Ladies' Fair: Irish Catholics in New York City, 1870–1900," in *The New York Irish,* ed. Ronald H. Bayor and Timothy J. Meagher (Baltimore: Johns Hopkins University Press, 1996), 234–51. In *The Irish Voice in America: Irish-American Fiction from the 1760s to the 1980s* (Lexington: University Press of Kentucky, 1990) and "The Heart's Speech No Longer Stifled: New York Irish Writing since the 1960s," in *The New York Irish,* 508–31, Charles Fanning pays tribute to the contributions of women writers, including Mary Ann Sadlier, Elizabeth Cullinan, Ellen Currie, Maureen Howard, and Alice McDermott.

2

Witnessing Two Worlds: Poems

Eamonn Wall

New Words

We hear our words transformed
to sidewalks, buoys, nickels and dimes,

but have we given up our right to name
by walking through the electric doors

into the gasoline air of Logan Airport?
Should we put aside our broken spades to mold

from scratched steel and broken timber
huge bridges, enormous words to talk of pain.

Hart Crane's Bridge

Rows of immigrants facing west
behind, the Bridge
city onto itself, world
within world, poem
of boats, steel, sailors;
Amen to seagulls, shifting
riverbeds hold this nest
of cars. Submarines to
Brooklyn come up for air
Thomas Wolfe's dead, body electric
of America. To the right
a lady of the harbour
swathed in centennial
Band Aid. The paper says
the French repairmen will not
go home when the work's done.
What does Whitman mean?
What have our bodies built for,

definitions through paper or
sunsets in familiar places?
Where in the forest grows
the Green Card?
Is it what surrounds the primrose
on the Wexford road?
Sit under a pine
with food and open lips,
hold this child of ours
upwards to the sky
to bronze his skin
any sky, any where
only the Irish pines and primroses
are mine.
America,
how she deals the cards.

Father, Father

Having crawled through
the tiled catacombs under
the Port Authority. Heard

balls clattering behind
glass, check-it-out merchants

but Isaac Bashevis Singer dead
was the word on the street.

Stalled buses. Traffic lights
stuck on yellow, brownies
hugging meters, the *Newsday*
sign shattered on the sidewalk,
the national debt headstone
flickering, a mocking pulse,
Girls, Girls, Girls, The
Croissant Shop, the
New York Public Library
Bryant Park, sauerkraut and
smoke from the vendor's carts.

You liked buildings with
courtyards like mine and

hearing your dead language
spoken in diners on Columbus Avenue.

I don't care much about my
dead language except the
poems of Nuala Ní Dhomhnaill,
the cupla-focail-merchants
killed the Irish lingo,
but, Father Singer,
I know what you mean.

The immigrant has witnessed two worlds
this much is true, the immigrant writer

is the witness' memory who pens lines
full of shame, lines full of hope.

Our leader has fallen. Our leader is dead.

Freewheeling by the Platte River: A Song

When I woke this Wednesday your hair
was spread on the pillow like the
many channels of the Platte River.

As I drive westward with the trucks
into the absence of trees, corn, cuts
in the horizon, I fix on the browned
grass flecked with the end of snow,
on those signs of our ageing into
the life of the prairie in winter—
this cloister of *Diet Coke*, draws,
artificial creamer for your coffee,
and too much country 'n western on
the radio. At night you roll against
me for my warmth. I trace from the
backs of your knees to your highest
vertebrae the cities of this state
from Omaha all the way to Chadron.
You turn towards me trusting in these
warming motions naming grasses
awakening the soil to the secrets
you have come to plant. The Land
The Land you sing straw hat on

your knees and yes I have heard it
talk to you and the Platte River
calls your name to me this afternoon
and I imagine you shin-deep and skirts
raised dancing on a shallow bar
in the middle of the flowing.

When I woke this Wednesday your hair
was spread on the pillow like the
many channels of the Platte River.

The Westward Journey

Setting out on the westward journey
with eight suitcases and two cats.
On this last night we sleep at the
La Guardia Marriott to swim in the pool,
and begin the busy work of forgetting
Mr. Pedro's large hands stuck in the
till as his fingers float among the
pennies. "You are leaving New York
to live in America," he says. "I would
be afraid of that, and the little ones
will lose their Spanish." At the end of
the street each Sunday morning bright
speedboats race for the early shadows
under the George Washington Bridge.

I have stored away your cries of
being born: from these ugly streets,
red paint on the old benches in
Payson Playground, to the sweet
brown eyes of an immigrant from
Galicia fumbling and cursing quietly
about for our change. My own childhood
unimaginable without the Slaney humming
"Son, you breathe" as I read the clock
each morning above Louis Kerr's shop.
Impossible that there was another life.

Tonight, my children are singing in the
water at the prospect of a plane ride to
another life, but someone must remember,
there must be someone to write this down.

Father and Daughter: Nebraska

My daughter's dancing at the
back door to the falling snow
picking up her rhythm I sway
from too tight-fitted western
boots and feel a sharp new
loneliness under high clouds
frosted tree branches in
Nebraska. Take it all away and
left will be shadows of trees,
ice & snow, birdseed,
a dancing child.

                    If I place
my hands on your shoulders,
you'll stop dancing.

                    Naked in
Nebraska without a paper
coffee cup, Uptown mothers
ring-a-roseying in the sun,
& I've moved around too much
opening the blinds at daylight
to search calm streets for
the view I've left behind me.
Blue-jeaned girl, barretted hair,
you are all I have—snow and ice,
trees and music—everything else
fell from the back of a Mayflower
truck somewhere between here and
there, reported to the police,
items considered lost, all
covered by insurance.
And shadows.

                    Snow brings
the children out. The world
feels good. Where were you hiding?
Why were your streets so quiet?
I bleed with the dry winter
air a thin blood, a paint-

flecked face, cream by an
upstairs mirror.

                    Darling,
I say, sweetheart and angel,
let's go driving just me and
you and we'll stop at Baskin-
Robbins on the way home to
eat—you a Party Cone, me one
scoop of vanilla—to watch
snow ploughs on Underwood
Avenue, and hold hands.

Easter Vigils, Easter Lights

At the Strategic Air Command Museum
on Good Friday we walked among
paint-peeled airplanes,
                    the largest
colossal in how their wings stretched
over concrete,
                    weeds sprouting through
their uniform gaps as once grass had
taken hold in a bonnet rust
hole,
          my old *Ford Escort,* BZR 891.

ICBMs
skeletons of hydrogen bombs
& in a shed beyond that
chain-link fence where the *Enola Gay*
had been assembled from piece A-1
to final piece, Z-2511.

Awesome, Cool, the kids shouted out.
Let's stop for burgers on the way home.

*

the flautist
& the fiddler
play a trio of tunes

though the singer's
the one trained
to make you weep

you are of the sea people
men and women
wrapped

in bitter seaweed
floating four green waves
behind the tide

*

A lone daffodil stands upright
in water in a silver vase, late
manna of the season on a rising
prairie between a full sugar bowl
and a half-empty shaker of salt,
a green table cloth on a bokety
kitchen table.
                        The music has reached
the end of its circuit though the red
light glows across this quiet room
on an Easter Sunday.
                        Winter has been
crushed by my son's bright face
at the back door & this is the line
I've been reading.
                        "There was
fog in the hollow places—white horses' tails
in wisps across the road," written by
Angela Bourke which reminds me to
ring home.
                        It's my father's birthday which
means Easter has come early this year.

Who Paved Paradise?

If you walked away from a place they tore it down.
   —Bernard Malamud, *The Tenants*

      And as shadows were moving
      from the warehouses,
                  our legs
      hung over the quay &

      we watched fishermen
      cast flies gurgling into pools,

      each repetition one line thrown
      across evening in July
                  blue
      river, Slaney air
      of another, shining July evening.

      I slipped into the cool sitting
      room—the Rosary said
      curtains moving steadily
      in the breeze.
               We shared
      a plate of toast & pot
      of tea, my grandmother
      and me.
               If you walk away,
      they will tear your
      hometown down, pave your
      squares for juggernauts
      & cars.
            You
      have to walk away,
                 you
      have to know of ancient
      hungers & bitter thirsts—

      your felled Cotton Tree,
      fished-out river flowing
      deeply as before through
      arteries to your finger

tips caressing her,
                    the
television turned off

a wild light coming off
a new moon in the centre
of the prairie, a month
beyond the solstice.
                    Boys
lean their legs over the
quay wall, shadows fall
from old buildings
dim as clay, limpid as air.

The Blackbird of Edermine
(after the Irish)

The call of the blackbird of Edermine
& the roar of a juggernaut on the N 11 that's
the chorus which carried Sharon and Darren
away & the wild duck of Wexford Sloblands

& the fast hare leaping over the Bare Meadows
& the otter whistling by the Fisheries
& the child singing under a clothes line
under Vinegar Hill & the warbling of the cuckoo

On Ballinesker Hill & the dogs barking
at the greyhound track & the screeching of brakes
on Friary Hill & the parade of mallards
returning early from Ferrycarrig bridge, downstream.

When Sharon and Darren were wild and young
they loved hill and shore more than they loved
falling on their knees before the rail of St. Aidan—

Sweeter to them the blackbird's call than the
shrill tongueing of the cathedral bell.

They oiled their bodies before an open fire
under state forest evergreens and the milky way

& the quiet sheep walking & the grass throbbing
motionlessly & french kissing & companions cooking
sausages & drinking cans of Furstenburg above the

Yellow lights of Bunclody & the boombox on the
bonnet of the Renault booming out a Waterboys/
Oasis/Counting Crows medley & the DJ quiet on 2 FM

& the summer's night ending in pitched screams
& the silence of the Nine Stones on the mountain
& the grey transmitter buzzing on the roof of the world

in Co. Wexford & carried on the breeze aloe & sesame &
safflower from "Nature's Harvest" in Enniscorthy.

Finding a Way Home

Expelled soft breath
collides with an early morning patch
of breeze come through a window
latched open

so what is breathed out
joins the wind, a slice of yesterday
when sent to fetch a grown-up's lighter
a child notices a flash of light
in the modest wake of a jet-ski
cutting across parallel to shore
the Irish Sea.

On the road you take an old blue bus
suddenly
hangs a right at the bottom of Topeka
on a wide busy street.

Out beyond the suburbs you look across
wide fields of Kansas through your window
and find trees whose names are known

to you and bales of hay covered in black
plastic and kisses as the road you travel
and the road you dream merge like

the numbers of the interstate,
so all share one way home like
fresh meringue inhaled on a city street
an ocean away

from the bakery through which you'd wandered as a child.

Winter has claimed the seaside,
the latch which squeaks and clanks
from salt air is locked to its frame
& narrow curtains are drawn across
the windows of mobile homes for
this is a lonely spot in winter. So

what is breathed out joins the wind,
a slice of tomorrow washing on the
tide from Wales—message in a bottle,
deep shells, smooth stones. Don't
you know your place? My home
is where I am, old wise blue bus.

Four Stern Faces/South Dakota

I was living in a bedsit in Donnybrook
when John Lennon was shot outside the
Dakota apartment building in New York
and that's what I'm thinking this morning
piloting my family through the hollow
darkness on Iron Mountain Road, trespassing
on the holy ground of the Lakota nation.

Four stern faces in the distance address
me and when I get stuck after rattling off
Washington & Lincoln I call on Matthew to
fill in the blanks and wonder how the hell
will I pass the civics test when I apply
for citizenship. I could tell you all
about Allen Ginsberg & Adrienne Rich
but presidents, state capitols and amendments
to the constitution would snooker me, and
I get the feeling the I.N.S. doesn't care
too much for postmodern American poetry.
Caitlin belongs to the woods—mosses,

pine needles, slow moving light and shade,
a bright face in the back of the car
breathing a fantastic language, this
slow mid-morning pilgrimage I drive
my loved ones forward and climbing.

When Lennon was dying I was typing
the forms to come to America: on this
journey through the Sandhills—Irish sand
dunes without the sea—to the Black Hills
to wild flowers with names so gorgeous
I cannot bear to hear you say them.
Native people, "Strawberry Fields Forever,"
Ryan White dying in Indiana. My children
craving this just as the matchsticks and
cats' eyes on the Gorey road mesmerized them,
howling now for lunch. Here the light is
different, the evenings shorter, Gods are weeping.

And there's no escape from caring or
from history: to lie on high plains,
prairie grasses, and Black Hills is to
be blown into their stories, drowned in
their summer rains. Just when I think I've
lost the Irish rings around the tree, I open
the door and find red clay stuck on the
tyres, the whole earth screaming, my children
breathing on the electric hairs above my collar.

Being woken one ordinary workday to Lennon
being dead, "Imagine" on the radio, remembering
the grown-ups weeping in late November '63,
one morning in Dublin when it finally struck
that heroes are flowers constantly dying on
these black and holy hills we spend the years
wandering towards till light reveals a universe
beyond stony victorious faces bolted to a rock.

3

That Special Place:
Poems and Stories from Irish America

Terence Winch

A Remarkable Impression of Harry Truman

on Labor Day weekend
Steve McHugh would perform
at the Emerald Isle House
he looked like a movie villain
with slicked down hair and a mustache
he used to sing "it must have been the Irish
who built the pyramids cause no one else could
carry all them bricks" but his big number was
"come in out of the rain, Barney McShane"
there was no one anywhere who could do better
hand farts than Steve McHugh and he punctuated
the pauses in "Barney McShane" with his
loud wet hand farts   sometimes he would sit next
to some very proper ladies at a bar and secretly let go
a few hand farts then he would give them a severely
disapproving look and move down the bar away from them
Jerry Lynch showed up on Labor Day too
and did a remarkable impression of Harry
Truman then one of Winston Churchill
he had an awful case of the gout
and sang an anti semitic parody
of "Little Spanish Town" which went
"in a little Yiddish town
twas on a night like this
all the Jews were eating matzos
and gefilte fish"
a very sweet old lady
in her seventies
played the piano
for the whole summer

even though she was almost
completely deaf
he knew he could get away
with it so Owen Lamb the owner
didn't pay her anything
except for
room and board

On the Fire Escape Naked

Mrs. McNally sold mass cards when somebody died
Mrs. Feeney would invite me in for oranges
Mrs. Cassidy threw water on kids who sat
on her stoop. Mrs. Keenan needed two clothes
lines because she had so many kids the clothespole
was as tall as our building and fell down from time to time
there were old men who roamed the backyards
of the Bronx chanting "fix the line!"
the backyards and alleys
were a geography that only kids knew
there were always shortcuts
if you knew your way around
once Scalley got caught in an alley
by some members of the Fordham Baldies
but they just roughed him up a little
some people's yards you had to stay out of
like Mr. O'Connor who farmed the back
yard of his building with great success
or yards with mean dogs in them
when we were small we would play
a lot in the yard and sometimes
we would yell for Maria
who lived on the first floor
to come out on the fire escape
naked and she would
and I would close my eyes
or look the other way

Introduction to Dead Mothers

Well, there's Connie Ryan's mother Agnes, dead just a month before. Nora
Keegan, Tommy Keegan's mother, passed away some time ago. Molly O'Leary
is gone too, God rest her soul. Her husband's with the buses now, a fine man.

And two grand kiddies, Ann and Dorothy. Tch, that was a terrible shame. There's
Katey Scanlon, dead these ten years. A great heavy woman with a bad heart, sitting always at her window, day and night. ("How did she die?" went the joke.
"She fell out the window.") Kitty Regan, old Mrs. Logan, Mary O'Brien (Paddy
O'Brien's wife), Butchie Ahearn's mother Mazie, May Monahan, Mrs. Duffy, Mrs.
Clark, Mrs. Flynn, Kathleen Fahey. Mrs. Sweeney, poor thing, was crippled with
varicose veins for years before her time came. And lovely Marian Casey, God be
good to her, was flattened by a bus on Southern Boulevard with her new mink
coat on.

Promises

> When they elevated our pastor Father Walsh
> to monsignor, the event became
> the parish dress rehearsal for the Second Coming.
> Everyone was mobilized. A big procession
> snaked through the neighborhood, with flags
> and banners, and virgins scattering flowers
> before the litter on which The Monsignor
> sat, perched on a throne carried by strong men
> of the parish. It was like Caesar entering Rome,
> Ike liberating Europe, Lindbergh landing in Paris.
>
> The bishop presided over the ceremony in the church
> after which the Monsignor could now dress in a red cape
> and wear a biretta with a little red ball on top.
> Scared of him before, now we were terrified.
>
> My father was custodian of the parish school,
> so the Monsignor was his boss. "What's your name,
> little boy?" he asked me on my first day of kindergarten,
> as we filed through the school doors. "Don't you know
> who I am?" I replied. "My father runs this place."
>
> Sometimes the Monsignor would roam the neighborhood,
> his red cape billowing behind him, hunting sinners
> as children hid or ran away, and adults crossed the street.
>
> When the Vogue movie house on Tremont Avenue offered
> me a job, I went to the rectory and asked the Monsignor
> to write me up a bogus baptismal certificate
> making me a year older, so I could get the job.

He loved the exercise of power, and in a flash
turned me from fifteen to sixteen.

At age seven, I went to him for my first confession.
"Bless me, father—" I began. "Monsignor," he corrected.
I confessed my misdeeds—forgetting my morning prayers,
talking back to my parents, fighting with my friends.

"Promise me you'll never do these things again," he said.
"I'll try, father, but I can't promise." "It's Monsignor,"
he said. "I'll try, Monsignor."

"I want you to promise, my child," he persisted.
I refused. I knew I had a long road
    of sinning ahead of me and didn't want to worsen
my soul's prospects by making promises I couldn't
keep, especially under the seal of confession.

He finally let me go, and I did indeed sin
more than I ever wanted to, the echo
of absolution growing fainter ever since.

What I Hear

My father's voice lost on the night
of the dance. My mother sexy in red dress
dancing on the sparks from his glance. Alone
together in her pink smoke. While aunts and uncles,
monsters with milky eyes, choked the skies.

In those days, everyone did last rites
near Tremont Avenue. Guests rested
in the parlor next to the saloon.
And soon the waterfall in Bronx Park
soothed our intoxicated hearts.

Near the Zoo I wandered through
the dawn of St. Raymond's
big gray rocks and remembered your songs,
turntable spinning out those years
of longing in your eyes and far away
in Rockaway faint sounds of surf
singing still in your ears

salting our moony bodies
in the wash and splash
of the hot day, the radio
crackling under that same sky
and I swimming back
to your open arms.

On the Sad Height
for mcw

Get old enough so you won't have much to fear.
By then, the music plays inside your head
and everything beautiful must be learned by ear.

In the bathroom mirror I behold my wear and tear.
In our bedroom I try to levitate in bed.
Get old enough so you won't have much to fear.

Meanwhile, my son at six wants to keep me near
and we sing together every night head to head.
So everything beautiful must be learned by ear.

His father's tunes, though, will one day disappear
beyond today's routines and daily bread.
But get old enough so you won't have much to fear.

Remembering my mother was my first career
and the songs surrounding her on which I fed,
knowing everything beautiful must be learned by ear.

We may waltz in the kitchen now, my dear,
or dance out of time in our sleep instead.
Get old enough so you have nothing left to fear.
Everything beautiful must be learned by ear.

Custodian
for charlie fanning

I ran the shovel along the street,
a razor path through the sidewalk's face,
snowy lather parting for me, for my father,
our feet crunching in the city night.

We grabbed the garbage cans from school
and church and dragged them up the iron
stairs. I lugged burlap bags stuffed
with bingo cards, light as cream puffs.

We swept the auditorium with green sawdust
from huge drums. We hammered and drilled
in his workshop, where tools hung on pegboard,
their images silhouetted behind them

For instant identification and placement.
Once he sawed his index finger in half
on the power saw in a moment of inattention
in a life otherwise constructed of skill and care.

Once a year the Monsignor made him climb inside
the giant boiler and clean it out
with enormous pipe cleaners till he was black
with soot that took days to wash off.

Sonny boy, he called me, and laddie buck.
He always said just do your best.
All of us loved to watch him fall asleep
on the couch, newspaper over his face

Snores filling the apartment
with the music of rest well deserved.
His finger took years to heal enough
for him to play again but a black scar

Ran down its center. He'd give me a rub
with his unshaven face, rough as sandpaper.
He'd pretend he didn't know me, scrubbed from
the tub, the lovely lie delighting me every time.

A Short History of Twentieth-Century
Irish Music in America

The Flanagan Brothers prospered, picking out tune after tune
in the bright light of New York, back when everyone could dance
the Stack of Barley and sing "the Old Bog Road" at the same time.
They strode into the Yorkville Casino, where their money
was no good. They took out their instruments, chose a key
(probably D), and tore into a paradise of jigs and reels.

The Clancy Brothers and Tommy Makem played no reels.
They dwelt within the universe of song, where no mere tune
held sway. Decked out in tuxedos, they lived on stage, the key
to the city in their pockets, sin in their hearts, the dance
of love in their beds. Ed Sullivan controlled all the money
till they made him give some up: "C'mon, Ed, it's time."

Where were the McNultys by then, but shrouded in the mists of time,
Pete and Ma dead, Eileen in exile, Rockaway just an old newsreel
in her memory, the glory days long over, applause gone, the money
spent, Ma's old accordions in a closet somewhere, no more tunes
from them. Pete living on in the hearts of the people—o, to see him dance
once more, his mother on the box, Eileen warbling slightly out of key!

Others took the stage. Mickey and Ruthie, each of them a key
contributor, reconstituted the cosmos in three-four time,
so that every Bingo hall in New York every weekend held a dance,
and it was the waltzes versus the foxtrots versus the reels,
and anybody in the parish who could remotely carry a tune
sang "Danny Boy," and the Monsignor left last with all the money.

You could sense the pace quicken by then, antennae out for the big money
the music could make. The Dubliners, the Chieftains, stuck the key
in and unlocked the loot, and suddenly at every turn the great tunes
took root—fiddles, flutes, accordions blazing, bodhrans marking time
in smoke-filled pubs, drunken pipers copulating with sets of reels
in the after-hours street, while feet entreated feet: let's dance!

Who can say what happened next? We are in Circuit City and "Riverdance"
is playing on seventy-five monitors, and the cold smell of money
is in the air. The ghost of the great sean-nos master Joe Heaney reels
around in confusion. Fat record-label moguls sport scary key
board size smiles. We hear spooky New Age confections every time
we turn around, hoping always to catch someone belting out a real tune.

So, we rant and rave about money and decline, berating everything, fumbling for
    the car key
when the dance is done, the century nearly at an end, our fragile sense of time
bolloxed up and reeling, when suddenly we hear—listen!—some distant, lovely
    tune.

The Upper Hand

The Irish women of my neighborhood, when I was growing up in New York in the 1950s, worked out an arrangement with the local German butcher. In return for their business, he made for them absolutely authentic Irish sausage and blood pudding, just like what you'd get back in Galway or Clare. As a result, I and my fellow narrowbacks, as we children of immigrants were sometimes known, grew up eating exactly what our counterparts in Ireland ate for their daily fry. Eggs, bread, bacon, sausage, and blood pudding, the latter now more euphemistically known as "black pudding."

But time passed, we all grew up and moved away, the women all died, and the butcher went out of business. By the time I reached adulthood, you couldn't really get the true Irish stuff over here anymore. In Washington, D.C., where I found myself living in my late twenties, no hope existed of a good fry like my mother used to make. It just wasn't that kind of town in the 1970s.

So my brother and I always kept alert for the pork of our past. Relatives and friends would bring bags of frozen meat back from Ireland, and we would slowly thaw out a bit of it, cook it up, and have nearly a religious experience at breakfast. We'd make it last for weeks, knowing it would be a long while until the next installment arrived.

One day, however, it seemed like the tide might be turning. There was an upscale little supermarket in my neighborhood, featuring high prices and slightly better fare than Safeway and Giant. I almost never went into this place. It was out of my price range, and, frankly, it intimidated me just a bit. Sometimes my origins in the working class mark me still.

But on this particular day, as I headed to the local drug store for cigarettes, a large sign in the window of this establishment caught my eye. I couldn't believe it. Luck had apparently decided to shine on me. There, amid all the items advertised in the store window, was one huge notice that called out right to me:

Special Today: IRISH SAUSAGE

I was thrilled. Wait till my brother Jesse hears about this! Finally, after all these years of waiting and yearning, Irish sausage right here in Washington, in my own neighborhood. Could blood pudding be far behind?

I stopped in my tracks and veered into the store, heading determinedly past a clientele who looked like they just stepped out of a *House & Garden* interior, and straight to the meat department to stock up on this unlikely treat being offered. Who cared if the people who owned this place were a bunch of rich Protestants? If they would supply me with Irish sausage, they were a fine lot of decent carnivores in my book.

I began rummaging around, flipping aside packages of filet mignon, deboned chicken breasts, lamb chops, and prime rib, hunting down the object of my desire. I was busy tossing meat in every direction, as excited as a lion about to bring down an unfortunate impala or slow-moving zebra, when a store employee asked if he could help.

"Yes," I said, in an imperious tone. "Where might I find the Irish sausage you have on special today?"

"Irish sausage?" he said back in bewilderment.

"Yes, you have a big ad in the front window for Irish sausage," I said impatiently. Jeez, you'd think the staff would be more up on this sort of thing.

He turned out to be very nice, actually, and once I had informed him that the store was blaring out news of the special by way of the sign in the window, he industriously joined me in my increasingly frantic search for those Gaelic links to my past.

No Irish sausage turned up, and I was now becoming annoyed, even a little angry. "This is ridiculous," I muttered, flinging about packages of meat. The employee met with no success either. "I'll get the manager," he said, finally giving up.

The manager soon appeared, a snooty, supercilious twit, the kind of person who spends half his time sucking up to the rich and the rest of it condescending to everyone else. Somehow I sensed immediately that he didn't live by that "customer is always right" principle.

"What seems to be the problem?" he sneered. I could tell straight off he didn't like the look of me and would not likely feel true compassion for my needs.

"The problem is," I sneered back, "we can't seem to find the Irish sausage you're advertising in your window." The word *asshole*, though not actually said by me at the end of that sentence, was clearly implied.

"I'm sure I don't know what you mean, sir. We are not offering this . . . this Irish sausage," he said, as though the very term were distasteful for him to have to utter. But I knew I had the upper hand.

"If you don't have any for sale, why do you have a six-foot-square sign in the window advertising it?" I rejoined, with deadly self-righteousness.

"Please, sir, show me this advertisement," he said, now with undisguised contempt.

"Gladly, *sir*," I snarled back.

The employee, the manager, and I exited the store, turned, and stood together in the street scanning the collage of ads in the big window.

When I saw my mistake, my heart sank, all the wind went out of me. The funny-looking "I" in "Irish" was actually an "F," and what these incredibly irritating people were offering was "Fresh Sausage." I had seen what I wanted to see.

"If you don't mind, I really have to get back to work now," the manager said, puffed up with rectitude.

We spend much of life saving face, but that doesn't mean we necessarily get good at it.

Later on, I thought I should have said to him, "Oh, I see, *fresh* sausage, as opposed to your usual stale crap?" But instead I said, "You oughta get a new sign maker," wit and the art of brilliant comeback deserting me, as they tend to do in these situations for all of us.

"Certainly, sir, we'll get right on it," the manager assured me.

That Special Place

After my badgering her for weeks, my mother finally agreed to buy me a black leather motorcycle jacket. I was ten years old and believed, with the absolute faith of children, that this article of clothing would solve all of life's problems for me.

We journeyed together to far-distant Manhattan for the prized jacket. This was not the sort of purchase that Alexander's, the most prominent Bronx department store, could be entrusted with. Never even mind Bobkoff's, the cut-rate army and navy store that supplied half the borough with its sartorial needs. We were a working-class family—by today's measurements, we would be considered poor. So buying such a jacket was a major fiscal undertaking. My mother handled the whole matter with the seriousness with which one might approach buying a new car today. Not that I, at ten, knew or cared what it cost. I just wanted that jacket to enter my life and drive out all that was bad.

To acquire the jacket, my mother concluded, it would be necessary to take the subway downtown to Bloomingdale's, the epitome of upper-class Wasp entitlement. This was an intimidating prospect for people of our station in life, and our embarking on this quest I see now as an act of love and devotion on my mother's part.

It has been one of the burdens of my adult life that my happy memories of my mother seem buried irretrievably beneath the stark and painful recollections I have of the long illness and suffering that preceded her death when I was sixteen and she fifty-five. But I do have some faded happy memories. I remember skipping down the street with her when I was a boy, the two of us singing "here we go loop de loo/here we go loop de lie." I remember helping her wax the linoleum floors till they gleamed. I remember her singing songs around the house, most of them calling to mind in some way her homesickness for Galway, though she disliked Irish farm life, which she fled in the 1920s for the promise of America, and left the New York City limits rarely and reluctantly.

Her brother Thomas repaired tracks for the New York subway system. Right through college, I could evoke the name "Tommy Flynn" to just about any employee of the subways and they would know immediately whose nephew I was. To distinguish him from his own uncle Tom back in Galway, he was called Thos by everyone in the family, except his wife, my Aunt Tess, who called him Flynn and Flynny, which I always thought was funny and slightly disrespectful of her, but, then again, Aunt Tess was a remarkable and often disrespectful human being.

I'm sorry to say I don't remember actually being in Bloomingdale's that day with my mother. What I do remember is sitting in the subway car with her, the two of us looking out the window, it being a sunny, clear day. We sat on those seats that always reminded me of shellacked corn on the cob. The train was still on the el tracks before going underground, when she nudged me and said, "There's your Uncle Thos. Give him a wave." As the train whizzed by, my uncle saluted us, and my mother and I waved to him, the entire exchange taking but a moment. It's one of those vivid moments that play over and over in my mind. My tall, lean, handsome uncle standing on the tracks, a universe away from Coorheen in Galway, giving his sister and nephew a smile and a wave as we rushed by on the IRT. Sweat shone on his arms, a handkerchief was tied around his neck, his pipe was stuck in his mouth. He smoked until a few years before he died, and I always loved the smell of his pipe. I credit him as a big influence in my own addiction to tobacco. I think he was holding a sledge hammer that day on the tracks. Brother and sister, so far from home, speeding past each other on the elevated train system of New York, not a green field in sight, nor a pig or a cow (at least as far as I knew) anywhere in the vicinity. That remembered scene has more voltage for me than a hundred videos about the Irish in America.

The coat itself measured up in every way to my ideal: it was buttery soft and sported about twenty zippered pockets. I found out only recently that my brother apparently resented my getting the coat and had to settle for imitation leather himself, the family coat fund having been no doubt seriously depleted by the purchase of my black leather beauty. I feel bad about that now, but back then it was every man for himself.

I don't think I went into Bloomingdale's again until around 1980, when the band was hired to join a number of other Irish musicians in providing entertainment for the gala opening of the store's huge marketing campaign to sell Irish-made products. The name of the campaign, announced via a giant banner that covered half the building's facade, was "Ireland—That Special Place." We musicians were placed around the store to add a bit of picturesqueness to the event, which featured big-name guests like the Irish ambassador and Hugh Carey, then the recent ex-governor of New York.

I remember that an old friend of mine showed up, a needy soul always in search of approval. She was on edge, and I told her to take a Valium. "Do you have any?" she asked with urgent hopefulness bordering on desperation. I looked in my band bag, and sure enough, there was Valium. The others in the group joke that I could make house calls, I lug around so much in the way of medicinal products. But my feeling is that pain is bad, can strike at any time, and it's best to be prepared. I gave her the pill, and an extra for later, and she was happy, if only very briefly.

Meanwhile, the rest of the musicians were guzzling the free drink and gobbling the free food, at first discreetly, but later with abandon. One old friend, but a mean drunk, slithered up to me at one point and hissed, "You're a snake." I'll never forget the venom he sent my way. The next day I asked him what he could possibly have been thinking, since I'd never done him a bad turn, but he said he had no memory of the incident, and apologized. Before the night was over, he smashed his guitar on the street, I guess so they could be smashed together.

But it was the inimitable fiddler Brendan Mulvihill who, in my opinion, displayed the most imagination and daring that night, as the event was winding down. Somehow managing to not attract the attention of the security guards and store staff who were patrolling the premises, Brendan crept up to a vignette featuring four life-size manikins in a fake horse-drawn cart, and rearranged the figures into obscene positions, with one male manikin's head disappearing under the dress of a female dummy, and another female nosing the fly of her partner. We all had fun that night, but the dummies had the most. Brendan moved the entire cart to a very conspicuous spot in front of an elevator, so that it would be the first thing seen by anyone getting off on that floor the next day.

I once ate a spoonful of my Uncle Thos's pipe tobacco. I hereby recommend smoking tobacco over eating it. I also bought a little pipe when I was eight and began experimenting with smoking, in preparation for taking up the habit full-time at thirteen. My uncle told me that during hard times in Ireland, they would sometimes smoke tea, and so I tried that too. I recommend drinking it over smoking it.

I don't remember what became of my motorcycle jacket. Such a prized item would certainly have had an extended life. I suspect my mother sent it to Ireland when I outgrew it. My family in Ireland tells me that my parents were always very generous and helpful through the years. Last month I visited my Auntie Nora, the last of my mother's siblings, who is now eighty-six. She lives in Kilchreest, not far from where she and my mother were born. I asked her what my parents sent over in the old days. "Wonderful things," she says. "Wonderful Yank things."

"Like what?" I ask. She thinks for a moment.

"Frocks," she replies. "The box would come and be filled with them."

They used to fight, she says, over the lovely frocks from America sent by my mother, the likes of which they couldn't even get in Dublin. She says she doesn't remember a black motorcycle jacket.

4

Joseph Mitchell's Irish Imagination

James Silas Rogers

In October of 1929, Joseph Mitchell, a young writer of Scottish and English descent, arrived in New York from North Carolina. The twenty-one-year-old Mitchell had been hired, sight unseen, for his first reporting job covering police affairs for the *World.* In the next decade, Mitchell moved on to reporter and feature writer positions at the *Herald Tribune* and, later, the *World-Telegram.* He joined the staff of the *New Yorker* in 1938 and remained there until his death in May 1996, where his extraordinary care in researching and composition helped to cement that publication's reputation for literary reportage. Calvin Trillin once dedicated a book to him as "the *New Yorker* reporter who set the standard."[1]

Although he lived in a city in which the Irish had dominated politics, the public safety departments, the unions, and construction for half a century—a city in which the census taken a year after his arrival disclosed some 220,000 foreign-born Irish living in New York City, 97,000 of them in the borough of Manhattan alone[2]—Mitchell's journalism holds limited value as a documentary source on the Irish in New York City. Yet a close reading of this most perceptive of journalists reveals that the Irish are nonetheless present as one of the "figures in the carpet" beneath his writing and, in a larger sense, beneath the city that he came to love. This figure comes to the fore in two ways: first, as an emblem of resistance to change; and second, as a tradition that reveres and is nourished by the spoken word.

That Mitchell was drawn to the Irish there is no doubt. After Mitchell's death, Brendan Gill recalled that, "Joe loved the Irish as a people, and he would sit talking by the hour to old tads at McSorley's."[3] He traveled to Ireland on several occasions and was an early and lifelong member of the James Joyce Society. In the introduction to *The Bottom of the Harbor* (1959), he identifies Irish literature as one of the great fascinations of his life.[4] He professed to have read *Finnegans Wake* "at least half a dozen times" and specifically cites Joyce as a major influence.[5] In his most autobiographical book, Mitchell recalled having, at the age of twenty-four, "come under the spell of Joyce's 'Ulysses'"[6] and wanting to write a comparable book that was equally encyclopedic about New York.

When we recognize Mitchell's affinity for the Irish, one of the questions that arises is why the group does not figure more prominently in his reporting. Two reasons—one temperamental and one sociological—suggest themselves to explain the relative paucity of Irish references in Mitchell's attempt to chronicle New York. The temperamental one is that he was, at times, a writer with a gift for overlooking the large; one able to write a detailed portrait of New York's skid row in the 1930s without mentioning the depression, and one able to omit all mention of World War II from his writing in the 1940s. The sociological explanation tells us more. Mitchell's arrival came at the very end of an era when, as a recent historian notes, "The Irish ruled New York. . . . They controlled its government and politics, dominated construction and building, moved into the professions and the managerial classes, and benefited, perhaps disproportionately, from the general prosperity of the times."[7] The creeping middle-class status of the Irish, their assimilation into conventional roles in society—public safety, education, and the professions—with an attendant draining of "color," probably kept Mitchell, with his innate taste for the offbeat, from paying more attention to them. The New York Irish were losing the distinctive characteristics that attracted Mitchell even as he was making them his own. Mitchell would have understood precisely what Lawrence McCaffrey meant when he said of a later generation's move to the suburbs that the Irish had moved "from somewhere to nowhere."[8]

Those Irish and Irish Americans who appear in Mitchell's journalism display many of the traits that Mitchell prized: a refusal to participate in commercial society, a heroic attempt to stay behind the times, a fear that the world passed on to future generations will no longer be, in one of his favorite words, "genuine." Thus, Mitchell's Irish perform a sort of literary ventriloquism; as they speak, they give voice to the author's own concerns and preoccupations.

At first blush, though, Joseph Mitchell's Irish appear to be not all that different from those presented by the image makers of the tourist industry—as a people who love drink and sentimental songs. One of his early newspaper features profiled John Hassett, a singing plumber's helper from the Bronx. Hassett, though only twenty-five, refuses to expand his repertoire beyond the "old Irish favorites" he learned at the Shamrock Democratic club. Hassett sings such chestnuts as "That's How I Spell Ireland" at the drop of a hat, anytime, anywhere; Mitchell meets him in the locker room of the Brooklyn Dodgers, where, despite being a no-field left-handed second baseman, he is getting a tryout because Casey Stengel likes to hear him sing "The Last Rose of Summer."[9] Music also appears in Mitchell's 1939 "Obituary of a Gin Mill," which laments the gentrification of Dick's Saloon, once beloved for its impromptu Friday "cabaret nights," when a "beery old saloon musician would show up with an accordion and a mob of maudlin rummies would surround him to sing hymns and Irish songs."[10]

Mitchell describes the all-male, Tammany-run fund-raising events of pre-Prohibition days known as "Beefsteaks" in "All You Can Hold for Five Bucks." Here, one of the chefs recalls, "At the old beefsteaks they almost always had storytellers, men who would entertain with stories in Irish and German dialect. And when the people got tired of eating and drinking, they would harmonize. You could hear them harmonizing blocks away. They would harmonize 'My Wild Irish Rose' until they got their appetite back."[11] In "Mazie," a 1940 piece set in a Bowery movie house where bums sleep off hangovers and retreat from the street, readers encounter a down-and-out "courtly old Irishman named Pop" who spends his nights singing ballads in "Irish gin mills on Third Avenue"—including "Whiskey, You're the Divil," "The Garden Where the Praties Grow," "Tiddly-Aye-Aye for the One-Eyed Reilly," and "The Widow McGinnis's Pig."[12]

Clearly, the face that the Irish presented to Mitchell was often a face found in a barroom. As it happens, the *New Yorker*'s "Irish saloon beat," if we may call it that, was already being well covered by his colleague John McNulty, who made a specialty of chronicling Irish watering holes in Manhattan and collected some of his most popular fictionalized stories in *Third Avenue, New York* (1946).[13] McNulty's stories feature Runyonesque Irish characters with names like Grogan the Horseplayer, Paddy Ferrarty the Bartender, and Little Mike and Grady, two cabdrivers. Mitchell turned his journalistic attentions elsewhere, but the sort of establishments that McNulty wrote about do appear in his work. For instance, Mitchell's fictional slice-of-life story "The Kind Old Blonde" opens in "Shine's, an Irish restaurant near the Pennsylvania Station."[14] The Native American bridge workers profiled in "The Mohawks in High Steel" hang out in Nevins Bar and Grill in Brooklyn, of which Mitchell admiringly notes, "The Nevins is small and snug and plain and old. It is one of the oldest saloons in Brooklyn. It was opened in 1888, when North Gowanus was an Irishtown, and it was originally called Connelly's Abbey. Irish customers still call it the Abbey."[15] Elsewhere he mentions a Bowery saloon called John McGurk's Suicide Hall.[16] He meets the Don't-Swear Man, a colorful antiprofanity crusader, when, as he relates, "One dank afternoon I dropped into Shannon's, an Irish saloon on the southeast corner of Third Avenue and Seventy-sixth Street, and ordered a split of Guinness."[17]

McNulty's and Mitchell's Irish differ in their degrees of participation. The Irish characters in McNulty's vignettes draw their energy from the hustle and vitality of urban life and, in turn, create part of the colorful ambiance that was New York in the 1930s. In contrast, Mitchell's Irish—like so many of the figures who inhabit Mitchell's New York—step away from the modern world and turn their gaze back to better days behind.

A revanchist in his outlook on the world, Mitchell wrote almost nothing about electoral politics. His 1938 anthology of newspaper features, *My Ears Are Bent,* however, contains a section called "Our Leaders" in which several stingingly ironic portraits of political hacks appear. One memorable Irish American, Peter J. McGuinness, a stevedore-turned-politician from the neighborhood of Greenpoint (famed as the birthplace of Brooklynese), provides the subject of one of these profiles, "Mr. McGuinness Puts a Stop to the Machine Age." Mitchell wrote:

> I like Mr. Peter J. McGuinness because he is hearty and outspoken, because he is one of the last of the old-time neighborhood statesmen, and because he will give an interview on any subject under the sun, no matter how abstruse, without a bit of hesitation. Mr. McGuinness once characterized himself as "the Fighting Alderman from Greenpoint, the Garden Spot of the World," and he prides himself on his incessant warfare against women cigaret smokers, Chinese coolies, cabaret cover charges and the abolition of the Greenpoint ferry.[18]

An honest politician, McGuinness was nonetheless what newspaper people call "good copy"; the aside about women cigarette smokers refers to a farcical incident in which New York cops thought that the legislation McGuinness had introduced had already passed and went out rounding up women who smoked in public. Mitchell recalls an interview with McGuinness on the subject of technocracy. The alderman lacks a sophisticated vocabulary of social analysis, but he knows very well what changing technology means for the people in his district:

> I told him [McGuinness] I wanted an interview on technocracy, and he said, "What is it?" I began a rough explanation, which he soon interrupted. He said that he was one of the original prophets of technocracy and that the 1928 minutes of the Greenpoint Peoples' Regular Democratic Club would prove it.
>
> "I seen it coming," he said. "Away back in 1928 I seen the machine age coming. One night at a meeting in the clubhouse I warned my constituents against the machine age. Technocracy is nothing new to me. As far back as 1928 I seen it coming. So far as I know I was one of the first to speak about it."[19]

McGuinness rants on about how draymen are being thrown out of work by trucks and how a pretzel factory in his district has laid off twenty women due to automation. Mitchell continues,

> The former alderman looked at his desk. The sight of his dial telephone made him angry. "And look at this," he said, "it's got so everything is hooked up to a machine." I asked him if he had thought of a way to put a stop to the machine age.
>
> "I have," he said. "Every machine the patent office down at Washington puts their O.K. on will do away with the work of men. There ought to be a stop put to the work done by the patent office. Just notify them they can't O.K. any more of these machines. We got to put a stop to the machine age, and so far as I know that's the best way."[20]

There is mockery here, yes—but there is also affection. Mitchell respects his subject's aggressive naïveté. McGuinness's suggestion that the patent office simply call a halt to the machine age is, of course, preposterous, and Mitchell de-

lights in the outrageousness of the idea. At the same time, Mitchell also understands that as times progress, decent men and women are losing familiar and cherished parts of their world. Mitchell's journalism often celebrates retreat: working men withdrawing to their taverns, the young man who sings only the old Irish
standbys, McGuinness fuming against technology, and the majestic anachronism
so warmly evoked in Mitchell's 1940 piece "The Old House at Home," collected
in his 1943 volume *McSorley's Wonderful Saloon.*

McSorley's, just off Cooper Square in Greenwich Village, was then (and remains still) the oldest bar in New York City. In many ways, it serves as the pro-
totypical Irish bar in the United States. Harrigan and Hart's musical comedy
"McSorley's Inflation" (1882) is set there. The bar's importance to the Irish community was examined in a 1987 documentary, scripted by Peter Quinn, which
shows how—despite having been opened to women, turned into a tourist mecca,
and subjected to standing-room-only crowds of young people every night—
McSorley's still trades on a reputation for changelessness.[21]

At the time of Mitchell's title story, the bar was eighty-eight years old, and in
that span had known only four owners, "an Irish immigrant, his son, a retired
policeman, and his daughter—and all of them have been opposed to change."[22]
It would no doubt please McGuinness that, when Mitchell reported on McSorley's,
the owner still refused to answer the telephone he had grudgingly installed in
1925. The bar that Mitchell cherished was at best a reluctant participant in modern commercial society or, indeed, in modern time at all: "There is no cash register. Coins are dropped in soup bowls—one for nickels, one for dimes, one for
quarters, and one for halves—and bills are kept in a rosewood cashbox. It is a
drowsy place; the bartenders never make a needless move, the customers nurse
their mugs of ale, and the three clocks on the walls have not been in agreement
for many years."[23]

In Mitchell's time, McSorley's was patronized by "a rapidly thinning group
of crusty old men, predominantly Irish, who have been drinking there since they
were youths and now have a proprietary feeling about the place."[24] The saloon
that Mitchell loved was founded on the backward look. John McSorley, Mitchell
tells us, "patterned his saloon after a public house he had known in his home-
town in Ireland—Omagh, in County Tyrone—and originally called it the Old
House at Home."[25] Mitchell catalogs the oddments hung reverentially on the walls
of McSorley's. They include such Irish-American tokens as shillelaghs, prints of
Irish prizefighters, and an engraving of the "Rescue of Colonel Thomas J. Kelly
and Captain Timothy Deacy by Members of the Irish Revolutionary Brotherhood
from the English Government at Manchester, England, September 18, 1867"[26]—
an original from the days when New York's Fenians caballed in the dim corners
of McSorley's. (Today, a framed chip of stone hangs behind the bar over a plaque
that reads, "This immortal specimen was presented to McSorley's by Joseph

McSorley's Back Room, by John Sloan. Reprinted with permission of the Spencer Museum of Art at the University of Kansas-Lawrence. Museum purchase: Peter T. Bohan Fund.

Mitchell and Brendan Gill." The stone is in fact a fragment from Nelson's Pillar in Dublin, which was blown up by the IRA in 1966.)

The Irish Americans to whom McSorley handed on his tavern were resolute in their unwillingness to change. In his later years, Mitchell would devote much of his energy to such causes as historic preservation and reforestation; it is not surprising that he would admire the sense of custodianship with which the founder's son Bill ran the bar.

> Throughout his life Bill's principal concern was to keep McSorley's exactly as it had been in his father's time. When anything had to be changed or repaired, it appeared to pain him physically. For twenty years the bar had a deepening sag. A carpenter warned him repeatedly that it was about to collapse; finally, in 1933, he told the carpenter to go ahead and prop it up. While the work was in progress he sat at a table in the back room with his head in his hands and got so upset he could not eat for several days.[27]

"The Old House at Home" concludes with a scene of the Bartender Kelly nudg-ing the old men who fall asleep in the afternoon sunlight of the wonderful saloon. Mitchell understands their rootedness in the familiar as a warm and humane blessing:

> Kelly makes jokes about the constancy of the old men. "Hey, Eddie," he said one morning, "old man Ryan must be dead!" "Why?" Mullins asked. "Well," Kelly said, "he ain't been in all week." In summer they sit in the back room, which is as cool as a cellar. In winter they grab the chairs nearest the stove and sit in them, as motionless as barnacles, until around six, when they yawn, stretch, and start for home, insulated with ale against the dreadful loneliness of the old and alone. "God be wit' yez," Kelly says as they go out the door.[28]

Like McSorley's, Mitchell himself elected not to be mastered by any clocks or deadlines. Virtually his entire output for the 1950s is found in one collection of six articles, *The Bottom of the Harbor*. In 1965 he published the enigmatic *Joe Gould's Secret*,[29] a book-length follow-up on a piece he had written twenty-three years earlier. After it appeared, Mitchell continued to go in to work at the *New Yorker*. However, until his death nearly thirty-two years later, he never again submitted a single word to the magazine.

If a journalist believes that the old ways are the best and that the contemporary world is less satisfying, less genuine, and less interesting than that which went before, then those convictions will shape the way in which he practices his trade. A corollary that follows from these convictions is that when a reporter tells a story, it is always derivative and by definition cannot hope to be as rich and full as is the original. In Mitchell's case, it seems clear that the original sources are informed by a particularly Irish privileging of orality. Noel Perrin has called attention to the "enormous courtesy" that pervades Mitchell's writing, a courtesy that translated into an innate respect for the role of the storyteller: "The ultimate courtesy is to accept people on their own terms—and more than accept them . . . to take them seriously, see them as they are or believe they are, and to value what you see."[30] When Mitchell wanted to learn about, for example, circus freaks or faith healers, he went to his subjects and let them speak for themselves.

And so, for instance, when Mitchell grew interested in gypsy fortune-telling, he opened a window on that world for his readers by letting them sit in on a lengthy disquisition by Captain Daniel Campion, the New York Police Department's expert on gypsies. Campion, a native of the Hell's Kitchen neighborhood, is "blue-eyed and black-haired, and he has a calm, ruddy, observant, handsome, strong-jawed, Irish face."[31] The account is given almost completely in a monologue by Campion as he instructs two young detectives. Although Campion alludes to written files that he maintains on gypsies, they are patchy and secondary; the world of the gypsies has come to Campion and now to us almost entirely through oral sources.

In the same manner, Mitchell created an exhaustive and factually detailed portrait of the Fulton Fish Market in his 1948 book *Old Mr. Flood*. In the three long chapters of this book, a ninety-three-year-old "tough Scotch-Irishman" named Hugh G. Flood hands on the lore and the poetic language and traditions of the fishing industry in New York in story after story. Mitchell was in fact testing the boundaries between fiction and journalism—or to put it another way, he was carrying his practice of literary ventriloquism to an extreme level. Old Mr. Flood was an invented, composite character—fictitious, but, the author asserted, "solidly based on facts."[32] The merits of such a journalistic strategy can be debated, but the relevant point here is Mitchell's sense of history. When challenged to introduce an unfamiliar subculture to his readers, Mitchell instinctively relied on spoken tradition: go to an old man and tell the stories that he tells you.

This heightened respect for storytelling came early to Mitchell, while growing up in the rural South, and it was a tradition that as an adult he found resonant in Irish life and literature. Most of Mitchell's brief introduction to his omnibus collection *Up in the Old Hotel* (1992) is given over to recalling how childhood in an oral culture influenced his "cast of mind"—a childhood in which, after picnics, his aunts Mary and Annie would lead a procession out to the family graveyard at Iona Presbyterian Church. He writes of his aunt that she "wore old-fashioned clothes and she often talked about 'the old times,' and we thought of her as our link to the past."[33] The family progresses from grave to grave, each accompanied by a story.

> "This man buried here," she would say, "was a cousin of ours, and he was so *mean* I don't know how his family stood him. And this man here," she would continue, moving along a few steps "was so *good* I don't know how his family stood him." And then she would become more specific. Some of the things she told us were horrifying and some were horrifyingly funny.
>
> I am an obsessive reader of Finnegans Wake—I must've read it at least half a dozen times—and every time I read the Anna Livia Plurabelle section I hear the voices of my mother and my aunts as they walk among the graves in old Iona cemetery and it is getting dark.[34]

An Irish preoccupation with listening lies at the heart of *Joe Gould's Secret*. Mitchell devoted six years of his career to writing this memoir of a Greenwich Village bohemian. Originally the subject of a 1942 Mitchell profile, Joe Gould is a Harvard-educated misfit who has lived on the streets of New York for decades. Among other foibles, he claims to be able to converse with seagulls and to have translated Longfellow into the seagulls' language. For decades, Gould has supposedly devoted his life to gathering materials for an enormous collection of transcribed conversations called the "Oral History of Our Times"—the first usage of the term *oral history*," incidentally. No one has ever seen the "Oral History," but by its compiler's count it consists of some nine million words. *Joe Gould's Secret* chronicles Mitchell's relationship with Gould and his mighty work-in-progress over more than two decades. Mitchell balances pity, annoyance, and respect for Gould until, at a certain point, we realize that Gould's vast project of collecting the speech of daily life parallels the author's own project of journalism. In some funhouse-mirror sort of way, the derelict Gould overlaps with Mitchell himself. Like Mitchell, Gould began his time in New York as an aspiring reporter. He tells Mitchell of the moment when the idea for the Oral History came to him:

> One morning in the summer of 1917, I was sitting in the sun on the back steps of [police] Headquarters recovering from a hangover. In a second-hand bookstore, I had recently come across and looked through a little book of stories by William Carleton, the great Irish peasant writer, that was published in London in the eighties and had an introduction by William Butler Yeats, and a sentence in Yeats's introduction had stuck in my mind: "The history of a nation is not in parliaments and battlefields, but in what the people say to each other on fair days and high days, and in how they farm, and quarrel, and go on pilgrimage." All at once, the idea for the Oral History occurred to me: I would spend the rest of my life going about the city listening to people—eavesdropping, if necessary—and writing down whatever I heard them say that sounded revealing to me, no matter how boring or idiotic or vulgar or obscene it might sound to others.[35]

Mitchell's writing abounds with genealogies—something of an Irish quality itself—and in this case, we can trace a line of descent that runs back from Mitchell, who began as a reporter, to Gould, who began as a newsboy, to Carleton, who first wrote for the *Christian Examiner*, and from there back to shanachies and storytellers of earlier ages—of whom, it would seem, journalists are merely the culturally impoverished heirs.

Mitchell's masterpiece, *The Bottom of the Harbor*, is suffused with the sense that the world is getting worse, and in aesthetic protest he portrays men who struggle to preserve a vanishing way of life—such as the shad fishermen of Edgewater, New Jersey, who, across the river from the Manhattan skyline, still hand set their nets as they have done for centuries; the fishing captain who "once threatened to fire a man in his crew because he worked too hard";[36] and the old African American tending a graveyard on Staten Island.

The general trajectory of Mitchell's career traces a movement from the eccentric to the elegiac, and in tracking the Irish figures sprinkled throughout his journalism we find the same pattern. The Irish New Yorkers in the early work of Joseph Mitchell—who exalt personality above success and refuse to go along with the times—prefigure Mitchell's great later themes. The old pensioners warming themselves by the stove in McSorley's introduce the deepest concern of Mitchell's mature work, his profound sense of mortality.

Joseph Mitchell's Irish form part of a project of bricolage—found objects pieced into an overarching story to present New York to the world. Mitchell constructed the Irish in a way that was informed by his deepest preoccupations. If we look closely, we find that Mitchell then took that construction and turned it around: in his taste for the eccentric, in his writings about those on the margins of society, in his admiration for those who resisted the increasing commercialism of the times, and in his celebration of oral tradition he went on to construct New York in Irish ways. If, from this, we can infer that there is an identifiably Irish way to practice the craft of reporting, then looking further along these lines might tell us something new about the Irish experience. For one thing, such an inquiry might suggest reasons why so many talented Irish Americans chose journalism as a profession.

Notes

1. James Rogers and Norman Sims, "Joseph Mitchell," in *American Literary Journalists, 1945–1995 Dictionary of Literary Biography* 185, ed. Arthur Kaul (Detroit: Gale Research, 1997), 199–210.

2. Ronald Bayor and Timothy Meagher, eds., *The New York Irish* (Baltimore: Johns Hopkins University Press, 1996), 560.

3. David Remnick, "Postscript: Joseph Mitchell: Three Generations of *New Yorker* Writers Remember the City's Incomparable Chronicler," *New Yorker,* 10 June 1996.

4. Joseph Mitchell, *The Bottom of the Harbor* (New York: Modern Library, 1994).

5. Joseph Mitchell, *Up in the Old Hotel* (New York: Pantheon, 1992), xii.

6. Ibid., 690.

7. Chris McNickle, "When New York Was Irish, and After," in Bayor and Meagher, eds., *The New York Irish,* 337.

8. Lawrence J. McCaffrey, *The Irish Diaspora in America* (Bloomington: Indiana University Press, 1976), 152.

9. Joseph Mitchell, *My Ears Are Bent* (New York: Sheridan House, 1938), 144.

10. Mitchell, *Up in the Old Hotel,* 246.

11. Ibid., 295.

12. Ibid., 33.

13. John McNulty, *Third Avenue, New York* (Boston: Little, Brown, 1946).

14. Mitchell, *Up in the Old Hotel,* 337.

15. Ibid., 285.

16. Ibid., 130.

17. Ibid., 232.

18. Mitchell, *My Ears Are Bent,* 263.

19. Ibid., 264–65.

20. Ibid., 265–66.

21. *McSorley's New York,* prod. and dir. Marcia Rock, Cinema Guild, 1987, documentary film.

22. Mitchell, *Up in the Old Hotel*, 3.

23. Ibid.

24. Ibid.

25. Ibid., 4.

26. Ibid., 7.

27. Ibid., 8–9.

28. Ibid., 22.

29. Joseph Mitchell, *Joe Gould's Secret* (New York: Viking, 1965).

30. Noel Perrin, "Paragon of Reporters: Joseph Mitchell," *Sewannee Review* 91, no. 2 (spring 1983): 169.

31. Mitchell, *Up in the Old Hotel*, 175.

32. Ibid., 373.

33. Ibid., xi.

34. Ibid., xii.

35. Ibid., 644.

36. Ibid., 544.

Part Two

*New Perspectives
on Pre-Famine Immigration*

5

From Ulster to Delaware: Two Poems
by James Orr about an Eighteenth-Century
Emigrant Voyage

Andrew Carpenter

Poetry, written as well as oral, played a major part in the life of eighteenth-century Ireland. Both English and Irish speakers often chose verse to tell a story or point a moral, to get across a political message, or to indulge in the pleasures of description. As we begin to read the poetry of eighteenth-century Ireland more attentively, we are gaining valuable knowledge about the cultural and social lives of people in all walks of eighteenth-century life that is not readily available elsewhere. In the early years of the eighteenth century, for instance, Murrough O'Connor described life on a farm in County Kerry in two most unusual Virgilian eclogues, and Matthew Concanen gave a vivid account of country sports in County Dublin—including an extended football match between teams from Rush and Lusk—in heroic couplets. James Sterling used verse for his politically motivated description of whale fishing off County Donegal in the 1730s, and Thomas Mozeen—a man of a social rather than a political turn of mind—wrote memorable songs about foxhunting and drinking in County Dublin in 1744. In addition, there are innumerable descriptions in verse of weddings and feasts and ramblings of various kinds, as well as detailed accounts of life in prisons, at fairs and at patterns, in poor houses and in rich houses, in city centers and in the depths of the country. Commentators on eighteenth-century Ireland cannot afford to overlook the information contained in its verse.

For instance, Laurence Whyte's long poem "The Parting Cup or the Humours of Deoch an Doruis," published in 1740, provides many fascinating details about life in County Westmeath, including information on diet, house furnishings, social customs, education, and language use in the area. Whyte also draws attention to the dramatic changes that had come about in rural life between the reign of Queen Anne and the 1740s, in particular lamenting the changing fate of the solid tenant farmer now subject to a new breed of landlord who, by racking rents on every possible occasion, was driving these farmers and their families, particularly those who sought to improve their holdings, off "their Native Soil."

> So Irish Landlords thought it fit,
> Who without Cer'mony or Rout,
> For their Improvements turn'd them out.
> Embracing still the highest Bidder.
> Inviting all Ye Nations hither,
> Encouraging all Strollers, Caitiffs,
> Or any other but the Natives.

Whyte goes on to explain that many of those forced off the land ended up traveling around the countryside until, almost inevitably,

> Whole Colonies, to shun the Fate
> Of being oppress'd at such a Rate
> By Tyrants who still raise the Rent,
> Sailed to the Western Continent,
> Rather than live at home like Slaves,
> They trust themselves to Wind and Waves.

The consequence of the behavior of these selfish and greedy Irish landlords is enforced emigration.

Many other eighteenth-century Irish poets—including Goldsmith in *The Deserted Village* and Samuel Thomson in "The Bard's Farewell"[1]—also mention forced emigration, and as the century proceeds, it is clear that emigration was increasingly the likely fate of many of those born into poor families. A few of the younger members of families forced off the land might emigrate for the positive reason of bettering themselves, but for most, and certainly for those who took their families with them, emigration was seen as the only alternative to starvation—an economic imperative. There are several poems in which the image of the emigrant ship waiting at anchor off the shore to take on board its human cargo, its tall masts visible from the surrounding countryside, leads to a gloomy description of the miseries of the moment of departure. In other poems, transportation of those convicted for petty offenses and the forcing to sea of those caught by press-gangs remind the reader of the sense of doom with which those living in eighteenth-century Ireland viewed any departure by sea for distant parts.

Among the most interesting eighteenth-century poems linked with the subject of emigration are two by James Orr, one of the most significant Ulster poets of the latter part of the century. Orr, who was born in 1770, was a weaver by trade and a Presbyterian by religious conviction. He came from the small County Antrim community of Broad Island and, although he did not attend school, was exposed to a wide range of books and ideas by his father, also a weaver. His poems show that he had read Scottish history and philosophy, and his elegy on the death of the Scottish philosopher Hugh Blair shows a considerable knowledge

of Blair's work, from sermons to literary criticism. Orr developed a strong social conscience and radical views in political matters; he joined the United
Irishmen and fought at the battle of Ballynahinch and at Antrim in June 1798.
After the collapse of the 1798 Rising, he went to America on the voyage described
below. However, he remained there for only a few months and took up weaving
again on his return to Ireland. His fondness for the bottle is said to have hastened his death, which came in 1816.

Although the two poems below describe the same voyage, from Larne in
County Antrim to New Castle in the state of Delaware, they are remarkably different. The first is in standard English and initially must disappoint the reader. It
has an unexciting title, "Song Composed on the Banks of Newfoundland," and
its vocabulary and imagery are conventional and predictable. The personified West
"smiles," Care "sits drooping" on a cheek (although one is perhaps not quite sure
how to visualize this), milkmaids are "blythe," the lea is "dew-sprinkled," and
there is even a kneeling parent "fondly praying" for the poet-swain. One remembers Dr Johnson's harsh comments on a certain type of pastoral poem—"easy,
vulgar and therefore disgusting."

The poem is, of course, skillfully constructed as a sentimental song for draw-
ing-room performance—the sort of song much appreciated by the delicate female
audiences that Tom Moore was to captivate within a few years—and it does have
energetic images in the second and third stanzas, where Orr is describing life on
the emigrant ship and the storm. But so wedded is the poet to late-eighteenth-
century notions of poetic diction and poetic decorum—the notions that Wordsworth so vigorously refuted in the preface to the *Lyrical Ballads* at the very time
this poem was written—that the poem fails to come to life. This is particularly
so when it is compared with the other poem Orr wrote on the same subject, "The
Passengers," a poem written for an entirely different audience in the language
which Orr and his countrymen spoke to one another every day, the language
known at the time as "Scotch," or even "Guid Scotch," and now usually as "Ul-
ster-Scots" or "Scots-Irish."

The most obvious characteristic of this second poem is its energy. The language Orr uses, in stark contrast to the language in the first poem, has an unin-
hibited freshness and freedom in both vocabulary and syntax, which allows it to
represent experience in a particularly vivid way. The relaxed and familiar nature
of the direct speech used throughout the poem is particularly striking, as are the
vivid lists of day-to-day objects and Orr's use of assonance and alliteration in
his descriptions. In addition, the directness of Orr's accounts of daily life on board
ship—the families at their open cooking place on deck, the outrageous behavior
of sailors on "the Banks,"[2] the fearful scurrying and hiding beneath piles of old
sails of those expecting to be press-ganged when the brig from Baltimore is
sighted, and the final poignant detail of the reaction of the Irish emigrants (or

rather immigrants by this stage of the poem) to the sight of people with black skin—all combine to make a poem of extraordinary power. If one wanted to know what life on an emigrant ship sounded like, felt like, almost smelled like, one need go no farther than this poem. Like so much of the verse that came out of eighteenth-century Ulster, it is a reflection of a vibrant poetic culture, one that deserves to be far better known than it is.

Song Composed on the Banks of Newfoundland

In Ireland 'tis evening. From toil my friends hie* all,   *hasten*
    And weary walk home o'er the dew-sprinkled lea;
The shepherd in love tunes his grief-soothing viol,
    Or visits the maid that his partner will be:
The blythe milk-maids trip to the herd that stands lowing,
    The West finely smiles, and the landscape is glowing,
The sad-sounding curfew, and torrent fast-flowing,
    Are heard by my fancy, tho' far, far at sea.

What has my eye seen since I left the green valies
    But ships as remote as the prospect could be?
Unwieldy huge monsters,[3] as ugly as *malice*,
    And planks of some wreck, which with sorrow I see?
What's seen but the fowl that his lonely flight urges,
    The light'ning that darts thro' the sky-meeting surges?
And the sad scouling sky, that with bitter rain scourges
    This cheek Care sits drooping on, far, far at sea?

How hideous the hold is!—Here, children are screaming,
    There dames faint thro' thirst, with their babes on their knee;
Here, down ev'ry hatch the big breakers are streaming,
    And, there, with a crash, half the fixtures break free:
Some court—some contend—some sit dull stories telling—
    The mate's mad and drunk, and the tar's task'd and yelling:[4]
What sickness and sorrow, pervade my rude dwelling!—
    A huge floating lazar-house,* far, far at sea.   *hospital*

How chang'd all may be when I seek the sweet village!
    A hedge-row may bloom where its street us'd to be;
The floors of my friends may be tortur'd by tillage,
    And the upstart be serv'd by the fallen grandee:[5]
The axe may have humbled the grove that I haunted,
    And shades be my shield that as yet are unplanted;

Nor one comrade live, who repin'd when he wanted
    The sociable suff'rer, that's far, far at sea.[6]

In Ireland 'tis night. On the flow'rs of my setting*   *birthplace*
    A parent may kneel, fondly praying for me:
The village is smokeless, the red moon is getting
    The hill for a throne, which I yet hope to see:
If innocence thrive many more have to grieve for,
    Success, slow but sure, I'll contentedly live for—
Yes, Sylvia! we'll meet, and your sigh cease to heave for
    The swain, your fine image haunts, far, far at sea.

The Passengers

Down where yon anch'ring vessel spreads the sail,
That, idly waiting, flaps with ev'ry gale,
Downward they move, a melancholy band,
Pass from the shore, and darken all the strand.
      —Oliver Goldsmith, *The Deserted Village*

How calm an' cozie* is the wight*   *sheltered / person*
    Frae* cares an' conflicts clear ay,*   *from / always*
Whase* settled headpiece never made   *whose*
    His heels or han's be weary!
Perplex'd is he whase anxious schemes
    Pursue applause, or siller,*   *silver*
Success nor sates, nor failure tames;[7]
    Bandied frae post to pillar
        Is he, ilk* day.   *each, every*

As we were, Comrades, at the time
    We mov't frae Ballycarry,[8]
To wan'er thro' the woody clime
    Burgoyne gied oure to harrie.[9]
Wi' frien's consent we prie't a gill,*   *took a small drink*
    An' monie* a house did call at,   *many*
Shook han's an' smil't; tho' ilk fareweel
    Strak, like a weighty mallet,
        Our hearts, that day.

On shore, while ship-mates halt, tho' thrang't,*   *busied*
    Wi' lasses hearts to barter;
Nybers,* an' frien's, in boatfu's pang't,*   *neighbors / crammed*
    Approach our larboard quarter;

Syne speel* the side, an' down the hatch   *immediately climb up*
    To rest, an' crack,* an' gaze on   *joke*
The boles o' births,* that monie a wratch   *small recesses for berths*
    Maun* squeeze in, for a season,   *must*
          By night, an' day.

'This is my locker, yon'ers Jock's,
    In that auld creel,* sea-store* is;   *wicker basket / provisions*
Thir* births beside us are the *Lockes*,[10]   *these*
    My uncle's there before us;
Here, hang my tins an' vitriol[11] jug,
    Nae* thief's at han' to meddle 'em.'   *no*
'L —— d, man, I'm glad ye're a' sae* snug;   *all so*
    But och! 'tis owre like Bedlam
          Wi' a' this day.'

'All boats ashore!' the mate cries stern,
    Wi' oaths wad fear* a saunt ay: *would frighten*
'Now Gude* be wi' ye, Brice,* my bairn'*—   *God / Bruce / child*
    'An' Gude be wi' ye, Auntie.'
What *keepsakes*, an' what news are sent!
    What smacks, an' what embraces!
The hurryin' sailors sleely sklent*   *slyly squint*
    Droll leuks* at lang wry faces,   *looks*
          Fu'* pale that day.   *full, very*

While 'Yo heave O!' wi' monie a yell
    The birkies* weigh the anchor;   *arrogant young men*
Ilk mammies pet conceits itsel'
    The makin' o' a Banker;[12]
They'll soon, tho', wiss to lieve at hame,*   *wish to live at home*
    An' dee* no worth a totam,*   *be / child*
When brustin'* breast, an' whamlin' wame,*   **bursting / heaving stomach*
    Mak' some wise men o' Gotham[13]
          Cry halt! this day.

Some frae the stern, wi' thoughts o' grief
    Leuk back, their hearts to Airlan';*   *Ireland*
Some mettle't bucks,* to work ay brief,   *bright young men*
    At en's o' rapes* are harlin';*   *ropes / hauling*
Some haud* aback frae dangers brow   *hold*
    Their toddlin' o'er, no* cautious;   *now*
An' some, wi' monie a twine* an' throe,   *entwining*

Do something wad be nauceous*   *nauseous*
  To name, this day.

Meanwhile, below, some count their beads,
  While prudes, auld-light sit cantin';[14]
Some mak' their beds; some haud their heads,
  An' cry wi' spite, a' pantin'!
'Ye brought us here, ye luckless cauf!*   *fool*
  ('Aye did he; whisht my darlin'!)
L —— d sen' me hame! wi' poke* an' staff,   *small bag*
  I'd beg my bread thro' Airlan',
    My lane,* that day'.   *on my own*

In twathree* days, the maist* cam' to,   *two or three / most*
  Few heads were sair* or dizzy;   *sore*
An' chiel's* wha scarce a turn cud do,   *young fellows*
  Begoud* to be less lazy;   *began*
At night (to tell amang oursel's)
  They crap,* wi' fandness fidgin',*   *creep / itching*
To court—or maybe something else,
  Gif* folk becam' obligin',   *if*
    Atween an' day.

Roun' the camhouse[15] what motley ban's
  At breakfast-time cam' swarmin'!
Tin, tankards, kettles, pots, an' pans,
  The braid* flat fire was warmin':   *broad*
The guid* auld rule, 'First come first ser't,'   *good*
  Was urg't by men o' mettle;
An' ay whan callens* grew mislear't,*   *youths / unruly*
  The arm o' flesh boost settle
    Th' affray, that day.

A bonie* sight I vow it was,   *bonnie, pretty*
  To see on some lown e'nin',*   *quiet evening*
Th' immense, smooth, smilin' sea o' glass,
  Whare porpoises were stenin':*   *leaping*
To see at night the surface fine
  That Cynthia* made her path on;   *moon*
An' snove, an' snore* thro' waves o' brine, *glided, and rushed*
  That sparkle't like a heath on
    A bleaze* some day.   *blaze*

But now a gale besets our bark,
  Frae gulph to gulph we're tumble't;
Kists,* kits, an' fam'lies, i' the dark,   *chests*
  Wi' ae* side-jerk are jumble't: *every*
Some stauchrin'* thro' a pitch lays laigh*—[16]   *staggering / low*
  Some, drouket,* ban* the breaker;   *drenched / curse*
While surge, on surge, sae skelps* her—Hegh!   *strikes*
  Twa three like that will wreck her
        A while ere day.

Win's,* wives, an' weans,* rampage an' rave,   *loved ones / children*
  Three score at ance* are speakin';   *once*
While blacks* wha a'* before them drave,*   *villians / all / drove*
  Lye cheepin' like a chicken.
'What gart* us play? or bouse* like beasts?   *made / drink*
  Or box in* fairs wi' venom?'[17]   *at*
Hear how the captain laughs an' jests,
  An' bit a bord between him
        An' death, this day.

'Tis calm again. While rightin' things,
  The heads o' births are bizziet,*   *busied*
The seaman chews his quid,* an' sings,   *plug of tobacco*
  An' peys his fren's* a visit.   *friends*
'Eh! dem my eyes! how is't, goodman?
  Got clear of *Davy*'s locker?
Lend me a facer* till we lan',*   *glass of whiskey punch / land*
  'Till blind as Newgate's knocker
        We'll swig, that day.'[18]

Here, gash* guidmen, wi' nightcaps on,   *respectable*
  At ance baith* pray an' watch;   *both*
An', there, for light, sits monie a loun*   *rogue, idler*
  At Cartes* beneath the hatch: *cards*
Here, some sing sangs, or stories tell,
  To ithers* bizzy knittin';   *others*
An', there some readin' to themsels,
  Nod owre asleep, while sittin'
        Twa fold* that day.   *folded in two*

Now Newfoun'lan's becalmin' banks
  Our ship supinely lies on;
An' monie a ane* his lang line fanks,*   *one / knots*

Whase heuk* some captive dies on: *hook*
An' now, disguis't, a fore-mast-man
   Shaves dry, the churls unwillin'
To pay the poll-tax on deman'—
   A pint, or else a shillin'
      A piece, that day.[19]

Aince mair* luck lea's* us (plain 'tis now   *once more / leaves*
   A murd'rer in some mess is)[20]
An English frigate heaves in view,
   I'll bail her board, an' press us:[21]
Taupies* beneath their wives wha stole,   *fools*
   Or 'mang* auld sails lay flat ay,   *among*
Like whitrats* peepi' frae their hole,   *weasels*
   Cried, 'Is she British, wat* ye,   *know*
      Or French, this day?'

'Twas but a brig frae Baltimore,
   To Larne wi' lintseed steerin';
Twa days ago she left the shore,
   Let's watch for lan' appearin':
Spies frae the shrouds, like laigh* dark clouds,   *low*
   Descried domes, mountains, bushes;
The Exiles griev't—the sharpers thiev't—
   While cronies bous't like fishes,
      Conven't* that day.   *convened*

Whan glidin' up the *Delaware*,[22]
   We cam' forenent* *Newcastle*,   *alongside*
Gypes* co'ert the wharf to gove,* an' stare,   *fools / gaze stupidly*
   While out, in boats, we bustle:
Creatures wha ne'er had seen a black,
   Fu' scar't took to their shankies;*   *legs*
Sae, wi' our best rags on our back,
   We mixt amang the Yankies,
      An' skail't,* that day.   *scattered*

Notes

1. Samuel Thomson, *Poems on Different Subjects* (Belfast, 1793).
2. Shallow "banks" off the coast of Newfoundland, famous as fishing grounds.
3. Probably referring to whales seen from the deck of the ship.
4. Sailors are yelling as they rush about their tasks.

5. In his imagination, the poet sees the land he knows taken over by some new land-owner, who plants fields and hedgerows where there are now houses.

6. Nor will any comrade still be alive who misses the company of the "sociable sufferer" (that is, the poet) out at sea.

7. Success does not sate him, nor does failure tame him.

8. The community in County Antrim where Orr was born.

9. To wander through the wooded countryside (in America) it was beyond Burgoyne's power to plunder. Orr uses the name of General John Burgoyne (1722–92), who surrendered his British troops to the forces of the American colonists at Saratoga in October 1777, marking a turning point in the War of American Independence, to symbolize the British forces defeated in America.

10. A note in the original edition explains that this family had sailed for America in 1798.

11. This must be a mistake for a "vitreous" jug, i.e., one made of, or looking as if it is made of, glass.

12. Every mother's child fancied that he had the makings of a "Banker" (one who fished on the Newfoundland "Banks") in him.

13. "Wise men of Gotham" is a traditional phrase meaning "fools"; the inhabitants of Gotham successfully prevented an English king from building a hunting lodge in their village by pretending to be half-witted.

14. Members of the "Old Light" (strict sects of the nonconformist churches) sit singing canticles or psalms.

15. Caboose, the cooking area on the open deck of the ship.

16. Some who were staggering are knocked down by the plunge of the ship into a wave.

17. These lines seem to mean: "What made us play around or drink like beasts or fight venomously at fairs?" The implication is that wrongdoers are suffering now for past misdeeds.

18. A "Newgate Knocker" normally describes a lock of hair, curled in a particular way. Here, however, the lines mean: "Lend me a drink until we land and I can get as drunk as a blind knocker on a prison door."

19. A note at this point reads: "It has been a long established custom for the seamen, on reaching the banks of Newfoundland, to exact a shilling, or a shilling's worth of liquor, from every passenger; and to shave, without soap, those who refuse to contribute their quota." A "fore-mast-man" is a sailor below the rank of petty officer.

20. It is plain now that a murderer is taking his meals in a mess (a group eating together) on board the ship.

21. I'm certain ("would go bail") that she will board our ship and press us into military service.

22. The Delaware River.

6

"Scotch-Irish" Myths and "Irish" Identities in Eighteenth- and Nineteenth-Century America

Kerby A. Miller

During the past half decade, I have been preparing for publication an edited collection of letters and memoirs written by Irish men and women who immigrated to North America between 1660 and 1814.[1] Because very little transatlantic correspondence written prior to the American Revolution—especially by farmers, craftsmen, laborers, and women—has survived, I have been obliged to include other documents, such as petitions and legal depositions. One example of the latter is the deposition given in 1806 by a Presbyterian woman, Mary Elizabeth McDowell Greenlee, who was born in west Ulster in 1711. In 1729 she emigrated with her parents to Pennsylvania, and in 1737 she accompanied her father, her husband, and other kinsmen to the Upper Shenandoah Valley on colonial Virginia's southwestern frontier, where they became the first settlers on the Borden Grant in what became Augusta and then later Rockbridge County, Virginia. In 1806 Mrs. Greenlee was nearly ninety-five years old, but her memory was still so clear and reliable that the local and state courts often requested her testimony in cases involving land-claim disputes among the descendants of Rockbridge County's earliest inhabitants, nearly all of whom she had known personally.[2]

Mrs. Greenlee's deposition describes in minute detail the initial settlement by Ulster men and women of what reportedly became "the most distinctively Scotch-Irish county in America." (One scholar estimates that, on the eve of the American Revolution, at least 75 percent of Rockbridge County's inhabitants were of northern Irish birth or descent.)[3] When I decided to reprint this document in my own work, I relied initially on transcripts published in the 1880s by J. L. Peyton, who was one of the first chroniclers of the Shenandoah Valley as well as an avid celebrant of the "Scotch-Irish" contribution to early American history.[4] Later, however, I procured a photocopy of Mrs. Greenlee's actual deposition, which enabled me to check the accuracy of the transcript. As a result, I discovered that Peyton—or some earlier scribe on whose transcription he had relied—had systematically altered or "Scotch-Irishized" the names of every early Rockbridge County settler who had been of "native" or Catholic Irish stock. Thus, Cullen had been changed to "Coulter," Quinn had become "Green," and so forth. Surely, this was

"Ulsterization" with a vengeance, and perhaps I may be forgiven for suggesting that this may represent one of the earliest—albeit one of the most extreme—examples of Irish historical "revisionism."

The anonymous tamperer with historical evidence was, of course, helping to create what Michael J. O'Brien and other early-twentieth-century Irish-American historians of "crude nationalist" sympathies once called "the Scotch-Irish Myth," an American cousin of one of what is now known in Ireland as the "two traditions" or even as the "two nations"—Protestant and Unionist, Catholic and Nationalist—eternally separate, impermeable, and inviolate.[5] To be sure, as the scholar James Leyburn wrote, "Scotch-Irish" is "a useful term . . . express[ing] a historical reality."[6] If employed carefully and neutrally, the "Scotch-Irish" label can reflect broad distinctions between, on one hand, Ulster Presbyterian immigrants to America of Scottish origin and, on the other hand, Irish Anglican, Quaker, Methodist, Baptist, and southern Irish Presbyterian immigrants primarily of English descent, as well as Irish Catholic immigrants of Gaelic, Norman, Scots Highland, or other backgrounds.

However, even in its most specific and careful usage the term "Scotch-Irish" homogenizes a complex historical reality. For example, it obscures the fact that eighteenth-century Ulster Presbyterian society was internally differentiated both by local circumstances and by the diverse regional, social, and cultural origins of a migration from Scotland that consisted of distinct waves from different Scottish regions during a period of at least one hundred years. Ulster Presbyterians whose ancestors had left the Scottish borderlands in the early 1600s and who themselves emigrated to the American colonies in the early 1700s may have differed in many significant ways from those whose parents had departed southwestern Scotland in the 1690s and who emigrated to the New World in the 1720s. If one also considers the regional, socioeconomic, cultural, and doctrinal differences that prevailed in eighteenth-century Presbyterian Ulster itself, then the possible variations and permutations among the American immigrants are practically endless. For instance, the varying backgrounds, outlooks, and proximity of migration from Scotland among Ulster Presbyterian immigrants to America who adhered to the orthodox Synod of Ulster, the liberal Antrim Presbytery, the evangelical Associated or Seceding synods, or the prophetic traditions of the Reformed or Covenanting congregations—or who were entirely "un-churched," as contemporary clergymen often complained—have scarcely been examined in terms of their socioeconomic, cultural, or political consequences in the New World.[7]

Moreover, the very origins of the term "Scotch-Irish," are highly problematic, both in the British Isles and in America. From the late sixteenth through at least the mid-seventeenth centuries, it appears that the term's most common British and Irish usage was pejorative, as both Irish Anglicans and Lowland Scots Presbyterians labeled as "Scotch-Irish" the Catholic, Gaelic-speaking MacDonnells and other Highlanders who migrated back and forth between Argyll and the Western Isles and the coasts and glens of north Antrim, causing political and military problems for Protestant officials in Edinburgh and Dublin alike. By contrast, Scottish Presbyterian settlers were then most commonly known in Ireland as the "Ulster Scots" or as the "Scottish Interest" or "Nation"; from the eighteenth century on the application to them of the term "Scotch-Irish" was extremely rare, revived to a very limited degree only quite recently in Northern Ireland, primarily to lure American tourists of Ulster Protestant ancestry.[8]

Likewise, among colonial officials in late-seventeenth- and early-eighteenth-century America the label often had negative connotations, perhaps because of its initial application to Catholic, Gaelic Highlanders. Unfortunately, scholars have not investigated the process in America by which the term "Scotch-Irish" lost its early "Catholic" associations and came to designate Ulster Presbyterian immigrants of Lowland Scottish origins. More importantly, perhaps, it appears that in eighteenth-century America prior to the Revolution, use of the label—favorably or otherwise—was quite uncommon. Leyburn located only a handful of recorded instances before 1776, and it is significant that the testament written in 1720 and later celebrated as the "charter document" of "Scotch-Irish" ethnicity—Rev. James MacGregor's famous petition from Londonderry, New Hampshire, to the Massachusetts Bay Colony's leaders in Boston—does *not* employ the term. Moreover, Leyburn concluded, after the Revolution the "Scotch-Irish" label virtually disappeared for at least several decades. Rather, the designations most prevalent in America during the eighteenth and very early nineteenth centuries were "Protestant Irish," "north Irish," or, most frequent and most inclusive, simply "Irish."[9] Thus, in a letter written in 1774 from Philadelphia to Ballymoney, in north County Antrim, the Ulster immigrant merchant James Caldwell designated as "Irish" both his "Countrymen [from] the North" and the original "native[s] of the Emerald Isle," and contrasted their American "patriotism" with "the unbounded loyalty" to George III expressed by immigrants from Scotland.[10] Such ecumenical definitions of "Irishness" were then increasingly common among political writers in Ireland itself, embroiled as they were in constitutional and economic controversies with Britain, and in the colonies Caldwell and other "patriots" of Irish Presbyterian origins clearly had additional "American" reasons to construct a pan-"Irish" identity and to shun "Scottish" associations.[11]

The "Scotch-Irish" label seems to have been reborn in America during the early mid-nineteenth century, but the precise causes of its resurrection are almost as obscure as its earlier history. Its reappearance and growing usage may have stemmed from the reemergence of overt Irish Protestant-Catholic conflicts on both sides of the Atlantic Ocean—for instance, after the failed 1798 Rebellion in Ireland. Certainly from the 1820s on, increasing numbers of new Irish Protestant immigrants to the United States had in Ireland been members of the Loyal Orange Order or had been embittered by Protestant-Catholic competition for land or, more broadly, by Daniel O'Connell's campaign for Catholic emancipation.[12] The most commonly accepted interpretation has been that, in the middle decades of the nineteenth century, Americans of Ulster Presbyterian birth or background "naturally" asserted and formalized their "Scotch-Irish" identity in order to distinguish themselves from the poor Catholic peasant immigrants of the Famine era, whose numbers, physical appearance, and behavior so shocked middle-class American Protestants.[13]

However, I would suggest that the "Scotch-Irish" designation owed its reappearance in the United States as much to social, cultural, and political tensions *within* the Ulster American Presbyterian community itself as to conflicts between this community and an Irish-American Catholic population that in the 1820s and even in the 1830s was still small and nonthreatening. For example, the historian R. S. Wallace has argued that the first, formal eulogies of "the Scotch-Irish Race" emerged during the early-nineteenth-century centennial celebrations of the first settlements of Londonderry, New Hampshire, and other New England villages that had been planted by Ulster men and women in the 1720s, in the first major wave of northern Irish migration. The authors of these published sermons, speeches, and "histories" were Presbyterian clergymen and other local notables who were closely associated with the Federalist—and later with the Whig—party and who were highly critical of both the Jeffersonian Republican political loyalties and the "uncivilized" and often sodden behavior that still characterized a large number of Ulster American farmers, frontiersmen, and urban workers.[14]

My hypothesis is that "Scotch-Irish" ethnicity was in part the product of an *intra*communal struggle for cultural and political hegemony, led by members of a conservative Ulster American bourgeoisie, whose primary goal was to expunge their communities of both the political radicalism and the social and cultural patterns that offended middle-class American sensibilities and that were, not coincidentally, similar to those traditionally deemed exclusively characteristic of the "native" or Catholic Irish. Indeed, it is revealing that in the 1790s Federalist polemicists applied the term *wild Irish*—laden as it was with historic connotations of *Catholic* Irish barbarism, treachery, and rebellion associated with their 1641 Rising—to *all* Irish Americans who opposed the Washington and Adams administrations, sympathized with the French Revolution, denounced Jay's Treaty, and supported the Republican Party in the United States and the United Irishmen overseas.[15] The Federalists well knew that the overwhelming majority of Thomas Jefferson's Irish adherents were of Ulster Presbyterian—not Irish Catholic—birth or descent. However, by stigmatizing their opponents as "wild Irish" the Federalists were, in effect, warning Irish-American Protestants that they were forfeiting their ancestors' claims to ethnic or religious superiority by behaving in ways that, in Anglo-Irish and Anglo-American popular culture, especially as interpreted by their respective elites, were traditionally associated with Irish Catholics alone. Likewise, it was probably no coincidence that the local Presbyterian clergy's first attempt to suppress Londonderry, New Hampshire's traditional semiannual fairs— boisterous events that unsympathetic observers decried in language similar to that applied to the infamous Donnybrook fairs in Ireland—occurred in 1798, the year of the Alien and Sedition Acts in the United States as well as of the suppression of rebellion in Ireland itself.[16]

Other possible links between the elaboration of Anglo-Irish-American political conservatism and sociocultural "modernization" on one hand and the emergence of "Scotch-Irish" ethnicity on the other also deserve exploration. For example, in late-eighteenth-century western Pennsylvania, the role of the Ulster-stock Presbyterian clergyman and arch-Federalist John McMillan in crushing the largely Irish "Whiskey Insurrection" of 1794 and in quarantining the Ohio Valley against United Irish exiles like Thomas Ledlie Birch after 1798—in combination with the Philadelphia Synod's "embargo" on Irish Presbyterian ministers and licentiates deemed infected by the "French disease"—suggests that the formulation of a distinct "Scotch-Irish" identity—linked to reactionary politics, evangelical religion, and bourgeois values—had its earliest origins in a broad ideological, social, and political movement that began in the 1790s rather than much later, in the mid-nineteenth century, as a simple revulsion against Famine immigrants.[17] The parallels—indeed, perhaps the actual connections—between these *American* developments and the triumph after 1798 of what Kevin Whelan has called the "counter-revolutionary" forces in Ireland itself deserve study, because conservatives on both sides of the ocean, and among Catholics as well as Protestants, sought to sunder the United Irish and the Jeffersonian Republican alliances between Presbyterians and "papists."[18]

Neither effort was entirely successful, at least in the short run. For example, in some parts of the United States, such as Crawford County in northwestern Pennsylvania, from 1796 at least through 1860 the townships that had been settled in the late eighteenth century by Presbyterians from Donegal and other Ulster counties voted consistently for Jeffersonian Republican and later for Jacksonian Democratic presidential candidates, thereby maintaining in America a political alliance with Irish Catholic immigrants that their ancestors had forged in the 1790s.[19] Likewise, the surprisingly large proportion of letters written by Irish Presbyterian immigrants of the pre-Famine and even the Famine eras that expressed liberal and even radical political sentiments suggests that the legacy of the United Irishmen was not so much diluted in Ulster as it was deported overseas.[20]

Eventually, however, ethnoreligious and political divisions between Ulster Protestants and Irish Catholics became stark and mutually reinforcing, on both sides of the Atlantic. In the United States, as early as the 1820s some Irish Protestant newcomers were conspicuous in the ranks of nativist organizations, temperance associations, and street mobs that demonized and assaulted Irish Catholic immigrants. Before midcentury it appears that a majority of Irish-American Protestants and Catholics were mobilized in opposite political camps as the middle classes in both groups found distinctly American reasons to marshal their adherents along ethnoreligious lines—for example, to sunder and suppress transethnic, working-class alliances.[21] Consequently, by the 1850s celebrants of "Scotch-Irish" ethnicity were drawing sharp and invidious comparisons between their Ulster Protestant ancestors and Irish Catholics.[22]

In their quest for "founding father" status alongside the Pilgrims and Puritans, the Scotch-Irish eulogists ignored Presbyterian immigrants (past and present) whose economic distress, political activities, and social behavior did not exemplify group prosperity, patriotism, or respectability. For instance, the important part played by Ulster Protestants in the Carolina and Georgia Loyalists' struggle against the American Revolution, and the even more prominent role of Irish Presbyterian immigrants such as George Bryan and William Findley in the Anti-Federalists' opposition to ratification of the U.S. Constitution, were downplayed or ignored altogether.[23] Instead, those who formulated the "Scotch-Irish Myth" projected the frailties of their own unfortunates and misfits onto Irish Catholic immigrants, implying that the "Scotch-Irish" could not have been failures or disloyal to "American values" because, by definition, the virtues inherent in both their religion and their British origins guaranteed their moral, cultural, and, hence, economic and political superiority. Thus, in 1850 the Rev. E. L. Parker of Londonderry, New Hampshire, blamed his community's now-suppressed fairs and formerly embarrassing drinking habits on its ancestors' exposure to "Celtic contamination" during their brief sojourns in northern Ireland.[24]

Furthermore, during the mid- and late nineteenth century, the term "Scotch-Irish" broadened in America beyond its narrow, initial associations with Ulster Presbyterians of Scottish descent. American historians have rarely explored or fully understood how this expansion happened, but surely it was associated with the dilution of Protestant denominational boundaries wrought by evangelicalism in both Ireland and America, and, in Ireland, with the emergence of a pan-Protestant political bloc in opposition to Irish Catholic nationalism. Again, possible transatlantic linkages—such as between American and Irish revivalism (often orchestrated by the same preachers), between anti-Catholic movements on both sides of the ocean, and with the parallel development of the Scotch-Irish Congresses in the United States and of Ulster Unionism in the north of Ireland—deserve investigation. In any event, the consequence by the late 1800s was that the group designated as "Scotch-Irish" had expanded to include not only Americans of Scots Presbyterian descent but also those of Irish Anglican, Quaker, or other Protestant antecedents (although most of the latter were of English—not Scottish—origins, and their ancestors often hailed from southern Ireland), as well as all those of Gaelic Irish or Hiberno-Norman descent who were currently *not* Catholic. Thus, by the early twentieth century, the authors of county histories as far afield as South Carolina and South Dakota were happily rebaptizing as "Scotch-Irish" the ancestors of respectable Methodist merchants and Baptist farmers who had embarrassingly "native Irish" names such as O'Hara and O'Brien![25]

Ironically, by making the "Scotch-Irish" group more inclusive, its eulogists inadvertently undermined the basic premise of the group "Myth" and demonstrated that the development of "Scotch-Irish" identity was obviously *not* the inevitable consequence of permanent conflicts between the inflexible adherents of two eternally separate and distinct historical traditions. And, of course, the question of ethnicity or nationality is not one of ancestral birthplace or religion but one of individual and collective identification, which in turn is subjective, situational, and variable, shaped by a multitude of shifting social, cultural, political, and even psychological circumstances. Indeed, one of the presumed benefits of migration from the Old World to the New is that it allowed immigrants to create or choose identities that might differ significantly from the categories imposed by public officials, landlords, clergy, or even kinsmen in their former homelands.[26]

Despite penal laws that mandated sharp legal distinctions, the actual ethnoreligious boundaries between Irish Protestants and Catholics, both in Ireland and in the American colonies, were much more flexible and permeable than they later became, as evidenced, for example, by the presence and intermarriage with Ulster Protestant settlers of a significant minority of "native" or Irish Catholic immigrants in the Shenandoah Valley and elsewhere in eighteenth-century America.[27] Similarly, the earliest Irish-American organizations—the St. Patrick's Society and the Hibernian Society in Philadelphia and other colonial seaports—included merchants (such as James Caldwell) and professionals of all denominations, reflecting a tolerance that stemmed from shared business and political interests as well as the influence of Enlightenment rationalism.[28] Among poorer migrants, the relative frequency of intermarriage and conversions reflected a pragmatic understanding that ethnic and religious affiliations were not absolute but were contingent on local economic and social circumstances. Meanwhile, in Ireland itself and on the more formal level of political culture, from the early mid-eighteenth century on, new, secular, and more inclusive definitions of "Irishness" temporarily promised to subsume Ireland's different religious and ethnic strains in a common "patriotism" that, as the Caldwell family's history and correspondence demonstrates, would flower on both sides of the Atlantic: in Ireland among the Volunteers of the late 1770s and 1780s and among the United Irishmen a decade later, and in America in the Revolution of 1775–83 and again in the Jeffersonian Republicanism of the 1790s and the early 1800s.[29]

Although these ecumenical blossoms withered and died, first in Ireland and later in America, the older traditions of tolerance and sociability, as well as the newer, inclusive notions of "Irish" ethnic and political identity, may have lingered longest in the southern regions of the United States. From the 1600s through the early 1800s there was a substantial migration from Ireland to what was later known as the Old South. Between the 1680s and the Revolution, as many as half of the one-quarter to one-third of a million emigrants from Ireland to British North America settled in the southern mainland colonies, primarily in the backcountry or frontier districts.[30] One scholar concludes that in 1790 at least one-fifth of white southerners were of Irish birth or descent, and that approximately two-thirds of these early Irish-American southerners were of Ulster Presbyterian origins, while most of the others (Anglicans and Catholics) had conformed to the dominant faith of their neighbors.[31] In addition, during the fifty years or so after the American Revolution, perhaps as many as one hundred thousand Irish—again, primarily Ulster Presbyterians—migrated to the southern states.

By the early twentieth century, of course, a popular and scholarly association between the white population of the Old South and the "Scotch-Irish" would be commonplace, symbolized by the prominence of Woodrow Wilson. However, during the colonial, revolutionary, and early national periods, the ethnic and political distinctions between the "Irish" of Ulster Presbyterian and other religious and regional origins appear to have been exceptionally vague. In late-eighteenth-century South Carolina, for example, the staunch "Scotch-Irish" resistance to ratification of the U.S. Constitution was led by Ædanus Burke, an emigrant from Galway of Catholic parents and indeterminate religion who, later in the 1790s, joined forces with the Leinster-born Anglican Pierce Butler to mobilize backcountry South Carolinians of Ulster Presbyterian descent against Jay's Treaty.[32] Similarly, in the early nineteenth century, most of the nation's most flourishing Hibernian and Irish-American nationalist societies were situated in Charleston, Savannah, and other southern cities, where usually they were led by Protestants of Ulster birth or descent.[33] During the same period, the Irish-born Catholic bishop of Charleston, John England, reported that Protestant-Catholic relations in his region were much friendlier than elsewhere in the country.[34]

In part, these residual patterns—anachronistic in the early-nineteenth-century context of worsening Irish Protestant-Catholic relationships in both Ireland and the northern states—reflected the general tendency of all southern whites to downplay internal differences for the sake of racial solidarity against the region's large and potentially rebellious slave population. Undoubtedly, they also reflected the relative paucity of Irish Catholic immigration to the Old South during the mid-nineteenth century, when the northern states were inundated by refugees from the Great Famine. In 1860 only 11 percent of the 1.6 million Irish in America resided in the southern slave states (primarily in "border" cities, such as New Orleans, Baltimore, and St. Louis), and they comprised merely 2.25 percent of the South's white population.[35] Consequently, the Catholic church was much weaker institutionally and much less aggressive politically in the antebellum South than in the North and was thus unable either to mobilize its own Irish flock or to frighten Irish-American Protestants away from secular alliances with their Catholic countrymen. Indeed, missionary priests in the early- and mid-nineteenth-century South often lamented the large numbers of Irish-stock families whose Catholic ancestors had abandoned the Church because of the dearth of priests and chapels in the region.[36] In Louisiana, the only southern state with a substantial Catholic presence, the primary cultural and political conflicts (aside from those associated with slavery and race) were between English- and French-speaking inhabitants, not between either Protestants and Catholics, generally, or Protestants and Irish Catholics, specifically.[37] Likewise, the kinds of socioeconomic competition conducive to white ethnoreligious antagonisms may have been less prevalent in an overwhelmingly rural South, where not only was cheap land relatively available but the urban-industrialization characteristic of the northeastern states was also comparatively underdeveloped.

Irish "revisionist" historians and their admirers on this side of the Atlantic should be assured that I am not asserting that Irish Protestant and Catholic immigrants and their descendants simply comprised a happy, homogeneous group in the eighteenth- or early-nineteenth-century South, much less in the rest of the country. However, I am suggesting that during this era, "Irish" ethnic identity in America, generally, was much more varied, flexible, and inclusive than it would later become; that the social and political issues that engaged the attention of Irish immigrants and prompted their ethnic self-definition often transcended the religious divisions that later became so prominent; and that these ecumenical patterns were especially marked in an Old South that, ironically, later came to be regarded as the very cradle or bastion of a "racially" distinct "Scotch-Irish" identity.

The lives of numerous "ordinary" emigrants from Ireland to the Old South illustrate the variety and mutability of early Irish identities in that region: John O'Raw, for example, in 1806 a Catholic emigrant from County Antrim to South Carolina, who in the "Charleston schism" of 1815–19 defied his archbishop's threats of excommunication in order to maintain his social and political links to that city's Irish Protestant immigrants, fellow Irish nationalists, and members of the local Hibernian Society. Or Andrew Leary O'Brien, a "spoiled priest" from County Cork and a former canal worker in Pennsylvania, who in 1838 removed to Georgia, converted to Methodism, and founded a college for students of that faith. Or, most remarkably, Samuel Burke, an Irish-speaker who was christened and raised in the city of Cork, who helped British officers in New York raise an Irish Loyalist regiment during the American Revolution and whose cultural and linguistic claims to "Irish" identity could only be mitigated by the fact that, genetically, he was an African American who had been born in Charleston and taken to Ireland in infancy.[38] However, the remainder of this essay will focus on the life of the Ulster Presbyterian immigrant William Hill, a merchant and farmer who lived in Abbeville District, South Carolina, from 1822 until his death, at age eighty, in 1886. Hill's career exemplifies the complex relationships between Irish and American influences and among the ideological, socioeconomic, and political circumstances that shaped the dynamics of "Irish" and "Scotch- Irish" identities in the New World.[39]

William Hill was born in 1805 in Ballynure parish, County Antrim, into a Presbyterian family that had been implicated in the 1798 Rebellion. According to family tradition, Hill emigrated from Ireland at age seventeen, primarily because he disliked his stepmother. In 1822 Hill arrived in Charleston with letters of introduction to an earlier emigrant from Ballynure, a Major John Donald, who had settled in Abbeville and fought in the War of 1812. After clerking for two years in Donald's store, Hill married his employer's daughter, Anna, and commenced farming land that the Major gave him as a wedding present. By the late 1820s, Hill was concentrating primarily on trade, selling goods in his own country store, although he continued to farm about 360 acres.[40] Sometime in the 1840s, he moved into Abbeville town, population four hundred, where he prospered as a merchant. Hill had no formal legal training, but he gained a reputation as an honest, competent adviser in probate law and estate administration, and in 1852 he was elected to the first of eight successive terms as Abbeville District's judge of the court of ordinary. According to the 1860 census, on the eve of the Civil War Hill owned real and personal property worth twenty thousand dollars, in addition to fifteen slaves.[41] However, the Civil War was a catastrophe for William Hill and his family; he claimed to have lost more than thirty thousand dollars in slaves, Confederate bonds and currency, and the general depreciation of real estate. In addition, two of his sons-in-law died of wounds or disease, and his own eldest son was severely wounded, while fighting for the Confederacy. Also, during South Carolina's postwar "reconstruction," the state's Radical Republican regime stripped Hill of his office as probate judge.[42] Hill continued to dabble in trade until about 1871, when he retired to his farm outside Abbeville town, where he died fifteen years later.

Fortunately, Hill wrote regularly to his brother David, back in Ballynure, and about a dozen of his letters have survived. Using that correspondence in conjunction with what can be discovered about Hill's career in South Carolina, we can reconstruct the changes in his sense of ethnic identity. One of Hill's obituaries described him as "a most enthusiastic Irishman, never being entirely weaned of his love for his native land."[43] However, Hill's emotional identification with Ireland is most evident in his earliest surviving correspondence, in which he often expressed poignant desires to return to his native land, if only to visit. In one letter, for example, Hill chided his brother for not writing more frequently: "There is little or nothing here [in South Carolina] to concern you," he wrote, but "every nook and corner of the neighborhood of Ballynure teems with absorbing interest to me. Although it is upwards of thirty-two years since I left 'the green hills of my youth,' I can still luxuriate in fancy, . . . young again, strolling over the old green sod."[44]

There are several likely explanations for William Hill's profound homesickness for Ireland. One is the circumstance of his emigration: at a relatively young age, and perhaps impelled less by ambition than by his deteriorating relationship with his stepmother. Another is Hill's romantic attachment to a woman he had left behind in Ballynure and to whom he referred in one early letter, when he recalled "whispering words of artless love to her who was—most beautiful, most lovely, but now alas, how changed." Hill asked his brother, "Do you surmise to whom I allude? Well then, tell me of her. Although the vase is long broken, yet still the fragrance of the once sweet flower remains."[45] By contrast, prior to 1867 Hill never even mentioned his wife in South Carolina in any of his surviving correspondence with Ireland. Thus, although Hill's obituary referred to his "beloved wife" and their "happy union for nearly sixty years," it appears that for many decades his deepest affections were reserved for someone "back home."[46]

Indeed, it is not improbable that Hill might have returned permanently to Ireland, as he claimed to desire, had he not married so young and so soon after his immigration, for although Hill's obituaries and other records provide little information about his first twenty or so years in South Carolina, during those decades he appears to have enjoyed little material success and to have made few or no public commitments to his adopted country. For example, Hill did not apply for U.S. citizenship until 1834, eight years after his arrival in South Carolina.[47] Likewise, he took no part in public life until 1836, when he joined Abbeville's militia company for service in the Seminole War. Significantly, it was just *before* those years, in 1832 and 1833, that John C. Calhoun and South Carolina's other leading politicians precipitated the "nullification crisis" and first challenged the federal government's authority. Both during and after that crisis, white South Carolinians experienced intense pressure to demonstrate communal loyalty and solidarity. However, because Hill's obituaries made no mention of any participation in the nullification movement, as they surely would have done had he been involved, it is likely that Hill was among the one-third of Abbeville District's voters (mostly poor men, as was Hill in the early 1830s) who opposed nullification. After the crisis, however, as a retailer dependent on elite credit and public approval, Hill probably hastened to conform to communal standards, and clearly it was during the twenty years following the nullification episode that Hill rose in prosperity and public esteem: by acquiring the military credentials, the membership in Abbeville's Presbyterian church, and the ownership of slaves that marked his entrance into the second tier of the District's elite and that made him electable to public office. By November 1860, Hill's local status was epitomized by his chairmanship, alongside the District's wealthiest planters, of the public meeting that sent Abbeville's delegates to South Carolina's Secession Convention.[48]

Likewise, in the decades that Hill became more "American"—which in Abbeville meant more "southern"—several specific developments in Ireland and South Carolina alike operated to mitigate or qualify Hill's identification with his homeland. During the nullification crisis, South Carolina's only Irish-American newspaper, the *Charleston Irishman and Southern Democrat*, was "violently anti-nullification," and Hill's attachment to Ireland may have been shaken by the consequent association of "Irishness" with "disloyalty" to South Carolina in the minds of many local whites.[49] More certainly, in the early 1840s, Daniel O'Connell—in alliance with Dublin Quakers, Ulster Presbyterian clergy, and Yankee abolitionists such as William Lloyd Garrison—publicly denounced southern slavery and urged all "true Irishmen" in America to join the American antislavery movement. In response, Hibernian and Irish-American nationalist societies in the South either shut their doors or repudiated O'Connell's leadership.[50] Significantly, it was during this period that William Hill's own letters to his brother denied vehemently that "slavery and Christianity were inconsistent," thus revealing the increasing gap between the antislavery sentiments that prevailed in Ireland and his own commitments both to his propertied interests and to the security of the white minority in a district where, between 1820 and 1850, the proportion of slaves in the population had grown from 40 to 60 percent.[51]

Also of crucial importance in the late 1840s and 1850s was the immigration to South Carolina of several thousand Irish Catholic peasants, impoverished refugees from the Great Famine. William Hill's "Irish" identity was shaped by the United Irishmen's republican and ecumenical ideals, which, in theory, submerged religious distinctions under the common name of "Irishman." Hill was true to that legacy: he named one of his sons after Robert Emmet, the United Irish hero and martyr, and in his letters he denounced England's "oppressive" rule over Ireland, expressed his detestation of Irish Orangemen for their bigotry and their loyalty to the crown, refused to consider permitting his son to attend one of Ireland's new Queen's Colleges because of its royalist associations, and eagerly anticipated Britain's defeat in the Crimean War.[52]

However, Hill's sense of "Irishness" had been shaped by a specific, local Irish environment—one that had been almost exclusively Protestant as well as relatively genteel. In the Ballynure parish of Hill's youth, 85 percent of the inhabitants were Presbyterians and merely 5 percent Catholics.[53] Perhaps it was no wonder, therefore, that Hill was shocked and embarrassed by what he described as the "poverty and want, rags, squalor, and wretchedness" of the Famine Irish who entered mid-century South Carolina and who, as he lamented, "reflect discredit on the better class of their countrymen." Hill admitted that "most of the [new Irish] emigrants . . . never had opportunity of polish," but for the first time he was forced to distinguish between his own people and what he called "the *real* Irish, of papist stock."[54] Subsequent events justified Hill's fear of guilt by association, for in the mid-1850s the nativist Know-Nothing Party, pledging to stem the influx of Irish immigrants and to curtail their political rights, briefly flourished in South Carolina, and in 1857 Hill was nearly defeated for reelection as probate judge by a Know-Nothing candidate who denounced his "Irish" origins.[55]

The South's defeat and South Carolina's devastation in the Civil War, plus the consequent damage to his own fortune and family, rekindled Hill's nostalgia for Ireland and made him yearn to "go back even in my old age to the dear land wherein I first drew breath."[56] Yet Hill's primary commitment to the South—as well as his actual estrangement from Ireland and its recent emigrants—was now evident. For instance, in his postwar correspondence Hill attributed the Confederacy's defeat to the "tens of thousands" of Irish Catholic "mercenaries," as he called them, who had joined the Union army to help the "accursed" Yankees "crush a people struggling for self-government regardless of anything but their filthy pay." Similarly, Hill was appalled that the Irish-American soldiers stationed in Abbeville allegedly "mingle[d] with the Negroes with as much affinity as if of the same blood."[57] Although Hill visited Ireland briefly in 1867, for the first and only time since his departure nearly half a century earlier, the letter he wrote to brother David, on his return to Abbeville, was so uncharacteristically unsentimental as to suggest that his visit had been profoundly disillusioning, memorable only for "the cough [with] which [he] had been so much troubled" in a wet, cold climate to which he was now unaccustomed. Perhaps tellingly, it was only in this and subsequent letters that Hill first made reference to his wife of forty years.[58] Thus, in 1867 William Hill finally came "home" to South Carolina, psychologically as well as physically. And given the evolution of his ethnic identity and nationalist sympathies—from "Irish" to white southern—perhaps it was inevitable that in the early twentieth century his granddaughter would write in a school essay that she was not of "Irish" but of "Scotch-Irish descent," although neither Hill nor the authors of his obituaries had ever employed the latter term.[59]

However, it is remarkable that today many of the descendants of the William Hills—and of the hundreds of thousands of other Ulster Protestants who settled in the Old South—now again regard themselves as inclusively, if vaguely, "Irish." In 1990 some 38.7 million Americans responded to a census question concerning their ethnicity by listing "Irish" as their response, and 13.3 million of these self-described "Irish-Americans," 34 percent of the national aggregate, resided in the South, although in 1860 merely 176,000 Irish immigrants, 11 percent of those then living in the United States, inhabited the slave states. From another perspective, in 1990 one-fifth of white southerners claimed Irish ancestry, yet on the eve of the Civil War scarcely more than 2 percent of white southerners had been Irish born. Even more surprising is that, in 1990, only 2.6 million white southerners, less than 4 percent, designated "Scotch-Irish" as their ancestry.[60] In light of the relative scarcity of Famine and post-Famine immigrants in the Old South, it seems reasonable to conclude that most of that region's self-designated "Irish" in 1990 were the descendants of the South's Ulster Presbyterian and other Irish Protestant settlers (including early converts from Catholicism) who had immigrated prior to the American Revolution or, at the latest, before 1830.

These data may provide Jesse Helms, Bob Jones, and the Rev. Ian Paisley's other southern friends with a few disquieting reflections, although of course contemporary professions of "Irishness" in Atlanta or Tupelo have quite different implications and consequences from similar declarations in north Belfast or Portadown. Yet the data clearly demonstrate once again both the mutable and situational character of ethnic identity and the significance of the *contexts* in which this identity is formulated—whether in Ireland or America, in the eighteenth or the twentieth century. Certainly, in recent decades Irish revisionist historians have applied this lesson of "contextualization" to deconstruct and destabilize the "Irish [and Irish-American] Nationalist tradition[s]." In fairness, I suggest that the same skeptical perspectives and methodologies should be applied more rigorously to the "Unionist [and "Scotch-Irish"] tradition[s]." As I argued in another venue, one may applaud the revisionists' desire to free us from what Roy Foster calls "imprisoning historical perspectives," but if the task of "objective" Irish scholars is to feed the popular heart with ambiguities and uncertainties, with paradoxes and contradictions, instead of traditional "myths," we should take care that this salutary diet and the consequent heartburn of confusion and guilt are equitably distributed among *all* those who share responsibility for Ireland's tragic past and troubled present.[61]

Notes

1. K. A. Miller, A. Schrier, B. D. Boling, and D. N. Doyle, *To Ye Land of Canaan: Letters, Memoirs, and Other Writings by Immigrants from Ireland to Colonial and Revolutionary America, 1660–1814* (New York: Oxford University Press, forthcoming).

2. Mary Elizabeth McDowell Greenlee deposition, *Peck v. Borden,* 10 November 1806 (District Court Record Book, September 1789–April 1793, in the Augusta County Clerk's Office, Staunton, Va.); for a copy of this document, I am grateful to Mrs. Katherine G. Bushman, Augusta County Historical Society, Staunton.

3. On Augusta and Rockbridge counties, see R. D. Mitchell, *Commercialism and Frontier: Perspectives on the Early Shenandoah Valley* (Charlottesville: University of Virginia Press, 1977); and A. H. Tillson, Jr., *Gentry and Common Folk: Political Culture on a Virginia Frontier, 1740–1789* (Lexington: University Press of Kentucky, 1991).

4. J. L. Peyton, *History of Augusta County, Virginia* (1882; reprint, Staunton, Va.: S. M. Yost & Son, 1902), 69–74; see also W. Couper, *History of the Shenandoah Valley*, vol. 1 (New York: Lewis Historical, 1952), 274–79.

5. M. J. O'Brien, "The 'Scotch-Irish' Myth," *Journal of the American Irish Historical Society* 24 (1925): 142–53. Reference to the "two traditions" is ubiquitous in recent scholarly and journalistic literature; on the "two nations," the classic text is British and Irish Communist Organization, *The Two Nations* (Belfast: British and Irish Communist Organization, 1975).

6. J. G. Leyburn, *The Scotch-Irish: A Social History* (Chapel Hill: University of North Carolina Press, 1962), 327–34.

7. The best recent book on the complexities of eighteenth-century Ulster Presbyterian society and culture is I. R. McBride, *Scripture Politics: Ulster Presbyterians and Irish Radicalism in the Late Eighteenth Century* (Oxford: Clarendon Press, 1998).

8. Leyburn, *Scotch-Irish;* see also D. Stevenson, *Scottish Covenanters and Irish Confederates: Scottish-Irish Relations in the Mid-Seventeenth Century* (Belfast: Ulster Historical Foundation, 1981). Ironically, although in the early eighteenth century Ulster-born Presbyterian students at Glasgow and Edinburgh universities were formally registered as "Scottus Hibernicus," in the frequent and occasionally violent conflicts between them and Scottish-born students and academic officials, they were denominated as "Irish" by both their critics and supporters.

9. Leyburn, *Scotch-Irish*; for the earliest published copy of Rev. James MacGregor's petition, see J. Belknap, *The History of New-Hampshire* (Dover, N.H.: O. Crosby and J. Varney, 1812), vol. 2, 260–63.

10. James Caldwell, December 1774, transcribed in John Caldwell, Jr., "Particular of History of a North County [Antrim] Irish Family" (1849), of which copies can be found in T.3541/5/3 in the Public Record Office of Northern Ireland, Belfast (hereafter cited as "PRONI"), and in the New York Historical and Genealogical Society, New York City.

11. See, for example, J. Leerssen, *Mere Irish and Fíor-Ghael: Studies in the Idea of Irish Nationality, Its Development and Literary Expression prior to the Nineteenth Century* (Notre Dame: University of Notre Dame Press, 1997), esp. 294–383.

12. K. A. Miller, *Emigrants and Exiles: Ireland and the Irish Exodus to North America* (New York: Oxford University Press, 1985), ch. 6.

13. M. A. Jones, "The Scotch-Irish in British America," in *Strangers Within the Realm: Cultural Margins of the First British Empire*, ed. B. Bailyn and P. D. Morgan (Chapel Hill: University of North Carolina Press, 1991), 284–85; H. T. Blethen and C. W. Wood, Jr., eds., *Ulster and North America: Transatlantic Perspectives on the Scotch-Irish* (Tuscaloosa: University of Alabama Press, 1997), 1.

14. R. S. Wallace, "The Scotch-Irish of Provincial New Hampshire" (Ph.D. diss., University of New Hampshire, 1984), ch. 1.

15. Edward C. Carter, II, "A 'Wild Irishman' under Every Federalist's Bed: Naturalisation in Philadelphia, 1789–1806," *Pennsylvania Magazine of History and Biography* 94 (1970): 331–46. On Irish-American loyalties to the Jeffersonian Republican Party, see M. Durey, *Transatlantic Radicals and the Early American Republic* (Lawrence: Univer-

sity Press of Kansas, 1997), esp. chs. 6 and 7; and D. A. Wilson, *United Irishmen, United States: Immigrant Radicals in the Early Republic* (Ithaca: Cornell University Press, 1998).

16. Rev. E. L. Parker, *The History of Londonderry* [New Hampshire] (Boston, 1851); Rev. A. L. Perry, *Scotch-Irish in New England* (Boston, 1891).

17. Wilson, *United Irishmen, United States,* 120–29.

18. K. Whelan, *The Tree of Liberty: Radicalism, Catholicism and the Construction of Irish Identity, 1760–1830* (Notre Dame, Ind.: University of Notre Dame Press, 1996), 133–75.

19. Extrapolated from S. D. Bates, *Our County and Its People: A Historical and Memorial Record of Crawford County, Pennsylvania* (Boston, 1899); [R. C. Brown], *History of Crawford County, Pennsylvania* (Chicago, 1885); and R. D. Ilisevich, "Class Structure and Politics in Crawford County, 1800–1840," *Western Pennsylvania Historical Magazine* 63 (April 1980): 95–119.

20. Miller, *Emigrants and Exiles,* chs. 6 and 7; see, for example, the Kerr family letters, 1840–58 (MIC 144/33-23, PRONI).

21. Miller, *Emigrants and Exiles,* ch. 6; D. Montgomery, "The Shuttle and the Cross: Weavers and Artisans in the Kensington Riots of 1844," *Journal of Social History* 5 (1972): 411–39.

22. Invidious comparisons between "Scotch-Irish" and Irish Catholic immigrants can be found in the historical and popular literature from the early nineteenth through the early twentieth centuries; see, for example, Parker, *History of Londonderry;* the ten volumes of the *The Scotch-Irish in America: Proceedings of the Scotch-Irish Congress* (Cincinnati, Ohio, 1889–1901); and M. Glasgow, *The Scotch-Irish in Northern Ireland and in the American Colonies* (New York: G. P. Putnam's Sons, 1936).

23. The historical literature on the southern loyalists is voluminous but see W. Brown, *The King's Friends: The Composition and Motives of the American Loyalist Claims* (Providence, R.I.: Brown University Press, 1965). On Bryan and Findley, see R. J. Ferguson, *Early Western Pennsylvania Politics* (Pittsburgh: University of Pittsburgh Press, 1938); J. S. Foster, *In Pursuit of Equal Liberty: George Bryan and the Revolution in Pennsylvania* (University Park: Pennsylvania State University Press, 1994); O. S. Ireland, *Religion, Ethnicity, and Politics: Ratifying the Constitution in Pennsylvania* (University Park: Pennsylvania State University Press, 1995); and H. M. Tincom, *The Republicans and Federalists in Pennsylvania, 1790–1801* (Harrisburg: Pennsylvania Historical and Museum Commission, 1950).

24. Parker, *History of Londonderry.*

25. For example, *Memorial and Biographical Record of Turner, Lincoln, Union and Clay Counties* [South Dakota] (Chicago, 1897).

26. The scholarly literature on ethnicity is voluminous. On Irish-American Catholic ethnicity, see K. A. Miller, "Class, Culture and Immigrant Group Identity in the United States: The Case of Irish-American Ethnicity," in *Immigration Reconsidered: History, Sociology and Politics*, ed. V. Yans-McLaughlin (New York: Oxford University Press, 1990), 96–129.

27. D. N. Doyle, *Ireland, Irishmen and Revolutionary America, 1760–1820* (Dublin: Mercier Press, 1981), 51–76.

28. J. M. Campbell, *A History of the Friendly Sons of St. Patrick and of the Hibernian Society for the Relief of Emigrants from Ireland* (Philadelphia, 1892); and R. C. Murphy and L. J. Mannion, *The History of the Society of the Friendly Sons of Saint Patrick in the City of New York* (New York: Society of the Friendly Sons of St. Patrick, 1962).

29. Leerssen, *Mere Irish and Fíor-Ghael,* 294–383.

30. For the contours of eighteenth- and early-nineteenth-century Irish (especially "Scotch-Irish") emigration and settlement, see Doyle, *Ireland, Irishmen;* and Miller, *Emigrants and Exiles,* chs. 4–6.

31. Doyle, *Ireland, Irishmen,* 51–76.

32. J. C. Meleney, *The Public Life of Aedanus Burke: Revolutionary Republican in Post-Revolutionary South Carolina* (Columbia: University of South Carolina Press, 1989).

33. M. F. Funchion, *Irish-American Voluntary Organizations* (Westport: Greenwood Press, 1983), 117, 141–45, 239.

34. On Bishop England, see P. Guilday, *The Life and Times of John England, First Bishop of Charleston, 1786–1840,* 2 vols. (New York: America Press, 1927).

35. J. C. G. Kennedy, *Population of the United States in 1860; Compiled from the Official Returns of the Eighth Census* (Washington, D.C.: Government Printing Office, 1864).

36. On the Catholic Church in the American South, see J. P. Dolan, *The American Catholic Experience: A History from Colonial Times to the Present* (Garden City, N.Y.: Doubleday, 1985), ch. 4; and R. M. Miller and J. K. Wakelyn, eds., *Catholics in the Old South* (Macon, Ga.: Mercer University Press, 1983).

37. E. F. Niehaus, *The Irish in New Orleans, 1800–60* (Baton Rouge: Louisiana State University Press, 1965).

38. On O'Raw, O'Brien, and Burke, see K. A. Miller, "'Scotch-Irish,' 'Black Irish,' and 'Real Irish': Emigrants and Identities in the Old South," in *The Irish Diaspora,* ed. A. Bielenberg (Harlow, Essex: Longman, forthcoming).

39. Unless otherwise cited, biographical data on William Hill in this and the following paragraphs are derived from information either contained in his obituaries in the *Abbeville Medium,* 21 January 1886, and especially the *Abbeville Press and Banner,* 20 January 1886, or communicated by Dr. and Mrs. William G. Hill of Abbeville, S.C., whose assistance I gratefully acknowledge.

40. U.S. Agricultural Censuses, 1850, 1860, 1880: Abbeville District, South Carolina (Columbia: South Carolina Department of Archives and History).

41. 1860 U.S. Census, unpublished ms. schedules, Abbeville Court House, South Carolina (microfilm), 21.

42. William Hill, 8 September 1865 (William Hill Correspondence, South Carolina Library, University of South Carolina, Columbia, S.C.; hereafter cited as "SCL-USC"). Quotations from Hill's letters have been modernized in spelling, punctuation, and capitalization.

43. *Abbeville Press and Banner,* 20 January 1886.

44. William Hill, 24 January 1855 (William Hill Correspondence, SCL-USC; and T.1830/3, PRONI). Also, see Hill's letters of 14 July 1847 (SCL-USC; and T.1830/1, PRONI), and of 21 January 1858 (SCL-USC).

45. William Hill, 24 January 1855.

46. *Abbeville Press and Banner,* 20 January 1886.

47. B. H. Halcomb, comp., *South Carolina Naturalizations, 1783–1850* (Baltimore: Genealogical Publishing, 1985).

48. On the nullification and secession crises, and antebellum South Carolina politics, generally, see L. K. Ford, *Origins of Southern Radicalism: The South Carolina Upcountry, 1800–1860* (New York: Oxford University Press, 1988); and "Republics and Democracy: The Parameters of Political Citizenship in Antebellum South Carolina," in *The Meaning of South Carolina History*, ed. D. R. Chesnutt and C. N. Wilson (Columbia: University of South Carolina Press, 1991), 121–45; W. W. Freehling, *Prelude to Civil War: The Nullification Controversy in South Carolina* (New York: Harper and Row, 1966); and S. A. Channing, *Crisis of Fear: Secession in South Carolina* (New York: Simon and Schuster, 1970). Information on Hill's leading role in Abbeville's secession meeting is from Dr. and Mrs. William G. Hill, Abbeville, S.C.

49. Freehling, *Prelude to Civil War,* 181–82.

50. G. Osofsky, "Abolitionists, Irish Immigrants, and the Dilemmas of Romantic Nationalism," *American Historical Review* 80 (October 1975): 889–912.

51. William Hill, 24 January 1855; demographic data on Abbeville District from Ford, *Origins of Southern Radicalism, 45.*

52. William Hill, 24 January 1855; William Hill, 7 March 1872 (copy of letter courtesy of Dr. and Mrs. William G. Hill, Abbeville, S.C.).

53. In 1766 Ballynure parish contained 383 Protestant and 8 Catholic families (T.808/15,264, PRONI). According to the 1831 Irish religious census, 3,380 of Ballynure's 3,549 inhabitants were Protestants, of whom 3,004 were Presbyterians (Report of the Commissioners of Public Instruction, Ireland, *British Parliamentary Papers,* 33 [1835]). On society in early-nineteenth-century Ballynure, see A. Day and P. McWilliams, eds., *Ordnance Survey Memoirs of Ireland, Vol. 32, Parishes of County Antrim, XII, 1832–3, 1835–40: Ballynure and District* (Belfast: Institute of Irish Studies, 1995), 31–73.

54. William Hill, 7 July 1859 (William Hill Correspondence, SCL-USC).

55. William Hill, 21 January 1858.

56. William Hill, 8 September 1865.

57. Ibid.

58. William Hill, 15 August 1867 (William Hill Correspondence, SCL-USC).

59. Mary Hill, "Who I Am" (undated school essay, copy courtesy of Dr. and Mrs. William G. Hill, Abbeville, S.C.).

60. *1990 Census of Population, Social and Economic Characteristics,* vols. CP-2-1 through CP-2-52 (Washington, D.C.: U.S. Dept. of Commerce, Economics and Statistics Admin., Bureau of the Census, 1993). The 2.6 million southern whites who claimed "Scotch-Irish" ancestry in 1990 represented 47 percent of all American whites who did so.

61. K. A. Miller, "Revising Revisionism: Comments and Reflections," in *Northern Ireland and the Politics of Reconciliation*, ed. D. Keogh and M. H. Haltzel (Cambridge: Cambridge University Press, 1993), 53.

7

The "Second Colonization of New England" Revisited: Irish Immigration Before the Famine

Edward J. O'Day

Marcus Lee Hansen, the pioneer American historian of immigration, in an essay published in 1929, wrote of the post-Revolutionary immigration of Europeans into the northeastern United States in now classic terminology. Immigrants to the new nation in the early years of the Republic, many of them Irish who had made their way across the Atlantic as passage-paying ballast in commercial ships plying the timber trade with British Canada, had constituted, in Hansen's words, no less than a "second colonization of New England."[1]

One hundred years before Hansen's essay appeared, the pages of Irish newspapers abounded with reports from America and advertising by transatlantic shippers, including one from 1828 that touted a copper-fastened vessel diverted from the East India trade as "the cheapest mode of proceeding" to the United States. There awaited for males willing to make the journey ten thousand jobs, promised by "the American Government" to complete the Chesapeake and Ohio Canals, and for young women, employment in the factories of Lowell, a "new village in Massachusetts," where more than a thousand other females under the age of thirty already labored.[2]

Such was the phenomenon that Hansen described, and so pervasive was it that only reports about Daniel O'Connell and the Repeal Association matched the space devoted to emigration in the early-nineteenth-century Irish press. By the mid-1830s, travel as ballast in ships of the lumber and flax trade began to give way to ships expressly devoted to passenger traffic, and Liverpool competed with Cork, Limerick, Galway, Londonderry, and Dublin for the profits to be made from carrying humans westward. By 1850, federal census takers counted nearly two hundred thousand inhabitants of Maine, New Hampshire, Vermont, Connecticut, Massachusetts, and Rhode Island who claimed Irish nativity. Their numbers reflected a swell of newcomers who had fled the Great Famine in their homeland during the previous five years.[3]

Hansen's essay on this Irish settlement of New England during the early Republic, although unaccompanied by detailed statistical analysis, was rich in insights and was thematically convincing. The first scholar to follow Hansen's suggestive lead was William Forbes Adams, whose *Ireland and Irish Emigration to the New World from 1815 to the Famine* (1932) drew upon British emigration statistics to depict the outflow of people from Ireland within the context of the rapidly changing economies of the British Isles and of North America during the first half of the nineteenth century. That early work, yet to be surpassed, demonstrated convincingly that the number of Irish arriving in North America increased steadily after the end of the Napoleonic Wars.[4] As Adams recognized, no one on either side of the Atlantic kept reliable count of those leaving Ireland or arriving in North America during this time, but their number approached, and may have exceeded, one million.

Thanks to the work of dozens of recent researchers, our understanding of Irish emigration in this period is much more complete than it was only a decade or so ago, and substantive studies of Irish migration to the Canadas have opened exciting opportunities for comparative cross-border studies between the United States and its northern neighbor.[5] Although much of that comparative work remains for the future, David Noel Doyle's essay on the Irish in the United States in volume 5 of *A New History of Ireland* (1989) and David Fitzpatrick's chapter on emigration in the same volume provide very useful summaries of the fresh perspective and mounting evidence now added to the pioneer findings of Hansen and Adams. Yet, with the exception of several valuable community studies, the Irish "second colonizers" of New England have received little attention in recent years.[6]

This study examines the naturalization records of more than five thousand Irish immigrants to the six most northeastern states of the United States, asks questions about them as a group, offers some comparisons between the group's experience and the general picture of early-nineteenth-century Irish emigration that has emerged since Hansen's essay, and suggests possible avenues for future study. What can be learned about the Irish origins of those who emigrated to New England? How did the flow of emigration to this region of the United States change from the founding of the Republic in 1783 until the mid-1840s? Where in New England did these Irish establish ethnic enclaves? What social and economic roles had they assumed in their adopted land prior to the Great Famine in their homeland? And finally, did the emigrant pattern before 1846 differ materially from the so-called new immigration of the Famine and post-Famine periods, and if so, how?

Early in the nineteenth century, U.S. citizenship could be acquired in several ways, including service in the military and residency in an area annexed to the United States. For most immigrants, however, a minimum five-year residency in the new land, accompanied by a two-step legal process, following provisions of a federal law of 1802, was the norm. This process involved a primary declaration of intent to become a citizen, followed two or more years later by an oath that forswore previous allegiance to any "foreign power or potentate." Those not yet eighteen years of age upon arrival in the United States could be administered the oath when they reached their majority, without the need of filing a prior declaration. All levels of the judiciary, from federal circuit courts to local police courts, provided they were "courts of record," were empowered to grant citizenship.

Photographic copies of all known naturalization oaths from the six New England states, made by the Works Projects Administration during the 1930s, were the initial basis for the present study. Original records of federal district and circuit courts in the New England Region National Archives, and those of state and local courts deposited in the Massachusetts State Archives, supplement the now-fading old photographs.[7] These files provide valuable thumbnail sketches of the emigrant passages of thousands of individuals and give occasional glimpses of their early lives in a new land. Although only a few list the port of departure, and fewer still enumerate all persons who traveled as a family group, a significant number give prior residences and provide evidence of occupation or employment. Of greatest value for the historian of immigration are the routine recording of age and birth date, the date and place of entry to the United States, and the Irish birth county of the prospective citizen. More than 90 percent of the records selected for this study contain these details, and two out of three provide more precise Irish origins by city, village, parish, or townland.

Because the documents give evidence primarily of male immigrants, no claim can be made that they are representative of Irish immigration as a whole, even on a limited American regional basis. This particular group of historical records is highly gender biased because most women did not become naturalized in their own right until the twentieth century. Only a handful of records provide data about immigrant females. The sample may be also socially unrepresentative, no doubt favoring propertied classes and skilled laborers over those who lacked the economic resources to pay for the services of clerks and the filing fees assessed by the courts.[8] Lastly, variations in precision and accuracy from court to court render some files hardly comparable. Although federal court records were usually more carefully prepared than those of lesser courts, that generalization did not always hold. While certain defects in the record could be corrected with relative ease, the rendering of some Irish place-names defied interpretation, while others were so common that they might refer to one of more than a score of Irish localities. Myriad spellings and misspellings make absolute certainty all but impossible, but the occasional mismatch that is bound to have crept in should not seriously damage the interpretations that follow. Records with dating anomalies, such as an arrival in the United States prior to the applicant's reported birth, have been omitted from calculations relating to age at immigration.[9]

Some of these records tell tales quite extraordinary, especially about the variety of routes by which these emigrant Irish reached New England. As David Fitzpatrick has pointed out, it took "alertness and ingenuity" to overcome the numerous obstacles to emigration existing in the early nineteenth century. Prior to the beginnings of a commercialized transatlantic passenger trade in the 1840s, humans were considered little better than an "unwelcome substitute for more profitable cargoes," forcing the overseas migrant to endure what Fitzpatrick aptly describes as a "torturous path" to their new land.[10] The naturalization records of New England Irish reveal many such paths. John Keefe, a tailor from Cashel who was naturalized in Boston in 1834, had arrived fourteen years earlier at Richmond, Virginia, while trader Henry Phillips's passage from Cobh had taken him to New Orleans before he found his way to New England. Tobacco and cotton no doubt took these men's places when the ships that bore them returned to England or Ireland. Antrim natives John Martin, Samuel Gilliland, and John White—all American citizens by 1833—had each followed a different commercial route between Belfast and North America, Martin landing at St. John, New Brunswick; Gilliland at Philadelphia; and White at Charleston, South Carolina. James Bannon of Dublin had lengthy stays in Quebec and in Odgensburg in upstate New York before he settled in western Massachusetts eighteen years after leaving his homeland. To reach the United States in 1831, John Fleming from Thomastown, Kilkenny, followed the Waterford–St. John's Newfoundland trade, and three months later that between Newfoundland and Newport, Rhode Island.[11]

While almost half of those 4,854 new citizens whose final papers state a port of entry reported arriving in the United States at Boston, many of them may have done so by transshipping from a Canadian port, as did Fleming. Three out of ten reported New York City as their port of entry to the United States, reflecting the growing importance of the Liverpool–New York route for passenger trade in the decade before the Famine. More than a thousand individuals, however, traversed scores of other routes, putting in at less frequented ports, including Portsmouth in New Hampshire, Newburyport and Duxbury in Massachusetts, and New London in Connecticut. Dozens of border crossing points between Canada and the United States appear in the records, stretching from Calais, Maine, through New Hampshire and Vermont to western New York State. When all of the expressed or implied Canadian traffic is calculated, some 15 percent of these new citizens of the United States can be shown to have first set sail for a Canadian destination. Each of Ireland's thirty-two counties sent someone by that route, and although such indirect passage was most common in the mid 1830s (accounting for 18.5 percent of arrivals during that time), the Canadian option continued to be exercised by one in ten on the eve of the Famine, especially by emigrants from counties of Ireland's west and southwest.

As David Fitzpatrick reminds readers of his essay on emigration in *A New His-*

tory of Ireland, migration often involves "reiterated if not 'perpetual' motion."[12] The naturalization files of Irish emigrants in New England add more evidence of this phenomenon, demonstrated countless times in numerous locales and among many different peoples. Bernard O'Cavanaugh, first resident pastor of Pittsfield in western Massachusetts, one of eight known Catholic clergy in the files, was surely the most traveled among the emigrants. He had spent twenty-nine years ministering to Catholics in South Carolina, Georgia, Maryland, Ohio, Michigan, Connecticut, and elsewhere in Massachusetts prior to taking the oath of citizenship in 1851. Thomas Bowes of Queens County, twenty-five when he arrived in New York City in 1832, had worked in three Massachusetts towns and as far afield as McHenry County, Illinois, before his naturalization seventeen years later. Michael Cottrell, but three years old when he came to Newport, Rhode Island, had traversed the continent, spending nearly two years in California at the height of the Gold Rush before returning to Rhode Island to claim his American citizenship. Other immigrants from Ireland had been in Georgia, Ohio, Michigan, and Wisconsin before proclaiming New England as their intended residence. Widow Anne Fogarty had arrived in Quebec in 1822 and Boston in 1823, accompanied by her son Daniel, then fourteen. She testified on his behalf in 1837 that three years later they had moved together to Sandwich, Barnstable County, where he had ever since resided, although she herself had by that time also lived "eighteen months in the State of Maine with another son."[13]

Michael Carroll arrived at Troy, New York, from Croom, Limerick, on his thirty-fourth birthday in July 1836, accompanied by his three children, the youngest, Catherine, not yet five months old. When he came to Boston, Timothy Hayes was single, a status probably characteristic of the majority of young laborers who found construction jobs, as he did on the railroad. Within a few years he married, and his firstborn entered the world in a labor camp near Pittsfield, Massachusetts, far from the father's native Lislevane in south-central Cork. When Edward Swiney left Cork for New York in 1826, his family remained in Macroom while he sought and obtained employment in the textile mills of New England. Filing his declaration of intent to become an American citizen eight years later, Swiney reported an odyssey that included five crossings of the Atlantic—three westward and two eastbound—and sojourns in four Massachusetts mill towns. He had first returned to Ireland to fetch his family, but they could hardly have been established in the factory village of Leicester when he again headed back to his native land. By the time he arrived in North America a third time, Swiney had apparently exhausted his resources, for it took two years to work his way from Quebec back to the family he had left in central Massachusetts. Eight years after he had first left Ireland, he reported to the court in 1834 that he was settled and wished to become an American.[14]

Shortly before Swiney's court appearance in early 1834, the *Jesuit, or Catho-*

lic Sentinel, predecessor of the Boston *Pilot,* featured an editorial and a letter from "A Naturalized Irishman" promoting applications for citizenship. Both pieces decried the special oaths that Massachusetts courts then required from Catholics and the constant reminders of inferior status that Boston's ten thousand Irish inhabitants faced in their daily lives. The letter writer, noting that "barely two hundred" of his fellow countrymen were "entitled to the privilege of citizens," called the path of naturalization "the most effectual means of establishing in Boston the respectability of Irishmen." Succeeding issues asserted that at least two thousand "could be naturalized tomorrow if they would" and urged them to come forward and claim their rights.[15]

Traders like Dennis Timoney and John McQuaid were especially active witnesses to the oaths of allegiance of other Irish in Boston who responded to the newspaper's appeal. Timoney, a Fermanagh native naturalized in 1826, kept a shop on Water Street and was secretary to Boston's O'Connellite organization, the Roman Catholic Mutual Relief Society. As witness to more than thirty citizenship declarations, Timoney had personally assisted a significant portion of the "barely two hundred" citizens mentioned in the columns of the *Jesuit.* The "Naturalized Irishman" letter writer to that paper may well have been Timoney. McQuaid came forth after the newspaper appeal to claim the citizenship for which he had filed his intent two years previously. Although he barely managed to sign his name on any of the forms, he would do so on numerous occasions in the next few years, often signing in the company of Timoney as witness for another Irishman becoming a new American.

Hugh Cummiskey of Crossan, County Tyrone, played a role in the textile town of Lowell at least as important as that of Timoney in Boston. A recruiter of labor for the mill town, Cummiskey served as intermediary between it, the port of Boston, and his homeland, helping to assure a substantial and continuing immigrant flow from south-central Ulster to the mills of Lowell and other towns in the Merrimack Valley.[16]

By 1822 every county of Ireland had sent to New England someone who remained there and would become naturalized five or more years later. Offaly and Wicklow in Leinster had sent few, and Clare and Mayo natives had but the tiniest of toeholds in New England by that time, but counties Dublin, Cork, Down, and Tyrone established an early lead as major contributors to the "second colonization of New England" (see table 1). Among the 882 immigrants whose arrival year is stated or can be estimated from other given data, 12 percent (590) arrived from Ireland in the forty-two years between 1784 and the end of 1825, Cummiskey, McQuaid, and Timoney among them. In the following two decades, pursuing economic opportunity in construction and in water-powered mills proliferating in nearly every valley of New England, the "Irish colonization" picked up tempo. More than 42 percent (2,176) of the sample arrived between 1826 and the end of 1837, a year of economic downturn that occasioned in the following year a brief ebb in the tide of arriving Irish men and women. The respite was brief, and the multiplication of naturalizations a few years later makes evident the quickened pace of immigration of the early 1840s. Another 42 percent (2,116) of individuals in the sample arrived from Ireland in the eight years preceding the Great Famine (1838–1845).

The naturalization records collected for this study tend to bear out the *Pilot*'s claim that early Irish immigrants had been slow to claim a stake in their adopted land. On average, those immigrants who arrived through 1825 had resided in the United States for more than sixteen years before they became citizens. Those who immigrated between 1826 and 1837 shortened the wait to slightly less than thirteen years, while the group that arrived after 1838 took oaths of allegiance after an average residency of nine years. As earlier examples illustrate, many an Irish immigrant of the earlier two of these eras was itinerant rather than place bound, a result of the temporary and shifting employment of mill work, the constant moving of labor camps as road or canal construction advanced, the seafaring required of mariners, the ministry to Irish settlements scattered across a vast and growing land, and similar factors. The itinerancy of their lives no doubt slowed the pace of naturalization, because a fixed abode and two character witnesses well acquainted with the applicant were essential elements of the naturalization procedure. Those arriving in the 1840s had the benefit of economic and civic support mechanisms within a growing Irish and Irish-American ethnic community, and they faced fewer obstacles than did their predecessors to claiming rapid status as new Americans. One in five of those who arrived after 1837 had become citizens before they had concluded their sixth year of residence in the United States.[17]

Where had they settled, this band of five thousand new Americans? Boston had become a major Irish-American hub well before the Famine, with the Irish filling the dockside and Fort Hill areas and pushing outward to surrounding Charlestown, Cambridge, Roxbury, and Quincy. The Massachusetts port and its expanding suburbs absorbed more than half the immigrants represented by this naturalization sample. But one-quarter of the immigrants in this group specifically defined their Irish roots in terms of townlands or villages of the Irish interior, and many of them were transplanted (to borrow John Bodnar's celebrated imagery) to numerous small New England communities. Dalton, Egremont, Middlefield, and Pittsfield in the Berkshires of western Massachusetts; Blackstone, the Brookfields, Oxford, Milford, Saxonville, and Ware Village in the central part of that state; Belfast, Columbia, Cherryfield, Pembroke, and South Berwick in Maine; and Barnard and Prospect in Vermont, Stafford in New Hampshire, and Smithfield in Rhode Island all had naturalized Irish in their populations prior to the Famine. In all, nearly four hundred New England towns and villages had become new homes for the Irish immigrants.[18]

Table 1: Naturalized New Englanders of Irish Nativity, 1784–1865

County/ PROVINCE	% of popu- lation 1841 census	1784–1825		1826–1837		1838–1845		Year Unknown No.	Total analyzed (5001)	% of full sample
		No.	% of known sample (590)	No.	% of known sample (2,176)	No.	% of known sample (2,116)			
Galway	5.39	9	1.53	50	2.30	121	5.72	2	182	3.64
Leitrim	1.90	11	1.86	44	2.02	36	1.70	3	94	1.88
Mayo	4.76	2	0.34	14	0.64	26	1.23	0	42	0.84
Roscommon	3.10	8	1.36	82	3.77	141	6.66	7	238	4.76
Sligo	2.21	5	0.85	54	2.48	38	1.80	2	99	1.98
CONNACHT	17.36	35	5.93	244	11.21	362	17.11	14	655	13.10
Carlow	1.06	7	1.19	11	0.51	13	0.61	1	32	0.64
Dublin	4.56	28	4.75	79	3.63	69	3.26	5	181	3.62
Kildare	1.40	10	1.69	36	1.65	43	2.03	1	90	1.80
Kilkenny	2.48	26	4.41	78	3.58	47	2.22	1	152	3.04
Kings	1.80	1	0.17	14	0.64	21	0.99	2	38	0.76
Longford	1.41	29	4.92	86	3.95	46	2.17	3	164	3.28
Louth	1.57	5	0.85	15	0.69	30	1.42	3	53	1.06
Meath	2.25	6	1.02	52	2.39	36	1.70	3	97	1.94
Queens	1.88	8	1.36	36	1.65	28	1.32	1	73	1.46

County										
Westmeath	1.73	4	0.68	41	1.88	1.75	37	6	88	1.76
Wexford	2.47	24	4.07	31	1.42	0.66	14	0	69	1.38
Wicklow	1.54	2	0.34	13	0.60	0.09	2	2	19	0.38
LEINSTER	24.15	150	25.42	492	22.61	18.24	386	28	1,056	21.12
Clare	3.51	1	0.17	34	1.56	2.88	61	1	97	1.94
Cork	10.45	46	7.80	397	18.24	18.76	397	12	852	17.04
Kerry	3.60	12	2.03	63	2.90	6.95	147	1	223	4.46
Limerick	4.04	16	2.71	55	2.53	2.60	55	6	132	2.64
Tipperary	5.33	32	5.42	111	5.10	4.16	88	6	237	4.74
Waterford	2.40	31	5.25	92	4.23	2.13	45	4	172	3.44
MUNSTER	29.33	138	23.39	752	34.56	37.48	793	30	1,713	34.25
Antrim	4.36	33	5.59	53	2.44	1.37	29	2	117	2.34
Armagh	2.84	14	2.37	26	1.19	1.04	22	1	63	1.26
Cavan	2.98	16	2.71	88	4.04	4.06	86	7	197	3.94
Donegal	3.63	18	3.05	95	4.37	4.30	91	7	211	4.22
Down	4.42	42	7.12	33	1.52	1.04	22	6	103	2.06
Fermanagh	1.92	14	2.37	60	2.76	2.32	49	4	127	2.54
Londonderry	2.72	15	2.54	69	3.17	2.65	56	6	146	2.92
Monaghan	2.45	11	1.86	63	2.90	2.55	54	3	131	2.62
Tyrone	3.83	71	12.03	107	4.92	4.63	98	7	283	5.66
ULSTER	29.15	234	39.66	594	27.30	23.96	507	43	1,378	27.55
County unknown		33	5.59	94	4.32	3.21	68	4	199	3.98
Total of sample		590		2,176			2,116	119	5,001	100.00

Apart from textiles and construction, economic activities that depended heavily upon immigrant labor in this era, what work did the Irish perform in these communities? Unfortunately, fewer than half the naturalization records give clear evidence of an applicant's economic or social status. Clerks were not required to list the occupation of a petitioner for naturalization, and many of them left the space for it blank on the form. As might be expected, slightly more than half (1,237 of 2,405) the records that include occupation information are those of laborers.[19]

Given the cost of the proceedings, the fact that so many day laborers are enumerated is revealing. Citizenship held value, and was worth the price. Many of the newly naturalized may have had skills or professions not revealed by the "laborer" designation, but only one, Richard Lloyd from Aughrim in County Galway, made sure that his record reflected that fact. With evident pride in his dual occupations, Lloyd reported that he was "by profession a Canal digger and Farmer."[20]

Second only to laborers as an occupation category were 151 "traders." They—together with three score shopkeepers, grocers, dealers, peddlers, an "inn-holder," a boardinghouse keeper, and a proprietor of a coffeehouse—indicate the presence of a class of property owners and small businessmen on the make among the pre-Famine Irish of New England. Artisans existed aplenty—ninety tailors, eighty-eight makers of shoes and boots (with various specialties from boot crimper to cordwainer), eighty-five builders of houses (carpenters, housewrights, lathers, and slaters), forty-five stonemasons, forty-one blacksmiths, and fifteen coopers. Some fifty mariners and sailors, together with stevedores, shipwrights and ship carpenters, lightermen, and rope and sail makers were to be expected from the coastal areas, but there was not a single Irish fisherman among those naturalized.[21] Twenty-six gardeners, sixteen curriers, and several hostlers and stablers evidenced those who had put their knowledge of plants and animals to work in an urban environment of a new world. Various blowers, cutters, and polishers of glass from Waterford and Tyrone had settled around Cambridge and in Sandwich on Cape Cod, centers of glassmaking. Numerous weavers of woolens and carpets, block cutters, and calico printers—along with cloth drapers, bleachers, dyers, and a few spinners—contributed to the area's burgeoning textile manufactories. Eight printers, five papermakers, a publisher, and a bookseller made and promoted the media of the day, while several dozen machinists and boilermakers, a variety of brass and iron workers, a whitesmith, a silversmith, and two gold beaters all worked with metals.[22]

Those in the learned and service professions were few among these Irishmen becoming citizens, but their number did include an architect, a sculptor, two physicians, a chemist, a student of law, four musicians, nine clergymen, and one comedian. A few—nine gentlemen, eight merchants, the nine who engaged in manufacturing (including brewing and distilling), and perhaps some of the seven farmers and twenty-nine yeomen—were men of means, although from the naturalization files alone there is no telling whether their apparently comfortable condition stemmed from Old World resources or New World opportunity.

Among those who settled in New England prior to the Famine, four out of five in this naturalization sample had been between sixteen and forty-five years old when they arrived in the United States. These were the most active work years, when a boy who turned sixteen earned a man's wage, and when a man expected to be, and often was, worn out at forty-five. Most of the 20 percent who fell outside that standard work range were under age sixteen, many of them young teens who might find factory work or enter apprenticeship at twelve or fourteen. From thirty of Ireland's thirty-six counties, more than half of those who had set out across the Atlantic for New England had been between the ages of fourteen and twenty-four.[23] Only fifty-nine individuals had emigrated after turning forty-six.[24] Not surprisingly, immigrants younger than eighteen often made more rapid progress up the social and economic ladder than did their older counterparts, sometimes with the benefit of American schooling behind them. Persons who had been under eighteen when they entered the United States accounted for 30 percent of the sample, yet these once youthful arrivals held 35 percent of those jobs described with a term other than the common "laborer."[25]

The average reported age for all those of working age when they arrived in the United States was almost twenty-five, but with marked variations by county. Statistics illustrating county and regional averages for immigrants of all ages are compiled in table 2, where the preponderance of the youth cohort (those ages fourteen through twenty-four) is amply demonstrated. The data indicate that adults emigrating from portions of Leinster and Munster were older on average than those originating in Connacht and west Ulster, or conversely that immigrants from the West were younger on average than those from other parts of Ireland. Emigrants from Kildare and Queen's (Laois) counties were on average over age twenty-six, while those from Roscommon, Donegal, and Galway, at twenty-two, were among the youngest.[26]

Such variations by region may reflect differing attitudes toward emigration, local differences in economic opportunity, regional population pressures, or a host of other factors, including presence or absence of a network between the homeland and previous emigrants. Some hypotheses, to be tested by additional study of regional push factors at work within pre-Famine Ireland, may be offered for the apparent age differentials. One may surmise that many an emigrant from the south and east during the period 1825 to 1837 had spent a decade or more in the labor market in Ireland or elsewhere in the British Isles before choosing the emigrant route. If indeed the move to the United States represented an attempt at a second chance in life after an inauspicious start elsewhere, there is seldom a hint of such prior employment (or unemployment) history in the records studied.[27] The outflow from Connacht, on the other hand, was an exodus among youth who

Table 2: Irish Immigrants to New England by County and Age, 1784–1865

County/PROVINCE	All immigrants this county	Age known	Under 14	14–17	18–24	25–45	Over 45	All Workers	% Aged 14–24	Average Age of Work Cohort
Galway	182	177	9	49	64	54	1	168	62.1	22.55
Leitrim	94	90	7	19	34	29	1	83	56.4	23.76
Mayo	42	41	2	8	21	10	0	39	69.0	22.82
Roscommon	238	238	15	67	90	55	4	216	66.0	22.12
Sligo	99	97	8	19	34	34	1	88	53.5	23.35
CONNACHT	655	643	41	162	243	182	7	594	61.8	22.70
Carlow	32	31	2	4	15	10	0	29	59.4	23.93
Dublin	181	166	16	28	73	44	5	150	55.8	23.89
Kildare	90	88	8	8	27	44	1	80	38.9	26.48
Kilkenny	152	144	3	22	60	58	1	141	53.9	24.87
Kings	38	36	2	5	15	14	0	34	52.6	24.58
Longford	164	160	12	35	67	43	3	148	62.2	23.00
Louth	53	49	4	6	19	19	1	45	47.2	24.95
Meath	97	93	3	10	48	31	1	90	59.8	24.06
Queens	73	69	3	7	24	32	3	66	42.5	26.10
Westmeath	88	81	3	8	44	23	3	78	59.1	23.02
Wexford	69	65	6	7	26	26	0	59	47.8	24.91
Wicklow	19	17	2	1	6	7	1	15	36.8	24.15
LEINSTER	1,056	999	64	141	424	351	19	935	53.5	24.37

Clare	97	94	7	8	44	35	0	87	53.6	24.69
Cork	852	834	75	116	307	330	6	759	49.6	24.75
Kerry	223	216	18	49	84	62	3	198	59.6	23.33
Limerick	132	123	12	29	42	39	1	111	53.8	23.31
Tipperary	237	226	18	27	92	87	2	208	50.2	24.50
Waterford	172	159	12	20	62	63	2	147	47.7	24.91
MUNSTER	1,713	1,652	142	249	631	616	14	1,510	51.4	24.44
Antrim	117	107	13	14	51	27	2	94	55.6	23.66
Armagh	63	59	6	15	16	22	0	53	49.2	24.69
Cavan	197	186	12	41	95	37	1	174	69.0	22.57
Donegal	211	200	13	49	98	38	2	187	69.7	22.19
Down	103	86	12	15	25	32	2	74	38.8	25.22
Fermanagh	127	121	11	34	37	34	5	110	55.9	23.05
Londonderry	146	139	9	32	57	40	1	130	61.0	23.23
Monaghan	131	127	5	19	56	46	1	122	57.3	23.97
Tyrone	283	266	31	52	104	76	3	235	55.1	23.55
ULSTER	1,378	1,291	112	271	539	352	17	1,179	58.8	23.31
County unknown	199	158	35	28	44	57	2	131	36.2	24.30
Total of sample	5,001	4,743	394	851	1,881	1,558	59	4,349	54.6	23.87

appear to have chosen long-distance emigration as a first resort. Such emigrant patterns suggest the emergence of a newer type of emigration in the west of Ireland in the decade before the Great Famine, one commonly associated with the "American wake" of the later nineteenth century and attributed to the social and economic aftermath of the Famine. Mass emigration of youth from parts of that region clearly predated the onset of that enormous economic and demographic disaster.

In the final years of the eighteenth century and the first twenty-five years of the next, emigrants originating in the northern province of Ulster constituted nearly two out of five of the Irish coming to New England represented in this sample. Given the heavy Ulster peopling of colonial North America, including New England settlements that still bear such Ulster place-names as Belfast, Colerain, and Londonderry, this dominance of immigrants from the north is not surprising. There is copious evidence (compiled since Hansen's pioneering essay) that, regardless of nationality, ethnic communities abroad serve as a powerful pull factor to new arrivals from the same area of the home country. What is surprising is how quickly Ulster was overshadowed by an outpouring to New England from Munster. Until the mid-1820s, the northernmost Irish province had contributed a disproportionate number of immigrants to New England when measured against Ulster's portion of the Irish population in 1821 (almost 40 percent of the immigrants from 29 percent of the island's populace). The emigrant flow from Leinster in this era was nearly consonant with its share of the total Irish population (24 to 25 percent), while Munster, which contained more than 28 percent of Ireland's inhabitants, was represented by only 23 percent of the naturalized citizens in this sample who reported arriving prior to 1826.

In the 1830s, no province could match the pace of the massive emigration from Munster, which then claimed the lion's share of Irish emigrating to New England, but early in the next decade, the data reveal Connacht and portions of the Midlands racing to catch up. As those southern and western provinces rose as sending areas, Leinster and Ulster, which had held the lead in the first decades of the century, declined in significance as contributors to the "second colonizing of New England." Ulster's overrepresentation among those emigrating to New England came to an end by the mid-1830s, the numbers from Antrim and Down trailing off annually, even as different Ulster men and women—from Donegal, Cavan and Monaghan—now headed for New England. For the province as a whole, the percentage of immigrants in this naturalization sample dropped to 27 percent (1826–1837), a figure slightly less than Ulster's share of the Irish population at the time. By the early 1840s, in a continuation of that trend, emigrants from Ulster had become fewer than one in four of the Irish entering New England.

Just as the Ulster element went into decline, Munster was hit by an exodus to New England of enormous magnitude. That province consistently represented one out of three Irish who became naturalized New Englanders in the three and one-half decades after 1825. The emigration from Munster was not without precedent, because Cork and Waterford natives were well represented in the small Boston Irish community before 1815, and a Kerryman naturalized in 1798, James Trant, reported that he had been a sailor out of Newburyport as early as 1782.[28] But emigrants to New England now came from throughout Munster—notably east and east-central Cork, south Tipperary, Kilkenny, and the Killarney and Dingle peninsulas in Kerry. Whether this was the result of more effective networking between the New World and the Old, an actual overrepresentation from Munster among all immigrants, or simply a higher propensity of Cork natives to claim a naturalized stake in their new homeland cannot be ascertained on the basis of the naturalization data alone. It may well have been a combination of those factors and others, including long-standing trade connections between Munster ports and the British colonies of northeastern North America during the eighteenth century. By the 1840s, three out of eight Irish settling in New England were Munster natives.

Connacht, as was generally recognized at the time and is demonstrable from other data, had not immediately caught the emigrant fever after 1815. Connacht's five counties, with slightly more than 16 percent of the Irish population in the 1820s, a figure that had reached 17.3 percent by 1841, accounted for less than 6 percent of this sample of immigrants to New England who arrived though 1825. Although that number nearly doubled during the next twelve years, Connacht was still underrepresented in the emigrant flow by 1837. That underrepresentation, the records indicate, was quickly corrected in the period just preceding the Famine, facilitated by a large out-migration to New England. In the period ending in 1845, 17.1 percent of the Irish entering New England originated in Connacht, two out of three of them in Roscommon and Galway.

From whence, more precisely than province or county, had these colonizers of urban and rural New England come? Reflecting on his study of Tipperary migrants to Canada, Bruce Elliott attributes part of the difficulty of tracking migrants to their propensity to settle (when they choose to do so) in regions where the maximum number of administrative and governmental boundaries intersect. Perhaps not coincidentally, a large portion of Irish immigrants in this sample came from just such places in Ireland—localities near county lines, parishes intersected by other administrative boundaries, and places on the economic or geographic margin. This phenomenon can be illustrated by identifying emigrants by the Irish Poor Law Union from which they originated. These unions—geographic divisions larger than the parish or town but smaller than the county, with boundaries revised several times after they were first defined in 1838—allow the mapping of emigration within a radius of market towns and commercial centers around which the unions were organized.[29] From such centers began the gathering—of information and of people—before the emigrants scattered to places unseen. It has been possible to identify the Poor Law Union base from which three out of five emigrants in this sample set out.

South-central Cork and the area astride the Munster-Leinster line poured out their young (and middle-aged) to New England in this period. With more than 350 emigrants from the adjoining County Cork unions of Bandon, Cork, Kinsale, Middleton, and Fermoy, this area provided one-third of the total inflow to New England from 1834 through 1837. More than one hundred additional emigrants from adjoining unions—Clonakilty, Macroom, Mallow, Mitchelstown, and Lismore—reinforced the already strong Cork element in this second colonization of New England. Former residents of these ten unions, although found throughout the six northeastern states by 1840, were most heavily concentrated in the counties of Hampden, Bristol, and Suffolk in Massachusetts (Springfield, Fall River, and Boston). From east Munster, along the divide with Leinster, from the valleys and hills of the Suir and Blackwater Rivers, in the unions of Waterford, New Ross, Carrick-on-Suir, Thomastown, Kilkenny, Callan, Cashel, and Clonmel, some 230 male emigrants set out for New England, the majority of them during the 1820s and 1830s.

When the numbers coming from these regions subsided, the Shannon borderland between Connacht and Leinster in west-central Ireland was ready to respond to New England's constant demand for labor in the early 1840s. The unions of Athlone, Roscommon, Ballinasloe, and Ballymahon contributed 164 emigrants to the second colonization of New England, while the neighboring unions of Granard, Longford, and Mullingar to the north and east sent another 110. The use of county-based statistics, the usual method of reporting (and of much subsequent analysis), could miss the significance of this four-county sending region of Galway, Longford, Roscommon, and Westmeath, although the known density and rapid growth of its population would suggest, even to the casual observer, that it might have been prone to emigration. The high level of new citizens of New England from these unions confirms that flight overseas had become general there prior to the Famine, and the new citizens' oaths of allegiance provide evidence of the places to which some from that area had scattered.

In marked contrast, neither the pull of jobs in the northeastern United States nor the political allure of "the Republic" seems to have affected north Wexford and south Wicklow (Gorey, Shilelagh, and Rathdrum Unions) in this period. Glin and Newcastle Unions in north Kerry also held their people (or sent them to places other than New England) during the pre-Famine era. Only thirteen of the new American citizens in this sample had come from these five unions. With the port cities of Dublin and Limerick within relatively easy reach, there was no lack of opportunity, and a reasonably healthy local economy or other factors may have kept emigration in check. Other regions, more remote from port access and often far from prosperous, also contributed only small numbers to the growing Irish population of New England before 1846. Two unions east and west of Lough Dergh—Scarrif (Clare) and Borisokane (Tipperary)—are represented in the citizenship files by only three former residents, even though the neighboring unions of Roscrea and Nenagh sent a steady trickle of people who had begun to reach New England as early as 1813.

Some regions on the Irish economic and geographic periphery, notably the Dingle and Inishowen Peninsulas, witnessed substantial out-migration to the northeastern United States. Thirty-four people from the former area in Kerry and forty from the latter in north Donegal found their way before New England courts to claim their American citizenship. Other overcrowded but remote regions, some ten unions of Ireland's Far West, from Cahirsiveen in Kerry to Dunfanaghy in Donegal, appear to have been left to face the Famine with their numbers scarcely diminished by New England–bound emigrants. There were but eleven naturalized New Englanders from these unions. Irish driven from most other parts of their homeland by the Great Famine, however, could find an established network of previous immigrants to assist them in nearly any part of New England. In summary, the evidence in these naturalization files confirms many commonly held positions about Irish emigration in the pre-Famine era. The data demonstrate a decline in emigration from Ulster by the 1830s and its rise elsewhere among a largely Catholic population from the southern provinces. From every corner of Ireland, a few pockets excepted, large numbers of Irish emigrants had begun new lives in New England before the Famine.

The regional origins of Irish immigrants to New England after 1815 as identified from naturalization files bear a striking similarity, in broad outline if not in exact percentages, to the pioneer findings of William Forbes Adams as well as to recent analysis of cohort depletion in Irish counties between the censuses of 1821 and 1841 by David Fitzpatrick.[30] The northeastern states of the United States appear to have been a typical immigrant receiving area, one whose Irish "colonists" mirrored closely the contemporary sending areas of the homeland from which they had come. In the rising emigration from Connacht and the outpouring from Munster, however, the region anticipated immigration characteristics usually associated more with the Famine and post-Famine emigration.

David Noel Doyle's essay on the remaking of Irish America after 1845 calls attention to a "new pattern [of emigration] that pointed to the future," a pattern already discernible in the 1841 Irish census returns. Emigration, Doyle notes, was shifting from earlier regions to an "epicenter" whose axis stretched from South Ulster and North Connacht southward to East Cork and Kilkenny.[31] American court records also illustrate that shift, one which on the eve of the Famine was giving new vigor and greater diversity to the Irish population that had streamed into the New England region since the founding of the Republic. The ever-increasing number of Irish-born New Englanders who had assumed American citizenship before the Great Famine struck, or who would claim it soon thereafter, helped prepare the transition for the unexpected and unplanned mass diaspora of the Famine years. To borrow Doyle's felicitous phrase, many areas that were hard hit by the Famine, Cork and Galway among them, were by then "equipped with their own bridges out of disaster," bridges secured in the northeastern states by immigrants of an older exodus, the "second colonizers" of New England, established throughout that once Puritan stronghold long before Black '47.[32] The naturalization records from New England courts give convincing evidence of an extensive network of Irish-American citizens in New England by that time, especially in the region's southern tier of Connecticut, Massachusetts, and Rhode Island, which was to absorb the bulk of the Famine emigrants.

Notes

1. Marcus Lee Hansen, "The Second Colonization of New England," *New England Quarterly* 2 (October 1929): 539–60, reprinted in *The Immigrant in American History* (Cambridge: Harvard University Press, 1942). Hansen, writing in the context of an anti-immigrant wave that had peaked with congressional passage of restrictive immigration laws in 1921 and 1924, may have felt some urgency to remind New Englanders—Irish Americans among them—that new peoples had been no less important to that region, and to the country, than had been the colonists of the seventeenth and eighteenth centuries.

2. "Ship 'John' for the beautiful city Quebec," *Connaught Journal,* July 31, 1828; "America," October 9, 1828. The young girls of Lowell were reported to be all "healthy, cheerful and moral," but in a silence that spoke volumes, no such claim was made about the boys and men of the construction camps, where violence sometimes flared and deaths from accidents and epidemics were common.

3. *Abstract of the 7th Census* (Washington, D.C., 1853), 18. Massachusetts, with 115,917 inhabitants of Irish birth, accounted for three out of five of the 196,609 Irish-born inhabitants in the New England states in 1850. Connecticut and Rhode Island jointly counted 42,633, while Vermont with 15,377 led the three states of the northern tier. There were 13,871 Irish men and women in Maine and 8,811 in neighboring New Hampshire.

4. William Forbes Adams, *Ireland and Irish Emigration to the New World from 1815 to the Famine* (New Haven: Yale University Press, 1932). Oscar Handlin's classic but now dated study, *Boston's Immigrants: A Study in Acculturation* (Cambridge: Harvard University Press, 1941; rev. ed., 1959), was the first to focus on the American side of the equation, using some of the naturalization records discussed here.

5. See Donald Harman Akenson, *The Irish in Ontario: A Study in Rural History* (Kingston, Ont.: McGill-Queen's University Press, 1984); David Noel Doyle, *Ireland, Irishmen, and Revolutionary America* (Dublin: Mercier Press, 1981) on the many connections between Ireland and America in the late colonial era and early national United States; and "The Irish in North America, 1776–1845," in *A New History of Ireland,* ed. T.

W. Moody, F. X. Martin, and F. J. Byrne, vol. 5 (Oxford: Clarendon Press, 1989), 682–785; David Fitzpatrick, *Irish Emigration 1801–1921*, Studies in Irish Economic and Social History, vol. 1 (Dublin: Economic and Social History Society of Ireland, 1984); and "Emigration, 1801–1870," in *A New History of Ireland*, vol. 5 (Oxford: Clarendon Press, 1989), 562–621; Ruth-Ann Harris, ed., *The Search for Missing Friends*, 8 vols. (Boston: New England Historic and Genealogical Society, 1989–1999); Kerby A. Miller, *Emigrants and Exiles: Ireland and the Irish Exodus to North America* (New York: Oxford University Press, 1985), the first comprehensive work relating to all of North America. In addition to Akenson's work, other Canadian scholarship includes Bruce S. Elliott, *Irish Migrants in the Canadas: A New Approach* (Kingston, Ont.: McGill-Queen's University Press, 1988); Cecil J. Houston and William J. Smyth, *Irish Emigration and Canadian Settlement* (Toronto: University of Toronto Press, 1990); and Thomas P. Power, ed., *The Irish in Atlantic Canada 1780–1900* (Fredericton: New Ireland Press, 1988).

6. Two of those local studies, both excellent, are Brian C. Mitchell, *The Paddy Camps: The Irish of Lowell 1821–1861* (Urbana: University of Illinois Press, 1988); and Vincent Powers, "'Invisible Immigrants': The Pre-Famine Irish Community in Worcester, Massachusetts from 1826 to 1860" (Ph.D. diss., Clark University, 1976).

7. National Archives and Records Administration, Northeast Region, Waltham, Mass., Record Group 85 (dexigraph records) and RG 21 (originals), hereafter cited as "NA New England," with corresponding record group number. Massachusetts State Archives records are cited as "MSA," with accompanying roll number for records that have been microfilmed. The author gratefully acknowledges the encouragement of James Owens, director of archival operations of the National Archives Northeast Region, and William T. Milhomme, reference supervisor of the Massachusetts Archives at Columbia Point. The exemplary assistance of the staffs at both repositories made lighter the arduous task of extracting data from the thousands of records they retrieved.

Naturalizations have been compiled from extant court files in all fourteen Massachusetts counties and federal-level circuit and district Courts of Massachusetts, Rhode Island, and Vermont. Records from Hartford County, Connecticut, eight counties in Maine, five in New Hampshire and six in Vermont round out the sample. In all, seventy courts are represented in the current study, and all surviving files in those courts were transcribed for all immigrants through the year 1838. After that date, all files through 1860 were compiled for rural counties, but the volume of records in urban areas precludes comprehensive coverage as immigration became heavier. A 10-percent random sample applies to Boston Municipal Court after 1842 and to the federal courts after 1848.

8. Filing fees, and those of a clerk to prepare the papers, amounted to about six dollars, and more if an attorney was employed. Throughout most of this period, that amount represented the weekly wage of a common laborer fortunate enough to have steady employment.

9. Many Irish place-names were recorded as the clerk heard them, as counties "Mead," "Teronna," and "DePrairie" evidence. A few clerks required written affidavits of prior residence of an applicant while others accepted vague responses, such as "The Parish" in Roscommon and "Notown" in Cork.

10. Fitzpatrick, "Emigration 1801–1870," 566, 581.

11. NA New England, RG 85, Box 347, Middlesex County MA Supreme Judicial Court, v. 1, #95 (Martin); Box 402, Boston Municipal Court, v. 21, no. 624 (Gilliland); v. 22, no. 840 (Keefe); Box 404, v. 29, no. 2970 (Phillips); Box 487, York County ME Court of Common Pleas, v. 39, no. 181 (White); Box 577. Providence RI Court of Common Pleas, 1838, no. 19 (Fleming). Fleming's wife joined him in Providence, where he had settled early the following year; the ship bringing her had docked in New York City.

12. Fitzpatrick, "Emigration, 1801–70," 562.

13. NA New England, RG 85, Box 223, Berkshire MA County Court of Common Pleas, v. 5, no. 30 (O'Cavanaugh); Box 425, Worcester MA County Court of Common Pleas, v. 2, no. 14 (Bowes); Box 574, Newport RI Supreme Judicial Court, 1852, no. 44 (Cottrell); Box 218, Barnstable County MA Court of Common Pleas, 1837, no. 1037 (Fogarty).

14. NA New England, RG 85, Box 321, Hampden County MA Court of Common Pleas, v. 1, no. 108 (Carroll); v. 1, no. 413 (Hayes); originals now in Massachusetts State Archives, Columbia Point, Boston. A transcript of Swiney's 1834 petition is in v. 81, no. 514, Worcester County MA Court of Common Pleas, Worcester County Courthouse. He had spent six months in Middlesex County and two years in Worcester County before filing his petition, but if he ever returned to take his oath two years later, the record has been lost.

15. *Jesuit, or Catholic Sentinel,* January 18, 1834, and January 25, 1834. Hereafter cited as the *Pilot.* Editorials and commentary promoting naturalization as the "only lever which can raise us to equality" (February 8) continued to appear for some weeks.

16. NA New England, RG 85, Box 402, Boston Municipal Court, v. 14, no. 209 (Timoney, 1826); v..22, no. 872 (McQuaid, 1834); Box 347, Middlesex County MA Court of Common Pleas, v. 1, no. 8 (Cummiskey, 1820). Brian Mitchell notes that only south-coastal Cork approached the rate at which Tyrone, Cavan, Leitrim, and Fermanagh sent emigrants to the Merrimack Valley. Mitchell, *Paddy Camps,* 20–21.

17. Computed on the basis of those who were sixteen or older upon arrival in the United States, Irish immigrants to the United States before 1826 were on average 16.1 years in residence before becoming citizens. For the 1826–1837 group, 162 had completed the legal process by the end of their sixth year in the country, but their average years in residence (12.9) remained relatively high. Later-arriving Irish made commitments to their new country more quickly, swearing allegiance to it after an average 9 years of residency. Almost one in five (407 of 2,116) of those arriving in the eight years immediately preceding the Famine had attained citizenship within a year after becoming eligible to do so.

As numbers of potential new citizens soared in the 1840s, private "naturalization specialists" developed a booming trade. Two—Thomas Rowean, who maintained an office at 129 Federal Street, and William F. A. Kelly—were especially active in the Boston area and may have accounted for half of the forms filed in federal district court in the early 1850s. Rowean's handwriting, often accompanied by the notation "paid my fees," appears on hundreds of forms of the era. First in 1843, and for a decade thereafter, he served as character witness to nearly one hundred of the Irish immigrants in this sample. Kelly was a "laborer" out of Westport in County Mayo when he filed his first papers in 1844, a self-styled "gentleman" by 1847 when he took the citizenship oath, and a justice of the peace by the early 1850s. NA New England, RG21, U.S. Circuit Court, Massachusetts District, v. 1, no. 85 (1847).

18. David N. Doyle, "The Irish as Urban Pioneers in the United States 1850–1870," *Journal of American Ethnic History* 10 (1990): 36–59, appropriately celebrates the Irish contribution to American urban life at mid-century but admits the attraction that small factory villages had for some immigrants. In a more recent essay, Doyle notes the lack of data about the "old" Irish immigration of the first half of the century and acknowledges that those "previous migrants may indeed . . . have stayed or migrated within the countryside." Doyle, "The Remaking of Irish America, 1845–1870," in *A New History of Ireland*, vol. 6 (Oxford: Clarendon Press, 1996), 741. The present study provides significant evidence that many of those whom Doyle characterizes as old Irish did exactly that.

19. The number of laborers among these new Irish-American citizens closely approximates the employment profile of the Boston Irish in 1850 that Oscar Handlin derived from the federal census of that year. Handlin viewed their numbers, more than 7,000 of the 14,595 Irish-born in the labor workforce, as evidence of an uprooted and "resourceless proletariat . . . a massive lump in the community, undigested, undigestible." Oscar Handlin, *Boston's Immigrants 1790–1865: A Study in Acculturation* (Cambridge: Harvard University Press, 1941), 60 and tab. 13, 237–38. Contrary to Handlin's assertion, the large number of laborers who claimed citizenship rights during the Famine decade were proving themselves both resourceful and digestible.

20. NA New England, RG 85, Box 577, Providence RI Court of Common Pleas, v. 1828, no. 6.

21. Although Handlin downplayed Irish successes, depicting them as victims of Famine, market forces, and an oversupply of labor in Boston in 1850, portions of his study reveal, as do the naturalization petitions, that many Irish had found niches in the American economy that were not being filled by native-born residents. As Handlin points out, until the Famine exodus depressed the Boston labor market, wages had been higher there than in New York, and Irish who settled in New England had by mid-century moved into significant positions in the infant heavy industry of the Boston area and had virtually dominated older crafts, such as roofing, smithing, and tailoring. Handlin, 81 and tab. 13, 237–38.

22. The printers included Patrick Donahoe, schooled in the United States, later publisher of the *Pilot* and numerous books by and for Irish Americans, and an active, if infrequent, witness for new citizens during the 1850s.

23. The naturalization records contain a number of sworn statements from witnesses who testified on behalf of a trusted employee that the employee had been in service since "only a lad."

24. Cornelius McManniman was over seventy when he emigrated, but the oldest new citizen was eighty-seven-year-old Thomas Brennan, native of Kilkenny, who had been thirty-three years in America before declaring allegiance to his adopted land in 1847. NA New England, RG 85, Worcester County Court of Common Pleas, Box 426, v. 1, no. 51 (McManniman); MSA, Hampden County MA Court of Common Pleas, v. 1, no. 52 (Brennan).

25. Mature emigrants may have been more reluctant than their children to adopt a new

national identity, and the known incidence of high mortality among the immigrant generation may have deprived many of them of the opportunity. The records evidence at least one such early death, documented in the file of Mary Dugan of Boston, a widow whose spouse had died without having taken the oath of allegiance. By producing husband Gregory's declaration of intent filed in Boston Municipal Court more than seven years earlier, under provisions of the law she claimed the citizenship that could have been hers had he lived. NA New England, RG 21, U.S. Circuit Court, Massachusetts District, v. 1, no. 543 (1850).

26. These differences deserve attention and further analysis, but all age calculations from naturalization records must be used with caution. They are indicative at best, because documents containing only a birth year and a year of entry into the United States might return a result a year or more off the actual mark.

27. Reported immigration dates to the United States may actually mask an emigration from Ireland that occurred years, rather than months, previously. A significant number of arrivals at the port of Boston were in ships of the coastal trade with the Maritime Provinces of Canada. Such indirect passage was common from Cork and Sligo, and perhaps other ports as well. A few naturalization files record the length of the Canadian stay, but most do not.

28. NA New England, RG 85, Suffolk County MA Supreme Judicial Court, v. 1, no. 48 (1798).

29. By the 1830s, according to William Nolan, the civil parish had often become "outdated and irrelevant to settlement and community." The new Poor Law Unions were intended to be more so. William Nolan, *Tracing the Past: Sources for Local History in the Republic of Ireland* (Dublin: Geography Publications, 1982), 17.

30. Fitzpatrick, "Emigration 1801–1870," 562–621.

31. Doyle, "Remaking of Irish-America, 1845–1880," 733–36. Citing S. H. Cousens, Joel Mokyr, and Fitzpatrick, Doyle recognizes a shift of migration patterns toward Munster and Connacht beginning before the Famine but contends that it was the impact of the Famine exodus that transformed Irish America at large. Contrary to Doyle's assertion that the Irish community of Boston was "but an overnight, famine-rooted one" (747), which echoes Handlin's classic study, this analysis of individual New Englanders of Irish origin indicates that the transformation of Irish America, especially in metropolitan Boston, was well under way before 1846. By then, 17 percent of the foreign born in Suffolk County (Boston proper) had become citizens, the vast majority of them—the records point to 90 percent—Irish immigrants. If the city suburbs in Middlesex and Norfolk counties are included, those born in Ireland who had acquired American citizenship exceeded 1,500, a sevenfold to eightfold increase from the "barely 200" of 1834. Doyle overstates the case in characterizing the Boston Irish community as an "overnight" phenomenon, although he is indeed correct that Boston, like the rest of Irish America, was transformed as a result of the Famine exodus.

32. Ibid., 734.

Part Three

New Sources for Diaspora Studies

8

Rites de Passage:
Rituals of Separation in Irish Oral Tradition

Grace Neville

After my father died, I went through his papers, which he had always kept in an emigrant's tin trunk that we were never allowed to explore. One might say that it was his memory box. I had to wait until he died in order to get access to it. In this trunk, among other belongings, I found two letters that had been written to his mother—my grandmother—in 1907, six years before my father was even born. They were written by a friend of my grandmother's (she signs herself "your friend Cissie") who was working for a family on Riverside Drive, Manhattan, probably as a servant girl. I do not know who exactly this correspondent was, nor do I know why my father kept these old letters when he must have discarded so many more recent ones. This essay is dedicated to the memory of these emigrants, some remembered, many forgotten, and the memory of their wider communities in Ireland and the United States of America.

Consciously or not, the need to mark important or liminal stages in life is deeply entrenched in most cultures, even in this modern age. Ceremonies of differing magnitude commemorate milestones like birth, marriage, and death, as well as intercalated stages like the advent of puberty and the reaching of citizenship age. Many of these milestones have been taken over by orthodox religion: arrival at what used to be called "the age of reason" becomes, in Catholic tradition, the time of one's First Communion; the onset of puberty is marked in different religious traditions by ceremonies like confirmation and bar mitzvah. They mark the community's public recognition and celebration of these key events; they are its way of saying, "This is important; things will never be the same again."

In Irish tradition, wakes have always constituted one of the major rituals, marking that most definitive of all boundaries: the crossover between life and death, between now and the hereafter. Folklorists from T. Crofton Croker[1] to Seán Ó Súilleabháin have left us rich and vibrant evidence to this effect. In the Irish context, as is well known, emigration drained the country of a high percentage of its young people, especially in the late nineteenth and early twentieth centuries. Statistics differ in detail but agree in broad outline: forty million contemporary Americans of Irish descent; one New Yorker in three in 1855 actually born in Ireland;

one immigrant in three arriving in New York in 1890 also born in Ireland; and so on. Terms like "hemorrhage" and "holocaust" are frequently used in order to depict the phenomenon perhaps more vividly than cold statistics ever could. The purpose of this essay is to draw together these two phenomena of wakes and emigration in order to shed some light on the *rite de passage* that was the so-called "American wake," the departure ritual for Irish emigrants leaving for the United States. Historian Kerby Miller sees it as a "peculiarly Irish custom, unknown in Britain or continental Europe."[2] The material analyzed here comes from the Archives of the Irish Folklore Commission.

A word at the outset about these archives. Housed in the Department of Irish Folklore at University College Dublin, they consist of approximately 1.5 million pages, largely handwritten and in Irish, made up mainly of interviews gathered in the 1930s and somewhat later by approximately two thousand collectors working with forty thousand informants. These informants, or sources, were overwhelmingly male and elderly, living throughout rural Ireland. The result is truly an Aladdin's cave packed with an astonishing range of eclectic material covering mythology and folk legends, recent history, folk customs and beliefs, songs and dance, accounts of folk habitations and furniture, sport and pastimes, and memories of long ago. Because many of the informants were born shortly after the Great Famine of the 1840s, their memories and experiences date largely from the second half of the nineteenth century and the first part of the twentieth century.

In the archives under discussion here, the conscious and widespread use of the term *wake* to describe the leave-taking ceremony underlines the user's awareness of this departure for America as momentous and, in most cases, definitive, for it was only one short step from waking the dead to waking a person still alive but who would probably never be seen in Ireland again, someone who could consequently participate in his or her own wake. The informants and their communities regarded emigration to America as a kind of death, indeed an early and thus unnatural death for the people involved, who were, overwhelmingly, young (in their teens and twenties): "You would know by them that they never expected to see you again. It was as if you were going out to be buried" (1411/92).[3] "When I came home [from America] they were as glad to see me as if I had come from the grave" (1411/95). In age-old Irish tradition, the Afterlife was situated, inter alia, over the Western Ocean, in the Isles of the Blest. This belief reinforces the image of the destination of most of these emigrants—America—as a kind of earthly paradise: "the great land beyond the sea," "God's own country" (1409/70).[4] Emigration or—in another parallel system of belief—death and arrival in Heaven had to be marked by some ceremony. This ceremony was the American wake.

There exists an interesting mismatch between, on the one hand, the remarkable homogeneity of descriptions of American wakes even from different parts of the country and, on the other, the lack of agreement surrounding the terminology used in order to designate this ritual. Among the names used here are "a spree," "a bottle drink," "a convoy," and "an American wake." As well as variants of these, Kerby Miller records other different names not mentioned in the archives I have consulted: "a live wake," "a farewell supper," "a feast of departure," "an American bottle night," and "a parting spree."[5] Apart from "American wake," the other names used in these archives do not necessarily have any sad or indeed ominous connotations. Some of them are merely factual:

- "A bottle drink" reduces the ritual to one of its main constituent parts: bottles of alcohol.
- "A convoy" can be used in other unrelated contexts. In these archives, this term is used as a verb ("to convoy someone") and as a noun designating the event or the group accompanying the emigrant to the port.
- "A spree" (from the Irish *spraoi*) can have positive connotations of merrymaking. *Spree* is also the term sometimes used to describe the party held to mark the joyous occasion of an emigrant's return, for example, on holidays.

In the interest of simplicity, the name "American wake" will be the main one used in this paper.

Asked when American wakes started, the informants' general perception is that they date from time immemorial: "The American wakes go back beyond living memory" (1430/216). Interestingly, for one female informant, the fixing in the memory of these ceremonies is women's work: "Bottle drinks are going on as long as people are going to America and that is longer than I remember or my mother or her mother" (1411/73). When asked whether the practice of holding American wakes still existed at the time of the collection of these archives (especially in the 1930s and 1940s), many informants reply that they have undergone a sea change and that the practice died out quite recently—in the previous generation. A somewhat more recent date is given by some informants: "The spree for intending emigrants was always held in North Longford even up till quite recently. Mrs Morris attended one only seven years ago" (1430/207). It would appear that, by then, one of the main features of the wake—that it was paid for by the neighbors—no longer applied: an informant refers to a spree held for a departing emigrant seven years earlier "but not subscribed for by the neighbours" (1430/211). The demise of the American wake was thus clearly imminent.

Perceived reasons for its decline are given: "They stopped in the last twenty years due to the slackening off of emigration to the USA" (1430/216). More specifically, "Mrs Morris gives as the reason for the non-continuance nowadays the fact that they would be too costly and also the fact that emigration to America is practically nonexistent today. The emphasis now is on emigration to England" (1430/209). The community knew that an emigrant was more likely to return, even temporarily, from England than from America. Hence, an elaborate departure ceremony was no longer needed.

For whom were American wakes held? They were held for individuals, male and female, and occasionally—for the sake of convenience—for a group leaving from the same parish: "The wakes were held for individuals going as well as for more than one person" (1430/217). The permission of the departing emigrant was sought before preparations were made. Emigrants heading for Australia or Canada were also waked in similar fashion: "There would be one [a wake] if you were going out to Australia or Canada just the same to America" (1411/92).

In his seminal study of rites of passage, the early-twentieth-century ethnographer Arnold van Gennep divides those attending funerals into two groups: not the living and the dead as one might have expected, but the dead and those mourning them on one hand and everyone else on the other hand.[6] This division can also be sensed in the American wakes described in these archives. Thus, an informant remembers how, when American money arrived to take someone to America, "there would be uneasiness in the house" (1411/35). In other words, two distinct groups were already discernible: the emigrant with his or her already grieving relatives, and the rest of the community. Elsewhere we read: "The intending emigrants also went around to the houses in the neighbourhood to leave goodbye with those who would not be coming to the wake, the old people and invalids and anyone else that they knew could not come" (1430/228). It was as if the intending emigrants were putting their affairs in order before leaving, like old people aware that their time is fast running out.

Once the intending emigrant agreed to be waked, the community took over the necessary arrangements, such as a collection to cover the cost of the wake. When questioned, one informant said that no invitations were given specifically. Pressed for details, she elaborated: "You would know there was a convoy and you went; no one would be turned away." Indeed, these wakes seemed to materialize out of nothing. Arrangements were made and everyone knew about them as if a common mind were working in a community where all were equal, no one taking the lead and no one being out of step; the community was acting as one.

When was the American wake held? The archives often inform us that emigrants left around April or May. Practical reasons are given for this timing, such as a safer crossing than in winter. Other less acknowledged reasons may also be glimpsed: this period of the year marks the new season, the time of a fresh start, of a new departure celebrated in folk song and lyric poetry the world over. The American wake "was always held the night before departure" (1430/207). "It started at seven or eight o'clock in the evening" (1430/216) and "continued all night until the emigrant (or emigrants) were due to leave" (1430/216). Interestingly, many informants specify these wakes "started soon after nightfall" (1430/228). In many societies, not just in traditional Irish society, night is believed to belong to the dead and the otherworld. A wonderfully evocative phrase used elsewhere in these archives states: "When the sun goes down, the spirits is as thick as the blades of grass in the field" (1845/159). Little wonder, then, that sensible people stay indoors and blot out this time by sleeping through it. It feels somehow appropriate that this ritual of the American wake should take place at a time believed to be controlled and peopled by the dead, thus heightening an awareness that the emigrants and the communities waking them now belong less to the realm of the living than to the dead.

Who attended these wakes? The emigrant's entire community seems to have attended this departure ceremony: "All the neighbours and friends attended the American wake" (1430/228). There are, however, fleeting references to people who did not attend these crowded affairs, either through choice or otherwise. One woman refers to occasional hooliganism at these wakes, explaining: "They'd be fellows who would be outside looking in through the windows" (469/400). These outsiders would hurl abuse and comments (for example, about underwear of the departing girl) in through the window. In other words, these "trouble-fêtes"[7] were outsiders in every sense of the term, deprived of the chance of traveling to paradise bestowed on the departing girl, larding their talk with taboo subjects (like female underwear) banned from normal conversations, reduced to spying on the personification of promise and future happiness through a window. Hence their rage, frustration, and jealousy, their need to bring her down to size by ridiculing her, by naming the unnameable.

These wakes were usually held in the emigrant's own house. One woman remembers, in an interestingly gendered account of her own space, that her own wake was held "in my father's house" (1411/92). Occasional variants are found on this pattern: "Sometimes when more than one person would be emigrating from the same district at the same time, the wake would be held for all in the one house for convenience sake or maybe two separate Wakes were held. There was no hard and fast rule about this" (1430/217).

The three main ingredients of the wake (apart from the person to be waked) were music, dancing, and drink. (I find it interesting that nowhere in the archives I have studied is there any mention of prayers or priests.) One informant remembered, "Mrs Morris was often at these American wakes and they followed the one pattern. . . . There would surely be two musicians at least, two of the neighbours, usually a flute player and a fiddler and perhaps an accordeon or concertina player" (1430/207). The songs that constituted such a central part of these ceremonies conjure up reluctant emigrants (for instance, "Noreen Bawn" and "My Charming Kate O'Neill") and emphasize the features of the darker side of emigration:

- the dangerous crossing ("that was the thing about the songs on the night of a Bottle Drink, they were all about ship wrecks and it would scare you even more than you had been for til I went to America I had never been passed [past] Carn and only then an odd time" (1411/93);
- family members abandoned and lonely at home; in particular, brokenhearted mothers grieving for their only son inevitably in America; consequent eviction and death through heartache;
- hard work and ill health encountered in America.

It is interesting to contrast these songs of doom and gloom with the enthusiasm recorded, often from the same informants, when emigration to America is discussed. The departure of the young is frequently depicted in these archives as an inevitable, natural, and even physical process: the young left "as soon as ever they were feathered" (1411/20), in the resonant phrase used by one woman to encapsulate the phenomenon. Most emigrants stayed in America, a fact that departing emigrants would themselves already have known and that historians have subsequently confirmed.[8] Why, therefore, this discrepancy between the overall haste of the emigrants to go and the pessimism of their songs? Perhaps at one level it would have been churlish and inappropriate to express overall delight (tempered, admittedly, by some misgivings) at the prospect of going. Kerby Miller goes so far as to state: "By declaring in verse that their lives in America, as well as their departures from Ireland, were or would be unhappy—riven with inconsolable homesickness—the emigrants further satisfied the demands of the exile convention and effectively deflected both communal and self-accusations of selfish and nontraditional behaviour."[9]

The songs constitute a parallel narrative running alongside the real one of the leave-taking being described. In these songs, similar scenarios are on view but they are heightened and, perhaps, exaggerated. This enhancement begs questions about the relationship between two narratives: Was the fictional one prompting the real-life actors as to the appropriate words, gestures, and reactions expected of them? Or were the real actors off-loading their reactions onto their songs, which they used to express themselves through the mouths and imaginations of others— either because to do it without this ventriloquizing would have killed them or because they lacked the vocabulary of emotion and directness?

At all events, the intensity of these songs is frequently pointed out: "People would sing the saddest songs they could think of" (1411/113); "all the songs that I ever heard about going away to America were sad and if you were going yourself and hear them it would break your heart. On the night of the Bottle Drink you would think that they were trying to see who could sing the oldest and saddest songs. You were listening to those songs from [when] you were able to creep and right enough it was terrible to think you would never hear them again" (1411/92).

These songs function like a heavy-duty drug to anesthetize the grief of all concerned, especially those departing. One woman says that "the sad songs nearly killed the poor wane that was going away" (1411/215). Another muses, "Imagine if you were going away the next morning and hear a song like that wouldn't it put you out of your mind" (1411/51). Perhaps that was precisely one of the functions of these songs: to stop people from thinking, to put emigrants "out of their minds" because these same minds had become such unbearably painful places. At another level, these songs probably had a cathartic effect sorely needed at a time of such intense emotion. They made people cry and perhaps allowed them to displace their grief onto the characters in the songs rather than onto the real emigrants around them, because the latter might have been too painful or even socially unacceptable in its intensity and directness. Most of the ballads cited here were dedicated to women: "The Maid of Coolmore" (1411/136), "The Maid of Galway Town" (1411/74), "Annie Laurie" (514/61), "Nora McShane" (1411/220), "My Lovely Irish Rose" (1411/230), "Nancy, Lovely Nancy, Ten Thousand Times Adieu" (1411/47). In their repeated depiction of men leaving their women behind, these overwhelmingly male-narrated songs give us a male perspective and may have been of help to the young men leaving. Men are portrayed as active, leaving some passive woman behind (never mind the social reality of this, given that women left and stayed away by the tens of thousands). If these songs were coping strategies, giving psychological help, where were the women's songs? Who, if anyone, did the women identify with in these songs: the departing males, the abandoned females or the females returning to Ireland in ill health, soon to die?

Dancing was the second major element of the all-night festivities under discussion here. The participants were mainly younger people, the emigrants themselves, for instance. Here again, the egalitarian nature of the proceedings is hinted at, as if the activities had materialized without any organizing, as if the entire community were acting as one: "There was no master of ceremonies but one of the neighbours would go around and get the boys and girls to dance, if they showed any hesitation in getting out on the floor. Anyone could call on any other person to sing or dance" (1430/207). The gendered nature of the proceedings is again clear:

At that time very often the boys would stand in the middle of the floor and wouldn't ask the girls out to dance. Two men would go around and make the girls get out on the floor. Thus every girl was compelled to get out to dance. When she did go out on the floor, she could go to any of the boys she liked, and dance with him. No girl was let sit down but had to dance. Apparently the boys were shy and wouldn't ask the girls out to dance. (1430/216)

This passage speaks volumes for the segregated rearing of boys and girls if the boys in question could not even pluck up the courage to ask girls they had known all their lives out to dance. These were the same young people who were about to cross the Atlantic for a new life in another continent. One wonders how, if ever, they ever managed to survive there.

Porter, wine, and tea are the three drinks mentioned repeatedly by informants. The status of these drinks and of the groups that preferred each is revealing. Here, as elsewhere, the gendered nature of these choices is evident: "The wine was for the women" (1430/207) states one informant. Another adds that alcohol was served to men and older women, suggesting that perhaps, with advancing years, women reached the status of men of any age! Tea was also a woman's drink, although not restricted by age: "It was mostly the women and girls who took the tea" (1430/216). Preparing tea was also a task for females: "The girls got the tae ready" (514/63). Another informant is more precise: "Tea was also provided, mostly for the womenfolk, as the men did not bother about tea when they had plenty of porter" (1430/207). If the porter ran out, the men went to buy some more. The usual quantity of porter provided is stated: "a barrell or half barrell of porter for the men" (1430/228). The alcohol was paid for on a bring-your-own principle: "The men supplied the drink only" (1430/216), which they then proceeded to drink. One text specifies that money for alcohol at these ceremonies was provided by heads of household only (1411/68) and could be collected at the ceremony itself: "At the spree the plate went around and everyone present of the menfolk put sixpence or a shilling on it to pay for the halfbarrell of porter" (1430/258). If women were heads of households, they were also expected to contribute drink money, their status conferring upon them a sort of honorary maleness: "The women did not pay except a woman happened to be the head of a house" (1411/5).

The result of this all-night drinking was predictable: "It was not uncommon for fights to occur at these American wakes, when the men would have got too much to drink" (1430/258). It is interesting to hear discordant echoes in these accounts of leave-takings, for the participants must have been very drunk indeed by morning if, as appears to have been the case and as is emphasized in the very term "bottle drink," they had had little or nothing to eat and too much to drink. The lack of food at the wake along with the overabundance of drink and the endless noise made up of talking, music, and singing must have brought about a kind of out-of-body experience for the departing emigrants. Like soldiers going into battle, they set out in a state of altered consciousness, anesthetized by alcohol, physically exhausted after a night's dancing, affected by a roller coaster of conflicting emotions, engaged with these emotions (if at all) through lines borrowed from songs written by someone else.

Daybreak marked the beginning of the end of the wake: "The spree would be over about five o'clock in the morning or later sometimes" (1430/251). It is interesting that first light should mark the start of the emigrants' new lives, for the morning after the night before, the young people about to emigrate were no longer the people they used to be: like children in some folktale emerging from the dark or the forest, they had suddenly grown up and become adults overnight.[10] Paradoxically, they were now older than their parents and elders would ever be: they were marked people, ancient before their time, heading for experiences and knowledge far beyond the wildest imaginings of their elders. In this motif of a new dawn, one senses the awareness of a new start not just for the emigrants but equally for the family and friends left behind. Quite simply, things would never be the same again.

Specifically, the horse and trap arriving to take the emigrant to the station or port is the deus ex machina that marks the beginning of the end: "The dance or spree went on all night till the car [explained elsewhere as "horse and trap"] came for the emigrant in the morning" (1430/228). Like someone condemned to death, the departing emigrant sometimes expressed a last request, for instance to see a favorite horse for the last time (1409/50). These texts stress the dramatic contrast that existed between the merrymaking of the previous evening and night and the trauma of the following morning: "*oidhche mhor cheoil a's spóirt . . . níorbh é sin do'n mhaidin. D'iompaigheadh an gáire 'na ghol acub*" (a great night of music and merrymaking . . . unlike the morning. Their laughter used to turn to tears [434/81]).

The leave-taking itself is described in detail. It was a noisy affair: "Then the weeping and wailing broke out" (1430/228). The gendered nature of the leave-taking is apparent in the role assigned to women, especially mothers. They seem to have functioned as lightning conductors for emotions such as grief on these occasions. These texts are full of mothers crying copiously on their doorsteps as their children leave for America (510/442), mothers clinging to their departing children's necks until someone would unclench their arms (1411/224), mothers screaming at trains about to take their daughters away (1430/229). This is how these women are remembered often by the children they were already mourning. But did those children not cry, too? If they did, the stories do not emphasize it. Like *mna caointe*, or keening women, these mothers are remembered as being physically and emotionally out of control. Perhaps they were expressing not just their own grief but that of the wider community at the unnatural loss of its young ones. The emigrants are often seen as trying to pacify their mothers. Who was the more wounded, the departing or the departed? One is left with the sight of the wounded trying to take care of the wounded: the paradoxical but common spectacle of the dying trying to console those left behind. "It was very sad when a young boy would be leaving after the Bottle Drink to hear him pacifying his mother and tell her of the grand clothes and the heaps of money he would send her the minute he would land" (1411/28). At one level, it is interesting to see how young men seem to have known how to console their mothers, what the latter's perceived weak points might have been (clothes and money). One is struck by how stereotypical this perception is. At another level, such promises evoke parallels with saints granting wishes (here for money, glamor, and status) from beyond the grave to their kinsfolk or to the deserving poor. The power imbalance between those leaving and those left behind, between present and future, is already clear.

Beyond all words and promises, however, one departing emigrant let out a "wild cry remembered to this day." The vocabulary of emotions is not afforded much space in these texts (one might discuss whether this is also the case elsewhere in traditional Irish society). This "wild cry" is a parallel and deeply expressive language uttered by a wounded animal, ripping apart the decorum, stepping outside the lines scripted for him, transgressing the boundaries pinning him in. Beyond all words and sounds lie other potent forms of communication, such as body language and gestures: "*Ni fhaca tú aon rud chomh cradhteach a riamh le sgaradh na gcaradh. Bhídíst a caitheadh a gcuid lámh thimpeal ar a chéile agus a pógadh a chéile*" (You never saw anything as pitiful as the friends' leavetaking. They used to throw their arms around each other and kiss each other [434/81]). This continues throughout the various stages of the leave-taking—in the family home and as they are getting into the coach. Beyond words and gestures lies silence. Emigrants, we read, would keep looking backward, silently, as long as their family home remained in view. They were now in a place beyond words, where words and gestures could not even begin to convey what they were going through, where—in a nation of speakers—silence is arguably the most powerful form of communication.

We are repeatedly told that a large group who had attended the wake would accompany emigrants part of the way and that a smaller group would remain with them all the way to the station or even to the port. Why did the larger group not travel the whole way? Practical reasons come to mind: the people in question, especially family members, were probably physically and emotionally drained, or they had to attend to work at home that could not wait. However, in a more positive sense, perhaps going part but not all of the way was the elders' way of launching their young—like fledglings out of a nest—and of letting them go in the realization that they could do no more for them, that the young people had to fend for themselves from now on, just as all young people have to be pushed or let go at some stage in order to become adults, although rarely in such a dramatic, public, or irrevocable fashion.

Anyone familiar with these archives will be struck by the unquenchable interest in the clothes of returned emigrants, especially those of the women. The effect these clothes had on the home communities was profound.[11] There are relatively few references, however, to the clothes worn by departing emigrants. Did they not change out of the clothes they had worn to dance the night away? One informant refers to the generosity of parents in dressing their daughters for emigration (1411/400). The parents' anxiety to dress their daughters in impressive clothes for their new lives brings to mind those photos of European peasants on decks of ships coming in to Ellis Island, standing erect and wearing all their finery in order to impress and salute their new homeland that, in many ways, was oblivious to this, the most momentous day of their lives, their arrival in paradise. Not that all elders agreed with such extravagance, however. One woman advises another about to send her daughter to America: "Don't bother dressing her up, for her clothes will only be burned when she gets to the far side anyway" (1362/139). The fragmented accounts of life in America scattered throughout these archives hint at the deliberate invention of new identities, especially by recently arrived young Irish women. One account states that they anglicized their names and pretended that they could not speak Irish (53/188–89). The reference to the burning of women's clothes in America further emphasizes this motif of the deliberate obliteration of the emigrant's original identity and the emigrant's subsequent transformation into a new one.

Items taken by emigrants on their journeys to America are remembered. Among these, food features prominently. It was usually prepared by the local women, who presented it to the departing emigrant at the wake: "All the women who attended the wake also brought something, a present for the emigrant . . . cakes, milk, or something like that" (1430/216), "griddle cakes of oaten bread buttered" (1411/393), "an oat meal cake, a fat hen (cooked)" (485/216). Here as elsewhere, one notes gender differences. Women function as nurturers; their gifts are altruistic, unlike the alcohol provided by male guests for their own consumption. One female informant "was very emphatic in pointing out that these gifts were in no way considered as charity but as presents" (1430/216). If drinking, dancing, and singing could all have had anesthetizing properties, work may have had these functions for the local women. One informant describes the women frantically baking for weeks before the emigrant's departure: "For weeks before the person would leave, all the neighbouring women would be coming to the house with oaten bread or butter or something of that sort to put in their barrell." The simple food, based on milk and wheat, recalls the food prepared in primitive cultures for the dead as sustenance on their long journey to the next world. Here again, the task of smoothing the passage to the next life falls to the women.

Alcohol also featured among the items taken by emigrants on their journey: "Sometimes the men would bring a bottle of whiskey for the emigrant. Usually the emigrant brought some of this whiskey with him on his journey" (1430/228); "a glass of whiskey in a small bottle in case of sickness" (485/218). Unsurprisingly, emigrants also took money with them. Some remarks spring to mind: Why was the money normally spent on alcohol at the American wake not given instead to the departing emigrant? One returned emigrant mentions having the meager sum of just five shillings with her on the boat that carried her westward. How much, one wonders, was spent on alcohol at her American wake? To object to what might seem to be a squandering of money on these wakes would be to miss the point, however. Even now, in late-twentieth-century (urban) Ireland, the dead must be given "a good send-off." Saving money in the process is not a priority.

Among the items of clothing taken by emigrants on the journey were garments made of tweed, a fabric that was believed to have been banned from America but that was unsurpassable for soaking up emigrant sweat in the Land of Opportunity. Particularly striking is the reference to departing emigrants perched on top of Bianconi coaches along with their bedclothes (434/83). Practical reasons, such as the wish to avoid the cost of replacements, may partly explain why emigrants took their bedclothes with them, but perhaps these bedclothes also functioned literally as a kind of security blanket with the feeling and smells of home, creating the illusion of safety and familiarity in the face of the unknown. At another level, this image of emigrants wrapped in their bedclothes is only one step removed from that of corpses wrapped in shrouds; once again in these archives, the New World and the next world become one.[12]

Along with food, alcohol, and clothing, books and manuscripts of Irish poetry were taken by emigrants. Could the emigrants actually read these works, or did these high-status objects function primarily as relics of homeland and family, as consoling reminders of past glories in the face of present destitution? Religious objects such as holy water also made the journey. Religion shades into superstition in the list of the additional luck tokens, such as blackthorn sticks and shamrock, taken along. Less clichéd are the references to relics and pubic hair sewn into undergarments "and worn as a protection when going into emigration" (469/411–13) as well as to the practice of taking along soil or turf cut from one's parents' turf bank. The soil could subsequently be worn in shoes in America, we are told, and thus the reality of America is denied as emigrants there continue to walk on Irish soil! The items listed were generally carried to America in canvas bags, whereas returning emigrants used tin trunks.

Rites of passage were not held for all emigrants. Some people simply did not give the required permission for them to be held: "Not every emigrant wanted the fuss of an American wake. Some asked to leave quietly" (1430/217). There is even a suggestion that one had to be deemed worthy of a wake, that it depended on the popularity of the individual. In the cases of some emigrants, the furtive manner of their leaving precluded the possibility of a wake: they were stowaways or were fleeing family or political problems. We read of the last daughter who "stole away" to America without informing her parents because she did not want to cause them distress (1409/6); one imagines that she caused them even greater distress by not telling them because they had no way of saying good-bye, no body to wake. Her disappearance must have seemed unnatural to them, like a suicide or a drowning. One senses, however, that these are just a minority of cases, which stick in the memory because of their sheer oddness. These exceptions emphasize that the norm for the vast majority of emigrants was a wake in the manner already outlined.

The repetitive, even choreographed, nature of these rituals is striking: "I was at plenty of Bottle Drinks but the one I remember best was my own" (1411/92). In other words, a series of dress rehearsals leading eventually to the opening night. In one text, a mother remembers the departure to America of the eldest of her fourteen offspring (434/234–35). One senses that this marks the start of the unraveling of this little clan, that the thirteen others will go too; not that thirteen additional American wakes will be held but that the initial one will be repeated thirteen more times. Linear time is here abandoned in favor of the circular time long favored by primitive societies[13] as the departure of one young person is endlessly relived by his mother, who repeats a pattern followed by countless of her peers, elders, and youngers as she says good-bye to all of her children. Less individuals than characters in a play, these people know all the words and gestures expected of them. Have they not witnessed them, day in day out, from a young age? After years of rehearsal, they are now word perfect when their own time comes at last.

The awareness of the American wake as the marker separating the old and new, East and West, past and future, is constantly emphasized throughout these archives. As a literary theme, the vast phenomenon of Irish emigration continues to haunt Irish and Irish-American literature, including twentieth-century Irish theater—from Lennox Robinson through Brian Friel to Martin MacDonagh—to the American side, including the Irish-American literature analyzed by Charles Fanning through such contemporary works as Margaret Atwood's highly acclaimed novel *Alias Grace*. Emigration and the profound seachanges it continues to generate on both sides of the Atlantic might best be understood through the contextualization of these literary works alongside the lived experiences remembered and preserved in the extraordinary and resonant memory box that is the Archives of the Irish Folklore Commission.

Notes

I am indebted to the Department of Irish Folklore at University College, Dublin, for permission to use material from the Archives of the Irish Folklore Commission in this essay.

1. T. Crofton Croker, *Fairy Legends and Traditions of the South of Ireland* (London, 1825).

2. Kerby A. Miller, *Emigrants and Exiles* (New York: Oxford University Press, 1985).

3. Irish Folklore Commission Archive MS no. 1411, p. 92. Information from the Archives of the Irish Folklore Commission is hereafter cited in the parenthetical format used here.

4. Grace Neville, "Land of the Fair, Land of the Free? The Myth of America in Irish Folklore," in *Exiles and Migrants: Crossing Thresholds in European Culture and Society,* ed. Anthony Coulson (Brighton, Eng.: Sussex Academic Press, 1997), 57–71.

5. Miller, *Emigrants and Exiles,* 557.

6. Arnold van Gennep, *The Rites of Passage,* trans. Monika B. Vizedom and Gabrielle L. Caffee (1908; London: Routledge and Kegan Paul, 1960).

7. Eugen Weber, *Peasants into Frenchmen: The Modernisation of Rural France 1870–1914* (London: Chatto and Windus, 1977).

8. Janet A. Nolan, *Ourselves Alone: Women's Emigration from Ireland 1885–1920* (Lexington: University Press of Kentucky, 1989).

9. Miller, *Emigrants and Exiles,* 565.

10. Bruno Bettelheim, *The Uses of Enchantment: The Meaning and Importance of Fairy Tales* (Harmondsworth, Eng.: Penguin, 1975).

11. Hasia R. Diner, *Erin's Daughters in America: Irish Immigrant Women in the Nineteenth Century* (Baltimore: Johns Hopkins University Press, 1983).

12. Neville, "Land of the Fair."

13. Mircea Eliade, *Le Mythe de l'Eternel Retour* (Freiburg: Herder, 1969); A. J. Gurevich, *Categories of Medieval Culture,* trans. G. L. Campbell (London: Routledge and Kegan Paul, 1985).

9

The Reynolds Letters: Sources for Understanding the Irish Emigrant Experience in America and England, 1865–1934

Lawrence W. McBride

The Reynolds letters is a collection of family correspondence that will interest historians of Irish emigration on both sides of the Atlantic. Consisting of approximately five hundred letters, greeting cards, postcards, legal documents, and photographs, the collection spans the period of 1866 to 1934. The materials stem from the activities of the family members of Mary Reynolds, a widow who took her family from Carrick, Mohill, County Leitrim, to Manchester, England, in 1849. The letters document her family's story as well as the stories of a network of relatives and friends who were swept out of Ireland during the Great Famine and who made their respective ways to the burgeoning cities of Manchester and Chicago and points beyond.

If the size and scope of the collection are enough to attract the initial interest of historians, its materials have the additional merit of meeting four criteria that measure the general utility of primary sources in any field of historical inquiry and that are especially important in the fields of local and family history. First, the letters project a narrative arc that intersects with history's great narratives and vital themes: patterns of social and political interaction across time and space; conflict and cooperation; the importance of values and beliefs; and the interaction of people with their physical environments. Second, the letters illuminate the important themes and significant events that constitute national history: in the Irish context, demographic issues and the resolution of the land and national questions; in the English context, issues in urban, social, and economic history; and in the American context, issues inherent in the experiences of the country's exiled immigrants both in cities and rural settings. Third, the letters tell an interesting story in their own right. They let today's readers hear the voices of Irish people—women and men, young and old, rich and poor—across three generations as they speak directly to one another without secondhand interpreters coming between the writer and the reader. As such, they help us develop habits of mind that increase our ability to understand more completely the human experience, specifically, to perceive the past as it was experienced by the people at the time and to respect their perspectives on events, two habits that help us avoid making excessive generalizations when we ask questions and search for answers about Irish emigrants during the process that has become known as the Irish diaspora.

The letters (currently in the author's possession until permanent archives can be found for them in Manchester and Chicago) fall into several integrated sections, although each section can stand alone and illuminate a particular aspect of the diaspora. At the heart of the collection, providing the stories that produce much of the collection's coherence, are approximately seventy-five letters exchanged between Mary Reynolds's family in Manchester and her son Laurence. He emigrated around 1860 from Manchester to Patterson, New Jersey, where he married before eventually settling in Chicago, Illinois, around 1865. Both ends of this correspondence, which covers the period of 1866 to 1908, have largely survived, thereby providing a dialogue between a mother and her son and between Laurence and his younger siblings—Mary Ann, Patrick, and William—who lived in Manchester with their mother.

These letters are valuable because they document the upward mobility of the Manchester Reynoldses as Mary's youngest son, William, developed a very successful career in the dyeing and dry cleaning trade. This first section of the collection also documents the fortunes of Laurence's working-class family living in Chicago's South Side neighborhood of West Washington Park. William Reynolds's letter book, with some seventy entries, constitutes the second section of the collection. It includes first drafts of some of the letters that were sent to his brother's family in Chicago and drafts of letters he sent to other family members, friends, and associates in other parts of England, Ireland, and the United States. The third section of the collection includes some twenty-five letters received by Laurence in Chicago from the family of Mary Reynolds's brother, John O'Toole, who emigrated from the townland of Carrick, Annaduff, near Mohill in County Leitrim to the hamlet of Schullsburg, in Lafayette County, Wisconsin. Although many of the letters from this farming family are undated, internal evidence places them in the 1875–1900 period. From 1894 to 1895, Laurence's eldest son, James Reynolds, spent a year in Manchester living with his grandmother's family. The purpose of his extended visit was to gain experience working in the Reynolds family business. During his stay, James sent at least one letter home to Chicago each week, and these letters constitute a very rich section of the collection. James's letters describe his experiences in Manchester, and the questions he asks about his friends in Chicago and the observations he makes about life there compared to life in Manchester provide valuable insight into the youth culture of the first post-Famine generation of Irish Americans.

A few years later, James's younger sister, Mary, visited her uncle William in Manchester and struck up a friendship there with Anne Masterson, a cousin. Anne's letters to Mary date from 1908, when they visited together in Ireland, and extend into the early 1920s. Constituting another section of the collection, Anne's letters provide a glimpse of the social life and other concerns of young middle-class women of Irish heritage in Manchester. James's and Mary's youngest brother, William, moved from Chicago to Boston around 1920 and began to correspond regularly about Irish and American political affairs and business matters with his uncle William, who was by that time in his seventies. Both ends of much of this correspondence—about twenty letters—have survived. When William Reynolds died in Manchester at age 84, James Reynolds returned to the city to settle the estate of his late uncle. This task took several months, and James wrote faithfully to his sister and brothers in Chicago explaining the status of the situation and commenting on a variety of matters pertaining to social life in England. He also sent about fifty postcards of Manchester street scenes to his nephew and nieces. Finally, there are a number of miscellaneous letters received in both Manchester and Chicago from various family friends, which constitute the final section of the collection.

This essay includes a representative sample from every section of the collection. The samples have been selected in large part because the themes of the respective national histories will be apparent in them and because each tells an interesting story in its own right. Each letter is transcribed here without any alteration in spelling, capitalization, or punctuation. The minimally edited texts are crucial because they allow the reader to hear the rhythms of speech and to appreciate the rhetorical style of the writers, thereby grasping something of the author's personality. I have indicated stops at the ends of sentences, where periods are absent in the originals, by a period in brackets. The text in the original letters, particularly the earlier ones, usually filled the stationery from top to bottom; I have created paragraph breaks to make the reading of some of the samples less arduous. I have also provided some brief background information about details within the letters.[1]

Letter 1
*Mary Reynolds in Manchester to her son Laurence
in Chicago, 30 October 1870*

The earliest surviving letter, dictated by Mary Reynolds to her son and daughter-in-law in Chicago, illustrates just how precarious life was for Irish emigrants. They had worked hard to escape from the area around the notorious Manchester slum "Little Ireland," which provided material for Friedrich Engels's classic *The Condition of the Working Class in England* (1845). This letter highlights health concerns, wages, and employment situations, each of which if gone awry could easily upset the family's attempt to gain the sufficient amount of capital required to enjoy a period of financial equilibrium. This letter was occasioned by Laurence's reply to an earlier one in which Mary had written, erroneously, that his brother had been killed. Laurence dutifully dispatched money to help meet the unexpected doctor bill and the presumed burial costs. Imagine, though, the emotional drain on the respective families in receiving both the prior and now the latest news. The final sentence was probably meant to be read aloud to Laurence's first child, Willie (who was actually named James). One small point: dyers were known colloquially in Manchester as "slubbers."

Manchester Oct 30/70

Dear Laurence

I rite these few lines to you hopeing to find you in good health as this leves us in at present thanks be to God[.] Dear Laurence I received your letter this mornhing and the check for 2 pounds and was very thankfull[.]

Dear Laurence it turned out better with Patrick than we expected[.] the report went everyware that he was killed[.] the cabman that took him to the infirmery brote word back that he was dead[.] Instead of that he was oneley 3 weeks under the Docter's[.] So wee ever can return thanks to God for his goodness[.] he is working for the Same Shop back again and there is no poorer work in the world working at 15 shillings per week[.] Maryann is getting pretty good health now[.] She was under a Docter for a wile[.]

Dear Laurence nothing would please us better than for us ale to Be together[.] if it wes a thing that wee would make up our minds time after time to go out thare[.] nothing would please us better than for us ale to be together[.] William cant Complain of his work[.] his wages is very tiday he is getting 26 shillings per week now[.] only for his wages wee would not be able to keep our House[.] they are always slack in the Spring of the year[.] Whenever he makes any over time gets 6/2 an hour for it[.] if Patrick had luck to have conStent work wee would be pretty well[.]

Dear Laurence in your next letter let William know what wages the Slubings Dyers have there[.]

Dear Laurence wee got a letter from John last week and a card de visit off hin ad his wife his wife went out last August and got a very good passage[.] he said he was going to rite a letter to you But whather he did or not wee dont know[.] I know his mind was not Settled tile his wife went thare[.] Prapps he will be diferant now[.]

Dear Laurence I get my health midling Considering one of my age[.] Since I came up here I think my health is nothing worse[.] I mite not be so bad only for ale the Sorrows I met with alethough I am further away from chapal I go every morning[.] Still the whather is very wet here[.] At present wee have not had a dry

night and day for these 3 weeks[.] Rite as Soon as you get this and let us know
Something about the Country[.] Wee Conclude By Sending our Love to you and
Maryann and the childering aspesheley little Willey that prays for his Grandmother[.]
direct 31 Gibson Street Hyde Road

Letter 2
*Laurence Reynolds in Chicago to his mother and siblings
in Manchester, 30 July 1879*

Laurence's letters to his mother, brothers, and sister in Manchester were brief
and to the point. His wife, Mary Ann, wrote more expansive letters from Chicago. Laurence settled his family in a small house in the West Washington Park
area on Chicago's South Side. He was a laborer in the Rock Island Rail Road
machine shops just to the west in the Englewood neighborhood. His mother encouraged him to find more healthful employment and gave advice on how he and
his wife should raise their growing family. He rejected the parenting advice and
worked almost continually for the railroad. Laurence and his wife passed along
news about the visits of Irish nationalist leaders to Chicago and reported on the
progress of the children's schooling. Their parenting was successful: four of their
surviving five children entered the professions. Among the interesting aspects of
this particular letter, however, is the description of fund-raising techniques employed by their parish priest as he constructed a new sacred space in St. Anne's
parish on Garfield Boulevard. Lissie is Alice, the wife of Laurence's uncle John
O'Toole, in Schullsburg, Wisconsin; John is Laurence's younger brother in
Manchester, who had married and moved a few streets away from Mary and the
other children who had remained in her home.

5234 Arnold Street
Chicago July 30th/79
Dear Mother
I received your letter on the 14th[.] we were glad to hear that you and Maryann were
going to Ireland[.] I hope that you will have a good time of it and get back all safe[.]
You will be able to let me Know how things are in Ireland and how my Uncle
William and Aunt Cicley is getting on[.] I expect to go up to Wis to see My Uncle in
September[.] his Daughter is going to be Mariade in the fall[.] we got a letter from
Lissie on the 15 of July[.] the are all well[.]
   Dear Mother[.] the children are all getting along good[.] the Baby is a fine stout
little felow he is over four Months old now[.] the old Woman is as supple as ever[.]
she was out Playing tig with the young girls last Night and she could bate them all
running[.] I am working 10 hours per day[.] I am getting twenty five cents an hour[.]

still we are getting along nicely[.] this sumer we had a few very hot days[.] it was over 90 in the shade[.] we are getting nice cool days for the last weeke[.]

Dear Mother things are prety sharp hare at present[.] there is every prospect of a good Harvest in this Country acording to the news from all parts of the Country at the present time[.]

We had a Jubliee in our church last weeke[.] our Parish Priest is building a new Church[.] he expect to have it redy by Desember[.] all the Priests studys in this Country is building big Churchs and trying all sort of Manes how the can Make a dollar[.] we had a fare for our Church[.] the had dancing and Walsing every Night untell 12 oclock for 9 nights and he had a bar there[.] I was tending bar[.] we sold beer pop and cigers[.] a boy 8 or 9 would come up and call for his beer & cigers like an old Man[.] That is the way the Majority of our Priest acts here[.] I give More Money in won year here than I would give in England in 20 years[.] They get the money so esay that the set no value on it and the think a poor man ought to get rich on a dollar a day[.]

Dear Mother I will conclude by sending our Kind love to you and Maryann[.] Patrick & William and John & wife[.] nomore at present but remains your Afectionate son & Daughter Laurence & Maryann Reynolds

Letter 3

Alice O'Toole in Schullsburg to Laurence
and Mary Ann Reynolds in Chicago, 30 June 1882

Mary Reynolds's older brother, John O'Toole, became a successful farmer in southern Wisconsin, owning several hundred acres of excellent land for crops and for raising livestock. He had several children, who were delighted when their Chicago cousins took the trip north through Galena, Illinois, to visit. These trips were of special interest to the Manchester Reynoldses because John rarely wrote to his sister. Mary Ann relayed pertinent information about John to her mother-in-law, who was always curious about how other branches of the family were faring. The postscript provided a bit of news (or gossip) about a family known to the Reynoldses and O'Tooles; perhaps the Gallophers and the Boyles were from one of the townlands near Mohill. The letters from Wisconsin to Chicago demonstrate that there were Irish emigrant farmers who were able to survive and prosper in the rural Midwest—weathering the severe winters and broiling summers, entertaining themselves on lonesome prairie spaces, and mastering the management techniques of large-scale agriculture. Henry, Bub, and Dan are John and Alice's sons; the Mound is a nearby town; White Oak is the name of the farm.

White Oak Springs
June 30th
1882

My Dear Niece

I had to make my letter short the other day for they did not tell me Henry was going to the hill till his horse was at the gate[.]

I forgot to tell you we get mail only three times a week in white oak since the railroad came to the burg & then it is one of the neighbors goes for it to the Mound[.]

Jim Kelley brother came from Ireland two weeks ago & his family are down with ship fever[.] our school is closed till after the fourth on that account. the scarlet fever is dying out. There was something strange about that scarlet fever in the New diggings[.] all that died were protestants[.] The majority of the school are protestant and they had a play in their school last winter[.] it was called the priest & the penitant[.] the teacher was the priest & fourteen of the little children that took part in that play have since died[.]

we got a letter from Bub yesterday & he says he is looking up a few carloads of cattle to ship to chicago[.] so you may look for him any time after the fourth[.]

Dan likes Iowa & if he gets good health there he will stay with Bub[.] the cattle are giving out to a man to heard at 75 cts. per head for the season[.] that leaves Dan & Bub free[.] Bub to buy cattle and Dan to tend the garden. They have potatoes. & lots of things planted. Bub has got on the right side of them young Englsh bollds that own Thousands of acres of land out there & they want him to buy cattle for them or go in as a partner[.] but Bub has not got money enough for that but he has good times with them[.] he says they live like Kings[.]

Dear Mary how much I wish you lived near enough to pick up that baby and run in heavens wouldent I make a cup of tea that would make you give milk for a week[.]

we are very busy Just now[.] the carpenters have things all their own way for the past week & will for weeks to come[.] I am writing this in the smoke house[.] That is our parlor now[.] the men sleep in the barn & they have lively times when it rains & that is avout every other day[.]

our mail comes to White oak on Monday, wednesday & friday[.] Henry went over for the mail today & and when there was no card from you he was teribley disapointed[.] he wanted Jim here for the fourth[.] I will mail this in the burg tomorrow. give my love to Laurence & the little ones & yourself[.] A O Toole

Rosanna galiger was married last week to John Boyle a brother of Mary Ann[.] They gave no wedding[.]

Letter 4

*James Reynolds in Manchester to his family
in Chicago, 18 August 1894*

The "returning Yank," either of the first or second generation, is a familiar male character in nineteenth- and twentieth-century Irish popular fiction in both the Irish and English languages. In fiction, the Yank rarely fits comfortably into his new Irish surroundings. Life followed art during James's year-long stay with his grandmother, aunt, and uncle in Manchester. James was homesick from the week he arrived. This malady was compounded by his amazement at how financially well-off and comfortable his relatives were, both in comparison to his family's satisfactory situation in Chicago and in absolute terms. James learned every day just how hard his uncle and aunt worked at the Reynolds' dye works in Longsight to maintain their social status in the upper-middle-class area around Dudley Place. Another source of unhappiness was James's belief that his privacy was not being respected by his hosts, who, always on the lookout for family news, liked to read his letters from home. In his letters, James resembles Chicago novelist James T. Farrell's famous character, young Studs Lonigan. Like Studs, James believed he was far superior to anyone who crossed his path; he could do anything better than they could. This cocky attitude precipitated two fights: one a fist fight at his uncle's works; the other, a scuffle on the city center's streets. His uncle was dragged into the latter mess and had to pay damages in court. Throughout his letters, James "talks the talk" of the rough-and-tumble West Washington Park Irish-American youth of the 1890s, foreshadowing the fictional Studs, who lived in the same neighborhood some twenty years later. James's siblings mentioned in this letter are Jack, Tom, Mary, and Willie. The term *polishing* refers to forging the steel spikes that secured the rails to the railroad ties. The Elliot Club was James's neighborhood social club.

Longsight Aug 18 1894

Dear Mother

Recd papers and tie all right yesterday, saw all about Father Pickham in them, that is a good picture of him is it not[.] I will wear that tie to morrow Sunday if all goes well[.] They are tickled here at me getting the tie[.] if not to much trouble buy a nice light one "four in hand" and send it to my Uncle in the same manner as I know it will pls him[.]

Still skating along in the same manner. I thought you would have written to Dudley Place as my Aunt expects a letter.

Remember to tell Jack to be a little foxy in writing to Longsight[.] that is change his hand use different ink as Uncle Wm got on to it at once, so I read it to him, not yours though.

How is Pop getting on[.] no work yet. that is to bad[.] how was it his name was not in it as a pall bearer[.] they missed him did they not[.]

Well the weather is rotten chilly here at present, but I am managing to get along with the help of a little Jamissons special[.] they keep it in the house and when I go home at night my aunt always doles me out a drop[.] ha ha[.] I am not the one to say no.

Well I hardly Know what to say[.] Grandmother still Keeps in good health, but is always saying goodnight James. I will shout when I come in[.] how are you[.] oh me gossoon[.] I am very poorly, that is always her story, she looks for petting like a child.

Well how are all de gang[.] So our George has the face to get married[.] the poor slob. who is the girl. is Terrance to be best man[.] he will be like an elephant at the wedding.

Tell Jack that I wrote to Goss and pretty near all the push[.] The are no good[.] they think it is to much to expend a few coppers on postage stamps[.] I will remember them in my will.

Mag Mac did not get married yet did she. tell her if she is going to I will try and make arrangements to get there in time to see the Knot tied.

How is the Shewbridges getting on, and Mrs Flynn.

I suppose Father Frank feels pretty blue over Father Pickhams death[.] it is pretty sad.

Do you ever see Mr Molloy & Mrs Molloy.

How is my old pal Charley[.] still as much a devil as he was when I left[.] I suppose you recd all my papers, and saw all our ads and every thing like that did you[.] Regards to all my young lady friends[.] also to the Elliott Club[.] in general tell them I am having a hell of a good time now regards to P.J.M[.] and the Hassetts[.]

How is the cat[.]

How is Tom, still chasing up Mag White or has he given over[.] heard Herb McLoud was cutting him out in that quarter[.] how about it Tom your easy to let any blooming bloody bandy legged sawed off Johnnie Bull get in ahead of you[.] my but your soft.

Jack is still polishing but why dont he get a move on him, get a job teaching swimming or some thing[.] tell him I said to practice and see what time he can swim a hundred yards in.

How is Mary[.] is she getting any heaverer[.] she should eat more. Billie I suppose still lets Hermy lick him does he is no good[.] why dont he learn to scrap, see it made a name for me over here, they think that pop was a daisy in his day to learn us all the Manley art.

Well[.] I suppose about Monday I will be getting a letter from you so then I will be writing to you again[.] tell them I am as always Your loving Son[.]

    James

Love to all
    regards to de gang
Also give my regards to all the Kids on the block

Letter 5

William Reynolds in Manchester to his brother Laurence
in Chicago, 13 March 1895

Mary Reynolds, the family's matriarch, died in February 1895 at age eighty-four. She died a contented woman whose family escaped the Great Famine that killed her husband and advanced from the poverty of its early years in Manchester to achieve respectability and security in an alien environment. Her youngest son, William, now owned one of the largest dye works, dry cleaners, and laundries in Manchester; he and his sister, Mary Ann, were active in Manchester's Irish nationalist political organizations. This letter paints an evocative picture of their mother's deathbed scene, a description that provided comfort for a brother and the rest of his family thousands of miles away. Still, there is a discordant note at the conclusion of the letter. Their brother John and his wife, who owned two green groceries and some rental properties, had become estranged from William and Mary Ann over the years. At their mother's funeral, John broke the customary rules of etiquette when he refused to ride in the hired coach with the priest and the rest of the family, thereby causing a great deal of embarrassment to his more socially conscious sister and brother. This tension among the family members in Manchester illustrates the opposing centripetal and centrifugal forces that were at work on families in industrial England, alternately pulling some members of families apart and causing other family members to work together to survive. The stationery had the customary thick black borders. St. Wilfrid's was the Reynoldses' first parish in Manchester.[2]

> 1 Dudley Place,
> Old Trafford, Manchester,
> March 13—1895

Dear Brother & Sister

Maryann and I received your letters last Saturday and we ware very pleased and thank you very hearthly for your kind Sympathy[.] it was the only real Sympathy we received Since mother died[.] We thank all the family Tom—John—Mary—Willia all for their good hearthed Sympathy[.]

Dear Laurence[.] we know you falt Mothers death extremely and we falt it[.] it was vary trying to us although She was a great age[.] Still at the last She went quicker than we expected[.] if it was possible for us to keep her living for a mutch longer time nothing in the world would have pleased us better[.] She received everything religion could do for—and She was well attended by the doctor & nurse[.]

She was allways praying from morning till night[.] that was the way She spent the principle part of her time[.] She gave us menay a good advise in our time as She was vary far seen in business mattars—and gave us a great example of patience[.]

Maryann was ill for about a week after the funeral but She is now mutch better and able to go to business for a few hours each day—we had some good friends at the funeral near friends Hughie and his Sister—Mr. & Mrs Masterson also Mr & Mrs Flannigan[.]

Mother died 11/30 Monday night Feb 11th[.] I went at once for Mrs Flannigan and boath came back at once and told me thay would go to London to assist us and Edward was quite broken down[.] Mrs Flannigan acted one of the best friends we mat with[.] She is one of the old Stock and we cannot forget her[.] All our friends were kind and had great Sympathy for us[.] all the people at ST Wilfrids—and all the Shopkeepers in Stretford Road even the people at old Trafford put down thair blinds the day of the funeral and Several of the Shops on Stretford Road put up thair Shutters till the funeral past. James assisted in every way possible and we ware vary well pleased he was over here at the time he was present when She died. Thare was Maryann[.] Hughie James & myself ware at the bedside when She died. Mother had a great Love for James as he Seen a good deal of her Since he has been here, up to 4 or 5 weeks before her death[.] She did not Show any great Signs of weekness[.] She used to tell us her time was getting Short but it was the very Severe frost it took a meney old people[.] She was quite prepared and resigned and even a day or two before She died She was Satisfied to accept the will of God—She had every care and attantion. and everything that could be done was done for her[.] She deserved all and the one great objact of our lives was if it was in our power to make her happy[.]

I think James told you how John acted—he done Something that was unworthy of himself it was a very discrasefull action in the presence of our Friends and Father Lynch[.] when Mother was very ill he had to be Sent for and than he came with a growl on his face—Maryann and I asked himn to bring his wife to the funeral but he Said She would not come for Father Lynch[.] but he had the worst action of all to act the day of the funeral—I had 4 coaches and Hearse ordered ample room for double the numberr who ware at the funeral Father Lynch John Maryann & myself in the first coach—when we arrived at the cemitary Father Lynch got out and than he said my wife has a coach and I am going home with my wife—you can imagine how we falt to receive this Stab when my Mother was gatting put down in the clay[.] A real brother would assist us and Say you must not bear all the expanse yourself[.] I am not Short of money and I will do my part No he never mentioned a copper[.] one would think that a Sister and brother who stood by the old home so well deserved better treatment[.] John is one of the meanest misers in this town[.] we forgive tham and we hope God will forgive tham.

I am Sorry I have obliged to write so mutch about a brother[.] Maryann is going to Send you a Letter[.] with love and best wishes I remain your effectionate Brother William

Letter 6

Mary Ann Reynolds in Manchester to Laurence's wife,
Mary Ann, in Chicago, 18 April 1895

Mary Ann Reynolds worked at her brother's side in the family business, and she shared the family's keen interest in politics and business. Addressing letters to each other as "Dear Sister," the sisters-in-law exchanged about two letters annually, augmenting the letters exchanged by the brothers. This letter is filled with family news about the three branches of the family: in Chicago, Wisconsin, and Manchester. Mary Ann used black-bordered stationery for this letter, and the text reveals that the death of the family matriarch was still keenly felt by Mary Ann and William and that John's affront was not yet forgiven. The advertisement mentioned in the letter is the announcement of Mary Reynolds's death that Laurence had placed in the Chicago newspapers. Mary Ann also passed along a bit of news about her nephew to his mother and made a sweet observation about the talents of her niece, Mary, and the youngest nephew, William, in a passage that was probably intended to be read to the children. Mary traveled to Chicago and Wisconsin to visit her relatives in 1897.

> 1 Dudley Place
> Old Trafford
> Apr 18th 1894 [1895]

My Dear Sister & Brother and family[.] I would have Writton to you Sooner but My health was very bad Since Mothers death[.] I am very much improved now thank god and able to go to the Shop Every day. We Still feel very Lonley without Mother. I feel it very Much because I was with her the Most. nearley all the day was Spent with her befor She died[.]

William is getting Round now he took Mothers death to heart very much. We thought that She Should never Leave us[.] We didnot consider her age because She was always interrested in the work.

Dear Sister James is getting on very well[.] he is a proper American[.] he cannot See aneything here Like America[.] I dont wonder at him[.] it is all work here not So gay as Chicago We had a letter this morning from Unkle John Otoole[.] he was very Sory about Mothers death[.] all his family are well and he Says they are doing very well[.] I suppose he did not think we new all about them from James William.

Dear Sister the weather is very fine just now. Easter Sunday and all Easter week was like Summer weather[.] James was saying if it was as fine in Chicago they would turn out in their very best but it is not So here. We were very busy befor Easter & we wair Glad of it we had So Much Slack time in the winter. We havnot Seen Johen Since the day Mother was buried and we donot want to See him[.] I hardly Know what to tell you[.] I Know James will tell you Every thing.

I was glad to See Marys Riting[.] it was very good[.] She will a very good writer[.] tell her I want a Letter from herselfe[.] I am Sure Willie is a good boy[.] his writing is very good[.] he must try and get up to Mary[.]

Dear Sister they advertisment in the Chicago paper was very <u>good</u>[.] We are getting they Letters on the gravestone of mothers death Soon. We will Send you a coppy of it.

Dear Sister I have nothing more to tell you this time[.] I will write oftner now that I am better in health, hoping you and Laurence and all they family are in they best of health. With Kind Love from William and Myselfe & James

Your affectionate Sister Mary <u>Ann</u>

Letter 7
James Curran, a family friend, in Boston
to William Reynolds in Manchester, 10 January 1911

James Curran makes several appearances in the Reynolds letters. He was a restless émigré who moved back and forth between an old world and a new one. The centerpiece of this letter, the lively passage describing his activities in New York, reveals his pride in the exemplary public conduct and self-discipline of Irish Americans. The letter also sheds light on the social and political activities on the eastern seaboard of such Irish-American organizations as the Ancient Order of Hibernia. In the closing passages, however, it appears that Curren was hoping William would send him a bit of money to ease his way into old age. William received similar "begging letters" from his cousins in Mohill, and he sent both financial assistance and clothing to them.

8 Marston St	Lawrence Mass
	U.S.A.
James Curran	Jan. 10 1911

My Dear friend,

Your Chrismas Greetings to hand. I dont Know how to express my feelings to you for your Kind remembrance. I often think about you and your Kindness towards me when in Manchester. Well how are you? are you in business yet? or have you got married?

I will give you a brieaf outline of my travels since I saw you, the first winter I went south to Florida amongst oranges groves[.] it was pleasent to go south to escape the cold of the north[.] I was in a fearfull storm going round Cape Hatress the most dangerous coast in the world[.] I sat locked in my State room all night expecting every minute to go down as it would be impossible to save yourselfe. it was anough to drive a person insane[.] I will never forget it. while there I sent My friends seven boxes of oranges 12 shillings per box. it takes 10 days to reaach Lawrence.

I often go to New York[.] two years ago I Saw the big parade of A.O.H. 40,000 in

line 200 open carriages headed by the 69th Reiment and the Jersey Irish Volunteers.
I went to see the one hundred anniversary of the Fulton Hudson celebration[.] the
greatest celebration the world ever Saw[.] it lasted two weeks. all Nations in the
world was represented[.] a parade every second day the Military was the most
interesting[.] it was headed by the finest body of men in the world[.] the N.Y.
Mounted Police[.] the English Soldiers and Sailors next and so on[.] the Germans
got a great recepton[.] The Military bearing was perfect 18 a brest all through but
when our Boys came along headed by the gallent 69 or as they are better Known as
the fighting 69th[.] next the Irish Volunteers of Jersey composed of Sons of
Irishmen[.] when they came in sight I never herd such cheering I never herd before.
The people took there places at 10 A.M. it was 4 P.M. when they came in sight[.] it
was worth the wait[.] $2^1/_2$ Millions of strangers in the city[.] 20 miles of grand
stands[.] 9 thousand Police on duty[.] one every 7 feet apart[.] it was a wonder that
hundreds was not Killed[.] the school childrens parade 500,000 in line the like neve
witnessed on this earth before[.] I was at 48th and 5 Ave. I went down to N.Y. last
June to see our Teddy Roosevelt come home[.] I saw him twice[.] no person ever got
such a reception in the country as he got[.] I saw him twice. I stayed 2 weeks on and
around New York. My Fathers youngest Brother is living in N.Y. 83 years old[.] in
N.Y. 67 years. he looks younger than I do; he is a splendid Man[.]

My Dear friend you can judge I am taking in all the sights[.] I will be a long
time up in the cemetary. I belong to the Nights of Columbus a Catholic organization[.] last summer about one hundred of us went up to New Hampshire to camp out
in the woods[.] we took 4 men with us to cook and wait on[.] we had a glourious old
time. we have secured Columbus day a leagel holiday Oct 12. we have it in 14
States[.] we are doing our best to get it a National one. we think the man that
discovered this country the greatest of them all deserves some reconition. our
Governer said he would not sign the bill[.] a delegation of the most influential
Catholic Ladies of Boston went to the Governs wife and told her if he did not sign
the bill to look out for the hand writing on the wall[.] that settled it[.] we celebreted
it in grand stile[.]

I spend most of my time in the club room. of course I have no home[.] you might
say I have my daughters but that is not my home[.] it is different with you. your rich
and can have what you please[.] My daughter family has hard luck[.] her Husband
underwent an operation[.] he was a long time before he was able to work[.] They
have 2 Girls in the high school one 14 the other 16 good Girls[.]

I help them some[.] I get discouraged at times[.] I am getting old but never felt in
my life[.] I was 70 Jan. 6 so I am liveing on borrowed time[.] I have lived through
the allotted time thank God I hope you will excuse to note[.] I dont Know that you
will be interested in what it contains[.] I am no letter writer.

In regard to business is very dull here for the last year[.] still the Keep building
Mills not halfe of the running[.] I might thousands out of employment.

I take inn all the good times that the K.C. has[.] I was at one this week at Lowell
10 miles from here[.] The K.C. Charted a White Star Steamer last year[.] went to
Rome[.] had a special audence with the holy Father[.] I would liked to have gone but

my means are limited[.] that is the reason I did not go[.] I hope you will be able to read this[.] My friends are after me to play wist[.] this is about all[.] I am alone in this cold world like yourselfe without Relative[.]

    with Sincere good wishes for your welfare I remain your

      Jas Curran

Letter 8

William Reynolds in Boston to his uncle William
in Manchester, 12 December 1921

William Patrick Reynolds was Laurence's youngest child (and my grandfather). After graduating from high school and finding employment in the food processing industry, the young businessman left Chicago for Boston. He hoped to market jams and preserves in England and sought his uncle's advice on how to proceed. An affectionate correspondence soon developed between the uncle and his namesake. Uncle William was especially eager to learn about the doings of his namesake's children, his grandnieces and grandnephew. Like the correspondence William had earlier enjoyed with his brother in the 1870s and 1880s, he now enjoyed the exchange of newspapers and opinions with his brother's son about matters affecting Irish Catholics and nationalists on both sides of the Atlantic. This letter describes the diversity that existed within Boston's Irish-American community and the discrimination that Catholics experienced in the workplace. William's older brother, Tom, also wrote to his uncle. Their uncle was a supporter of Michael Collins and the pro-Treaty side in late 1921–22, arguing that the Irish Free State offered a reasonable opportunity for political unification of Ireland and for economic progress in the future.

                  21 Arbington Ave
                  North Beverly
                  Mass.
                  December 12th 1921

Dear Uncle William

I received your letter this morning also package of newspapers. I noted the marked columns in the Catholic Times. Father OFlanagan received quite a reception everywhere he went. It is unfortunately true however that there is quite a feeling of bitterness in America on the question of religion and the Irish question here is practically decided here in the minds of non-Catholics to a great extent to be entirely a religious one. I have not discussed Irish Freedom with one single Protestant but what was apposed to it. It is needless to argue the point with such persons as almost one hundred percent Protestants are intensely bigoted and only believe what they like to believe.

Boston is truly a great Irish Catholic City. Tomorrow is election day here for Mayor of Boston. The candidates are Murphy—Curley and O'Connor so you will note how the Irish stand here. It is remarkable however how many people with destinctly Irish names such as O'Brien—McCarty—O'Hara—Murphy that are non-Catholic. In the daily papers you will often see such names or similar to them as members of some lodge of Freemasons. This is not the case in Chicago as there almost always a name distinctly Irish usually devotes a Catholic.

When my wife and I first came to Boston we looked for a Catholic church on Saturday so we would know where to go to Mass on Sunday[.] We came to a church with a cross on it. It had a sign on the outside telling the hours of the masses also mentioned Benedictions—also said Pastor-Rev. Father Edward <u>Sullivan</u>. To be sure we were right we enquired if it was a Roman Catholic church and to our surprise learned it was not.

There is fortunatly not as much bigotry now as there was when I was a little boy, or when I was employed by Libby McNeill and Libby (Meat Packers)[.] To get along there one almost had to be a Freemason. All the Masons and they were in the great majority wore Masonic emblems of some description or other. I was there thirteen years and although everyone knew I was a Catholic and further more a Knight of Columbus nevertheless I got along very well indeed but I can truly say that no Catholic outside of myself ever was given a position of responsibility there. It just so happened I was with a man of big broad ideals who would not entertain anything in his mind but a mans own capability regardless of religion and I came up along with him.

The newspapers here along the coast are more friendly to England than the insular papers and hence the feeling here against the thought of Irish Freedom, while further in the country the papers are in sympathy. If you could only take a walk with me here and see the many streets named after Irish men you would really believe Boston is an Irish City. Admiral Beatty did not get much of a reception. In fact the poorest of all. Foch-Diaz-Jacques—were received with great fervor and enthusiasm. They are all Catholics. The Knights of Columbus as you probably know is a great Catholic Fraternal order. Its members now total over a million which is very. good for a young society.

The weather here is still very warm for this time of the year. We have had only one very slight fall of snow. Usually it is very cold at this time. Business is very very dull and depressing. We all hope that after the first of the year it will be brisker.

My wife and children are still in the best of health—also myself. Torn is a very good dentist as I can testify from experiencing some work done by him. He is very gentle and his work is as painless as possible. I am writing from my house which is a few miles outside of Boston. It is a quiet place—just the place for the children. I hope you have received their pictures by this time. We did not have a picture of my wife but as she expects to have some taken soon will send one to you. Hoping your good health continues and with love from us all.

I am Yours affectionately
    William

Letter 9

Anne Masterson in Manchester to her cousin Mary Reynolds
in Chicago, 18 June 1922

Anne Masterson's letters to her friend and cousin Mary Reynolds began shortly after the two young women met when Mary toured Ireland and England in 1908. Most of Anne's letters center on the social events that kept her busy and that she believed would interest Mary. The letters also served another important function. After 1904, William Reynolds had no immediate family members left in Manchester, and by 1908 his relationship with Mary's brother James had cooled. Until Mary's brothers Tom and William began to write to their uncle, Anne's letters kept alive the link between the two branches of the family, and she regularly supplied information about William's continued good health and his full schedule of activities in Manchester and travels abroad. The letters she wrote during the First World War and in the aftermath of the Irish War of Independence reveal another side of Anne's character. This letter combines family news with some observations on Irish political affairs. One of the two little girls mentioned at the end of the letter is my mother, Anita (Reynolds) McBride. The Reynolds letters and the other materials in the collection were saved in the first instance by James and Mary Reynolds, and then by Anita, who has passed them on to me.

Telephone
Rusholme 883

                                    Danebury,
                                    Levenshulme,
I see you are   Manchester.
at the same   18th June 1922
address.

My dear Mary.

Don't get too great a shock when you see my writing again! I feel very much ashamed when I think of my long negligence. I have been thinking of writing ever since I got your welcome card at Xmas and now I have broken the ice.

How are you all these ages? I have often thought about you and wondered how you were faring, and really it does not seem such a very long time since you were over though there has been a nasty little war in between. Thank God, our two boys came safely through. Tom was in the thick in France with the "Royal Irish" but I think he has forgoten all about it now. Joe went back to college after the Armistice and is now in Rome. He will be ordained in three years time. Willie is still at home on one [illegible]. Tom is married and has three lovely little kiddies. Maureen Denis & Billie. The three girls are still here. Kathleen and Celia quite grown up. Kathleen graduated at the Liverpool University and got her degree. She is teaching at the Xaverian College (Boys)[.] Celia is an Instructress of Domestic Science and teaches

Cookery and Laundry at the Prestwick Council School. I am still at home, not married or gone before or anything like that. Now what about yourself Mary dear? I expect you will soon be getting holidays. Where are you going this time? Do you never think of taking another trip over to this side. I have not seen your Uncle for some time, but the last time he asked me up to see him so some of these days I will be walking across. His house is about fifteen minutes walk from here. He looks splendid and does not appear to have changed a bit.

Father and Mother got back from their holidays this week. They have been all over the place. Starting from Ostend, through Belgium, Germany, Bavaria (Passion Play) Austria and Italy[.] They stayed with Joe in Rome for eleven days and came back through Switzerland staying at Lucerne.

I do not know where to go this year. I suppose it will be Ireland in the finish[.] I am only back from there about 6 weeks. When I was there things were not at all settled, but I suppose there will be peace soon. Terrible things happened during the Troubles as you will have learned in the papers and even how in Belfast the daily toll of life is awful. I do hope things will soon be alright and from then Mary for me—no politics. In Ireland at present, it is hard to know what to accept. Some are for the Treaty, others against. Some for the Free State and more down and out Republicans. I wonder what will be the end of it all. Sometimes I wonder what I am. I woble between the Free State and the Republic. I think for the present until Ireland gets on her feet the Free State will be the best. I wonder what you say?

We have had most glorious weather here for the last month but now it is turning cold again. Have played a lot of tennis this summer.

Don't be long before you write to me. I will try and have some snaps ready for my next letter. I hope all at home are well. Your brother Willie is married I know. I saw two lovely photograps of his little girls. Aren't they sweet? Are any of the others married. Kindly remember me to all and to your Mother.

I don't think I have any more news now. Please do write soon with all news.

With love from Father Mother and all at home.

> I remain
> Yours affectionately
> Anne

Letter 10

James Reynolds in Manchester to his brothers
and sister in Chicago, 22 October 1934

When James Reynolds was settling his uncle William's estate over a five-month period in 1934–35, he kept his sister and brothers in Chicago posted about the status of the sale of the dye works, the house in Fallowfield, his uncle's other real estate holdings, and related probate matters. This letter was the first substantial one he sent home. His cousin William Masterson, who was Anne's father, conducted the legal business. The executor of the estate was William's parish priest and best friend, Canon James Rowntree of St. Cuthbert's, Withington. William bequeathed the parish seven hundred pounds for the construction of a new high altar. Perhaps the most interesting part of this letter, however, is the description of Lena Sullivan, the Irish servant who first alarmed James of his uncle's illness in a most touching letter and who remained devoted to her employer during the closing days of his life. She then looked after James during his second stay in Manchester. William's net worth at the time of his death was about twenty thousand pounds; he lost a great deal of money during the Depression, and his dye works needed capital improvements. All of his property and holdings were auctioned. A few days after this letter was posted, James discovered the box containing the correspondence that the Manchester Reynoldses had received over some sixty-five years from their relatives in America and Ireland.

Oct 22—1934

Dear Folks

Well I am here. had a fine trip—Southhampton about 8:45 Thursday then to London—across London in a taxi then to Manchester arriving here at 4:30 am. Friday[.]

Everything in the hands of <u>Administrators</u> Wm Masterson & Canon Roundtree[.] Masterson is in France and I cannot tell how things will be till we meet and I see the will. The Government men are taking Inventory of all assets—there are no debts I understand.

Yesterday we went to the cemetary[.] there is a new stone over them—which uncle bought & had made in Italy—costing $2500.00. Now all that has to be done is put is name on it.

From what Lena tells me is at there a lot of bequests—to workers, Masterson, the Canon, different charities[.] after this is taken care we get the rest. So I will mark time.

"Lena Sullivan"

Irish, born in Cork, came to England to work[.] worked two places before coming to my uncle[.] has been with him about 5 years, went with him on is different holidays, when he got feeble she took him for his daily walks, she was always with him, she dressed, washed, and put him to bed, of late she changed is clothes 3 times a day, sometimes she would sleep at the foot of is bed, when he was bad. If fact she never left him alone—by his side always. And she is for us now and always.

She says about two weeks before she wrote, she says why dont you have one of your own here, he says Ill ask the Doctor, the Doctor did not want to worry him so passed it off[.] Miss Sullivan thought, he would ave urged him to do so[.] So I'm mad say's she because I did not post the Lr. When she did write, she said to Uncle, your know what I am going to do, I am going to write to your Nephew James. he says, will you, do[.] When she did, he watched the maid, till she crossed and posted the letter. then he was watching the days for the answer. when he got my letter, she

says he read it, then he read it again, then he says I am ten years younger[.] it made
him very happy. When he died in her arms, the Canon wanted to "cable"[.] she said
not yet, She was afraid that I would not come if he was, dead, and she wanted me
here, as it was my right, and she says that I would not be in doubt, as I could now
see everthing. He left her £500. She earned it many times over. She is a great cook—
"Boy oh Boy".
Allways. Remember, "<u>Lena Sullivan</u>" as a very dear friend.
I will write, as soon as, hear anything
Love to you all, and Bill Jane & the little ones
    Jim

Letter 11

James Reynolds in Manchester to his brother William
in Chicago, 6 January 1935

In the remaining letters from Manchester, James passed along a good deal of information about aspects of his new experiences in Manchester. He had a good
deal of time on his hands and seemed to enjoy the city much more the second
time around. Lena Sullivan's great menus and his late uncle's supply of bever-
ages were among the delights of his stay. Thus, his second batch of letters from
Manchester lacks the flinty edge of those letters dating from 1894 to 1895, but
James had not lost his appetite for criticizing the English. He did not hesitate to
pass along advice to the daughters of his youngest brother, William, who had returned from Boston as an executive with his old firm, Libby, McNeill, and Libby.
The young ladies—the "Debs"—were William's daughters, Josephine and Anita;
"Bud" (Laurence Reynolds) was his son. Jane was William's wife, and Janie was
his youngest daughter, Jane. James's sister and brothers, like many of the Irish
Americans who had lived earlier in West Washington Park, had migrated farther
south, to the city's South Shore neighborhood; hence the reference to 7236, their
home on Prairie Avenue. William's family lived ten blocks farther south, on
Paxton.

Manchester Jany 6th 1935

Dear Bill
Yours of the 21st ultmo to hand yesterday[.] glad to hear that all are well[.] I rec'd
the "Blind Barber"[.] Probably I am as Blind has him because I could not find him[.]
However I enjoyed it.
    I also rec'd the cigars[.] smoked two already today, they have these over here
beat a mile[.] I had to pay 8 cents apiece duty but they were well worth it. Talking
about radios, some of the artists are awful[.] they would not allow they on the old
Olmpic stage on a Monday night[.] it would be a case of get the "Hook"[.] they are

so rotten that you listen to them to see what d—— fools they can make of themselves[.]

So the young ladies are stepping out[.] as long as they dont step out with the
wrong Kind everything ought to be "Jake"[.] tell [them] to confine themselves to the
meek ones, then they can boss them[.]

Nothing new, only the will has been probated[.] So "Bud" can look for his bit
before long as those will be taken care of first.

I was invited over to Tom Mastersons last Saturday night. I was induced to play
poker[.] I told them I was no poker player, that I had not played in years, they would
not believe it so I sat in[.] all "Jacks"[.] sixpence limit. Now they dont believe me at
all[.] I collected all the money[.] about 18 Bucks[.] every little bit helps[.]

Well I got to write to 7236 and Janie[.] So thanks a lot for the smokes and love to
Jane, Janie Bud and the "Debs"[.]

Yours

Jim

The letters selected for inclusion in this chapter provide a glimpse of the scope
and sequence of the Reynolds letters. They give an indication of the family members' varied interests and concern for one another. Other representative samples
could have easily been chosen: letters on politics that describe labor strife in England and America, events in the Land War in Ireland, or reaction in England
and Ireland to the famous Parnell split; letters that describe William Reynolds's
entrepreneurial spirit and Laurence Reynolds's continual effort to create a better
life for his children; letters that describe the family members' perspectives on
the respective social and economic environments of Manchester and Chicago and
points beyond. This collection of emigrant letters will shortly be made available
to other scholars, who will ask new questions of the authors about life in the past.
It will be interesting to hear the answers.

Notes

1. A thorough explanation of the Reynolds family in Manchester and a description of
the city between 1850 and 1935 is found in my book *The Reynolds Letters: An Irish Emigrant Family in Manchester, England, 1878–1904*, Irish Narrative Series (Cork: Cork
University Press, 1999).

2. This letter is included in my *Reynolds Letters*.

10

Bridget and Biddy: Images of the Irish Servant Girl in *Puck* Cartoons, 1880–1890

Maureen Murphy

Courage, resourcefulness, and self-sacrifice characterize Irish domestic servants in Irish-American literature. These virtues, particularly self-sacrifice, distinguish the fiction about Irish servant girls from the fiction about Irish immigrant boys that adheres to the following formula: young man wins fortune and happiness through hard work and by demonstrating his moral character, usually over a matter concerned with money. While the Irish male role model succeeds, the Irish female sacrifices: for her parents, her siblings, her extended family, her church, and her employer's family. The servant girl in nineteenth-century Irish-American fiction is usually rewarded with marriage to a kind, steady man and occasionally with a return visit to Ireland; however, it is the survival and prosperity of her family, of her father, mother, and siblings, that promise her the greatest satisfaction and pleasure.[1]

If self-sacrifice defines the Irish servant girl in Irish-American fiction, what defines her in popular culture—in drama and film, in fine arts and cartoons? Visual representations of Irish servant girls offer as much idealized imagery as do the portrayals of the girls in literature. In her pioneering essay exploring the representation of women in the Irish pictorial tradition, "The Real Molly Macree," Margaret MacCurtain considers the series of paintings by Thomas Alfred Jones called "The Irish Colleen," with particular attention to "Molly Macree" (1860). MacCurtain argues that the colleen image was at once sentimentalized and exploited.[2] Although she is idealized in Jones's watercolor, contemporary engravings, photographs, and written accounts describe Irish girls living in the countryside as little more than beasts of burden, transporting creels of turf on their backs and harvesting seaweed and wrack from freezing water.[3] Arranged marriages were the rule for the dowered daughter, and those undowered faced lives as unpaid servants in the houses of male relatives or widowed mothers.

Irish-American popular culture had its own colleen image. She appeared as a dark-haired beauty sitting demurely amidst harps and shamrocks in book illustrations, in periodicals, and in sentimental postcards, especially the "across the miles" variety that the Irish in America sent home as St. Patrick's Day greetings. It was the perceived libel of that image that caused the United Irish Societies, in 1907, to form the Society for the Prevention of Ridiculous and Perversive Misrepresentation of the Irish Character and to target the Russell Brothers' Irish servant girls routine that had been their signature piece for thirty years.[4]

The servant girl was the colleen, and the colleen was Ireland. That she was rescued from humiliation by male protectors reflected the convention of the *aisling,* the Irish vision poem that promised the restoration of Ireland's rightful kingdom by a male deliverer. In defending the reputation of the Irish servant girl, the men of the United Irish Societies were coming to the rescue of Cathleen ní Houlihan.

L. Perry Curtis has demonstrated in *Anglo-Saxons and Celts* (1968) and in *Apes and Angels: The Irishman in Victorian Caricature* (1971)[5] that nineteenth-century British political cartoonists appropriated the image of Ireland as a vulnerable colleen who required protection from Fenian beasts by a solicitous Amazonian Brittania. Curtis established the link between the negative images of the Irish and the shaping of English public opinion about Ireland in his analysis of the political cartoons of the English and the American cartoonists John Tenniel (1820–1914), Thomas Nast (1840–1902), and Frederick Opper (1857–1937). These cartoonists created images of the Irishman as a simian creature who occupied a biological and cultural rung below the Victorian English gentleman.[6] Tenniel's beauty and the beast-type cartoons, which include "The Fenian Pest" (1866) and "Two Forces" (1881), show a frightened colleen (Ireland) protected from the dangerous Fenian, an anarchist ape-man, by a stalwart, resolute Britannia.[7]

In his essay "Paddy and Mr. Punch," Roy Foster has challenged Curtis's theory arguing that the cartoons were more concerned with religion and class than with race and that the portrayal of Ireland as a classical beauty reflected the *Punch* editorial position that Hibernia was Britain's Cinderella sister but that "neither Mr. Punch nor his cartoonists ever followed through the implications of the metaphor that Britain was therefore Hibernia's ugly sister exploiting her at home and keeping her from the ball."[8] "Cinderella," however, is not the narrative of the ugly sister; it is the narrative of the degraded sister who eventually triumphs over the sisters who have exploited her.[9] Such a narrative is the feminine counterpart of Ireland's most popular folktale narrative type: the restoration of the rightful kingdom, the story of the young hero deprived of his lands who gains ownership again by successfully meeting tests that often involve combinations of courage, cleverness, and generosity. This folk tradition has a counterpart in the rhetoric of nineteenth- and twentieth-century Irish nationalism.

American cartoonists Thomas Nast (*Harper's Weekly*) and Frederick Opper

(*Puck*) appropriated the British simian stereotype to create negative images of the Irish in America.[10] While Curtis has examined the Ireland-as-colleen figure, he has not considered other representations of Irish and Irish-American women in American cartoons. John J. Appel's "From Shanties to Lace Curtains: The Irish Image in *Puck* 1876–1910" mentions the appearance of Irish domestic servants "in endless variation on the theme of the funny, disorderly, hardworking but unpredictable servant girl" as an example of the "ignorant but harmless drudges" who make up the majority of *Puck's* Irish types.[11] Appel offers no analysis of the servant girl images, no examination of the different styles of the various *Puck* artists who drew Irish domestics, no consideration of the social or political contexts for certain cartoons or cartoon series, and no attention to gender differences. This essay will examine the imagery in the cartoons featuring Irish women that appeared in the pages of *Puck* (1877–1916) during the decade of the 1880s.[12]

Keppler, Opper, and fifteen other cartoonists contributed 130 drawings that featured Irish women: shantytown wives and mothers, women working outside the home (usually doing laundry), and especially domestic servants.[13] The cartoonists' attitudes toward the women ranged from humor to ridicule, from bitter indignation to biting satire.

Fifty-nine (45 percent) of the cartoons of Irish women were by Opper, and thirty-nine (66 percent) of them were of Irish domestic servants. There is no defining Opper domestic servant image. Instead, his domestic servants are of two figures—a younger Bridget and an older Biddy—and they fall into four distinct types, whose features become more simian when Opper's point becomes more bitter, a demonstration of what art historian E.H. Gombrich calls "mythologizing . . . by physiognomizing."[14]

Opper's most innocuous type is Bridget, an untidy, freckled, somewhat slack-jawed girl lately arrived from rural Ireland. She is a cheerful innocent, the subject of countless jokes. The older Biddy comes in three varieties: a sturdy, plain, bossy woman with a broad face, a pug nose, a topknot, and beefy forearms; a squat simian-featured woman with a grizzled muzzle and big feet who is given to helping herself to the household resources and to supporting Irish revolutionaries; and most simian of all, Biddy Tyrannus, an enormous, menacing figure who threatens her employer. Occasionally, Opper's servants are comely Irish girls, but they are the biddable Bridgets who know their place and who sensibly refuse to have anything to do with Irish nationalist agitators. Notice the contrast in "How to Keep a Girl" between the simian Biddies and the pretty young cook who looks a bit apprehensive as she takes instructions from her mistress (January 30, 1884, center; plate 1).

Before considering the cartoons of Irish domestic servants, it is useful to examine the wider view of Irish women by *Puck* cartoonists. First, there are the graphic varieties of the international "numbskull" tales, whose humor turns on a newcomer's misunderstanding of words or on an individual's following directions literally with comic results. Most of these cartoons were *Puck's* filler cartoons, the $5 black-and-white drawings of immigrants and minorities done by *Puck* artists and freelancers.[15] Many of the numbskull cartoons are good-natured; however, some of the numbskull cartoons play to the negative "pig in the parlour" image associated with the Irish. In F. M. Howarth's "A Slight Misunderstanding" (October 21, 1885, p. 124), a Board of Health officer has returned to cite Mrs. McGuinnis for keeping a pig in her apartment and to tell her that the nuisance would have to be abated. Her startled response is, "An' sure Oi've abayed yer insthructions. Oi've bin a-bating th' poor baste wid a club since th'occasion of yer last visit."

Another group of more nativist cartoons ridicules Irish immigrants by reinforcing the negative beliefs, values, and stereotypes associated with the Irish urban poor: their dirt, their ignorance, their neglect or abuse of their children, their penchant for drink and violence. In a color cartoon condemning the Irish radical nationalists' bombing campaign that began in England on St. Patrick's Day in 1883, Opper's "A Bombardment That Would Paralyze Them" (April 18, 1883, back cover; plate 2) shows a shower of soap, brushes, and towels descending on terrified Irish shanty dwellers. In Bisbee's "Lost in Admiration" (*Pickings from Puck,* supplement, 1887, p. 25), a simple-looking woman marvels at a rat running off with a piece of cheese and says, "Next toime I'll be afther puting the chaze *inside* of the trap where he can't get it at all."

The truant officer in Apheus's "Compulsory Education" (April 28, 1886, p. 138) who is inquiring about the Mulvany children is told by their mother, "Is it imployed in the day-times they are? Shure it *is*. Phelim bees down at the parruk drownin' kittens. Norah an' Terence are chasin' fer cinders at the doomp below, an' Michael is soberin' the ould man aft from McGinty's wake last night. To the divil wid your questions!" In E. S. Bisbee's "Mississippi Martyrs," an Irish mother shouts from the roof of a flooded house to save her pig rather than her children because the pig is "the only wan" (April 26, 1882, p. 118).

Michael Angelo Woolf used his cartoons of battered and neglected waifs to keep the issue of children's welfare before the public.[16] "Unaccountable" (December 14, 1881, p. 234) depicts an untidy woman looking at her two bedraggled children and saying, "I bate thim from mornin' till noight to put a little loife and spirit into them, but it don't seem to do 'em any good." Finally, domestic violence is portrayed in fights where women give as good as they get. In Opper's "A Shantytown Anniversary" (April 5, 1882, p. 74), an Irish Shantytown woman reassures a policeman that the rocking shanty with objects, including a child, flying from the windows is "only the Clancys celebratin' their wooden weddin'."

Although they are portrayed as slatternly and simple, Irish women are more favorably treated than Irish men. It is the women who work, usually at washing, while the men loaf. The exasperated wife in Louis Dalrymple's "A Good Sitter" (June 13, 1888, p. 262) pauses over her scrub board to say to her dozing husband, "Och, if yez be going ter sit all day long, go out and sit on thim eggs that ould hen has left. It's some use ye'd be." A washerwoman is a central figure in Opper's "The New York Tenement House-Fire Escapes" (June 24, 1885, back cover); the men are sleeping and lounging.[17]

Opper had a series of cartoons featuring an ambitious but ridiculous, squat, pipe-smoking shawlie who sets up different street corner enterprises: a peanut and apple emporium she supervises from an easy chair (December 15, 1880, p. 54), a peanut stand raised over slush-flooded Third Avenue (January 26, 1881, p. 354; plate 3), a Bible stand with a sign reading "Mrs. Casey formerly in the peanut line" and the caption "No change of Heart—Change of Business" ("The Revised Bible Boom," June 1, 1881, back cover), a shack in Shantytown called "Rosedale" that sits in the shadows of the hotels built as part of uptown development ("The Growth of New York," May 24, 1882, p. 120), and finally a peanut stand cum claim agency to join the other start-up pension agencies ("The Pension Agency Industry," December 12, 1883, p. 231).[18]

Opper's "Crowding in Cars" (September 29, 1880, p. 52) and C. J. Taylor's "She Took the Wrong Bundle, or Heroic Treatment for Gout," (May 8, 1889, p. 181) protest the inconvenience that laundry women burdened with bundles cause to other passengers on city streetcars. On the other hand, the Irish washerwoman is a powerful figure in J. A. Wales's sympathetic cover cartoon "Where Mr. Field's Subscription List Would Do the Most Good" (July 20, 1881) that shows a bedridden, badly injured railroad worker surrounded by his rail-thin wife standing over an enormous washtub with hungry, crying toddlers clinging to her. A little girl with a very old face irons nearby.

In both the graphic humor and the popular culture of Irish domestic servants, Bridget is most often the subject of numbskull jokes that turn on the servant girl's lack of familiarity with American cooking or household ways. Such jokes were told *by* Irish domestic servants as often as they were told about them.

Some stories that Irish servant girls told about themselves later became family anecdotes, such as the one about Lucille Quinlan recently arrived from Clare, who took her employer's words literally when the employer said she wanted potatoes baked in their jackets for Saturday night dinner. Lucille spent the afternoon making little woolen jackets to cover them.[19] A joke that turns on literal language is the one where Bridget is dispatched to the butcher to see whether he has pigs' feet. She returns saying, "I couldn't tell. He had his boots on." Another story, probably apocryphal, tells of the servant girl's conversation with the family doctor about the condition of the man of the house. He asks, "How are the bowels?" She responds, "Sure, sir, we had soup last night and there's not a clean bowl in the house."[20]

Puck, too, featured numbskull Irish domestic stories. Samuel Ehrhart's "An Irish Duster" (May 30, 1888, p. 231; plate 4) depicts Bridget dusting furniture with the dustpan. Syd B. Griffin, who specialized in numbskull cartoons about Shantytown matrons in aprons and boots, drew the same image for a numbskull servant joke in "A Cold Day for Terrapin" (March 5, 1890, p. 19), where Honorah the cook drops a turtle out the window while she says over her shoulder to the woman of the house, "The butcher-boy's afther playin' wan o' his jokes on me, Ma'am. He left a basket in th' basment wid six o' these lizards wid boxes on their backs, t' frighten me."

Numbskull stories involving kerosene mishaps had a perverse appeal for *Puck* cartoonists. In Ehrhart's "Those Pretty Dresden Decanters" (June 18, 1890, p. 266), Bridget's employer discovers that Bridget has mistaken a crystal decanter for an oil lamp and filled it with kerosene. The mishap is discovered before there is any harm to the family; however, in the other kerosene cartoons, the Irish servant is the victim, and her injury or death is part of the joke. Opper's "Modern Miracles" (December 8, 1880, p. 224; plate 5) satirizes the apparitions reported at Lourdes (1858), Knock (1879), and the Monastery of the Passionist Fathers in Hoboken (1880) by describing some modern New York City miracles. One shows a grinning Irish simpleton pouring kerosene directly into the stove. Opper commented:

> It is said that the greater portion of the population of Heaven consists of servants girls who have gone, prematurely, thither through the medium of coal oil.
>
> We once knew of a Milesian servant girl who built her fire with kerosene—no explosion followed, and she did not feel in the least bit the worse for it.
>
> Such a curious circumstance cannot be accounted for by natural means, the supernatural must have done the business.
>
> Perhaps the angel or imp who takes petroleum under his special protection did not desire the presence of this particular Biddy in his stamping grounds; but, endeavor to explain it as we may, the fact of her not being blown up is, to our minds, a miracle of the very highest order, and as such deserves to be handed down to posterity to become an ancient miracle in due time.

Opper's "The King of Destroyers" (August 24, 1881, p. 419) appears more sympathetic to Irish servants in identifying the stove as a danger to those working in the kitchen. A servant girl with an oilcan for a head stands in front of a wood-fired stove while a man with a leering skull face and wearing an undertaker's hat holds a coffin marked "For the family." The caption reads, "The Real Irish Infernal Machine." The cover of the previous week's *Puck* provides the context for the cartoon; it features smoke labeled "Irish infernal machine" wafting from upturned dynamiters' hats.

That the infernal machine was a device, often innocuous in appearance, designed to explode and to destroy people or property not only condemns terror-ists' indifference to innocent suffering from political violence but also rebukes employers for their indifference to the safety of their servants. It suggests an ex-ample of employers' attitudes toward Irish domestic servants: that they were an interchangeable unit in the household economy. Some Irish domestic servant in-formants report that employers did not even bother to learn their names but called them by generic names: Biddy, Bridget, or Maggie.[21]

Opper's "European Notions of American Manners and Customs" (November 16, 1881, p. 169) mocks a number of American conventions, including table man-ners, business ethics, and weak coffee. A panel called "American Plan of Kin-dling Fires" shows Bridget blown into the air by an exploding kerosene can. In a similar cartoon by ABS (A. B. Shultz) titled "Amplified 'Ads'" (April 21, 1886, p. 118), another Bridget reels from the flames shooting from a burning kerosene lamp. The caption: "WANTED— An Irish Girl to do Light Work."[22]

The cruelty of making light of pain and suffering to Irish servants can be em-phasized by setting these cartoons against the dangers of household fires. In her study *Serving Women: Household Service in the Nineteenth Century,* Faye E. Dudden points out that while kerosene was the preferred fuel after it was intro-duced at mid-century, its virtues of brightness and longer light were qualified by its explosiveness. Catharine Beecher told the readers of her *Treatise on Domes-tic Economy* (1841) that the care of kerosene lamps was so exacting that the woman of the house often chose to do that work herself.[23] Contemporary news-papers carried stories of injuries and deaths from lamp and stove fires. For ex-ample, there was an account in local papers of the agonizing death of seventeen-year-old Mary McDonough in West Newton, Massachusetts, in 1887 when a kettle of fat went ablaze and set her clothes on fire.[24]

Household fire safety was considered such an important subject for girls at-tending Irish National Schools in the 1880s that the first part of the four-part "Du-ties of Female Servants" in the *Girls' Reading Book* featured lessons designed to familiarize pupils with basic fire safety, including the properties and dangers of cooking and heating fuels and what to do were one's own clothes to catch fire.[25] With the *Puck* cartoonists' exploitation of household fires as a source of humor, the usually innocuous numbskull cartoon becomes crude and malicious.

Cartoons exploiting negative stereotypes about Irish domestic servants focus on both Bridget, a young housemaid or a children's maid, whose foibles usually come in for mild ridicule, and an older Biddy, almost always a cook, who is the target of more pointed mockery. Bridget is a slapdash cleaner who dusts the room with the feathers on her hat in Dalrymple's "Utilization" (June 1, 1887, p. 226), or even with dust itself in Opper's "She Dusted" (February 29, 1888, p. 7). In two Opper cartoons, Bridget neglects the child she has taken to the park in order to flirt with a policeman ("In the Park. An Episode," April 29, 1885, p. 133; and

1. "How to Keep a Girl," by Frederick Opper. *Puck*, January 30, 1884, center.

2. "A Bombardment That Would Paralyze Them," by Frederick Opper.
Puck, April 18, 1883, back cover.

3. "The Streets of New York—No. IV," by Frederick Opper. *Puck*, January 26, 1881, p. 354.

4. "An Irish Duster,"
by Samuel Ehrhart.
Puck, May 30, 1888,
p. 231.

5. "Modern Miracles,"
by Frederick Opper.
Puck, December 8,
1880, p. 224.

6. "No Nurse-Girl Should Be Without One," by Frederick Opper. *Puck,* May 5, 1886, p. 149.

7. "The Last Reception of the Season," by Frederick Opper. *Puck,* September 11, 1882, back cover.

(Opposite page):
9. "Our Self-Made 'Cooks'—
From Paupers to Potentates," by
Frederick Opper. *Puck,* January
30, 1884, back cover.

8. "The Universal Piano," by Frederick Opper. *Puck,*
September 20, 1882, p. 270.

10. "The Irish Declaration of Independence," by Frederick Opper. *Puck*, May 9, 1883, cover.

11. "The Goose That Lays the Golden Eggs," by Frederick Opper. *Puck,* August 22, 1883, cover.

12. "Another Blind for the Biddies—The Dynamiters' New Device," by Frederick Opper. *Puck*, March 11, 1885, back cover.

"A Long-felt Want Supplied—Puck's Hand-Book of Etiquette for 'Help,'" January 16, 1889, back cover); however, no harm is done to her charge. In a third Opper cartoon, "No Nurse-Girl Should Be Without One" (May 5, 1886, p. 149; plate 6), a clever Bridget has a windlass-like contraption fastened to a little girl, and as she talks with her policeman, she reels in the child.

While Bridget may be dismissed as irresponsible, *Puck* cartoonists never suggest that she does harm to the children of the house as the cartoonists do in "The French Maid" (October 14, 1885, p. 92), in which the parent/speaker prefers the French Maid to "the rude Hibernian [who] make[s] the house her own," but wonders whether the baby's unbroken sleep since the maid's arrival is "because she chocks him up with laudanum."

Cartoons about Bridget and Biddy suggest some petty pilfering or "borrowing" from the family. Two C. J. Taylor cartoons feature servants who appropriate family possessions to wear to mass. In "Christian-Like," Bridget wears her mistress's dress to church and rationalizes it with the verbal acuity for which she was known, "Thinks I to mesilf if ther missis won't go to church, I'll go and represint her absence be ther dress she wears!" (November 24, 1886, p. 136). In "It is a Sunday Morning," Biddy decorates her hat with her master's shaving brush (March 10, 1886, p. 20).

In cartoons, Irish domestic servants are portrayed as generous and hospitable to their families and friends, but they are not the self-sacrificing heroines of fiction; the resources of the household subsidize their kind impulses. A number of cartoons feature Bridget or Biddy entertaining their family and friends often while their employers are away.[26] Opper's "The Last Reception of the Season" (September 11, 1882, back cover; plate 7) finds four Biddies entertaining an assortment of gentlemen callers, including three Irish policemen and a grocer, to drinks, conversation, and music. Opper's cartoon reinforces the stereotype that Biddies cannot be trusted; it also implies that the idea of Irish servants wearing party clothes and hosting a party in a middle-class sitting room is preposterous. The presence of policemen visitors suggests that the guardians of civic authority and virtue are kitchen cronies of Irish domestics, who view them as attractive marriage partners.

These Biddies do not have the usual Opper simian features that he gives his Irish women. Biddies in party dresses, jewelry, and bows are sufficiently ridiculous. He uses the same device in a panel of "A Long-felt Want Supplied—Puck's Hand-Book of Etiquette for 'Help,'" (January 16, 1889, back cover), in which Biddies wearing hair ribbons and ruffled dresses and holding a fan or balancing a cup daintily serve tea to male visitors in the kitchen. The caption reminds Biddy as hostess that she should offer her chair to her mistress should she arrive in the kitchen during Biddy's reception.

F. Graetz's verse and drawing "Out of Town" (June 28, 1882, p. 265) along with two more Opper cartoons suggest that Irish domestics do not merely enter-tain in their employers' absence, but that they also allow their relatives to move into the house. A mistress discovers Bridget's cousins, aunts, and siblings in clos-ets, in barrels, and even in the coal bin ("Our Unexpected Return from the Coun-try—and How We Found Bridget's Relations all over the House," September 12, 1883, p. 281). A simian Mrs. Brophy explains to an inquirer that her family lives in Shantytown only during the winter, for, "It's Beyant over there we spind our summer. When the payple lave, yer know, me Bridget is lift alone thin" ("Over-heard in Shantytown," June 6, 1883, p. 212).

When the Irish began to raise their standard of living, *Puck* used ridicule to suggest the absurdity of the Irish adopting middle-class mores. Griffin and Dalrymple specialized in cartoons describing the social pretensions of the poor Irish as they begin to improve the quality of their lives. Dalrymple's self-satis-fied, simian "McGarragan's Family Group" (*Puck Annual,* 1888, p. 21) and Syd B. Griffin's "He Got a Negative" (December 19, 1888, p. 24), in which Mr. McPhlynn thinks that a surveyor is a photographer and calls out, "Will ye plase howld on a bit, sor, till Oi git the goat and the rest av the childer in the group," lampoon the middle-class respectability of the family portrait. The acquisition of decorative objects is another sign of Irish middle-class pretensions. Mrs. Reilly thinks Mrs. McPugh's china pug is a statue of the man of the house in Griffin's "They are Strangers Now" (January 23, 1889, p. 648), and the sine qua non of middle-class life—the piano in the parlor—is the subject of Opper's "The Uni-versal Piano" (September 20, 1882, p. 270; plate 8), in which two Shantytown men watch two other men measure a shanty doorway. One explains to the other that they are measuring for "Mary Ann's new pianny."[27] Even a basic comfort like a bed is fair game for *Puck.* In Syd B. Griffin's "More Than He Bargained For" (March 19, 1890, p. 38), the agent coming to repossess a box spring finds that it has become a dog pen.

The cartoons about ambitious domestic servants are more biting because ser-vants' mobility was regarded as threatening and disruptive to householders. *Puck* readers would have had more direct experience with the independent Irish do-mestic servant than with the Irish Shantytown dweller, and *Puck* used that expe-rience to present Irish servants as objects of satirical humor and as metaphors in some of their political cartoons. As a rule, the younger Bridget, usually the sub-ject of the numbskull jokes and sometimes of the purloined hospitality cartoons, is treated more sympathetically than the older, more formidable Biddy, who has worked her way up in the household, usually to the position of cook. It is Biddy who allows *Puck* artists to exploit the negative Irish female stereotype. She is bellicose, bossy, and frequently, like her male counterpart, boozy.

The figure of Biddy did not originate with the cartoonists. Biddy was a char-acter in vaudeville routines like George Munroe's monologue "Aunt Bridget,"[28] and one of the spectacles of the Grand Duke Opera House featured a drunken Biddy thrown out a window. Biddy the brawler would make her appearance in one of the earliest silent films, the 1903 *Washerwoman's Daughter,* when a neighborly visit turns into a punch-up.[29]

Opper's two-panel cartoon "Our Self-Made 'Cooks'—From Paupers to Potentates" (January 30, 1884, back cover; plate 9) satirizes Biddy's rise from a barefoot girl in an Irish cabin who wrings her hands at the doorway as she watches the agent arrive with an eviction sign to a fashionable—if too elaborately dressed—servant who dominates her kitchen, entertains an Irish cop who sits under a drawing of a simian Pope Leo XIII, and orders her meek and somewhat frightened mistress from the room. The caption reads "But in America They Do All the Evicting Themselves."

Opper's running gag about Biddy's ambition and her imperious behavior appears in the double-page center cartoon in the same issue. The servant girl upstart returns in an almost identical cartoon the following year that is titled "A Miraculous Metamorphosis or Bridget's Sudden Rise" (September 23, 1885, p. 59). In the top panel, an old lady, who is smoking a pipe, and a pig watch a barefoot Biddy dropping potatoes into a pot over an open fire. A sign that reads "Eviction for non-payment of rent" hangs on the wall. In the lower panel, a well-dressed Biddy with a brooch and a bow in her hair stands at the stove while the cop on the beat enjoys a cup of tea. Her mistress is opening the door, but Biddy's determined expression and her stance with her hand on her hip and a strong forearm holding a frying pan make it clear who is in charge.

Irish women did not equate domestic service with servility, so it did not have the negative associations that it did for some other ethnic groups. What was responsible for such an attitude? The demand for domestic servants and servants' high mobility contributed to be sure, but it was also the servants' sense of egalitarianism. The national schools can be faulted for their class-limited curriculum, but their textbooks included readings that fostered the opinion that servant girls were anybody's equal. The nineteenth-century Anglo-Irish poet Felicia Dorothea Hemann's poem "Sunbeam," which appeared in the *Girls' Reading Book* (1887) and later in the *Fifth Reader* (1897), reminded the young reader that the sunbeam visits all: the monarch's palace and the peasant's cot. The *Girls' Reading Book* offered advice for the domestic servant that emphasized the dignity and the professionalism of service: "Let it be borne in mind that a good servant, one who is mistress of her work, will always command good wages, for she is a treasure to her employers."[30]

Not only was Biddy in charge of the kitchen, but the Irish were in charge of American urban politics. Irish-born William R. Grace was elected mayor of New York in November 1880; Hugh O'Brien followed as the first Irish-born mayor of Boston in 1885. The emergence of the Irish as a political force in American cities coincided with the papacy of Leo XIII (1878–1903), a period of remarkable institutional growth for the Roman Catholic Church in America, a church dominated by the Irish. Nowhere were these interests more closely linked than in New York, where the Catholic hierarchy had conspicuous links with the Democratic political machine. America's first cardinal, John McCloskey, was elected archbishop of New York in 1875; his niece married "Honest John" Kelly, the New York Tammany leader between 1871 and 1882. Kelly and Tammany were a favorite prey of *Puck* cartoonists. Anticipating Grace's mayoral election, J. A. Wales's "The Cath'lics Are Coming," an allusion to the warning to patriots on the eve of the American Revolutionary War, was *Puck's* October 27, 1880 cover (p. 190), which featured a renovated city hall in the shape of the papal crown with its three gold diadems representing the Tax Office, the Parochial School Fund Office, and the Police Office. Clerics do city business, and even the Irish scrub woman is dressed in a religious habit.

In Opper's "The Tammany Bridget Re-engaged" (November 22, 1882, p. 187), Biddy herself is the metaphor for Tammany politicians. A smirking, simian Bridget, hand on her hip, holds a broom upside down as she surveys the room: spider webs hang from the ceiling, paint peels from the walls, a looking glass shatters. Pleased with herself, she announces, "Begorra, I'm here for another two ye-urrs."

Opper's most simian and most menacing Biddy, the hussy who intimidates her employer in "The Irish Declaration of Independence" (May 9, 1883, cover; plate 10), is a metaphor for the Irish threat to nativist America. Biddy, the bullying cook, is an enormous redhead with simian features: wild eyes, upturned nose, and long upper lip. Her buckteeth and protruding tongue make her more fierce, for it is Biddy's verbal abuse that is one of her most terrifying features. Biddy's dress, decorated with shamrocks, is kilted over her knees to reveal a red petticoat, the red petticoat with the black bands that is associated with the dress of the women of the time in the west of Ireland. Fists raised, she threatens her slender, blond employer, who cringes in fear, arms extended and hands clasped in a gesture of supplication. Part of her dress, or perhaps a matching bonnet, lies crumpled at her feet.

The writer of the "Cartoons and Comments" column in the "Declaration of Independence" issue linked the Opper cartoon with the first meeting of the Irish National League of America, which was founded in Philadelphia in April 1883:

> We do not clearly see why the Irishmen of Philadelphia should have made a little declaration of independence of their own. We in this country are already pretty fairly familiar with the principal that an Irishman is as good as any other man, and as much better as the other man will permit him to be. The Irish Declaration of Independence has been read in our kitchens many and many a time, to frighten housewives, and the

fruits of that declaration are to be seen in thousands of ill-cooked meals on ill-served tables, in unswept rooms and unmade beds, in dirt, confusion, insubordination and general disorder, taking the sweetness out of domestic life. Declaration of Independence! Why, the Irish in this country have made a declaration of Autocratic Supremacy, and are acting upon it. (May 9, 1883, p. 146)

The writer continues in a nativist tirade to condemn journalists who capitulate to the Irish vote, "trucking to a handful of ignorant emigrants who, without a particle of sympathy for our political aims and ambitions"; to rage about the Irish in municipal government, "by sheer audacity and unprincipled impudence"; and to call for a new Declaration of American Independence. The "Declaration of Independence" refers, of course, to the American Declaration of Independence with its lines "all men are created equal." Opper alludes to the independence of the Irish domestic servant of the day, who knew that her services were in demand and that she could easily find another job. Opper's cartoon, in the context of his other domestic servant cartoons, suggests that if Americans could not control Bridget or Biddy, America would not be able to control the immigrant population, particularly the Irish, who posed a threat to nativist interests by their emerging political power.

Not only was Biddy a household tyrant and a metaphor for the Irish domination of urban politics, but she was also linked to the violent wing of the Irish nationalist movement. This Biddy made her appearance long before *Puck*. An early *Harper's* cartoon, "The Fenian Joan of Arc" (December 2, 1865), the contribution of a cartoonist described only as "our Canadian artist," features a slatternly Biddy with her broom raised, threatening "Arrah, Johnny Bull, we're after yez! Willaloo! Wist!" She has the familiar ape features and wears a bottle of rye atop her disheveled hair. This identification with an Irish domestic servant and St. Joan points to the subversive qualities of independence and autonomy that George Bernard Shaw developed later in his characterization of St. Joan.

While Opper did not make the Irish domestic servant a terrorist in his cartoons, her reputation for self-sacrifice is given a sinister turn in the cartoons, for he and the other *Puck* cartoonists believed that they were themselves the prey of Irish revolutionaries, particularly Jeremiah O'Donovan Rossa, a *Puck* bête noire, who combined a dedication to Irish independence through violent means that *Puck* associated with anarchy and a sleight of hand it associated with Tammany rascals.[31]

In 1875, Rossa started a "Skirmishing Fund" to finance the Irish radicals' campaign to blow up English jails to free Fenian prisoners. On the *Puck* cover for March 27, 1878, "The Rival of St. Patrick" (p. 55), Rossa (Sir Skirmish Tyranius) sits on a lion dangling a bag marked "Skirmishing Fund." Later that spring, Blather O'Blunderbuss, the narrator of "Triplet's" "The Great Fenian Movement"

(May 15, 1878, p. 5), describes the sources of support for Rossa's Skirmishing Fund as the "generous self-denying, sacrificing spirit of the stupid Irish servant girl and trusting Irish laborer, toiling harder than any animal used in civilization. They are *our* big bonanzas and we use 'em.'"

On May 6, 1882, in Dublin's Phoenix Park, the chief secretary for Ireland, Lord Frederick Cavendish, and his undersecretary, T. H. Burke, were murdered by Irish radicals known as the Invincibles. Four Opper cartoons, two published within six months of the murders, elaborate on the Irish domestic's generosity—and gullibility. His "American Gold" (May 22, 1882, back cover), which plays on the myth of America as the land with gold in the streets, suggests that the Irish immigrant's hard-earned money did not make it back to the poor lazy Irish with too many children but instead went to political terrorists.

In Opper's "The Irish Skirmishers 'Blind Pool'" (September 6, 1882, back cover), simian Paddys and Biddy and small children offer their money to hands reaching through a wooden barrier with a poster saying "Subscribe Here and Ask No Questions." Behind the barrier, Rossa and his well-dressed friends, sporting shamrocks in the bands of their top hats, drink up the contributions. *Puck* was not alone in its distrust of Rossa; the *New York Tribune* (April 20, 1883) shared the view that Rossa was profiting from the Skirmishing Fund.[32]

In 1883, the year that Irish radicals began their Dynamite Campaign of bombing English public buildings, Anglo-American relations were strained because the U.S. government was unable to produce the evidence linking Rossa with the Dynamite plots.[33] That year Opper's *Puck* cover "The Goose That Lays the Golden Eggs" (August 22, 1883, cover; plate 11) identified Rossa's benefactor as the Irish servant girl. Rossa feeds slips of paper marked, "Pay the Bearer $5 when Ireland is Free" to a goose dressed in a dress, apron, and slippers. If there is any question about the identity of the goose, "Bridget" is written on her apron strings. Rossa chortles, "Begorra, we'll never kill her while her appetite lasts."

A later Opper cartoon shows the ever resourceful Rossa behind yet another scam for Irish domestic servants: "Another Blind for the Biddies—The Dynamiters' New Device" (March 11, 1885, back cover; plate 12). A long line of simian-faced ladies, two of whom wear the cook's long white apron, appear at the Irish Liberator's Café that features a poster proclaiming "Aid for the MAHDI. Subscriptions wanted for an IRISH regiment to crush the BRITISH!" The Biddies file past a mechanical Mahdi, who sits atop a box labeled "The Mahdi Bank." They put their Mahdi pence in his dish, which, in the manner of an old-fashioned toy bank, drops the pennies into the bank below.[34] The Biddies are drawn into support for the Mahdi, believing that "British misfortune is Ireland's opportunity"; however, the figure of O'Donovan Rossa lurks behind the door. He has invented the ruse to get money from the Biddies to fund his dynamite campaign.

The important aspect of this cartoon is that the women have control over their own money. Opper chose to portray the Biddies as dupes of O'Donovan Rossa's in "American Gold," "The Goose . . . ," and "Another Blind . . . ," but in fact, the money from Irish domestic servants, from Bridget and from Biddy, financed two far more revolutionary movements. They sent home the rent as they would send the money home that allowed for the purchase of land authorized by the Wyndham Act of 1903 and subsequent land purchase legislation. Their money created an Irish peasant proprietorship. Their money also provided a good deal of the bricks and mortar for the Devotional Revolution at home and the Irish church in America, the dominant force in American Roman Catholicism until Vatican II in the 1960s.

Roger Fischer's analysis of political cartoons in *Those Damned Pictures: Explorations in American Political Cartoon Art* includes a chapter called "Aliens," which considers Irish, Jewish, and African American cartoons in American comic papers, including *Puck.* He argues that the ethnic stereotype reinforced the sense of the ethnic other, the unassimilated alien. *Puck* cartoons perpetuated the Bridget and Biddy stereotypes to maintain such a fiction. The fact is that by the 1880s, the Irish *were* assimilating, and many Irish servant girls were marrying and moving into the American middle class. *Puck* might ridicule their mobility and use its cartoons to try to distance Irish servant girls from their employers' families, but Irish domestics were virtually indistinguishable from other female members of the household. Servant girls' literacy, their wit, their sense of style, and the appreciation for what was "nice" that they learned in service eased their way from "lately landed" to lace curtains for themselves and, especially, for their children.[35]

Notes

1. See the discussion of the Irish servant girl in fiction in Maureen Murphy, "The Irish Servant Girl in Literature," in *America and Ulster, A Cultural Correspondence, Writing Ulster,* vol. 5, ed. Bill Lazenblatt (1998), 135–36.

2. Margaret MacCurtain, "The Real Molly Macree," in *Visualizing Ireland* (Boston: Faber and Faber, 1993) 9–21.

3. The American traveler Asenath Nicholson visiting Valentia Island in 1845 observed with distress the sight of girls and women wading in chest-deep water to gather seaweed; however, Nicholson noted with approval that girls who returned to Ireland after working in service in America refused such labor. "She ceases to become a beast of burden, and the basket on her back, which she then throws off, she will never lift again." Asenath Nicholson, *Ireland's Welcome to the Stranger: or, Excursions Through Ireland in 1844 & 1845* (London: Charles Gilpin, 1847), 321, 318.

Harsh physical labor continued for another century. Photographs in Thomas H. Mason's *The Islands of Ireland,* 3rd ed. (London: Batsford, 1936) show girls on Inishere carrying heavy baskets of seaweed on their backs.

4. Geraldine Maschio, "Ethnic Humor and the Demise of the Russell Brothers," *Journal of Popular Culture* 26, no. 1 (summer 1992): 81–91.

5. L. Perry Curtis, *Apes and Angels: The Irishman in Victorian Caricature* (Washington, D.C.: Smithsonian Institution Press, 1971).

6. Frederick Burr Opper (1857–1937) was the son of an Austrian immigrant who settled in the Midwest. He started his fifty-seven-year career in the comic weeklies in 1876, at the age of nineteen, as a cartoonist for *Wild Oats*. He worked on *Puck* for eighteen years (1881–1899) before moving to the Hearst dailies for twenty-five more years, where he created "Happy Houligan." In *A History of American Graphic Humor*, vol. 2 (New York: Whitney Museum of American Art, 1938), 177, William Murrell characterized Opper's work as "grotesque—the low comedy school if you will, but his comic line is one of the greatest of all times."

7. Curtis, *Apes and Angels*, 25, 41.

8. R. F. Foster, *Paddy and Mr. Punch: Connections in Irish and English History* (New York: Penguin, 1995), 193–94.

9. Bruno Bettelheim, *The Uses of Enchantment: The Meaning and Importance of Fairy Tales* (New York: Vintage, 1977), 236.

10. The late Dennis J. Clark contributed the text to a study of negative stereotypes of the Irish in America. It appears in a teaching kit called "Images of Indignation: How Cartoons Shape Our Views," which examines anti-Irish cartoons. The kit was prepared by the Center for Irish Studies and distributed in cooperation with the Balch Institute for Ethnic Studies (Philadelphia, n.d.).

11. John J. Appel, "From Shanties to Lace Curtains: The Irish Image in *Puck*, 1876–1910," *Comparative Studies in Society and History* 13, no. 4 (October 1971): 367.

12. *Puck* was founded by Joseph Keppler, an Austrian immigrant to St. Louis, who founded a comic German language paper called *Die Vehme* (Impetuous) which folded after one year. Keppler went to New York, where he joined the staff of *Leslie's Illustrated Newspaper* in 1872. In 1876, Keppler and Adolph Schwartzmann, a printer, founded the German comic weekly *Puck*; the English language version was launched in 1877. Its color cartoons and caricatures made *Puck* the leading American humor magazine.

13. Keppler, a major influence on American graphic humor, was in turn influenced by European satirical cartoonists.

14. Roger Fischer quotes Gombrich's phrase in *Those Damned Pictures: Explorations in American Political Cartoon Art* (North Haven, Conn.: Archon Books, 1996), 11.

15. Ibid., 70.

16. While he drew for *Puck*, Woolf's drawings of slum children also appeared in J. A. Mitchell's *Life* during the decade 1886–1896. Murrell, *History of American Graphic Humor*, vol. 2, 99, 100.

17. Fischer, *Those Damned Pictures*, 76, describes the *Puck* Paddy as an innocuous daydreamer "living in constant fear of his better half, a beefy Bridget."

18. *Puck* took on the powerful pension lobby in its cartoons by Dalrymple, Keppler and Opper. Murrell, *History of American Graphic Humor*, vol. 2, 86.

19. The story was collected from Lucille Quinlan's relatives at State University of New York, Stony Brook, 16 November 1989.

20. This version of the story was provided by Dr. June Davison, who said it was a family story. Grace Neville of University College, Cork, includes another version of the anecdote in her essay "'He Spoke to Me in English; I Answered Him in Irish': Language Shift in the Folklore Archives," in *L'Irelande et ses langues,* ed. Jean Brihault (Renne: Presses Universitaires de Reeme et Centre d'Études des Irlandaises, 1992), 30.

21. The *Oxford English Dictionary* defines Biddy as "an Irish domestic," and Irish women who looked after generations of Harvard undergraduates were known as Biddies. Maggie was the name for Irish domestics in Fall River, Massachusetts. When Lizzie Borden was standing trial for the murder of her parents, she and the District Attorney Hosea Knowlton referred to Bridget Sullivan, the Borden servant girl, as "Maggie." Arnold Brown, *Lizzie Borden: The Legend, the Truth, the Final Chapter* (Nashville: Rutledge Hill, 1991), 140.

22. Stove explosions feature in Irish joke books. H. P. Kelly's *Gems of Irish Wit and Humor* (New York: George Sully, 1906), 25, includes this exchange between servant and mistress:

> Mary Ann: "I've come to tell you, mum, that th' gasoline stove has gone out."
> Mistress: "Well, light it again."
> Mary Ann: "I can't. Sure it went out through the roof."

23. Faye E. Dudden, *Serving Women: Household Service in the Nineteenth Century* (Middletown, Conn.: Wesleyan University Press, 1983), 129.

24. The incident was reported in the *Newton Journal,* March 12, 1897. I am grateful to Charles Bowen for providing me with this account.

25. *Girls' Reading Book* (Dublin: Alex. Thomas, 1887), 40–42.

26. Conrad Arensberg, *The Irish Countryman: An Anthropological Study* (1937; reprint, Gloucester, Mass.: Peter Smith, 1959). In his classic study of rural Clare, the Harvard anthropologist Conrad Arensberg describes the Irish system of extended kinship and its reciprocal obligations, which include hospitality. The custom is well documented in nineteenth-century literature. Mary Leadbeater refers to the intense sense of extended family that includes sharing the table with all members, in *Cottage Dialogues,* vol. 2 (London: Johnson, 1811), 259. Mrs. Anna Hall's "It's only the Bit and the Sup" counsels offering extended hospitality only to those who need it, in *Stories of the Irish Peasantry* (London: W. & R. Chambers, 1878), 114.

27. See Finley Peter Dunne's "The Piano in the Parlor," Mr. Dooley's sketch of the arrival of Molly Donahue's piano in Bridgeport. Charles Fanning, ed., *Mr. Dooley and the Chicago Irish: The Autobiography of a Nineteenth-Century Ethnic Group* (Washington, D.C.: Catholic University of America Press, 1987), 143–45.

28. Joe Laurie, *Vaudeville* (New York: Holt, 1953), 89.

29. Joseph Curran, *Hibernian Green on the Silver Screen: The Irish and American Movies* (Westport: Greenwood Press, 1989), 18.

30. *Girls' Reading Book,* 88.

31. Jeremiah O'Donovan Rossa (1831–1915), a Fenian exile member of Clan na Gael, represented the most revolutionary wing of the Irish nationalist cause in the United States.

Rossa founded the Phoenix Society of Skibbereen (1856), which was later absorbed by the Fenians. He came to the United States for a short time as a Fenian agent in 1863. After he returned to Ireland, he was arrested with other Fenians in 1865 and sentenced to twenty years in an English prison, where he was brutally treated. Elected to Parliament from Tipperary in 1869, he was not seated because he was a convicted felon. Given early release in 1871, with the proviso that he go into exile, Rossa returned to the United States in time to run against Boss Tweed for the New York State Senate. His reputation for chicanery may have started there, for the legitimacy of his claim to American naturalization was challenged. Florence Gibson, *The Attitude of the New York Irish Toward State and National Affairs, 1848–1892* (New York: Columbia University Press, 1951), 235.

32. See Opper's cartoon "Fired from the Feast" (*Puck,* XIII, 321, 2 May 1883, back cover), where Rossa skulks off in disgrace from a nationalist banquet. Thomas Brown called Rossa "a highly frivolous administrator. His conduct lacked even that measure of decorum demanded by those who sympathized with his bloodthirsty projects." *Irish-American Nationalism 1870–1890* (Philadelphia: Lippencott, 1966), 70.

33. Gibson, *Attitude,* 337.

34. Mohammed Ahmed Ibd el Sayyia Abdullah, the Islamic Messianic hero, appeared in 1881, declared a jihad, and led his followers through the Sudan, where they swept through the Egyptian garrisons. When Gen. Charles George Gordon was dispatched to get the Egyptians out of Khartoum in 1884, he decided to hold out for British reinforcements. The Mahdi and his followers took Khartoum in January 1885. The Mahdi was dead by late spring, but his followers ruled for thirteen years until they were defeated by General Horatio Herbert Kitchener.

35. Kerby Miller gives some idea of the kind of mobility the Irish experienced in American cities. He writes that in Boston, in 1890, 10 percent of the Irish born were white-collar workers, while 40 percent of the second generation became white-collar workers. He also notes that between 1900 and 1910, one-fifth of all the teachers in northern cities, including one-third of all the teachers in the Chicago public schools, were Irish-American Catholics. Miller, *Emigrants and Exiles* (New York: Oxford University Press, 1998), 496.

11

"Slide, Kelly, Slide":
The Irish in American Baseball

Richard F. Peterson

Baseball historians have long recognized the ascendancy of Irish players in the early history of baseball. By the end of the nineteenth century, Irish stars dominated baseball and its greatest teams. The legendary Baltimore Orioles, managed by Ned Hanlon, won consecutive National League pennants in 1894, 1895, and 1896 with Hall of Famers Big Dan Brouthers, Hugh Jennings, and John McGraw in the infield and Joe Kelley and Wee Willie Keeler in the outfield. A decade earlier, so many New York Irish fans came out to see the stellar pitching of Tim Keefe and Smiling Mickey Welch, both winners of more than three hundred games in their professional careers, and the slugging of "The Mighty Clouter" Roger Connor, the Babe Ruth of his day, that the bleachers at the Polo Grounds were called "Burkeville." At other ballparks, the Irish sat in "Kerry Patches" to watch the colorful Mike "King" Kelly, generally regarded as the most popular baseball player of the nineteenth century. A. G. Spalding's sale of Kelly in 1887 from the Chicago National White Stockings to the Boston Beaneaters for the unheard-of price of ten thousand dollars was the biggest and most controversial deal of the era. Kelly's baserunning was so spectacular and his behavior on and off the field so flamboyant that he inspired the popular song "Slide, Kelly, Slide" and often performed on the vaudeville stage to packed houses during the off-season.

This predominance of Irish players in baseball's evolution into America's national pastime is most frequently interpreted within the traditional and popular view of the game as both an opportunity for individual success and a melting pot for ethnic groups. Conventional historical wisdom has it that once organized baseball shook free of both its amateur beginnings in the 1840s and the Knickerbocker hold on the game as a polite pastime for Protestant gentlemen, it opened its fields, especially after baseball became professional in 1869, to an increasing tide of immigrant players. The first immigrant wave of Germans and Irish supplanted the English and Scottish and transformed the game in the last few decades of the nineteenth century from a rural diversion and class signifier into an expression of America's democratic character and its competitive spirit. By the twentieth century, baseball had further evolved to the point that the ethnic origins of players had become an essential part of baseball's character and even a matter of pride. Of course, even as German and Irish players became assimilated into the national game and some of them emerged as ethnic heroes, other ethnic and racial groups, such as the Italians, Jews, and African Americans, would face the same prejudices and obstacles but would also have the same opportunity, when their time came, to prove themselves on the playing field. A 1931 editorial in *Sporting News*, baseball's bible, declared, as if in anticipation of Joe DiMaggio, Hank Greenberg, and Jackie Robinson, that the "Sons of Erin" had "better beware. . . . They will be challenged to prove their racial superiority one of these days."

The problem with this theory of the melting pot and the ethnic hero, besides its paradoxical nature, is that it relies heavily upon a romantic vision of baseball as a moral and heroic proving ground, an immigrant field of dreams. This vision, while one of the formative principles for baseball histories, perhaps finds its perfect expression in Lucy Kennedy's *The Sunlit Field*, generally recognized as the first adult baseball novel written by a woman. Published in 1950, two years before the appearance of Bernard Malamud's *The Natural*, Kennedy's historical romance, set in 1857, follows its runaway sixteen-year-old Irish heroine, Po (for Pocahontas) O'Reilly, from Fall River, Massachusetts, where the capitalist Eaters and their thread mills threaten her spirit, to Brooklyn, where she discovers that her dying father's dream of America as "a fabulous place—like a great open sunlit field" comes to life on a baseball field, where "the men flashed about, stretching their bodies in long beautiful arcs, or leaped into the air to catch the ball with easeful sureness in bared cupped hands. Yes, these were the tall men!"

In *The Sunlit Field*, baseball also becomes an epic battlefield for ethnic clashes and class rivalries when Kennedy turns one of the most celebrated events in early baseball history—the 1858 three-game Fashion Race Course Series between what A. G. Spalding in *America's National Game* described as "picked nines representing the foremost clubs of New York and Brooklyn"—into a bloodletting, to-the-death contest between the hirelings of the Knickerbockers and Po Reilly's tall men. The real series, the nineteenth-century precursor to the modern-day World Series, was played over a span of three months and was remarkable not only for its fierce rivalry but for the demand by its organizers for a fifty-cent admission fee and for the heavy amount of gambling on player performance and the outcome of the games. In her novel, Kennedy does not change the historical outcome of the series—New York won the deciding third game after the teams split the first two—but she does condense the series into a three-day event and transform the games into a ruthless attempt by the upper-class Knickerbocker Club to buy baseball supremacy by hiring "shooting stars" or "revolvers" to beat the upstart, working-class Brooklyn nine by any means, including bribery, cheating, and dirty play.

The dream of baseball as a field for individual opportunity and social assimilation survives Brooklyn's loss in *The Sunlit Field*. By the end of the novel, the game of baseball as a professional sport emerges as the immigrant's best hope for participating successfully in the democratic and competitive spirit of America. But Lucy Kennedy's novel remains to the end far more historical romance than historical writing. While *The Sunlit Field* envisions baseball as heroic ground for immigrants, baseball histories, even when celebrating the glory of the game, have tended to see baseball's assimilation of ethnic and racial groups through the distorted lens of ethnic and racial stereotypes—and this has been especially so for the Irish. Lawrence McCaffrey in *The New York Irish*, observing that "Irish players came to represent American adaptability and their skills in this arena gave them a more acceptable persona," also notes, "but athleticism also reinforced nativist opinion that the Irish were strong of back and weak of mind."

One of the most blatant, if not outrageous, examples of the historical stereotyping of Irish ballplayers occurs in one of baseball's most popular historical texts, *The Bill James Historical Baseball Abstract*. In writing about the Irish domination of baseball in the 1890s, James at first appears to reject nativism and stereotypes by declaring that "many people, in the same stupid way that people today believe that blacks are born athletes, thought that the Irish were born baseball players." But in the very next sentence, after observing that "of course people also associated the roughness and unruliness of the players with their ethnic background," he notes that "the Irish have, indeed, always been known for that." In other words, while it is stupid to think of the Irish as born baseball players, to think of them as born rowdies may be another matter.

Adding ethnic insult to injury, James, beginning with his section on baseball in the 1880s, a decade where the players were "mostly eastern, mostly Irish, and a little rough," sets up a special category for baseball's "Drinking Men." The category, with its listing of Charlie Sweeney, King Kelly, Curt Welch, and Duke Farrell among its eight most notorious drunks, is obviously tilted toward the Irish. In the next section on the 1890s, James, in writing about the decade most dominated by Irish players, continues his category for Drinking Men. By listing Tom McCarthy, Marty Bergen, and Willie McGill among his five baseball lushes of the 1890s, the category once again raises the glass to the Irish. When James gets to the 1900s, the decade when baseball "gradually began to shed its Irish flavor," his category for the game's Drinking Men disappears, apparently no longer required. And, notes James, with baseball becoming more temperate and respectable, baseball attendance dramatically improved: "Whereas baseball in the nineteenth century was in danger of becoming a game of the Irish, by the Irish, for the Irish, it now began to appeal to a broader cross-section of the public."

The Bill James Historical Baseball Abstract obviously relies on blatant stereotyping in its association of baseball's early rowdyism with the predominance of Irish players in the 1880s and 1890s, but there is ample historical evidence to support James's attitude toward the Irish, an attitude shared by baseball historian Benjamin Rader, who in his own commentary on late-nineteenth-century ballplayers in *Baseball: A History of America's Game* notes, "(at least for the Irish) drinking, brawling, and display were a conspicuous part of their male homosocial world." Curt Welch, listed among James's Drinking Men, once purportedly dedicated his season to beer. His heavy drinking forced him out of baseball at the age of thirty-one, and he died three years later of alcoholism. Also on James's list, Charlie Sweeney, according to the biographical entry in the Society for American Baseball Research's (SABR's) *Nineteenth Century Stars,* "was vilified in the press for his public drunkenness and for assaulting another player." Several years after his career was over, Sweeney was convicted of manslaughter and sentenced to ten years in prison for killing a man in a barroom argument. But Sweeney's conduct and fate pale beside that of Marty Bergen, a brilliant but emotionally disturbed player who, in the middle of an erratic career and nine days after the turn of the century, used an ax to kill his son and daughter and then cut his own throat with a razor.

Even baseball's earliest historians had no trouble finding and displaying examples of Irish misconduct on and off the playing field. In *America's National Game*, published in 1911 and generally regarded as the first official chronicle of baseball, A. G. Spalding uses, as one of the turning points in baseball's development into the national pastime, a meeting between William Hulbert, president of the National League, and Jim Devlin, one of four Louisville players banned from baseball for conspiring with gamblers to throw games. According to Spalding, Devlin, after being reduced to abject poverty by his expulsion, came to Hulbert's office and fell to his knees to plead for mercy on behalf of his starving family. Moved to tears, Hulbert put a fifty-dollar bill into Devlin's palm but told him: "That's what I think of you, personally; but damn you, Devlin, you are dishonest; you have sold a game, and I don't trust you. Now go; and let me never see your face again; for your act will not be condoned as long as I live."

The banning of Devlin, despite the claims of Spalding, hardly kept baseball free of gambling and scandal, but, thanks to Spalding's chronicle, Devlin became baseball's most conspicuous example of the crooked ballplayer, at least until the fixing of the 1919 World Series. Devlin, a thirty-game winner for Louisville in 1876 and 1877 and one of baseball's emerging stars at the time of his expulsion, was further proof that the Irish were prolific in the late nineteenth century, not only for their playing skills, competitive nature, and success on the ball field, but for their alcoholism, hoodlumism, and self-destructiveness. They have provided historians with the best examples of the "poor moral conduct and . . . ill-mannered behavior both on and off the field" that Steven A. Riess in *City Games:*

The Evolution of American Urban Society and the Rise of Sports, his study of sports in the Progressive Era, sees as the cause for ballplayers' low prestige in the early history of professional baseball.

The epitome of the nineteenth-century Irish ballplayer for baseball historians is the colorful and controversial figure of Mike "King" Kelly. Listed by Bill James as the most handsome and dashing ballplayer of the 1880s, Kelly is described in SABR's *Baseball's First Stars* as "the brainiest, most creative, and most original player of his time." The most spectacular base runner of his day, Kelly once stole a remarkable 84 bases in just 116 games. He was also an excellent hitter, leading the National League in batting twice and in runs scored three times. During his Major League career, he led Cap Anson's Chicago club to three straight National League pennants from 1880 to 1882 and to two more in 1885 and 1886. He was elected to the Hall of Fame in 1945.

Yet when baseball historians portray Kelly, their accounts draw far more attention to his heavy drinking, his flaunting of baseball rules, and his troublesome and often unmanageable behavior than to his accomplishments. In *Baseball: An Illustrated History*, the book derived from Ken Burns's popular television documentary on the history of baseball, the narrative relates story after story of Kelly's drunkenness and trickery. Readers, after looking at a cartoon of Kelly in the clubhouse sleeping off a nightly bender, learn about the time Kelly, when asked if he drank while playing, replied, "It depends upon the length of the game," and about the time he held up a game while he and "several wealthy gentlemen in box seats toasted one another." The narrative also quotes the solemn words of Henry Chadwick, baseball's pioneer journalist and an early reformer of the game, condemning Kelly's outrageous conduct: "To suppose that a man can play properly who guzzles beer daily, or indulges in spiritous liquors, or who sets up nightly gambling or does worse by still enervating habits at brothels is nonsense."

The stories of Kelly when he was sober enough to play ball are usually about his trickery and cheating. On the base paths, he routinely skipped second base on his way to third if the umpire was watching the ball being retrieved in the outfield. When he was the catcher for his team, he would cover home plate with his mask to prevent the base runner from scoring. But the most apocryphal story of Kelly's on-the-field cunning has to do with his leaping, game-ending catch in the twilight gloom to save a Chicago victory. When he came off the field and was asked for the ball by his manager Cap Anson, Kelly supposedly replied, "The ball? . . . It went a mile over me head." Of course, there is also the story of the time Kelly, sitting out the game because of a hangover, saw a foul pop fly heading toward the bench, cried out, "Kelly catching for Boston," and jumped up and caught the ball for an out.

Kelly, however, was a piker compared to the infamous Baltimore Orioles and their galaxy of Irish stars and miscreants. The Irish-dominated Orioles were led on the field by the pugnacious John McGraw, who was called Muggsy by his enemies for his foul mouth and dirty play. In the Ken Burns history, McGraw is described in the words of the sportswriters of his day as "the toughest of the tough . . . an abomination of the diamond." Bill James in his *Baseball Abstract* named McGraw the best third baseman of the 1890s but also listed him as the decade's least admirable superstar. McGraw's own biographer, Charles Alexander, called him the worst umpire baiter in the history of baseball.

McGraw's Baltimore Orioles may have been one of the best teams in the early history of baseball, but they are also generally regarded as one of baseball's most infamous nines. Although they were the era's most skilled team at playing inside or scientific baseball, they have been historicized for abusing umpires and intimidating, and even maiming, opposition players. In his highly regarded history of baseball, *Baseball: The Golden Years,* Harold Seymour cites a complaint by the *Sporting News* that the Orioles were "playing the dirtiest ball ever seen in the country" and summarizes its description of such dirty tactics as tripping and spiking base runners or grabbing their shirts as they went by. The Orioles would also bunt between the mound and first base to run into and spike opposing pitchers. They bowled over infielders as they rounded the bases, and they crowded around and jostled any catcher waiting for a throw home. As for umpires, one of their favorite targets, John Heydler, who was an umpire during the 1890s and later became president of the National League, offers the following indictment of the Orioles:

> We hear much of the glories and durabilities of the old Orioles, but the truth about this team seldom has been told. They were mean, vicious, ready at any time to maim a rival player or an umpire, if it helped their cause. The things they said to an umpire were unbelievably vile, and they broke the spirits of some fine men. I've seen umpires bathe their feet by the hour after McGraw and others spiked them through their shoes. The club never was a constructive force in the game. The worst of it was they got by with much of their brow beating and hooliganism. Other clubs patterned after them, and I feel the lot of the umpires never was worse than in the years when the Orioles were flying high.

The most obvious, albeit superficial, way to counter the historicizing of the Irish ballplayer in the nineteenth century as something of a cross between an irresponsible drunk and a vicious hooligan is to offer examples—and there are many—of Irish ballplayers who, despite the ethnic stereotype of the "Sons of Erin," were not alcoholics, rowdies, or blackguards. For every Irish ballplayer in SABR's two-volume biography of nineteenth-century stars who fits the stereotype of the Irish born to drink, brawl, and break the law, there is a player like the idolized The

Only Nolan, the respected Billy McLean, or the redoubtable Connie Mack, each greatly admired for his skill, his integrity, or his career achievements. For every Irish ballplayer who qualifies for James's list of Drinking Men, there is an enshrined Hall of Famer like Orator Jim O'Rourke. A Yale Law School graduate, O'Rourke, when told that to sign a contract with Boston and its Protestant financial backers he would have to drop the "O" from his name, responded: "I would rather die than give up my father's name. A million dollars would not tempt me." For every Jim Devlin, banned from baseball for life for throwing games, there is a Kid Gleason, who retained his reputation for fairness and honesty as a manager even after eight of his Chicago White Sox players threw the 1919 World Series. Among the overflow crowd of five thousand in attendance at Gleason's funeral were Baseball Commissioner Kenesaw Mountain Landis, who had banned Shoeless Joe Jackson and his fellow Black Sox from the game, and fellow managers and Irishmen John McGraw and Connie Mack.

Among the nineteenth-century greats listed position by position in Alfred H. Spink's *The National Game*, first published in 1911, are several Irish players praised for their "sterling character," "excellent disposition," and "splendid habits." James Deacon McGuire, who caught and managed for over thirty years and later coached at Albion College, was known to have "never been fined, never put out of a game by an umpire." Long John Reilly, one of the early power hitters in his years with Cincinnati, won public acclaim for his modest conduct and was widely regarded as a model for self-discipline and team play in an era characterized by its rowdiness. Tommy Burns, the third baseman for Cap Anson's pennant-winning Chicago teams of the 1880s, never drank or smoked and was respected for his fairness and honesty as a player and a manager. Silent Mike Tiernan, who starred as a slugger and a base stealer with New York in the 1890s, earned his nickname for his dignity and his calm. In a 1902 article in the *Gael,* he was described as being "as honest as the sun, a sober gentlemanly professional player, . . . a credit to his team, . . . possessed [of] a record of never having been fined for disputing an umpire's decision."

Other Irish ballplayers in Spink's *The National Game* are singled out for their "braininess" and were instrumental in revolutionizing the professional game. Irish-born Tommy Bond, who won forty or more games in three consecutive seasons from 1879 to 1881, was one of the first to "throw the ball rather than pitch it" and is credited with perfecting the curveball after learning how to throw it from Hall of Famer Candy Cummings. Another Hall of Famer, Charles A. Comiskey, destined to become one of the most dominant and controversial baseball magnates of the twentieth century, revolutionized the position of first base in the late nineteenth century by playing far off the base when fielding his position. James Fogarty, a left fielder described by Spink as one of the "greatest who ever lived" was one of the first outfielders to earn a reputation for his defensive play because of his great speed, powerful throwing arm, and ability to make sensational catches. Tim Murnane, popular with his teammates because of his cheery disposition and credited with the first stolen base in National League history, eventually, after a brief stint umpiring, became one of the leading baseball writers of his day. He became renowned as a champion of the game's traditions and its old-time ballplayers and is credited with writing the first baseball column.

There were many stellar Irish ballplayers important to the early history of American baseball whose conduct did not conform to an ethnic stereotype, but the real historical issue of the Irish in baseball resides not in the character of the Irish but in the character of the professional game in the late nineteenth century. Steven Riess has pointed out that "the professionalization of the sport did not begin in earnest until after the Civil War in response to the strong demand by upper-middle class amateur clubs for winning teams." These ringers or revolvers were not only given money, but they were often given jobs or placed on company payrolls. As baseball in the 1870s became a means to earn money, it attracted young men who were poor and uneducated and otherwise trapped economically and socially within their underprivileged class.

That baseball's origins were in the Northeast and that professional play was concentrated in seaboard cities—Philadelphia, New York, Brooklyn, Baltimore, and Boston—also had a major impact on the character of baseball in the nineteenth century. Riess notes that 83 percent of the players in baseball's first professional league came from cities, and 40 percent of those players were from cities along the eastern seaboard. With baseball's professional game emerging as one of the few ways of escaping urban slums, it is hardly surprising, considering the waves of Famine and post-Famine Irish immigrants settling into shantytowns in America's cities, that the "Sons of Erin" seemed to have a natural affinity for baseball and its rowdy play.

As for the rowdyism in baseball, the obvious cause, rather than the ethnic character of the ballplayers, would seem to be the loosely organized, financially unstable, and fiercely competitive nature of the early professional game. With the biggest payouts and profits going to the most successful players and teams, with the most skilled players rotating to the highest bidder, and with less successful teams going bankrupt and failing to meet their payrolls, baseball quickly became a cutthroat business on and off the field. The Pittsburgh club earned its team name not because of its swashbuckling play but because it stole players under contract to another team.

When baseball formed the National League in 1876 and took its first major step toward becoming a business monopoly, the owners, who now saw themselves as magnates, instituted within a few years a reserve clause to gain absolute control over player movement and salaries. With players now in virtual bondage to the owners, the game became even more combative—Spalding applauded it as "war"—because victory or defeat determined a player's survival in the game and his livelihood. If extra money could be made by associating with gamblers, some players were willing to take the risk.

The early professional game may have been something like a war, but not because of the ethnic stereotype of the Irish as drunken brawlers. That the stereotype of the Irish seemed to fit the early character of baseball is undeniable, but it is also undeniable that the game's economics demanded a combativeness from its players and victories on its playing fields. Once baseball became a money-making opportunity, created ironically by the same class that had turned Irish immigrants into servants and day laborers, the Irish were among the first—and became the foremost—in seizing upon the game as a means to rise out of the urban ghetto. It is true that some Irish players in the first decades of professional baseball could not handle their new financial success and celebrity status and ended their careers and sometimes their lives in disgrace and tragedy. But it is also true that many performed so well and conducted themselves with such integrity that they became a major reason for the advancement of baseball into a major sport, a big business, and a national pastime worthy of the support and passion of the American public.

While baseball historians are fond of their stories of the wild Irish and the rowdy days of the early professional game, the Irish, in reality, played the game as they found it. Once they became a major part of early baseball, however, they played with such fierce determination and success that, although they were early targets for nativism, many of them also were eventually elected into baseball's hallowed Hall of Fame. The Irish belong in Cooperstown, not for their notoriety but for their achievements on the field and their contributions in the transformation of a leisurely pastime for gentlemen into *America's National Game.*

Works Cited

Ivor-Campbell, Frederick, Robert L. Tiemann, and Mark Rucker, eds. *Baseball's First Stars*. Cleveland: Society for American Baseball Research, 1996.
James, Bill. *The Bill James Historical Abstract*. New York: Villard, 1986.
Kennedy, Lucy. *The Sunlit Field*. New York: Crown, 1950.
McCaffrey, Lawrence J. "Forging Forward and Looking Back." In *The New York Irish*, edited by Ronald H. Bayor and Timothy J. Meagher, 213–33. Baltimore: Johns Hopkins University Press, 1996.
Rader, Benjamin G. *Baseball: A History of America's Game*. Urbana: University of Illinois Press, 1992.
Riess, Steven A. *City Games: The Evolution of American Urban Society and the Rise of Sports*. Urbana: University of Illinois Press, 1989.
Seymour, Harold. *Baseball: The Golden Years*. New York: Oxford University Press, 1960.

Spalding, A. G. *America's National Game.* New York: American Sports Publishing, 1911.

Spink, Alfred H. *The National Game.* St. Louis: National Game Publishing, 1911.

Tiemann, Robert L., and Mark Rucker, eds. *Nineteenth Century Stars.* Cleveland: Society for American Baseball Research, 1989.

Ward, Geoffrey C., and Ken Burns. *Baseball: An Illustrated History.* New York: Knopf, 1994.

Untitled and uncredited material from the *Sporting News* and the *Gael* provided by the National Baseball Library.

Part Four

*New Perspectives on Irish
Diasporic Communities*

12

The Irish of Chicago's Hull-House Neighborhood

Ellen Skerrett

A settlement looks about among its neighbors
and finds a complete absence of art.
  —Jane Addams, "A Function of the Social Settlement"

My grandmother contributed 25 cents toward a stained
glass window in [Holy Family Church]. She was proud
of this all of her life.
  —James T. Farrell, personal correspondence

Determined to live meaningful lives among the poor of Chicago's Nineteenth Ward, Jane Addams and Ellen Gates Starr (plates 1 and 2) founded Hull-House on September 18, 1889. The story of how two middle-class women brought beauty and refinement to a slum district captivated audiences around the country and focused positive attention on the settlement house movement. Indeed, Hull-House quickly achieved a reputation as "Chicago's Toynbee Hall," the famous London settlement organized in 1884 by Rev. Samuel A. Barnett.[1]

Addams and Starr began their work in Chicago with an unshakable belief in the transforming power of art and beauty. A *Chicago Tribune* feature in 1890, among the first of thousands of articles on Hull-House, praised the two women for sharing "their books, pictures, learning, gentle manner, esthetic taste" with the "uncultivated." In her own eloquent account written for the *Ladies' Home Journal,* Addams recalled the excitement she felt on discovering "a fine old house standing well back from the street . . . [with] pillars of exceptionally pure Corinthian design and proportion." Clearly influenced by John Ruskin and William Morris, Addams and Starr decorated the old Hull mansion on Halsted Street with "photographs and other impedimenta . . . collected in Europe, and with a few bits of family mahogany." And they hung their "best and largest photographs," the Madonnas of Raphael, where children in the day nursery and kindergarten could see them (plate 3).[2]

Like middle- and upper-class Protestants of their generation, Addams and Starr regarded European cathedrals and their artistic treasures as powerful symbols of refinement and beauty. In the 1880s, they had spent considerable time together in Munich, Rome, and Madrid, studying great masterpieces and church interiors. Indeed, thanks to Ellen's aunt, Eliza Allen Starr, Chicago's most famous Catholic convert, the young women secured coveted tickets to ceremonies in St. Peter's in Rome in conjunction with Pope Leo XIII's jubilee in 1888. It was during this trip abroad that Addams resolved to establish a "cathedral of humanity," a place both large and beautiful, dedicated to human solidarity.[3]

On their return to Chicago, the young women formulated plans for a settlement and committed themselves to making "the aesthetic and artistic a vital influence in the lives of their neighbors." Personal experience only deepened their conviction that rich and poor alike had a right to art and beauty. In working with children at Hull-House, Starr noted that the mind of the young responds "almost miraculously . . . to what is beautiful in its environment, and rejects what is ugly . . ." Addams observed the same thing in the settlement nursery. She recalled that, surrounded by reproductions of Raphael, Donatello, and Della Robbia, the neighborhood children "talk[ed] in a familiar way to the babies on the wall, and sometimes climb[ed] upon the chairs to kiss them."[4]

Less than two years after beginning their work in Chicago, Addams and Starr had persuaded a wealthy donor to finance an art gallery, the first new structure in what became a complex of thirteen buildings by 1907. Reverend Barnett, vicar of St. Jude's and the internationally known founder of Toynbee Hall, was the featured speaker at the opening of Hull-House's Butler Art Gallery on June 20, 1891 (plate 4). Praising the work of Addams and Starr, he recounted his own success with "Free Picture Shows" among the poor of London's notorious Whitechapel district. "Pictures were invaluable for poor people," Barnett told the "public-spirited and distinguished people" who gathered in the old Hull mansion, reminding them that "the common enjoyment of common treasures would make a common life the strength of great cities." Art Institute president Charles L. Hutchinson agreed, especially since art "brings home to the people conceptions of the great realities of Christ and immortality, and . . . develops taste and the higher purposes and instincts of humanity."[5]

Although journalists and social reformers described Hull-House and the Butler Art Gallery as the only places of beauty in the neighborhood, this was hardly the case. Just a few blocks away stood Holy Family Church, a landmark on Twelfth Street since its dedication in 1860 (plate 5). And right next door was St. Ignatius College (1870), a massive four-story structure with an ornate library, museum, and meeting hall. The Gothic church of Holy Family, built by Irish immigrants, was a working-class "art institute" with stained glass windows, intricate stencils and frescoes, elaborately carved altars, and statues. Indeed, one of its most prominent features was a copy of Murillo's "Holy Family," which hung above the main altar. Also nearby were the parishes of St. Francis of Assisi (German), St. Wenceslaus (Bohemian), and Notre Dame (French). Considerably smaller than Holy Family, each church nevertheless was a place of beauty and refinement. And others would follow. In 1899, Italian Catholics began worshiping in Holy Guardian Angel Church and, by 1910, a second Italian parish, Our Lady of Pompeii, organized to meet the needs of the growing population.

As a result of Addams's skills as a writer and lecturer, Hull-House soon became "one of the most useful and most widely known institutions in the world for the uplifting of the neglected masses." In an address before the School of Applied Ethics in Plymouth, Massachusetts, in 1892, Addams discussed the underlying motives behind settlement work and its attraction for educated young men and women who "long to give tangible expression to the democratic ideal." Drawing upon her own experience on Chicago's Near West Side, she asserted that the poor "live for the moment side by side, many of them without knowledge of each other, without fellowship, without local tradition or public spirit, without social organization of any kind." And she lamented that "The people who might [remedy this situation], who have the social tact and training, the large houses, and the traditions and customs of hospitality, live in other parts of the city."[6]

Addams's harsh assessment of neighborhood life would have confounded the twenty thousand Irish men, women, and children who belonged to Holy Family, the most highly organized English-speaking parish in Chicago. Not only did they worship in one of the most beautiful churches in the city, but they came into regular contact with educated people, Jesuit priests and brothers, the Religious of the Sacred Heart, and the Sisters of Charity of the Blessed Virgin Mary, who taught five thousand young people in Holy Family's schools, fully 15 percent of the entire Catholic school population in the city in 1890. Equally significant, the "mother parish" of the Near West Side had already fostered religious vocations among the children of Irish immigrants, providing leadership in the immediate neighborhood as well as in new Catholic parishes beyond.[7]

That the Irish of Holy Family remained virtually invisible in the early scholarly literature on Hull-House is not surprising. By her own account, Addams preferred newly arrived Italians who reminded her of the picturesque quarters she had visited in Naples and Rome. In March 1889, for example, she began "looking up different slums" in Chicago with an attendance officer from the Board of Education. While expressing compassion for the poverty of the North Side Italians, she noted that the "mild eyed Madonnas . . . never begged nor even complained, and in all respects are immensely more attractive to me than the Irish neighborhood I went into last week."[8]

In light of Addams's apparent dislike of the Irish, it is a mystery why she opened her settlement just blocks from Holy Family, the most prominent Irish Catholic church in the city—and the most Roman. While she shared many of Starr's ideas about beauty and art, Addams remained deeply suspicious of elaborate Catholic ritual. During her 1888 trip to Rome, for example, she wrote her sister lengthy descriptions of a beatification ceremony in St. Peter's Basilica. Although clearly awed by the decorations in the chapel "ablaze with candles, thousands of them on all sides," the procession of "thirteen gorgeously red cardinals," and the very fine music, she concluded that it was "absurd . . . to connect all this pageant and pride with the religion which Christ himself taught." Moreover, Addams characterized the veneration of saints' relics as "depravity," wondering, "how in the world sensible people ever got into it."[9]

This photographic essay explores the neglected Irish dimension of the Hull-House neighborhood. It is an attempt to describe the Irish of Holy Family as they saw themselves, not as impoverished slum dwellers without fellowship or organization, but as urban, practicing Catholics whose church and schools invested neighborhood life with meaning and beauty. The photographs published here, many for the first time, will address three questions: what did Holy Family parish look like in the nineteenth century, how did it become a sacred place in the lives of Irish Catholics and their neighborhood, and what difference did it make for the larger city?

Creating Sacred Space on the Prairie

It is no exaggeration to say that the Jesuit parish of Holy Family put the Irish on the map. When the Catholic diocese of Chicago was established in 1843, there was a single parish in the city, St. Mary's, at Madison Street and Wabash Avenue. Between 1846 and 1856, ten more parishes organized, but even these were inadequate for the rapidly expanding Irish and German Catholic population. The extent of the problem was clearly revealed in August 1856 when Rev. Arnold Damen, SJ, preached a mission. Twelve thousand men, women, and children received Communion, but "[none] of the churches could accommodate the multitude that crowded from all parts of the city." Even with its new galleries, St. Mary's Cathedral was too small, and the mission was transferred to the Irish parish of Holy Name on the North Side.[10]

After conferring with his Jesuit superiors in St. Louis, Father Damen agreed to establish a parish in Chicago but refused the bishop's request to take over Holy Name as well as his offer of property at Madison Street and Ogden Avenue. Instead, the forty-two-year-old priest purchased thirty-two lots near the intersection of Blue Island Avenue and Twelfth Street, directly south and west of the city's business district, convinced that "Here we will have a large Catholic population at once, sufficient to fill a large church." And he was right. Between 1857 and 1860, 151 men and women were married at Holy Family and 1,462 babies were baptized.[11]

While sacramental records confirmed Father Damen's optimism, they tell only one part of the Holy Family story. When the *Chicago Daily Journal* announced that a church, college, and free school would be constructed "on a scale of magnitude equal to any of the same character in the United States," the *Chicago Tribune* struck back. In its lead editorial of May 25, 1857, the widely respected abolitionist newspaper "beg[ged] Protestants to think twice before they aid in any way the founding of Jesuit institutions in this city." Reflecting nativist sentiments of the day, the *Tribune* claimed: "We do this not in a spirit of intolerance, but upon the warrant of facts which show that the Society of Jesus is the most virulent and relentless enemy of the Protestant faith and Democratic government."[12]

The anti-Catholicism of the *Tribune* notwithstanding, there was another, equally compelling, obstacle. As the Depression of 1857 deepened, Chicagoans of all classes began to feel the effects of bank failures in the East and Midwest. Nevertheless, Father Damen raised thirty thousand dollars in pledges toward the new church and college on Twelfth Street, informing his provincial in May that "people are astonished that I can get money at all." The cornerstone laying of Holy Family Church on August 23, 1857, set the tone for parish life for decades to come. Press accounts commented favorably on the large crowd that gathered for the "appropriate and imposing ceremonies" conducted by Bishop Anthony O'Regan, "assisted by the entire body of the Chicago Catholic clergy." Moreover, the presence of "several military groups and the Hibernian Society" confirmed Holy Family's status as an Irish parish.[13]

Although newspapers in the nineteenth century routinely characterized Catholic devotion as spectacle, providing readers with detailed accounts of rituals and their meaning, there were limits to such favorable coverage. The *Tribune,* for example, regarded it as scandalous that Irish Catholics sacrificed to build beautiful churches. An 1857 editorial claimed that "nine-tenths of the beggars" in Chicago were Irish and that "hundreds of poor servant girls and laboring men, now in want of food, shelter, and fire" have spent their hard-earned money on the Catholic Church. Indeed, the newspaper suggested that Bishop O'Regan ought to turn Holy Name Cathedral "into a workshop for the unemployed." Yet as construction proceeded on Holy Family Church, the *Tribune* began to sound a different note. When the parish sponsored a five-day fair in Metropolitan Hall downtown during the Christmas season of 1857, the newspaper conceded that "the Church will be one of the finest stone edifices in the West and will add greatly to the character of our growing city for architectural taste and grandeur."[14]

According to Father Damen's written reports, by August 1858, approximately eight thousand men, women, and children worshiped in the temporary frame church every Sunday and "quite a number of them assist at the holy sacrifice of the mass every day." Nearly 400 children had been prepared for their First Communion and 258 confirmed. He reported, "We have also commenced two day-schools for the poor," with an attendance between 300 and 400 children. Despite these signs of spiritual success, however, Father Damen noted, "times have turned out in such a manner that we foresee nothing but misery and poverty. Last winter we . . . [relieved] about 3,000 persons or families. This winter the poverty will be greater and we must be prepared to relieve a greater number of poor people."[15]

Considering the material circumstances of Holy Family parishioners, did it make sense to invest so much money in a permanent church capable of accommodating six thousand people? Far from being a luxury, the new edifice was essential because the temporary wooden structure was filled to overflowing—even on weekdays. During May 1859, for example, "about eight hundred persons, for the most part women, came to mass [and devotions in honor of the Blessed Virgin Mary] and in the evening as many men to the sermon." These numbers were all the more significant because they reflected the profound changes wrought by the "Devotional Revolution" in Ireland. After the Great Famine of the 1840s, Irish Catholics became more regular in their practice of religion, contributing to the erection of new churches and enthusiastically supporting such devotions as novenas, rosaries, benediction, and Stations of the Cross. Just as important was the growing presence of Irish males in the pews of American Catholic churches. That working-class Irish men attended mass week in and week out amazed—and sometimes puzzled—social reformers. But as the Holy Family experience makes abundantly clear, the benefits of attending church were cultural as well as spiritual.[16]

With its price tag of two hundred thousand dollars, Holy Family was the most expensive church erected in Chicago in the 1850s—and the most beautiful. As news accounts confirmed, creating this sacred space was not a pious activity for the fainthearted. It involved cooperation, commitment, and money—lots of it—as well as competition. That Holy Family compared favorably with the Gothic edifices built by Protestant congregations was no accident. Father Damen hired John Van Osdel, the city's leading architect, to complete the interior, and he specified that Robert Carse, the noted New York stained glass expert, create windows equal in quality to those in St. James Episcopal Church on the North Side! Moreover, the brickwork of Holy Family was to be "of best possible character," and Patrick O'Connor's workers were instructed to fill the joints "solid with good lime and clean lake shore sand mortar."[17]

Contrary to conventional wisdom, investing scarce resources in refinement and beauty paid dividends. In addition to providing jobs for immigrant laborers, the construction of the Gothic edifice actually helped to build community in the developing neighborhood. Accustomed to "penny-a-week" collections for new chapels in Ireland, the Chicago Irish responded enthusiastically to appeals for Holy Family Church. Right from the start, the parish was divided into seventeen districts (much like the precincts of a city ward), each with its own volunteer collector who went door-to-door soliciting funds. Twelve more men served as "rovers" in the city at large, relying on their own personal contacts to raise funds in offices, hotels, saloons, and factories. The campaign to complete Holy Family did more than strengthen the link between parish and neighborhood; it also boosted the political careers of aldermen "Honest John" Comiskey and Patrick Rafferty. During their tenure on the city council, the immigrant Irish aldermen voted for public works projects that materially improved the neighborhood. And Comiskey and Rafferty also used their influence to ensure that the spacious grounds of Holy Family Church and St. Ignatius College remained intact.[18]

The annual fairs in the parish played a crucial role in establishing Holy Family as a place of culture, according to the *Tribune,* "in the outskirts of the city." The lavish exhibition and concert, which opened in the unconsecrated nave of the Gothic church in June 1859, for example, began a tradition that continued for decades. Part highbrow entertainment and bazaar, Holy Family's fairs featured drama and music as well as the sale of domestic goods, everything from fancy needlework and homemade delicacies to rosaries, paintings, and statues. Few congregations—Protestant or Catholic—were as successful in raising funds, and Chicago newspapers regularly reported the proceeds, which ranged from $8,500 in the 1860s to a phenomenal $20,000 in the 1890s. Beyond their significance as an important source of revenue, these events contributed to Holy Family's growing reputation as a center of neighborhood life and refinement.[19]

The completion of Holy Family Church in three years' time was a remarkable accomplishment for a predominantly working-class Irish parish. (The much larger St. Patrick's in New York, begun in 1858, for example, was under construction for twenty more years.) Although the *Tribune* characterized the exterior of the Gothic edifice as "huge and unattractive, [looming] above the humble [homes] . . . like a stately ox among so many sheep," the newspaper praised its interior as "one of the most elegant we . . . have seen, and will challenge comparison certainly with any in the Northwest." The prediction was soon fulfilled, thanks to Anthony Buscher's craftsmanship.[20]

According to neighborhood legend, Father Damen found the German immigrant carving cigar store Indians and persuaded him to devote his artistic talents to Holy Family Church, with dazzling result. Buscher began his work at a time when American Protestants were debating the propriety of ornament in their churches, especially such marks of refinement as stained glass windows and frescoes. That the Irish of Holy Family had no such qualms when it came to enriching the interior of their Gothic edifice became clear in 1861 when they took up a collection for a statue of St. Patrick. Buscher's carving of the patron saint of Ireland didn't disappoint: the only gold-leafed "St. Patrick" in Chicago, it constituted a positive symbol of group identity in an era when the Irish were still being portrayed as crime-ridden and drunken sots. And that was merely the beginning.[21]

Buscher's masterpiece (plate 6), financed by the contributions of eight hundred men and women, was a fifty-two-foot-high main altar, a veritable "Communion of Saints" that symbolically linked parishioners with God in heaven. Just above the gold tabernacle that held the Blessed Sacrament stood figures representing the Greek and Roman doctors of the Church. At the very top were statues of Faith, Hope, and Charity, the cardinal virtues to which all Catholics aspired (each statue bearing its own distinctive symbol). But for many parishioners who had left behind beloved parents and siblings in Ireland, the main altar took on new layers of meaning. Surrounding the traditional oil painting of the Holy Family were statues of Jesus' maternal grandparents and cousins—reunited under the watchful gaze of celestial cherubs and God the Father. And, over the years, more than a few mothers and fathers sitting in the pews must have thought, "Sure weren't they the Holy Family, they only had the one!"[22]

Despite the fact that the ritual blessing and mass took the better part of Sunday, October 15, 1865, crowds remained behind long after bishops from Milwaukee, Detroit, Alton, and Pittsburgh had left the church. Why? Part of the reason had to do with the illumination of the main altar by gas jets, a marvel of technology. Because Buscher worked in wood, rather than marble, he was able to create an altar of massive proportions, one that nearly touched the ceiling of Holy Family Church. Press accounts were lavish in their praise, describing it as "the most beautiful altar ever erected on the soil of the new world." But there was more to it than that, asserted the *Chicago Republican*. Explaining that Catholicism was "a religion of symbols," the newspaper insisted that "it appeals to the soul through the senses . . . employ[ing] poetry and music, sculpture and painting, and the symbolism of color to reach the feelings, and connect them with the divine by a bridge of beauty."[23]

In terms of its structure and organization, Holy Family was clearly a Jesuit parish, yet it was also unmistakably Irish—with one important difference. Very few of its members had ever worshiped in such a magnificent church in Ireland. Indeed, the Gothic edifice on Twelfth Street was wholly an American creation, supported by voluntary contributions, and, thanks to Father Damen, it enjoyed a national reputation. Born in Holland in 1815, Father Damen emigrated in 1837, determined to become an American Jesuit missionary and preacher. And he did. Although English was his second language, Father Damen gained a reputation as a speaker of "uncommon eloquence." His sermons in the College Church of St. Louis University between 1847 and 1857 drew "all classes of persons," and a newspaper dubbed him the "Catholic Beecher," after the famous Presbyterian minister Lyman Beecher. Moreover, during his first two decades in Chicago, Father Damen personally conducted more than two hundred missions, making Holy Family a household name in cities across the country.[24]

Catholic Schools in the Urban Neighborhood

Far from being a "ghetto" parish that limited the aspirations of poor Irish families, Holy Family set new standards for church building and decoration as well as for Catholic education. At the same time that architect Van Osdel was completing the interior of the Gothic edifice on Twelfth Street, the Religious of the Sacred Heart commissioned him to draw up plans for their new convent and academy on Taylor Street (plates 7 and 8). Significantly, although the *Tribune* continued to criticize the Jesuits of Holy Family, the newspaper had looked favorably on the girls' school because it also served the city's Protestant elite. Under the heading "West Side Improvements," in January 1860, for example, the *Tribune* noted that the nuns were building a sixty-thousand-dollar structure "in the same style they have at New Orleans, Philadelphia, Baltimore, St. Louis and other cities in the United States. . . ."[25]

Mother Margaret Galwey, RSCJ, a native of County Cork, Ireland, welcomed the opportunity to establish a foundation in the Jesuit parish. Not only had the sisters' boarding school on the North Side become crowded, but its location near the Rush Street Bridge was a danger to students. On the sparsely settled West Side, however, the "Seminary" would enjoy landscaped grounds with ample room for expansion. Although there were obvious class differences between parishioners and the teaching sisters, the Irish of Holy Family held the Religious of the Sacred Heart in great esteem, as events in August 1860 revealed. In their convent journal (written in French), the nuns commented favorably on the crowds of parishioners who turned out to help them move. "Never before had the city of Chicago witnessed such a parade," they claimed. The daily newspapers concurred, noting that "this removal of ordinary household goods, chattels and fixtures was made quite imposing by a procession of forty drays and thirty-five express wagons, in all seventy-five loaded vehicles."[26]

In contrast to the publicly active Irish Sisters of Mercy, who were known as Chicago's "walking nuns," the Religious of the Sacred Heart remained semi-cloistered. Nevertheless, through their work in the classroom they influenced thousands of young people in Holy Family parish, using tuition from boarders to pay the costs of educating the poor. While the Constitution of the Society of the Sacred Heart clearly established that impoverished children enjoyed "additional claims to the tenderness and zeal" of the sisters, the depth of their commitment was astonishing: from 1867 through 1899, the "Madames" (as they were often called) annually taught nine hundred students and also prepared classes for First Communion and confirmation. Father Damen noted, gratefully, in his reports to his Jesuit superiors that in addition to contributing toward the construction of Holy Family, the Sacred Heart nuns "render immense service to our church. They teach the parochial school of the girls . . . and they do it for nothing. . . ."[27]

Catholic schools strengthened parishioners' ties to the neighborhood and deepened the bonds of community. Yet from the Protestant vantage point, there was little reason to celebrate the growth of parishes such as Holy Family. On the contrary, warned Baptist minister Warren Randolph, DD, of Boston. At a national meeting in Chicago in May 1867, he asserted that the future of America as a Christian country was imperiled by "Romanists who have already come up like the frogs of Egypt, into all our houses, and who are still pouring in upon us at the rate of almost a thousand a day."[28]

To ensure these arrived immigrants would have access to Catholic education, Father Damen sought more teaching nuns from a predominantly Irish order, the Sisters of Charity of the Blessed Virgin Mary (BVMs). Founded by Dublin native Mary Frances Clarke in Philadelphia in 1833, the community had grown dramatically since the nuns established their motherhouse in Dubuque, Iowa, in 1843. Despite initial setbacks, the BVMs prospered to such an extent that they were able to make a foundation in Chicago in 1867, a decision that had profound consequences for the city as well as for their order. Father Damen's request was characteristically blunt. "We would like to get nine Sisters," he wrote the nuns' spiritual director, "but try to send three or four at once if possible and let them be good teachers, so as to make a good impression, for the first impression is generally the lasting one."[29]

The task fell to Sister Mary Agatha Hurley, a native of Cloyne, County Cork, and a small band of sisters who arrived in Chicago in August 1867. The contrast with Iowa's rich farmland could not have been more shocking. Nearly sixty years later, Sister Mary Scholastica McLaughlin still recalled with clarity the brutal heat wave and the sight of "three hundred children whose laughs grew stronger the louder they screamed, jumping over gates." She remembered the taste of lukewarm Lake Michigan water, noting poignantly that "those days we lived like the poor who never buy ice nor did we want it." Within two months, the community of eleven nuns could point with pride to an enrollment of 850 students in two schools, "with 150 more striving for entrance." Sister Agatha and her BVM colleagues continued to live and teach in makeshift quarters until 1870, when the modern brick school and convent of St. Aloysius opened on Maxwell Street (plate 9).[30]

What difference did these women religious make in the lives of Irish immigrants? No clearer example exists than the career of Mary Kane (plate 10). Born in Carrigaholt, County Clare, Ireland, in 1855, she came with her widowed mother to Holy Family parish in 1865. As a student under the care of the Religious of the Sacred Heart, Mary participated fully in the sacramental life of the parish, making her First Communion and confirmation in front of the massive altar in the Gothic church on Twelfth Street. In August 1867, she joined hundreds of children gathered to welcome Sister Agatha Hurley and was entrusted with the altar

1. Jane Addams (1860–1935), c. 1889. Jane Addams Memorial Collection, Special Collections, The University Library, The University of Illinois at Chicago.

2. Ellen Gates Starr (1859–1940). Jane Addams Memorial Collection, Special Collections, The University Library, The University of Illinois at Chicago.

3. Photograph of the Hull-House nursery showing the Madonnas of Raphael that Jane Addams and Ellen Gates Starr hung on the walls. Jane Addams Memorial Collection, Special Collections, The University Library, The University of Illinois at Chicago.

4. Hull-House and Butler Art Gallery, c. 1892. Jane Addams Memorial Collection, Special Collections, The University Library, The University of Illinois at Chicago.

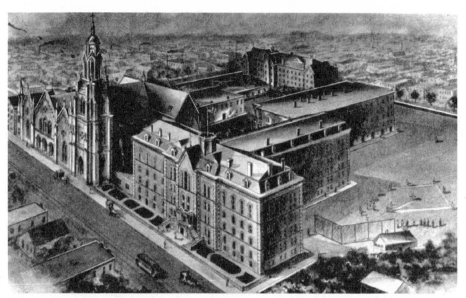

5. Engraving of the Holy Family complex from Blue Island Avenue, 1890s. Reprinted from *Holy Family Parish: Priests and People*, by Brother Thomas Mulkerins, SJ (Chicago: Universal Press, 1923).

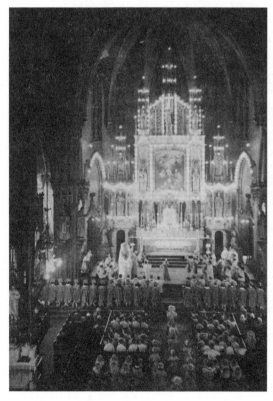

6. Anthony Buscher's 1865 main altar in Holy Family Church was illuminated by electric lights in 1899. Sisters of Charity, BVM Archives.

7. View of Sacred Heart Convent Academy and grounds, later the Chicago Hebrew Institute. Chicago Jewish Archives, Spertus Institute of Jewish Studies.

8. Sacred Heart Convent Chapel, 1879, a rare example of women's sacred space. Photo courtesy of Woodlands Academy of the Sacred Heart.

9. St. Aloysius School, 631 West Maxwell Street, c. 1880. Sisters of Charity, BVM Archives.

10. Mother Isabella Kane, BVM (1855–1935). Reprinted from *Holy Family Parish.*

11. Holy Family Church, St. Ignatius College, 1892.
Reprinted from *Holy Family Parish*.

12. O'Leary house and neighborhood, c. 1871. Special Collections and Preservation Division, Chicago Public Library.

13. St. Joseph wearing a derby hat, side altar, Holy Family Church. Author's collection.

14. Mother Elizabeth Sheridan, RSCJ (1847–1926). Reprinted from *Holy Family Parish.*

15. Confirmation Day Parade, 1890s. Reprinted from *Holy Family Parish.*

16. Cartoon of Alderman John Powers (1852–1930) throwing a rock through Hull-House window. *Chicago Times-Herald,* March 5, 1898. Chicago Historical Society (ICHi-30814). Courtesy Chicago Historical Society.

17. Aerial view of Hull-House and Holy Family Church prior to urban renewal, c. 1960. Jane Addams Memorial Collection, Special Collections, The University Library, The University of Illinois at Chicago.

stone for the nuns' chapel on Halsted Street. Mary Kane not only became a diligent BVM pupil, but in 1870 she joined the order, among the first of 196 young women from Holy Family parish to take the veil during the next fifty years.[31]

Her working-class origins notwithstanding, Sister Mary Isabella Kane became an accomplished musician and art teacher and she steadily rose through the ranks of her community, eventually serving as superior in academies in Iowa and Kansas. Elected head of her order in 1919, Mother Isabella was directly involved in opening thirty-three new schools in the Midwest and California. But two Chicago institutions bore her special imprint: Immaculata High School (1922), designed by the noted architect Barry Byrne; and the Art Deco skyscraper known as Mundelein College (1931). Not only did Mother Isabella arrange financing for the million-dollar liberal arts college during the depths of the depression, but she took an active role in decorating the fifteen-story limestone "temple of classic beauty in the heart of a great city." Shortly before Mother Isabella Kane's death in 1935, Loyola University awarded her an honorary doctor of law degree, publicly acknowledging her role as an "eminent builder."[32]

That Holy Family parish also succeeded in educating the sons of Irish immigrants was due in no small part to the "Brothers' School" directed by Jesuits Andrew and Thomas O'Neill. As Famine refugees from County Wicklow, Ireland, the O'Neill brothers knew firsthand the difficulties facing newcomers in America. From the 1860s through the 1890s, their school earned a reputation for preparing nearly thirty thousand boys to function in the larger society, with no distinction made for students unable to afford the tuition of fifty cents a month. In terms of its physical plant, the Brothers' School on Morgan Street compared favorably with local public schools, and it enjoyed several advantages. The eleven-month course of study emphasized mathematics and bookkeeping, skills that had practical application in Chicago's expanding economy. And at a time when there were few Catholic teachers in the public schools, the faculty at Holy Family included Irish schoolmasters as well as young women who had grown up in the parish.[33]

Revising Stereotypes

To an extent that historians have not fully appreciated, parishes represented a new beginning for immigrants who had escaped Famine and eviction. By building and decorating churches and establishing schools and charitable organizations, the Irish created a place for themselves in Chicago. Moreover, as the case of Holy Family demonstrates, participation in religious rituals and parish organizations contributed to a more positive image of the Irish city wide. From the 1860s through the early 1900s, Chicago's newspapers routinely commented on the crowds at Sunday mass, the decorations at Christmas and Easter, and the devotions, such as the Stations of the Cross and the May crownings. But year after year, it was the Corpus Christi and Confirmation Day parades that received the most attention. The sight of hundreds of children dressed in white marching through the neighborhood—models of order and decorum—offered visible proof that the Irish were becoming devout, disciplined urban dwellers.[34]

One of the most cherished traditions to emerge in Holy Family was the annual St. Patrick's Day celebration. In contrast to the official parade and banquets downtown, which were predominantly male oriented, these events brought together thousands of Irish men, women, and children. What attracted them? Primarily entertainment, which was remarkably broad in range. An early program, for example, featured such crowd pleasers as traditional Irish airs and music by the juvenile band along with selections from Mestrino sung by eight choristers "dressed in Jewish costume." Among the dramatic presentations were "The President and the Office-Seeker," a farce entitled "The Spectre Bridegroom," and "The Brigade at Fontenoy," a patriotic ballad beloved by Irish nationalists. The evening, termed a "brilliant success" by the *Chicago Times,* concluded with four grand tableaux vivants depicting scenes from the life of St. Patrick. Far from being stuffy, staid affairs, the March 17 celebrations were a source of genuine delight for adults and children alike. Particularly memorable were the first-night performances by children in the primary grades, who sang songs and answered catechism questions. In addition to bridging the gap between Irish immigrants and American-born sons and daughters, these performances fostered pride in a common Catholic identity. Audiences eagerly awaited Rev. Andrew O'Neill's query, "What is the One True Church?" Invariably, a boy or girl would reply with great enthusiasm, "Holy Family," bringing the house down with laughter.[35]

Holy Family's commitment to beauty and refinement was further enhanced in 1870 with the opening of St. Ignatius College (plate 11), the forerunner of Loyola University. According to one Jesuit visitor from Europe, the $230,000 building just east of the Gothic church was begun "on a large scale to make it possible to compete with the Protestant colleges and the public schools, which are like palaces." While few Irish parishioners could afford the luxury of a college education, they enjoyed the benefits of art and culture. The first production in Chicago of Mozart's *Twelfth Mass,* for example, occurred at the dedication of Holy Family in 1860, no small feat in a city that lacked a symphony orchestra. But it was the organ, with its sixty-three stops and nearly four thousand pipes imported from Paris, that assured Holy Family's reputation for fine music. Built by Louis Mitchel of Montreal, "The Largest Church Organ in the United States" was inaugurated with a great concert on October 20, 1870, featuring selections from Rossini, Mendelssohn, Haydn, and Handel.[36]

Had it not been for the Great Fire of October 1871, Chicagoans may have remained unaware of the modest circumstances in which many Holy Family parishioners lived. All that changed when a fire in the barn behind Catherine and Patrick O'Leary's frame house on DeKoven Street roared out of control and spread eastward, eventually destroying the city's business district as well as residential areas on the north and south sides of the river. Newspaper reporters quickly pinned the blame on Mrs. O'Leary and her cow, creating perhaps America's first urban legend. In recounting his search for the O'Leary home, a *New York Daily Tribune* correspondent drew on accepted stereotypes of Irish Catholic immigrants as poverty-stricken and superstitious. He described the neighborhood of "shabby wooden houses, with dirty dooryards and unpainted fences falling to decay" and "[s]latternly women [whose] bare-legged children skirmished with the geese." Proclaiming that "there was no shabbier hut in Chicago nor Tipperary," the reporter informed his readers that the O'Leary house (plate 12) bore a curse as powerful as any in Greek mythology. Moreover, in characterizing Catherine O'Leary, a respected member of Holy Family Church, as "Our Lady of the Lamp," the *New York Tribune* account denigrated Irish Catholic veneration of saints, especially Mary.[37]

Lingering anti-Irish and anti-Catholic sentiment may explain, in part, why Holy Family parishioners soon embraced a different myth about the Great Fire of 1871. It involved Father Damen, who was preaching a mission in Brooklyn when he learned that Chicago was in flames. During the night, while "praying for the safety of his church and the homes of his parishioners," Father Damen sought the intercession of Our Lady of Perpetual Help. If Holy Family were spared destruction, he promised to light candles in front of her statue. Whether the Gothic church and St. Ignatius College were directly threatened remains unclear, but the wind did shift and crossed the river, burning down huge sections of the city. Popular belief in the myth of divine intervention was apparent within weeks: at a special ceremony, parishioners sang "the Miserere to atone for the faults, committed during the last year, and . . . the Te Deum, to extend thanks to God for 'all blessings received.'" Moreover, according to the pulpit announcements, there were collections "after all the masses to keep lights constantly burning before the statue of Our Lady of Perpetual Help," fulfilling Father Damen's vow.[38]

Investing in the Future

However despised by Protestants, Catholic material culture continued to matter to Irish men, women, and children, and it also had long-term consequences for the larger city. In contrast to mainline Protestant churches and Jewish synagogues that sought new locations after the Great Fire of 1871, for example, Holy Family parishioners reinvested in their neighborhood. The litany of improvements to the church alone was impressive, indeed: new side altars (plate 13); Stations of the

Cross; intricately carved confessionals; imported statues from Europe; and in 1874, a massive 266-foot tower built by parishioner James P. Tracey. Equally significant was the expansion of the parish's school system to include three new institutions—Guardian Angel on Forquer Street, St. Joseph on Thirteenth Street, and St. Agnes on Morgan Street. In an increasingly urban neighborhood, these branch schools not only reduced the distances smaller children had to walk, but they also helped to build up the parish. (By his own account, Father Damen estimated that the sisters reached at least four-fifths of the congregation through the Catholic schools.) While critics continued to lambaste the Irish commitment to "brick-and-mortar" Catholicism, Holy Family's success could not be ignored. Far from being a burden to taxpayers, one newspaper noted, the parish had filled up the neighborhood "with a dense and closely settled population—thus swelling the assessed value of the property by many millions and increasing the revenues of the city and county in a corresponding ratio."[39]

Although continued immigration from Ireland during the late 1870s and 1880s brought new life to Holy Family parish, depressions in the local economy and labor strikes profoundly affected the neighborhood. A Jesuit census taker put the matter succinctly by expressing the hope that "before the end of this long and tedious Visitation of the Parish not more than 300 families had struck their tents & pitched them elsewhere."[40] Left behind were many destitute Irish men and women, as the Little Sisters of the Poor—a third community of nuns in the neighborhood—discovered in 1876 when they opened a home for the elderly in the Hull mansion on Halsted Street (the same red-brick building in which Addams and Starr would later begin their social settlement).

Almost immediately, however, the Little Sisters of the Poor made plans to erect a new complex because their rented space had become overcrowded and "badly adapted to the present requirements." Using donations from their daily rounds of begging, they purchased a large tract of land along Harrison Street, and before long, sixteen nuns, many of them of Irish birth, were caring for upwards of two hundred men and women without "distinction made as to creed or nationality." A few weeks after Hull-House opened, Archbishop Patrick A. Feehan dedicated yet another brick building for the growing number of elderly. He praised the sisters' devotion to the poor and commented on the beauty of the chapel where the aged and infirm would worship. And the archbishop reminded the great crowd at the dedication that "it would be well for all of every class and condition" to see for themselves the good work being done by the Little Sisters of the Poor.[41]

As far as the Irish of Holy Family were concerned, there was not anything unusual about men and women who chose to live among the poor, caring for the aged, teaching in classrooms, and preparing children to receive the sacraments. In contrast to Irish politicians, whose exploits provided colorful copy for newspapers and grist for reformers, men and women religious neither expected nor sought public notice. Yet the presence of nuns, especially, did not go unobserved or unappreciated by neighborhood residents. Indeed, even Jane Addams of Hull-House benefited. While riding the streetcar home one evening, she discovered that an Italian laborer had paid her way. Drawing comfort from this "little courtesy," Addams asked the Irish conductor to point out her benefactor and was told, "I cannot tell one dago from another when they are in a gang, but sure, any one of them would do it for you as quick as they would for the Sisters."[42]

Elizabeth Mary Sheridan (plate 14) and Thomas S. Fitzgerald offer classic examples of the way in which "homegrown" talent provided leadership and continuity in an Irish-American neighborhood. Born in London in 1847, Lizzie Sheridan came to Chicago as an infant. She made her First Communion in the original frame church of Holy Family and was the first girl from the parish to enroll in Sacred Heart Convent Academy in 1860. After graduation, Sheridan began her teaching career in the Brothers' School in a classroom of seventy-five boys. The experience stood her in good stead after she joined the Religious of the Sacred Heart and was appointed principal of the girls' school on Taylor Street in 1878. Maintaining order and educational standards for nearly one thousand students was a challenge, but Mother Sheridan "quickly [won] the esteem and confidence of both parents and pupils . . . [and] her name was a household word throughout the parish for more than twenty years."[43]

Having grown up in Holy Family, Sheridan was well aware of class distinctions between girls in the Sacred Heart Convent boarding school and those in the "poor school." But she also understood and valued the power of Catholic ritual to mediate difference. Her staff made sure that girls from the parish were as properly outfitted as the boarders in white dresses and long white veils for First Communion and confirmation, the sacraments that symbolized their "coming of age" as Catholics. That the Religious of the Sacred Heart took great pride in this work is undeniable. In reports to their motherhouse in Paris, they described "the grand parish school" in Holy Family as "the principal work of our mission." Indeed, a high point of Mother Sheridan's tenure occurred in 1886 when "all the nuns and pupils from the Academy had the privilege" of joining nine hundred girls from the "ecole" (parish school) in the first mass celebrated in their new chapel.[44]

Thomas S. Fitzgerald, born in Tipperary during the Famine, came to Chicago as an infant in 1849 with his parents, who became respected members of Holy Family parish. After attending the Brothers' School, he studied at St. Louis University, formally joining the Jesuit order in 1869. (Four of his sisters also chose religious life as BVMs.) Recognized as a scholar and administrator, Fitzgerald completed assignments at Marquette College in Milwaukee and at Creighton College in Omaha before returning to his boyhood parish in 1891, where he served dual roles as rector of the church and of St. Ignatius College.[45]

Like Lizzie Sheridan, he had spent countless hours as a child inside Holy Fam-

ily Church, attending Mass and participating in processions and feast day celebrations. The experience of this sacred space with its illuminated main altar and
stained glass windows had clearly left its mark: Fitzgerald devoted much of his
energy to reviving old traditions such as the "elaborate but artistic decorations"
at Christmas and during the month of May to honor Mary the Blessed Mother.
He also spearheaded a major fund-raising campaign to refurbish the grand pipe
organ, renewing Holy Family's reputation for sacred music. And, once again, the
parish's bazaars merited coverage in the daily papers for their exhibits of "handsome, rare, and costly [articles], artistically arranged as to gratify the most fas-
tidious taste."[46]

Thanks to the creation of new Catholic parishes in emerging residential districts, Holy Family's extensive boundaries had been reduced to little more than
one square mile by the late 1880s.[47] No longer a prairie, this part of the Near
West Side had become a densely populated urban neighborhood, home to increasing numbers of Eastern European Jews and Italians. All the more reason, perhaps, that the Irish continued their tradition of elaborate celebrations, especially
the Confirmation Day parades (plate 15). These processions were public acts of
faith that provided immigrants and their children with an opportunity to create a
more positive group image. And they did. Throughout the 1880s and 1890s, Chicago newspapers carried detailed accounts, column inch after column inch, describing the sight of hundreds of girls in white dresses and veils and boys in wide
collars and new suits marching in formation to meet the carriage of Archbishop
Patrick A. Feehan. In 1895, for example, a platoon of policemen, mostly Irish,
led the parade, followed by 1,800 members of the Married Men's Sodality; the
Father Mathew Temperance Society; the Emerald Cadets in their colorful military uniforms; and the First Communicants, organized by school. The second division of the parade featured more Total Abstinence bands, Holy Family's Cadets, and members of the Ancient Order of Hibernians. And bringing up the rear
were members of the Catholic Order of Foresters, the fraternal group founded
by John F. Scanlan, one of Chicago's most famous Fenians. In addition to praising the order and decorum of the parade, press reports invariably commented on
the special stops made by the archbishop at Catholic institutions in the neighborhood—the Sacred Heart Convent on Taylor Street; St. Joseph's Home for Working Girls; Sodality Hall; and St. Ignatius College, where he reviewed the march-
ers before proceeding into Holy Family Church for the confirmation ceremony.[48]

Despite the regular public parades and processions that filled the streets in Holy
Family parish, the Irish were conspicuously absent from *Hull-House Maps and
Papers,* the pioneering sociological study published in 1895 by Jane Addams and
the settlement residents. Whereas investigators devoted entire chapters to the
neighborhood's Jews, Bohemians, and Italians, discussing the synagogues,
churches, and religious schools these groups had created and the special prob-

lems they faced as immigrants, there was no mention of the Irish—nor of any of their institutions, such as the great Gothic church, St. Ignatius College, or any one of the parochial schools with their annual enrollment of five thousand children.[49]

What possible reasons could there be for neglecting the neighborhood's largest and oldest ethnic group? Perhaps after living in the area for five years, Addams and Starr believed that the Irish did not need—or want—their help or that there were more deserving ethnic groups in the immediate neighborhood. And they may have been right, judging from the settlement's aggressive, but unsuccessful, campaigns to unseat "Johnny" Powers, the boss of the Nineteenth Ward since 1888. That an Irish immigrant politician was "teach[ing] political methods to the other foreigners living in an oppressed industrial quarter" was bad enough. But Powers had become something of a folk hero, finding patronage jobs for Irish and Italian residents, contributing prizes to church bazaars, attending baptisms and weddings, and arranging funerals for impoverished neighbors. According to the *Tribune,* on Christmas Eve, 1896, the saloonkeeper-alderman personally distributed twenty-five thousand pounds of turkey, chicken, goose, and duck to 2,600 families in his ward. Hull-House residents and members of the Municipal Voters' League steadfastly maintained that the alderman's generosity was the direct result of unethical conduct, payments he received for granting municipal franchises to traction companies.[50]

During the 1898 campaign, Chicago newspapers were filled with stories about Powers's alleged vow to drive Hull-House from the Nineteenth Ward (plate 16). While he received a barrage of negative publicity, there was one vote of support and it came, surprisingly, from Finley Peter Dunne, the most well-known Irish Catholic journalist of the day. As an editorial writer, Dunne had been a vociferous critic of Irish "boodler" politicians, yet in one of his most memorable dialect columns, he denounced as naive and hypocritical the campaign to replace Powers with a reform candidate. Mr. Dooley explained to his friend Hennessy that "I'm not settin' up nights wishin' f'r th' desthruction iv Jawnny Powers an' th' likes iv him." The philosopher of Archey Road painted a sympathetic portrait of the Nineteenth Ward alderman as a quiet, "innocent little grocery-man that knew no thieves but thim that lurked along alleys with their hats pulled over their eyes, bein' inthrojooced to bigger thieves [on the city council and in business] that stole in th' light iv day, that paraded their stovepipe hats an' goold watches an' chains in Mitchigan avnoo."[51]

Thanks in great measure to Addams's writing and lectures, especially her 1898 classic, "Why the Ward Boss Rules," Powers achieved notoriety beyond Chicago's Nineteenth Ward. In clear language that national audiences could understand, Addams explained why an immigrant population preferred his "big Irish heart" to the "big guns who are always about talking civil service and reform." While

Addams conceded that Powers "understands what the people want, and ministers just as truly to a great human need as the musician or the artist does," she never wavered in her belief that "the many small personal favors done in the ward by Mr. Powers blind the voters to their real rights and interests."[52]

It is ironic, indeed, that Addams was so perceptive when it came to Alderman Powers yet ignored the institutions Irish Catholics created and sustained in the Hull-House neighborhood. As the photographs in this essay attest, it would have been hard to miss the massive Gothic church of Holy Family (plate 17), whose bells rang three times a day, or the Confirmation Day parades with their brass bands and American flags. And yet Chicago's largest Irish parish in the 1890s is all but invisible in the literature on America's most famous urban neighborhood. Addams's 1906 memoir, first published in the *Ladies' Home Journal,* provides an important clue to this omission.

Although fifteen years had passed since she and Starr had opened the doors of their settlement, Addams still remembered in vivid detail her search for the Hull mansion. On the way to a Congregational mission in the Pilsen neighborhood in the spring of 1889, she caught a glimpse of the house from the window of her carriage. Convinced that this would be the perfect place for the settlement, she set about the next day to retrace her steps—but to no avail. For the better part of a week she searched for "the fine old house," and then nearly a month passed before she discovered it by accident. Addams finally realized her mistake: she had left Halsted Street a block too soon and followed "Blue Island Avenue into the Bohemian quarter."[53] Few, if any, middle-class readers of the *Ladies' Home Journal* would have known—or cared—that in her search for Hull-House, Addams had passed by Holy Family Church and St. Ignatius College not once but several times. She could not have failed to notice them. Yet Addams left the distinct impression that Hull-House was the only place of refinement and culture in the neighborhood. What then, was the great Gothic church of Holy Family, built with the nickels and dimes of Irish immigrants and decorated with imported oil paintings, statues, elaborate carved altars, and Victorian stenciling? Or the convents and chapels of the nuns who educated thousands of children every year?

Did it matter that Addams never publicly mentioned the sacred spaces of her Irish Catholic neighbors? Absolutely. Not only have historians perpetuated the myth that Addams and Starr alone brought art and culture to the poor, but they have missed an equally compelling story: by building ornate churches and establishing schools, working-class Catholics created community and identity—and put their imprint on the urban landscape.

Notes

I am deeply grateful to Dr. R. Scott Appleby, director of the Cushwa Center for the Study of American Catholicism, University of Notre Dame, for financial support provided by the 1998 Hibernian Research Award. I also owe special thanks to the following individuals who aided me in locating photographs and new material: Brother Michael Grace, SJ, archivist, Loyola University; Mary Ann Bamberger, assistant special collections librarian, University of Illinois at Chicago, and library technical assistants Patricia Bakunas and Zita Stukas; Sister Anita Therese Hayes, BVM, archivist, Sisters of Charity of the Blessed Virgin Mary, Dubuque, Iowa; Sister Elizabeth E. Farley, RSCJ, chief archivist Sister Margaret Phelan, RSCJ, assistant archivist and Sister Catherine R. McMahon, RSCJ, researcher, Society of the Sacred Heart, National Archives, St. Louis; Carol J. Callahan, director of advancement, Woodlands Academy of the Sacred Heart, Lake Forest, Illinois; Joy Kingsolver, archivist, Spertus Institute of Jewish Studies, Chicago; Andrea M. Telli, senior archival specialist, Special Collections & Preservation Division, Harold Washington Library, Chicago; Julie A. Satzik, assistant research archivist, Archdiocese of Chicago's Joseph Cardinal Bernardin Archives and Records Center; Suzy Beggin, executive director, Stephenson County Historical Society, Freeport, Illinois; and Paula Christine Murphy, research services librarian, and Matthew Cook, rights and reproductions, Chicago Historical Society. And for their continuing friendship and interest in my research, I am indebted to John C. O'Malley, Suellen Hoy, Charles Fanning, Joan Radtke, Dominic A. Pacyga, Joseph C. Biggott, Lawrence J. McCaffrey, Jeanne M. Follman, Ann Durkin Keating, Jean M. Glockler, and Steve Rosswurm.

1. Jane Addams visited Toynbee Hall in June 1888. For the Hull-House connection to Toynbee Hall, see "To Meet on Common Ground: A Project to Bring the Rich and the Poor Closer Together," *Chicago Tribune*, 8 March 1889; "They Help the Poor," *Chicago Times*, 23 March 1890; and "Chicago's Toynbee Hall," *Chicago Tribune*, 21 June 1891.

2. "Two Women's Work," *Chicago Tribune*, 19 May 1890. The exterior description of Hull-House appeared in "Jane Addams's Own Story of Her Work: Fifteen Years at Hull House," *The Ladies' Home Journal*, March 1906, 14. See also Addams, *Twenty Years at Hull-House* (New York: Macmillan, 1910), 94; and *Hull-House Maps and Papers* (1895; reprint, New York: Arno, 1970), 225.

3. Eliza Allen Starr (1824–1902), author of such books as *Patron Saints* and *Pilgrims and Shrines*, was also the city's most well-known female artist. The *Chicago Tribune*, 17 March 1889, claimed that she "rocked the cradle of art in Chicago." For an account of Jane Addams's tribute to Eliza Allen Starr, see the *New World*, 18 October 1902. Quoted in James Weber Linn, *Jane Addams: A Biography* (New York: Appleton-Century, 1938), 85–86; and Addams, *Twenty Years at Hull-House*, 149.

4. Addams, "The Art-Work Done by Hull-House, Chicago," *Forum* 19 (July 1895): 614; and *Hull-House Maps and Papers*, 165, 225.

5. For information on the Hull-House complex, see Mary Ann Bamberger, "Hull-House: Its Growth and Development," in *Hull-House: The Urban Conscience* (Chicago: University of Illinois at Chicago, 1989). Lengthy accounts of the dedication of the Butler Art Gallery appeared in "Chicago's Toynbee Hall," *Chicago Tribune*, 21 June 1891;

and "Pictures for the Poor," *Chicago Inter-Ocean*, 21 June 1891. See also Dorothea Moore, "A Day at Hull House,"*American Journal of Sociology* 2, no. 5 (March 1897): 629–42.

6. Editor's note, "The Art-Work Done by Hull-House, Chicago," *The Forum* 19 (July 1895): 617; Addams, "The Subjective Value of Social Settlements," quoted in *Jane Addams: A Centennial Reader* (New York: Macmillan, 1960), 10–12.

7. In his benchmark study *The Education of an Urban Minority: Catholics in Chicago, 1833–1965,* James Sanders called Holy Family the "single great Irish workingman's parish" (New York: Oxford University Press, 1977), 91–92.

8. Jane Addams to her sister Mary Catherine Alice Linn, 13 March 1889, quoted with permission of the Stephenson County Historical Society, Freeport, Illinois. Microfilm reel 2-1043 at Jane Addams Memorial Collection, Special Collections, the University of Illinois Library. For a typical romantic view of Italians, see "At Naples the Beautiful," *New York Times,* 4 March 1888.

9. Jane Addams to her sister Sarah Alice Addams Haldemann (AH), 12 February 1888, quoted with permission of the Stephenson County Historical Society. Microfilm reel 2-740 at Jane Addams Memorial Collection. Addams asked that the letter be forwarded to "Mary & Weber . . . [because] I am quite sure I never could write it out at such length the second time." For a differing view of Addams and ritual, see Jean Bethke Elshtain, "A Pilgrim's Progress," *Journal of Religion* 78, no. 3 (July 1998): 339–60. Ellen Gates Starr's account of her conversion to Catholicism appeared in "A Bypath into the Great Roadway," *Catholic World,* May/June 1924.

10. *St. Louis Leader,* 26 August 1856, quoted in Brother Thomas Mulkerins, SJ, *Holy Family Parish: Priests and People* (Chicago: Universal Press, 1923), 1. According to the *Chicago Daily Times,* 9 August 1856, "immense crowds" were attracted to St. Mary's Church by Father Damen, "one of the most zealous and forcible preachers we have ever heard." Between 1850 and 1860, Chicago's population increased from 29,963 to 109,260.

11. Quoted in Rev. Gilbert J. Garraghan, SJ, *The Jesuits of the Middle West,* vol. 3 (New York: America Press, 1938), 398–99. For sacramental statistics, see Mulkerins, *Holy Family Parish,* 26.

12. "Jesuit Religious and Educational Institutions in Chicago," *Chicago Daily Journal,* 19 May 1857; "Proposals for a Jesuit College," *Chicago Tribune,* 25 May 1857. The *Weekly Chicago Times,* 28 May 1857, commented at length on the *Tribune*'s "intense hatred of [Catholicism], and the low, base and unmanly assaults it has committed upon that denomination of Christians." See the *Weekly Chicago Times,* 4 September 1857, for its expose of the *Tribune*'s "Literary Larceny" regarding Bishop Anthony O'Regan.

13. Damen correspondence with Rev. John Druyts, SJ, quoted in Garraghan, *Jesuits,* vol. 3, 402.

For information on the cornerstone laying of Holy Family Church, see *Chicago Daily Times,* 23 August 1857, and *Chicago Daily Tribune,* 24 August 1857.

14. "An Irish Relief Society," *Chicago Daily Tribune,* 23 November 1857; "Fair for the Church of the Holy Family," *Chicago Daily Tribune,* 24 December 1857.

15. Damen to Rev. Peter Beckx, SJ, August 1858, quoted in Garraghan, *Jesuits,* vol. 3, 404–5.

16. Damen to Beckx, 11 May 1859, quoted in Garraghan, *Jesuits,* vol. 3, 409. Emmet

Larkin's seminal essay "The Devotional Revolution in Ireland, 1850–75" first appeared in the *American Historical Review* 77 (June 1972): 625–52. See Larkin's introduction for the reprint in *The Historical Dimensions of Irish Catholicism* (Washington, D.C.: Catholic University of America Press, 1984). For a discussion of "The Workingman's Alienation from the Church," see *American Journal of Sociology* 4, no. 5 (March 1899): 621–29.

17. Quoted in Garraghan, *Jesuits,* vol. 3, 410. Contract between Patrick O'Connor and Arnold Damen, 23 May 1860.

18. See Mulkerins, *Holy Family Parish,* for information on the volunteer collectors, 54–58; biographical sketches of Comiskey, 772–74; and Rafferty, 791. For the city ordinance vacating Aberdeen Street, see *Chicago Times,* 26 July 1870.

19. The *Chicago Tribune,* 16 June 1866, termed the net proceeds of $8,500 "a magnificent success"; "Exhibition and Concert at the New Church of the Holy Family," *Chicago Daily Times,* 25 June 1859. The tradition at Holy Family was established nearly twenty years before the Great Bazaar at New York's St. Patrick's Cathedral that Colleen McDannell discusses in *Material Christianity: Religion and Popular Culture in America* (New Haven: Yale University Press, 1995). I am grateful to Suellen Hoy for finding an account of the 1895 Holy Family bazaar that netted "a trifle over $20,000," *Chicago Inter-Ocean,* 10 November 1895.

20. For cornerstone laying of St. Patrick's Cathedral, see *New York Times,* 16 August 1858; an account of the dedication appeared on 26 May 1879. Quoted in *Chicago Tribune,* 27 August 1860. See also 17 July 1860 and 4 January 1861.

21. Biographical information on Buscher appears in Mulkerins, *Holy Family Parish,* 293, 296–98. See especially Richard L. Bushman, *The Refinement of America: Persons, Houses, Cities* (New York: Knopf, 1992); and Daniel Bluestone, *Constructing Chicago* (New Haven: Yale University Press, 1991).

22. See Mulkerins, *Holy Family Parish,* for a description of the main altar, 284–88; and a list of contributors, 59–72.

23. For accounts of the dedication of the main altar, see *Chicago Times,* 16 October 1865; *Chicago Republican,* 16 October 1865. My thanks to Joseph Bigott for pointing out the significance of Buscher's craftsmanship.

24. Quoted in Garraghan, *Jesuits,* vol. 3, 236; and vol. 2, 78; and Mulkerins, *Holy Family Parish,* 124. See especially the biographical sketch of Arnold Damen in Garraghan, *Jesuits,* vol. 2, 77–102; and vol. 3, 232–38 and 393–420.

25. *Chicago Tribune,* 4 January 1860.

26. *Chicago Daily Journal,* 29 May 1860; *Chicago Evening Journal,* 23 August 1860. I am grateful to Sister Margaret Phelan, RSCJ, for finding the description of moving day in the *Lettres Annuelles, 1859–1862,* cited by Louise Callan, RSCJ, in *The Society of the Sacred Heart in North America* (London: Longmans, Green, 1937), 630–31. For background information on the society, see Nikola Baumgarten, "Education and Democracy in Frontier St. Louis: The Society of the Sacred Heart," *History of Education Quarterly* 34, no. 2 (summer 1994): 171–92.

27. *Constitutions and Rules of the Society of the Sacred Heart of Jesus* (Roehampton, Eng., 1890), 192. Quoted by Callan, *Society of the Sacred Heart,* 631. I am grateful to

Sister Catherine McMahon, RSCJ, for verifying the statistics of the parish school from 1859 to 1905.

28. Quoted in *Chicago Republican,* 23 May 1867.

29. Quoted in Mulkerins, *Holy Family Parish,* 423. For the early years of the BVMs, see Sister M. Jane Coogan, BVM, *The Price of Our Heritage: 1831–1869* (Dubuque, Iowa: Mount Carmel, 1975); and Sister Jane McDonnell, BVM, "Terence J. Donaghoe: Theology and Spirituality of Nineteenth Century BVM Spiritual Director," in *Terence J. Donaghoe: Co-founder of the Sisters of Charity, BVM* (Dubuque, Iowa: Mount Carmel, 1995). Thanks to Sister Mary DeCock, BVM, for sharing her research on the Iowa roots of the BVMs.

30. I am grateful to Sister Mary Therese Hayes, BVM, for providing me with biographical information on the nuns who accompanied Ellen Hurley (Sister Mary Agatha) to Chicago: Margaret Dunphy, Ann Quigley, Maggie Collins, Bridget McLaughlin, Kate Hannon, Bridget Walsh, Letitia Burke, and Catherine Dunn. Quoted in Sister Mary Scholastica McLaughlin, BVM, "Historical Notes of Our Missions in Chicago," BVM archives, Dubuque, Iowa, and *The Price of Our Heritage,* 384–85. According to "Supplementary notes" in the BVM archives, the walls of St. Aloysius school were constructed of "nice cream-colored Milwaukee pressed brick . . . [and] all the floors, doors, windowframes, cabinet work, etc. were of the finest white pine."

31. Mulkerins's statistics include 54 women from Sacred Heart, established as a separate parish in 1872, 480–86. According to Ada K. Gannon, "B.V.M. Sisters Close Sixty Years As Teachers in Schools of Chicago," *New World,* 19 August 1927, 635 of the nearly 3,000 BVMs had entered from Chicago.

32. Biographical information on Mary Kane appears in Mulkerins, *Holy Family Parish,* 475–76; and Sister Mary Aquin, BVM, "Woman of Decision," *BVM Vista,* September 1959; and "Thousands Mourn Death of Mother Isabella, B.V.M.," *New World,* 8 November 1935. The BVM archives in Dubuque has preserved Mother Isabella's small black diary with notes of her dealings with George Cardinal Mundelein and specifications for Mundelein College. The 6 November 1930 letter from Mundelein to Mother Isabella approving the loan of $1,800,000 for the new college is located in the Archdiocese of Chicago's Joseph Cardinal Bernardin Archives and Records Center, Chicago. See also *New World,* 8 August, 29 August, and 12 September 1930.

33. *Chicago Post and Mail,* 20 April 1876, quoted in Mulkerins, *Holy Family Parish,* 432–37. According to the *New World,* 12 May 1894, Holy Family School on Morgan Street included sixteen large classrooms and "an assembly hall, with a seating capacity of 1,400, complete with stage and scenery."

34. According to Mulkerins, *Holy Family Parish,* 42, the first Confirmation Day parade took place on 19 July 1863. For accounts of Easter, see *Chicago Times,* 2 April 1866 and 22 April 1867; for Christmas, see *Chicago Times-Herald,* 26 December 1895, and *New World,* 23 December 1899.

35. "St. Patrick's Day," *Chicago Times,* 18 March 1870 and 21 March 1870; *New World,* 28 March 1896 and 26 March 1910. See also Mulkerins, *Holy Family Parish,* 879–80; 888–91.

36. Cited by Garraghan, *Jesuits,* vol. 3, 419. See also *Chicago Tribune,* 26 August

1870. For an account of the organ dedication, see *Chicago Times,* 21 October 1870. The concert program is reproduced in Mulkerins, *Holy Family Parish,* 98–100; description and history, 307–15.

37. The *Chicago Evening Journal,* 9 October 1871, reported that the fire began when a cow kicked over a lantern in a stable on DeKoven Street in which a woman was milking. Five days later, the newspaper asserted, "From this small beginning, the great city has been laid in ruins." See also "The Cradle and the Grave of the Fire," *New York Daily Tribune,* 17 October 1871. Despite the findings of an official inquiry, Catherine O'Leary continued to be blamed for the fire long after her death in 1895. See the *Chicago Sun-Times,* 11 September 1997, for the city council resolution absolving Mrs. O'Leary.

38. Mulkerins, *Holy Family Parish,* 103–4; and pulpit announcements, Holy Family Church, Feast of the Circumcision of Our Lord, 1 January 1872, at Loyola University Archives.

39. See Father Damen's 1878 retreat sermon to the sisters at St. Aloysius Convent, Chicago, in BVM archives. A brief biographical sketch of James P. Tracey appears in Mulkerins, *Holy Family Parish,* 783–84. 27 March 1875 news clipping, "Our Religious Orders, the Jesuits in Chicago."

40. My gratitude to Brother Michael Grace, SJ, Loyola University archivist, for alerting me to the parish census, and to Paul Djuricich, for hours of photocopying.

41. Quoted in *Chicago Tribune,* 2 December 1877, and *Chicago Inter-Ocean,* 2 November 1889.

42. Addams, *Twenty Years at Hull-House,* 84–85.

43. I am grateful to Sister Margaret Phelan, RSCJ, for locating biographical information on Elizabeth Mary Sheridan in *Lettres Annuelles, 1927–1929,* in the Society of the Sacred Heart, National Archives, St. Louis. See also Callan, *Society of the Sacred Heart,* 634–35.

44. According to the *Vade Mecum for Parish Schools: Chicago—Holy Family School, 1895,* in RSCJ archives, "During Lent, [students] are encouraged to save, in order that they have the merit of helping needy First Communicants." The document stresses the necessity of "keeping up with the times" to compete with Catholic and public schools, and warns teachers: "Never permit the expression 'Poor School' to be heard, and use every righteous means that it is not used in the Community." See also 12 September 1886, entry, house journal, RSCJ archives.

45. Biographical sketches of Father Fitzgerald appeared in *Chicago Evening Post,* 6 July 1892; *New World,* 29 September 1894; and Garraghan, *Jesuits,* vol. 3, 429–31. See *New World,* 17 February 1900, for information on the Fitzgerald family and the daughters who joined the BVM order: Sister Mary Wendelin, Sister Mary Thomasina, Sister Mary Lamberta, and Sister Mary Angela.

46. Mulkerins, *Holy Family Parish,* 172, 527, 171, and 202–3.

47. According to the *New World,* 6 April 1895, although the boundaries of Holy Family had been reduced three times, the population of the district numbered seventy-five thousand, about a third of whom were Catholic.

48. See, for example, *Chicago Inter-Ocean,* 10 June 1895 and 1 June 1896; *New World,* 12 June 1897. In their house journal for 18 June 1882, the Religious of the Sacred Heart

described "la grande procession paroissiale" in front of their convent, with particular reference to the maneuvers of the Irish military group headed by Captain Burke.

49. In *Jane Addams and the Men of the Chicago School, 1892–1918* (New Brunswick, N.J.: Transaction Books, 1990), 66, Mary Jo Deegan argues that "*Hull-House Maps and Papers* marks the intellectual birth of Chicago sociology."

50. According to Mary Lynn McCree Bryan, Addams discussed ward politics and Johnny Powers at the New York City Social Reform Club on 7 December 1898, and the Chicago Ethical Society on 23 January 1898; *The Jane Addams Papers: A Comprehensive Guide* (Bloomington: Indiana University Press, 1996), 134. Addams's view of Powers is quoted in Linn, *Jane Addams,* 172. For differing views of Powers's Christmas charity, see *Chicago Tribune,* 25 December 1896; and *New World,* 2 January 1897.

51. *Chicago Times-Herald,* 8 March 1898, published detailed information on John Powers provided by the Municipal Voters' League. See also "All Vote to Stand By Powers," *Times-Herald,* 7 March 1898; and "Hoodlums Work For Powers," *Chicago Tribune,* 27 March 1898. Finley Peter Dunne's sympathetic view of Powers appeared in the *Chicago Evening Post,* 15 January 1898. See especially Charles Fanning's pioneering work, *Finley Peter Dunne and Mr. Dooley: The Chicago Years* (Lexington: University Press of Kentucky, 1978), 121–24.

52. Addams, "Why the Ward Boss Rules," *Outlook* 58 (2 April 1898): 879–82. See also "Still Opposed to Powers," Addams's lengthy letter published by the *Chicago Evening Post,* 20 February 1900.

53. "Jane Addams's Own Story of Her Work: Fifteen Years at Hull House," in *Ladies' Home Journal,* March 1906, 14.

13

Epidemics, Influenza, and the Irish: Norwood, Massachusetts, in 1918

Patricia J. Fanning

"The Doctor's Son" is a John O'Hara short story set in rural Pennsylvania during the 1918 influenza epidemic. In the story, the narrator, whose father is a physician, brings a young medical student to visit patients in the "patches," small mining villages where the epidemic had spread rapidly. Here, the medical student, Dr. Myers, learned the practice of "wholesale medicine" at Kelly's, an Irish saloon in a patch of about one hundred families: "It was easy enough to deal with the Irish: a woman would come to the table and describe for Doctor Myers the symptoms of her sick man and kids in language that was painfully polite. . . . After a few such encounters and wasting a lot of time, Doctor Myers more or less got the swing of prescribing for absent patients."[1]

The 1918 pandemic was no trifling matter. It was responsible for more deaths—twenty to thirty million worldwide—in a shorter period of time than any epidemic in history. To put this in perspective, the United States alone lost over six hundred thousand residents, more than were lost in World War I, World War II, Korea, and Vietnam combined. Still, despite its scope and size, this pandemic displayed the same characteristics evident in instances of epidemic disease throughout history.

As early as 1794, Dr. Benjamin Rush observed that all nations believed disease originated in foreign countries. Certainly this was the case in America where, by the late eighteenth century, colonists had internalized the notion that the American continent was a virginal territory, free of corruption and disease. Thus, when illness struck, people looked elsewhere for a cause and found it in the immigrant populations. Historian Alan Kraut, in his work *Silent Travelers: Germs, Genes, and the Immigrant Menace,* confirms that, in the United States, "there is a fear of contamination from the foreign-born."[2] This fear is heightened in the instance of epidemic disease when such medicalized nativism can result in the stigmatization of entire ethnic groups. Haitian, French, German, Asian, Italian, and Irish immigrants have each in their turn been blamed for outbreaks of deadly epidemics, ranging from yellow fever to cholera, bubonic plague, polio, diphtheria, influenza, and AIDS.

An epidemic is, after all, not merely a medical occurrence; it is a truly frightful experience that challenges people's senses of well-being. The essential arbitrariness of an epidemic forces people to explain the occurrence in order to quell their panic. Consequently, outbreaks of epidemic disease are usually characterized first, by denial, an unwillingness to recognize the disease as serious; and second, by assigning blame. Blame makes the disease appear less random and its victims more identifiable. People are seen as culpable; they deserve the disease because they have done something wrong and are being punished by God. This pattern of behavior is particularly evident in America, where immigrants provided a readily available population to blame. It is no surprise, then, that in the nineteenth and early twentieth centuries, the Irish were a particular target of those who associated epidemic disease with immigrants and divine punishment.

By the time the cholera epidemic of 1832 swept across the United States, inhabitants had no difficulty pointing out that the Irish, who were the primary sufferers, deserved their fate. Alan Kraut explains, "Irish immigrants felled during the 1832 cholera epidemics were believed by many of the native-born to have died of individual vices typical of their group, a divinely determined punishment. . . ."[3] The vices, in this particular instance, were intemperance, lack of cleanliness, and Catholicism. Even those who did not adhere to the direct association of vice with disease often felt that the lifestyle of the Irish was an inadvertent violation of natural law and, hence, punishable by God.

Charles Rosenberg, in his study *The Cholera Years,* agrees.[4] The link between cholera and the Irish was an immediate and immutable one. It became the subject of church sermons, newspaper editorials, and public sentiment. Anti-Irish biases hardened amid cries for immigration restriction and quarantine. Such actions symbolize the third phase of epidemic behavior: social action. A society's response to an epidemic often results in regulations aimed at increased surveillance and control of the victims, thus dehumanizing and segregating them even further from the larger community.

By the mid-1850s, America's social response to continued epidemic crises was twofold. First, more intensified inspection procedures were instituted at various ports. Vessel quarantines were supplemented by individual examination of disembarking immigrants. Second, new public health policies emerged at the local, state, and federal levels. Many of these new measures were intrusive and controlling, and they were rarely implemented without moral implications.

Americans had come to equate disease with immigrants, and in an attempt to eradicate the first, they sought to blame, restrict, and exclude the second. But, as sociologist W. I. Thomas argues, situations that are defined as real become real in their consequences.[5] Such ostracism and restriction of the Irish, and of immigrants in general, became a self-fulfilling prophecy. The correlation between immigrants and disease continued, yet it can be attributed in large part to factors related to prejudice and exclusion.

As studies have indicated, the lower the hierarchical status of a group within a community, the higher the group's morbidity and mortality rates. Marginal groups work and live in more hazardous environments, they are less knowledgeable about disease, and they have less access to medical care. Even in situations where care is available, they are less able, due to economic or social circumstances, to utilize health services. Other studies indicate that the higher the degree of ethnic exclusivity, the greater the group's distrust of outside medical authority. The more parochial the background, the more likely members will be to overlook symptoms and delay treatment. In essence, this social isolation makes the group more vulnerable to disease.

This construction of epidemic disease continued into the twentieth century and the influenza pandemic depicted in O'Hara's short story. My own research into the 1918 influenza epidemic centers on the town of Norwood, Massachusetts. I chose this community because my paternal grandmother died there during the epidemic, leaving a husband and five small children. I was curious about the epidemic and its omission from most history books, until I found that the populations within American society that were most severely affected during the 1918 epidemic were young adult, lower class, and foreign born, those groups most ostracized and isolated from the social mainstream.[6] Norwood's victims correlated perfectly with these general statistics: the vast majority were between ages twenty and forty, almost all were lower class, and 75 percent were foreign born. This in a town where 30 percent of the population consisted of immigrants.

Norwood in 1918 had several ethnic neighborhoods.[7] Two of these neighborhoods, Dublin and Cork City, were Irish. Most of these residents had come to Norwood to work in the industrial factories—tanneries, printing mills, and ink works—that abounded in the area. Here they were ostracized and stigmatized for their language, religion, customs, and political beliefs. In 1913, the police chief was forced to resign when charged with extortion and influence peddling among the immigrant population. In 1914, when municipal reform was promoted by progressive businessmen in Norwood, ethnic and class animosities surfaced. The Irish were the most vocal of the immigrant groups. At an open hearing on proposed town charter changes, Daniel J. Collins voiced his concern. According to Collins, "The statement had been made that the working class were incapable of serving on a committee." He protested that, in fact, "there are men in the factories capable of filling any position."[8]

As the debate heated up, reformers appealed to Irish residents with a poorly written parody of a Finley Peter Dunne "Mr. Dooley" column entitled "Mr. Hooley on the Town Charter," in which Mr. Hooley, a shopkeeper, *not* a saloonkeeper, seeks to persuade his friend Mr. Hennessey of the merits of political reform. Approved in October of 1914, the new town charter centralized government power in the hands of selectmen, at the expense of the town meeting process. In this way, new citizens lost a major forum to voice and redress their grievances.

When the United States entered the war in Europe, the situation became worse as immigrants were accused of being "alien slackers" and un-American, further polarizing the community and isolating the immigrants. Once the epidemic struck, in the fall of 1918, and it became apparent that Norwood's immigrant laborers were dying, the official response was quick and sharp. The Committee on Public Safety was placed in charge of the town's relief efforts. This organization had been formed months earlier to monitor the activities of presumed political subversives. A subcommittee of the Committee on Public Safety, known as the Night Riders, had patrolled industrial sites, ethnic neighborhoods, and immigrant social clubs in search of anarchists and anti-war radicals. Yet this committee was placed in charge of the town's influenza response. Such a step immediately equated illness with undesirable political activity. What is more, the response itself was far more military than medical.

Immigrant neighborhoods, and only immigrant neighborhoods, were canvassed and searched. The sick were transported, sometimes against their wills, to an emergency hospital, located at the headquarters of the Civic Association, an organization founded in 1912 for the Americanization of immigrants. Once at the Civic, the patients were denied visitors and placed on army cots, and they received minimal attention because the volunteer staff was overwhelmed by the number of victims. Thus, while town physicians visited door-to-door with the middle and upper classes, many of Norwood's poor were not allowed this luxury. Instead, they were exposed to yet another form of "wholesale medicine." Newspaper reports suggested that unsanitary living conditions, deficient personal hygiene, and lack of assimilation were the causes of the epidemic.[9] New public health regulations and public assembly restrictions aimed at the immigrant populations were instituted. As a consequence, uncertainty and fear increased, and many immigrant families failed to report cases of illness and even deaths.

Uptown merchants and stores took note of the epidemic by offering sales. Orent Brothers advertised winter coats to "help stem the epidemic," assuring their customers that it was the board of health's advice to "provide yourself with plenty of warm clothing. Buy your overcoat now and avoid suffering from influenza." H. E. Rice & Co., a dry goods store, known a few years later for placing "No Irish Need Apply" signs in their store window, was promoting a fine selection of "mourning hats."

Thursday, September 19, 1918, marked the beginning of the epidemic in Norwood, when a thirty-three-year-old housewife, Bridget Flaherty, died at her home in the Dublin section of town.[10] She was survived by a husband and two children. Within the next thirty-eight days, more than one hundred others died. It was a terrifying month.

Seventy-five years later, some residents were still reluctant to talk about what it was like to be Irish and ill. Others were relieved to share their experiences.[11] One resident recollected her neighbor repeatedly tearing a quarantine sign off his door until he was threatened with arrest. Another, a child at the time, recalled: "I remember [they] came up to the house with a great big white sign and on the sign it said INFLUENZA in red letters. And they nailed it to the door. I'll never forget it. . . . It was as if, I don't know, we'd done something wrong. We'd done something wrong and we were being punished."

Scattered images, indistinct fears, and an overwhelming sense of doom dominate the reminiscences. One Irish-American woman recalled the walk between her home and her workplace as a frightening journey: "I remember I'd go up the street, walk up the street, with my hand over my eyes because there were so many houses with crepe draped over the doors." Still another recollected: "I remember it was horrifying; not only were you frightened you might come down with it but there was the eerie feeling of people passing away all around you." And, indeed, many were. John Connolly, age forty, was survived by a wife and seven children. Walter Coady, thirty-four, born in Ireland, had recently filed his final naturalization papers. Coleman Keady, a thirty-one-year-old worker at the Readville Car Shop, left a wife and two children.

As more people succumbed, a well-nursery was opened for children whose parents were sick or dead. Coffins were in short supply, and a ban was placed on public wakes and funerals. One resident who had contracted influenza described sitting by her front window during her convalescence: "And I remember sitting in the chair and watching funerals go by. They were hacks, . . . horse drawn carriages and it seemed to me they were constantly going by . . . one after another." Even in death, the immigrants were ostracized. Most were buried in single graves on the perimeter of Highland Cemetery, a spot reserved for the poor, alien, orphan, or black. Often their names were spelled differently on death certificates; in town records, newspaper reports, and cemetery listings; and on the gravestones themselves. Many were buried with no markers at all or in the Catholic Free Lot, forever nameless and invisible.

The toll continued to mount. Richard Ryan, a forty-six-year-old painter, died on October 6, two days after his wife had passed away. The couple was buried in a joint service. The local newspaper noted that "much sympathy is felt for the little ones [they had two children] now bereaved of both parents." Julia Roberts, forty-nine, left a husband and several children. She lived in the Cork City section of town, as did Cornelius Coughlin, twenty-eight, who was survived by a wife and a daughter only a few days old; and Bridget Sheehan, forty-three, who left a husband and three sons.

Another woman had an even more tragic tale to tell. Her mother, Julia Drummy, then only twenty-four, had been married for eighteen months. She and her husband had recently moved into a new house in the Cork City neighborhood and were anticipating the birth of their first child. The woman gave birth to a baby girl on September 20 but contracted influenza. In accordance with the Committee on Public Safety regulations, her husband was not allowed to go into the hospital to visit her. But, as recounted by her daughter, "sometimes they would bring her to the window so he could wave." The new mother died on October 8, and the child was brought up by her mother's parents. "Oh, my father would visit now and then," she recalled, "but I lived with my grandparents and they raised me."

Many immigrants had similar experiences and outcomes. Orphans, and often even children with one surviving parent, were dispersed among relatives or adopted by middle- and upper-class families. In my own family, my grandmother's youngest child, Joseph, was sent to relatives, where he lived until he was sixteen.

Author Mary McCarthy offers some insight into what life may have been like for these displaced children. She and her siblings lost both parents to influenza in 1918. Although never told directly of her parents' deaths, McCarthy reports in her memoir, *Memories of a Catholic Girlhood:*

> We became aware, even as we woke from our fevers, that everything, including ourselves, was different. We had shrunk, as it were, and faded, like the flannel pajamas we wore, which during these weeks had grown, doubtless from the disinfectant they were washed in, wretchedly thin and shabby. The behavior of the people around us, abrupt, careless, and preoccupied, apprised us without any ceremony of our diminished importance. Our value had paled. . . .[12]

Such reminiscences may also provide a clue about this epidemic's absence from the collective social memory of Americans. Despite the massive loss of life, no legends, no significant art, no body of literature emerged from the experience. The epidemic is missing from most general histories of the period. There are two factors that need to be considered to explain this phenomenon: the brevity of the epidemic and the social location of its victims.

The 1918 pandemic lasted for little more than a year. At a time when the world was at war, and later, celebrating the end of war, the epidemic may have seemed simply another aspect of the conflict, another hardship to withstand. This brevity may also help account for the lack of literature, art, or legend built up around the disease. It may only be when a disease continues for years, ever present, accumulating a steadily increasing number of victims (as in the plagues of medieval Europe or AIDS today) that it makes its way into our collective memory, that artists begin to capture the tragedy.

Coupled with this notion of brevity, however, is the reality of who the primary victims were. They were, for the most part, unimportant. As Alfred Crosby, the most noted historian of the epidemic, asserts in his study *Epidemic and Peace, 1918:* "If the pandemic had killed one or more of the really famous figures of the nation or the world it would have been remembered. . . . Spanish influenza killed young adults and therefore rarely men in positions of great authority. . . ."[13]

In his article "Plagues, History, and AIDS," Robert Swenson's description of the pandemic is similar: "Despite being the largest epidemic in history, it had little long-term effect, because, . . . the influenza epidemic was relatively short-lived and the population losses were rapidly replaced."[14]

But mothers, fathers, sisters, brothers, sons, and daughters are never rapidly replaced. Yet, we have only to return to the community of Norwood to understand the reality of Crosby and Swenson's words. The vast majority of the victims struck down in Norwood during the epidemic were between twenty and forty years old; nearly 30 percent were single foreign-born adults, far from home and alone in an unwelcoming land. Who was going to memorialize them in prose and poetry? Another 40 percent were young marrieds, many with children. Surviving spouses remarried, many out of necessity. One family defended their father's remarriage: "It was hard, you know. He had to work, he had to keep going." The children's mother was rarely mentioned. Another respondent was an adult before he learned of his mother's death during the epidemic. He had always assumed his stepmother was his biological mother. Who was going to remember these young mothers and recount how they died?

This is not to say that influenza victims were forgotten entirely; family stories and memoirs are testimony to that. It is simply that these survivors were not capable of a public expression of their suffering or an institutionalized memorial to their grief. And the nation at large had moved on to other things. Just as the belief that the victims were somehow culpable had tempered the scale of the tragedy, so it also allowed the victims and their families to remain invisible. They were poor and they were immigrants. Many did not speak English; others were illiterate. How were they to speak of their pain or memorialize their grief?

Analyses of social memory have shown that nations do not remember spontaneously; social memory is created by an elite and then reinforced by the media, historians, and public institutions. Through these sources, memory filters down and becomes embedded in the collective consciousness of a culture. Yet, those living on the margins of a society or a community do not have access to these memory makers. Consequently, their stories are often omitted. The influenza epidemic of 1918 was too brief and its victims too marginalized for their experience to earn a place in America's social memory. They were unimportant and replaceable. They were, ultimately, people for whom the practice of medicine was wholesale and who came to recognize that their "value had paled."

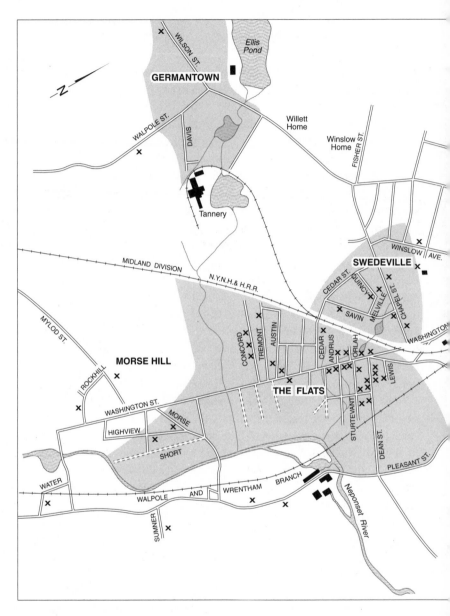

Map of Norwood neighborhoods, 1918, showing locations of influenza victims (marked "**x**").

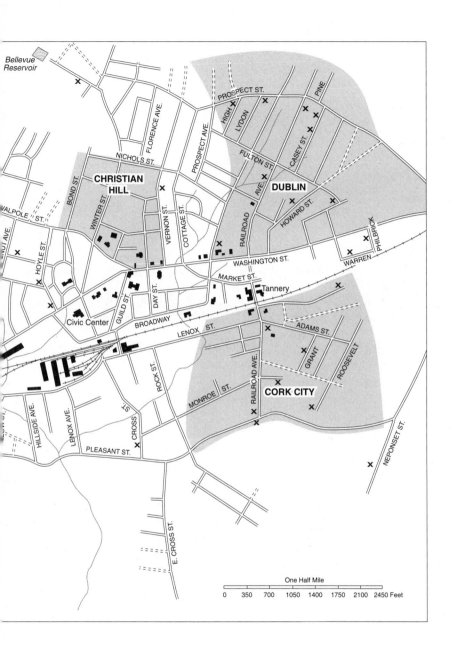

Bellevue
Reservoir

CHRISTIAN
HILL

DUBLIN

CORK CITY

Civic Center

Tannery

BROADWAY

PROSPECT ST.

PINE

HIGH

LYDON

CASEY ST.

FULTON ST.

PROSPECT AVE.

FLORENCE AVE.

NICHOLS ST.

BOND ST.

WINTER ST.

VERNON ST.

COTTAGE ST.

RAILROAD   AVE.

HOWARD ST.

PHILBRICK

WARREN

WASHINGTON ST.

MARKET ST.

WALPOLE   ST.

AVE.

HOYLE ST.

GUILD ST.

DAY ST.

LENOX   ST.

ADAMS ST.

GRANT

ROOSEVELT

ROCK ST.

MONROE   ST.

RAILROAD AVE.

NEPONSET ST.

HILLSIDE AVE.

LENOX AVE.

ST.

CROSS

PLEASANT ST.

E. CROSS ST.

One Half Mile

0   350   700   1050   1400   1750   2100   2450 Feet

The Norwood Civic Association building on Washington Street, around 1918. Photo courtesy of Norwood Historical Society.

Help Stem the Epidemic

The Health Board's advice is to "Provide yourself with plenty of warm clothing."

Buy your Overcoat now and avoid suffering from Influenza. Our Suits and Overcoats are moderately priced when you consider the fact that we guarantee the fabrics to be all-wool. It is pretty hard to do that and we can do that only because they are made by houses that would prefer not to sell any at all rather than lower their old time standards.

Hart Schaffner & Marx
————AND————
Adler's Collegian Clothes

Are tailored right and styled to suit every man from 17 to 70. These suits range from

$25.00 and higher

Other Suits are priced $16.50, $18.50, etc.

Boys' Suits
Made in the latest style and are sure to give service.
$6.95 up to $12.50

Corduroy Suits
Well made, well tailored, and are made from the very best corduroy.
$7.50 and $8.50

Children's Hats
We show a large variety of every description.
65c up to $2.00

Sweaters
That will keep you warm.
$3.50 and up

Suits at $12.50	Flannel Shirts	Sweaters
First long pants suit for young men. Good looking and serviceable. Specially priced.	We are prepared to offer you at less than the present cost. $1.15, $1.45 up to $5.50	All-wool, are the best grip preventors. To make sure they are all-wool, take no chances and get them here at $7.50, $8.50 and up.
Regal Shoes The finest and best for style and wear. $5.50, $6.00 up to $8.50	**B**UY **B**ONDS	**Lamson & Hubbard Hats** All styles and colors $2.50 to $5.00

Home of Hart Schaffner & Marx Clothes **ORENT BROS.** Next to Postoffice NORWOOD

Orent Brothers advertisement from the *Norwood Messenger*, 5 October 1918.

H. E. Rice & Co., advertisement from the *Norwood Messenger,* 12 October 1918.

Notes

1. John O'Hara, "The Doctor's Son," in *Collected Stories of John O'Hara* (New York: Random House, 1984), 10–11.

2. Alan M. Kraut, *Silent Travelers: Germs, Genes, and the Immigrant Menace* (New York: Basic Books, 1994), 3.

3. Ibid., 33.

4. Charles Rosenberg, *The Cholera Years* (Chicago: University of Chicago Press, 1962), 30, 136.

5. W. I. Thomas and D. S. Thomas, *The Child in America* (New York: Knopf, 1928), 572.

6. It should be noted that although it is popular belief that the influenza epidemic indiscriminately cut across all economic, ethnic, and regional lines, statistics do not bear this out. A much higher incidence of sickness and death occurred among certain populations, such as Italian, Irish, and Russian immigrants in cities like Boston, New York, Philadelphia, and Chicago; Hispanics in San Diego; Japanese immigrants in Oregon and California; and Mexicans in New Mexico and Texas. Eskimoes and Native Americans were particularly hard hit.

7. Most of Norwood's ethnic neighborhoods, such as Germantown, Swedeville, Dublin, and Cork City, are fairly self-explanatory. Christian Hill was the neighborhood where many middle-management, store owners and professionals resided—mainly white, Anglo-Saxon, and Protestant. "The Flats," situated in the southernmost section of town, was populated primarily by Eastern Europeans—Italians, Russians, Lithuanians, and Syrians—who had recently arrived in town.

8. *Norwood Messenger,* 7 February 1914.

9. This sentiment was widespread. During the epidemic, for example, the *New York Post* intoned, "Epidemics are the punishment which nature inflicts for the violation of her laws and ordinances." Quoted in A. A. Hoehling, *The Great Epidemic* (Boston: Little, Brown, 1961), 46.

10. Unless otherwise noted, all information regarding victims and their families was found in the official town death records, cemetery records, and the *Norwood Messenger.*

11. For the purposes of this essay, I have focused on the experiences and recollections of Irish informants. Other ethnic groups in Norwood, primarily Lithuanian, Polish, and Italian groups, suffered greatly as well and had comparable recollections.

12. Mary McCarthy, *Memories of a Catholic Girlhood* (New York: Harcourt, Brace, 1957), 36.

13. Alfred Crosby, *Epidemic and Peace, 1918* (Westport: Greenwood Press, 1976), 322.

14. Robert M. Swenson, "Plagues, History, and AIDS," *American Scholar* 57 (spring 1988): 186.

The Last Word: Reflections
on *Angela's Ashes*

George O'Brien

From beginning to end, possession of the last word is both a basic feature of the world of *Angela's Ashes* as well as an essential and revealing artistic strategy in the representation of that world. Whether in stating on the opening page that "worse than the ordinary miserable childhood is the miserable Irish childhood, and worse yet is the miserable Irish Catholic childhood,"[1] or in making the concluding and conclusive affirmation of "'Tis,"[2] referring to how great a country America is, the sound of the final word is seldom far away. It is fundamental to the author's social and institutional experiences of Limerick, and it underpins his response to those experiences. The most common reaction by the countless readers of *Angela's Ashes* is one of amazement and a vague kind of gratitude on finding the bathos, and even the pathos, of the bad old days of exclusion and deprivation irradiated by the wit, charm, spiritedness, and resilience with which McCourt talks back across the years. Finally, he gets to have the last word, although in doing so he also shows, perhaps unwittingly, the complicated and, from a certain point of view, dubious forms that securing the last word can take.

Time and again in Limerick, the child's world is shown to be overshadowed by the twin powers of utterance and finality. These powers make themselves known, typically, because they present themselves in combination. In life beyond the lanes, where teachers, priests, dispensary clerks, and their kind officiate, utterance is finality. It may be possible to speak back—it may be only natural, as the saying goes. But doing so only confirms powerlessness. Attempts to respond bespeak a kind of social illiteracy, the domestic counterpart of which consists of the ashes of a language—sighs, coughs, wails, and when it reaches the verbal level, the husks and crusts of cliché. (The ashes are Angela's; the hollow forms are Malachy's.) The parents cannot speak, or are so impoverished they have nothing to say for themselves: the children starve. That is the way of the Old World.

Not surprisingly, the child-narrator who is father of the man-author of *Angela's Ashes* (both born in the New World) is equipped with a language whose impetus and animus redress even as the language recapitulates his parents' impoverished speech and attempts to undo or—by virtue of the finality of print—to outdo the authorities that imposed it. McCourt breaks the verbal monopoly of Limerick's powers that be with a repertoire of put-downs, comeuppances, and backchat generally so comprehensive as to constitute a rhetoric of retaliation. There is no doubt about who is really having the last word, and the last laugh that is its predictably derisive sidekick.

In Frank McCourt's Limerick, access to language is almost always the result of the kindness of strangers. Kindness amounts to an offer of language and permission to speak. This secular gesture of solidarity and fellow feeling clearly makes a stark contrast to the arctic moralism of the materialist conception of charity practiced by the Church and affiliated do-gooders. More often than not, however, these strangers also happen to be ill: Mr. Timoney, who hires Frank to read to him and who ends up in the City Home (he mentions *A Modest Proposal,* itself a rather heterodox reading of charity and of how it may begin at home); Patricia Madigan, who introduces Frank to Shakespeare, and who dies of diphtheria; and—once removed—Seamus, the balladeering janitor who acts as go-between for Frank and Patricia, although, "I'm not supposed to be bring anything from a diptheria [*sic*] room to a typhoid room with all the germs flying around and hiding between the pages. . . ."

These people give quasi-social status to, and make Frank self-consciously aware of, the compensatory exchange of physical weakness for imaginative resource. (The primary embodiment of this economy is, of course, Frank's father, alcoholic and mythologist.) Frank's discovery that "it's lovely to know the world can't interfere with the inside of your head" is also a realization that the privacy of reading requires the isolation of hospital. And in its reliance on voice, *Angela's Ashes* implicitly repudiates the withdrawal, silence, institutionality, and passivity of the hospital context. Voice insists, in effect, on raising itself above the nonstop white noise of poverty in order to relieve and overcome the ways of poverty rather than carry out the more detached and interrogatory act of reading those ways.

Clearly, the need and desire to have one's say is fundamental to writing an autobiography and presupposes the possession of a voice and a language, a rhetoric of presence and selfhood. It seems equally obvious that, to engage the reader and maintain artistic viability, autobiography should be expected to sound like something as resonant and unanswerable as the last word. In the case of *Angela's Ashes,* such a verbal construct becomes not merely understandable but inevitable, because its function is to redeem—that is, to reclaim and transfigure, to make good—material whose original social, historical, and cultural deformities gave rise to a structure, or habitus, consisting of no more than last straws.

Yet authoritative as the last word is, and readily as one acknowledges Frank

McCourt's desire to possess it and to exercise the rights that it entails—the power to order, to allocate, to accommodate, to decide on an appropriate place for the broken furniture of life—transmission and reception are not necessarily as unproblematic and, so to speak, natural as *Angela's Ashes* encourages us to assume. The encouragement comes from three sources. One is the almost irresistibly persuasive case for triumphant accomplishment alleged by the *post facto* spectacle of the book's success. And not only by its success merely, but by its inexplicable success, because the spectacle of an international audience gorging itself on backstreet misery in interwar Limerick—not even Dublin itself (to use one of the book's favorite locutions), much less Belfast, needless to say, never mind Boston or Chicago or Liverpool or Glasgow, places that might be conventionally thought of as lending themselves to the kind of story Frank McCourt has to tell—is certainly not easy to explain. Canonization by the marketplace has given the book something of a sacrosanct status, making it seem more phenomenon than commodity, ironically fetishing its origins in poverty and conferring on it a uniqueness that makes criticism seem beside the point. It is as if now that the twin powers of fame and fortune have said their last word on *Angela's Ashes,* what more needs to be said?

Obviously, Frank McCourt could not have foreseen his book's success, and even if he had, one would hardly wish to deny or begrudge him it. The unimpeachable fact of its success, however, has the unintended effect of acting as the culmination, or ratification, of two areas within the text—its readability and the nature of its narrative voice—each of which encourages the view that the material is being presented in an unproblematical manner, or is being presented as though there are no problematic issues of presentation concerning not only the material as such, despite all its pain, loss, and damage, but also the writing of memoir generally, with all its unavoidable formal hybridity.

The second source, then, for the assumption that the last word may be conveyed with ease is the book's readability. The disarming facility with which young Frankie's presence is established, the directness of the access provided to the distant and unknown world of the slums concealed within the distant and unknown world of Limerick, the frank and persistent focus on the body and its functions and appetites, comprise an elaborate articulation of naturalness. This articulation is obviously endorsed and substantiated by the fact that *Angela's Ashes* is a festival for the voice. The structuring of sentences around free indirect speech and the historic present tense of the verb, the expertise with which such syntactical tendencies as run-on and repetition are reproduced, the manipulation of tone and idiom, convey the tempo and immediacy that give the informal and the demotic the incontrovertible air of natural speech. Because this speech is the idiom of the moment, of unmediated experience, rather than the language of reflection or argument or evaluation, the reader is powerless before it. To interrogate the moment risks denying the improvisatory, restless, insecure, unstructured nature that typifies McCourt family life. A valediction forbidding innerness, the affect of naturalness in McCourt's language functions as a medium for the last word, as even the mock conclusiveness and asseverative finality of such frequently used chevilles as "surely," "itself," "entirely," "altogether," and "at all, at all" attest.

All the reader can do before this type of language is to listen passively. Engaging with the content of what's being said, rather than being in thrall to the saying, will divert the verbal flow into channels that McCourt may be understandably keen to avoid. Let us just take one example: "Mam says she wants to join the library too but it's a long way from Laman's house, two miles, and would I mind getting her a book every week, a romance by Charlotte M. Brame or any other nice writers."[3] In the first place, this language is not necessarily an accurate reproduction of the way anybody, including the author, spoke in the Limerick or even the Brooklyn of his youth, much less the New York City of his adult years. It does not have to be. Such authority as it possesses derives less from any interest the author might have in total recall, much less in ethnographic authenticity, than from the performative dimension of *Angela's Ashes*. The McCourt family story originally took the form of a pub cabaret, and the book has remained true to those origins, beginning with the depiction of the father as ballad singer and storyteller and repeated in cameos of the stereotypical carrying-on of schoolteachers, learning Irish dancing, going to the movies, hearing Shakespeare on the radio, and uncle Ab Sheehan doing "The Road to Rasheen."

Moreover, in view of the relationship between Angela and Laman Griffin, "romance" seems a particularly pregnant choice of reading. And is it the nature of that relationship, and not just the two miles, that makes Angela disinclined to carry out the routine transaction of borrowing a book from the library? Maintaining the focus exclusively on the immediacy of Angela's speaking tends to defer or deflect such perspectives, particularly when what she says does not stop there but goes on to formulate what sounds like a definitive defense of her taste in reading: "She doesn't want any books about English officers looking for salmon or books about people shooting each other. There's trouble enough in the world without reading about people bothering fish and each other."[4] The odd conjunction of data (fish, officers, violence) and a reliance on last-word rhetoric—"there's enough"—gives Angela her say in a manner so immediate and final that to dwell on any other aspects of her situation, or to consider it retrospectively, is not so much out of the question as it is insufficiently in question. The effective silencing of the question—the obviation of reflection upon and inquiry into motivation, personal knowledge, and systems of behavior—not only leaves what is problematic at a latent, undeveloped state, it also gives an impression of overlooking levels of awareness that writing, as distinct from speech, exists to identify and serve. The performative voice tends to overshadow the speculative mind.

Just as Angela is represented essentially through being "voiced," so is everyone else in the story. All participate in a patter that is as universal, as unavoidable, as persistent, and as capable of saturating as McCourt's Limerick rain. Of nobody is this more true than the author himself. In his case, however, the point is not voice as such but the type of voice chosen. But why would Frank McCourt elect to present himself as a child? It is not too difficult to appreciate the voice's appeal to the reader; without it, *Angela's Ashes* would certainly be less reader friendly. This version of himself as a Cagneyesque angel-with-a-dirty-face also imbues the material with an air of naturalness, spontaneity, innocence, and resilience, despite the artifice of its cinematic prototype. The child-narrator, then, is the third reason that *Angela's Ashes* appears to express itself unproblematically. The child is sentient, but without knowledge. The child is innocent, but stigmatized. The child is vigilant, but subjective. The child is not responsible; his story is incorruptible. But it is also worth considering the ways in which presenting himself in the guise of a child is a useful strategy for the author to address the tasks of writing. The author's portrait of himself as a young urchin not only constitutes the book's most comprehensive performance, it also is fundamental to the overall shaping of the story. The child is the sign of a future. The child dreams.

By *future* and *dream* are meant America, the place that never should have been left, as the book's opening sentence asserts and its closing sentence affirms. That closing sentence, consisting of the word "'Tis," is given a chapter of its own, which certainly makes its status as the last word unmistakable. How is the reader intended to hear that last word? It comes after Frank and some of the ship's company—the Irish contingent, as it happens—have been welcomed ashore in Poughkeepsie, where Frank finds himself promptly naturalized by a certain lady liberty of that fair city. Back on board, the wireless officer says to him, "My God, that was a lovely night, Frank. Isn't this a great country altogether?"[5] And as though to take a deep breath before replying, the penultimate chapter ends there, leaving the narrative to conclude in that one-word final chapter.

It is tempting to hear that last word as a typically two-toned Irish statement, concessive and ironic, affirmative but with an edge of incredulity—the kind of complicated acknowledgment of difference that an emigrant, in particular, facing in two directions at once, might be likely to make. But that does not seem to be the intention. Rather, "'Tis" rectifies the statement with which the book opens—"My mother and father should have stayed in New York where they met and married and where I was born"—by making an "is" of its "ought." The last word contains no ambivalence, no uncertainty. These are forbidden by the theory and practice of the last word, as well as by the magnitude of the dream that America embodies.

"Day and night I dream of America."[6] America is the inner life source and guarantor of the narrator's distinctiveness, his needs, his goals, his viability, his deliverance; all very understandable under the circumstances. As the lengths to which he goes in order to pay for his passage suggest, America is the necessary and sole inspiration to rise above the flotsam and jetsam of his Irish home. To believe that his destiny is to sail, not drown, there has to be a destination. The unadorned directness and simplicity of "'Tis" enacts the young emigrant's embrace of the idea of America and conveys the positive thinking that derives from that idea. As a result of his unfortunate Irish landfall, the child has to look forward. Thanks to his fortunate American landfall, the man is sufficiently secure to make what he will of a childhood in which insecurity was a byword. America is not only the last word in the sense of being a dream come true—the last word and the dream embody an identical integrity. It also provides the basis for having the last word about pre-American conditions.

> But the saviour of Frank McCourt—and all that in him which made *Angela's Ashes*—was not a person but a place. The United States of America is the heroine of this book—longed for for years as the place of health and opportunity. . . . If, therefore, this is a great Irish book it is also one which could not have existed without America. The suffering is Irish: the genial entertainer who puts it before us is Irish-American.[7]

In order that the American dream sustain and nourish the child, it seems necessary—judging by the way *Angela's Ashes* is organized, that is—that it have an equal and opposite entity with which to be compared and contrasted. The name of this entity is Ireland, and of course it is a nightmare. When the child dreams of America, he speaks the naive and plausible language of hope:

> Some day I'll go back to America and get an inside job where I'll be sitting at a desk with two fountain pens in my pocket, one red and one blue, making decisions. I'll be in out of the rain and I'll have a suit and shoes and a warm place to live and what more could a man want?[8]

When the child lives in Ireland, he speaks impishly, emits Bronx cheers, and sticks his tongue out at all and sundry, in the hope, difficult for a child to realize, of being "the way I'd like to be in the world, a gas man, not giving a fiddler's fart."[9] As his brother Oliver is being buried, the graveyard full of jackdaws, he reflects: "I hated jackdaws. I'd be a man someday and I'd come back with a bag of rocks and I'd leave the graveyard littered with dead jackdaws."[10] In a certain sense, *Angela's Ashes* realizes that ambition by subjecting Limerick's ill-omened birds of a feather, all tainted with the same unlovely ideological color, to the nonstop fusillade of the author's powers of mockery and burlesque.

The basis for what might be called this "cheeky monkey" disposition, which reveals a child distinctly underwhelmed by his Irish context (as opposed to being overawed by the sight of New York: "I'm on deck the dawn we sail into New York. I'm sure I'm in a film"),[11] is a statement that, again, has the ring of the last word about it: "Worse than the ordinary miserable childhood is the miserable Irish childhood, and worse yet is the miserable Irish Catholic childhood."[12] Just as America as inner world is a necessary invention, so is the book's outer world of Ireland and Irishness. Not that the Ireland of slums, poverty traps, lack of opportunity, and so on did not exist—in Ireland and elsewhere, including the United States, as the opening of *Angela's Ashes* makes clear. And not that the depiction of those conditions is not sufficiently arresting—a Breughel bled of color by the rain.

Once the level of expectation created by the last word—"worse yet"—has been introduced, however, it seems difficult to operate outside its discursive limits, particularly when it has been given the prominent place of an opening gambit. One of its effects is clear and immediate, when in order to earn its keep, so to speak, it is supported by a certain amount of imaginative embellishment. In this way, the author can account for events that took place before he was born. The scenes of Angela's father dropping baby Patrick, of Frank's own conception in a "knee-trembler," of Angela and Malachy's betrothal and marriage, reinforce a sense of fated haplessness that is apparently endemic to the line of Irish Catholics from whom the author descends (lest there be any doubt, his father was also dropped as a baby) and that underwrites the finality of "worse yet."

Similarly, in the representations of the mentalities with which the youthful Frank McCourt is surrounded, it is not that people in Limerick did not invoke the Famine, the English, the Protestants, the faith of their fathers, freedom, Northerners, and all the rest of it. But they did not do so as consistently as they are said to have done. Nobody could. No community does. The consistency is alleged to align this Limerick outlook within the framework of the last word, and then to undo the power of that outlook's pronouncements—"Mr. Benson hates America and you have to remember to hate America or he'll hit you,"[13] for example—by filtering it through the superior, more natural, ideologically innocent lens of the child's perspective and tonality. The child can talk back. But what he says is structured around inevitably simplistic binaries—Ireland and America, Northern and Southern, drunkenness and sobriety, Cuchulain and Malachy, Angela's fertility and the ashen destiny to which her children are born, the sanctimonious sodality and that poor man's Wurlitzer, the fiddler's fart. "It is in the memoir's strange combination of the remembered with the stereotypical that its appeal and its problems lie."[14]

The compositional authority exerted on the material of *Angela's Ashes* by the pursuit of the last word—the means, that is, by which the data of memory is finalized in the shapeliness of text—has the paradoxical effect of calling into question the ultimate conclusiveness and reliability of what is evoked. As instability is the core of the story, strategies to stabilize that core make it both accessible and clichéd, vivid and repetitive. Frank McCourt—Montaigne he ain't. As an artistic utterance and an aesthetic accomplishment, *Angela's Ashes* is more an illustration of than an engagement with some of the expressive problems and opportunities generated by the writing of memoir. These openings and challenges concern the imaginative and conceptual transactions between now and then, here and there, youth and age, the collective and the individual, home and abroad, truth and memory, and how active the negotiations between these various zones need be to present the maximum degree of commitment on the part of the autobiographical subject to the totality of material at his disposal. Being true to life is a more complicated undertaking than *Angela's Ashes* makes it.

Despite such considerations, and also despite certain reservations expressed directly and indirectly regarding the narrator's reliability, *Angela's Ashes* is certainly a noteworthy cultural document.[15] The reservations in question focus not only on matters of documentary veracity but also on issues of emphasis and attitude. Other grounds for wondering about reliability arise from the fictional scenarios already noted as well as from the book's omissions. As to the latter, the thought of applying for charity in Brooklyn doesn't arise, although the agencies exist (his parents "found a steamer trunk at the St. Vincent de Paul Society").[16] Also, the lanes of Limerick are remarkably crime-free—men are drunk but not disorderly; despite obvious need, there is no theft (except that carried out by Frank and his brothers); the one policeman in evidence is the well-meaning truancy officer.

In addition, Limerick seems to be a city without a history. There are ruins—signs of history as terminus—but there are no stories, no expressions of history as continuity. Or rather, the only stories are the father's, and they have nothing to do with history—except remotely, secondarily, as they continually sublimate the energy of resistance into the transcendental stasis of myth. Yet, the history of twentieth-century Limerick city contains such memorable and unique episodes as anti-Jewish demonstrations in 1904 and the organization of a soviet fifteen years later.[17] Nothing of either remains in communal memory, apparently. No association is suggested between the events of 1904 and comments from men in the pub "talking about concentration camps and the poor Jews that never harmed a soul,"[18] just as none is made between the community's evidently endemic anti-British sentiment and the notorious shooting by Crown forces of George Clancy, mayor of Limerick, in 1921.[19] McCourt's is not the first book in which a comprehensive account of the complexity of the local in Ireland is passed over in silence. The silence of the lived, particularized past is no doubt one of the cultural costs of emigration. And it is all the more audible because of the scarcity of elderly people in *Angela's Ashes*—the greater number by far of the book's adults belong to the generation of Frank's parents.

Of course, the claim for *Angela's Ashes* being a noteworthy cultural document rests not on what is missing from it, obviously, but on what it discards. Its happy American ending not merely draws attention to what the text looks back on but highlights what it gladly forsakes. It is not just that the author turns his back once and for all as soon as he possibly can on the conditions that gave his childhood its particular character and coloration. By doing so, he is also dismantling the structures of the Irish and the Catholic that to all intents and purposes upheld and maintained those conditions.

Of these two sets of structures, the Irish comes in for by far the most comprehensive undoing—so much so that it is tempting to think of its treatment as systematic. But McCourt's capering is too fitful to carry out anything as clear-cut as a critique. Broader perspectives or evidence of general cultural awareness emerge only by default, accidentally, inconsequentially. Yet it is through their presence, rather than as a result of McCourt's artistic choices, that *Angela's Ashes* has a final say that does engage the reader and earns for the book a place in the contemporary Irish cultural mix. Although the attitude toward the overall context of his experiences is to a large extent disguised by McCourt's fondness for the performative and the deleteriously carnivalesque, a set of considerations can be detected behind the mask that should perhaps be taken all the more seriously by the reader because their covert presence suggests the author's uncertain sense of responsibility for them.

Among the subtexts that form a latent, underdeveloped, but nevertheless persistent, critical discourse are nationalism, class, sectarianism, various forms of the Christian commandment of charity, citizenship, and the nature of public policy in the emerging nation state of Ireland. Together, these overlapping and interrelated conceptual, ideological, and juridical structures act as a portal, passage through which is intended to secure a sense of being at home in the cultural, political, and social realities of the day. Yet in *Angela's Ashes,* each of these structures is shown to be in a terminal condition, no longer able—assuming it was ever willing—to live up to its promise or discharge its function. Not surprisingly, the resultant panorama of impoverishment, futility, and inadequacy has been credited with the power to bring about a radical adjustment to the Irish collective (or selective) memory:

> I think *Angela's Ashes* is set to become one of the vital Irish documents of the twentieth century. So many Irish people will have read it that a view of society, not just Lim-

erick society, will have been planted in everyone's mind. . . . The power of the book is that it offends respectable Irish memory, it challenges silence. In a country that idealises the past with so much soft-focus art and poetry, it offers a fine broad canvas of dry toilets.[20]

Whatever the form taken by the complicated and difficult negotiations between the affluent society of Ireland today and the effluent society of McCourt's Ireland—negotiations undoubtedly made more culturally fraught by such Third World–like asides in *Angela's Ashes* as visiting officers of the St. Vincent de Paul Society saying, "That's not Italy they have upstairs, that's Calcutta"[21]—it will necessarily be more hard-edged, shame making, conscience pricking, and explicit. To bring about such a change in taste and disposition certainly seems tantamount to having the last word.

As a result of the portrait of the father, for example, it becomes quite difficult to continue to take die-hard nationalism at face value. Malachy McCourt's version of the patriot game, the basis of his identity and self-awareness, succeeds only in stripping itself bare of the glory it claims for itself. His faith is exposed as self-deceiving pride, and his tradition is no more than a set of cultural expressions exhausted from a repetition that only confirms their irrelevance. This nationalism can only register its vocabulary of freedom, independence, and integrity as a repertoire of bleak ironies. This nationalist is comradeless, alienated, and with merely the mystique of activism to substantiate his affiliation (the circumstances of how "he wound up as a fugitive with a price on his head"[22] not only remain untold, they remain unimagined—unlike, for instance, the circumstances of Angela's birth). Malachy the nationalist warrior embodies a form of spiritual death. And his condition is all the more abject because he can neither abandon nor renew his attachment to this lapsed source of power and purpose. Northern, with an odd manner, himself alone: it is impossible not to wonder if an attitude to other Northern activists of a more recent vintage is reflected in this portrait. Obviously the character and personality of Malachy McCourt cannot be viewed solely in terms of his nationalism. But in his nationalism we see a path— a dead end—traced on which the son cannot conceivably follow in the father's footsteps. Here is a history that has killed the soul. And feeding the heart on fantasies is not enough.

"This is an Ireland men died for."[23] And this is a society that fails. The collective triumph of nationhood has apparently obscured the particular needs of citizens. Rather than produce a future, history has only managed to come up with an aftermath. In painfully obvious ways, "cherishing all the children of the nation equally," as the Easter 1916 Proclamation "guarantees," has not been possible.[24] The agents and officers of the public realm—the sanitation department clerk, hospital nurses, the librarian, postal workers, Mr. McCaffrey of Eason's—

are all characterized by a need to control that is so vigilant and exacting as to define an essentialist view of the unfitness and disentitlement of those with less control. Allied to this reductive and impermeable code are the Church's expectations and prescriptions—its judgmental paternalism, the condescension of its charity, the iciness of its virtue, its vocabulary of infantilism. And although the emphasis throughout *Angela's Ashes* is less on the effects of clerical authority than on the penalties of class, and although there are notable exceptions to the author's typical public experiences (one teacher, one Franciscan friar), the combined procedures of Church and State are shown to militate against the integrity of that supposedly homogenous entity, the Irish people. This concept too, like the nationalist ideal from which it grew, has its obituary inscribed here.

Other components of Irish culture and history will also be more difficult to see in quite the same way—meaning, to take for granted—as a result of how they are represented in *Angela's Ashes*. The manner in which hunger resonates with allusions to the Great Famine—as in how an old acquaintance, Mrs. Clohessy, greets young Frank: "You look like one left over from the Famine itself"[25]—introduces that human disaster as an image of Irish experience counter to that of the authoritarian triumphalism of Church and State (and not just because the book's publication coincided with the Great Famine's 150th anniversary, when for the first time in Irish public discourse the dire event received anything approaching appropriate commemoration). The applicability of the designation "men of no property" (Wolfe Tone's phrase) not only to the McCourts but to all their friends and neighbors suggests the configuration of social classes in Ireland and the existence there of a class system. Suddenly, less distance exists between present-day sensibilities and the caricatured poor (one of the staples of Irish cultural iconography); between the reader and a character such as, for instance, Danny Mann in Limerick's most celebrated literary work, Gerald Griffin's novel *The Collegians* (1829), with his "look of pert shrewdness which marks the low inhabitant of a city."[26] The intimate squalor of *Angela's Ashes* makes it more difficult for the poor to be represented in terms of archetypal physiognomies alone. Even Irish orality is no longer merely a medium of song and story. The mouth may be just as obviously associated with drink- and hunger-induced pathologies (not to mention tobacco addiction).[27] And speaking of iconographic staples, the image of the mother, beloved of both Church and State, source of shelter, succor, and ease, comes under severe pressure in the Laman Griffin sequence—so much so that as a result, son abandons mother, a move that turns out to be a necessary overture to emigration.

From the sustained manner in which every area of Irish social life is revealed to be inadequate, repressive, discriminatory, and essentially inhumane, there emerges an exhaustive view of a humiliating collective failure. This revelation is not the whole story of *Angela's Ashes,* needless to say. Given the McCourt family's dysfunctionality, however, the public sphere has an obvious pretext to act for the common good and is clearly unable to meet its obligation to do so. The expression of that inability as additional terms in a series of irreversible completenesses and finalities is yet another instance of how the last word is applied. It may be argued that McCourt's documentation of the ways in which Ireland is, here again, the old sow that eats her farrow is too comprehensive, too consistent, too repetitious over too many years—perhaps, as the aptness of Joycean tag seems to suggest, too derivative—to be entirely persuasive, so that what appears to be a showing up is a mere piling on. But even supposing that the aim is simply to accumulate, to leave no deprivation unremembered, no indignity unrecorded, that in itself is one more attempt to leave nothing unsaid, once and for all; to leave the reader speechless, to leave the material itself to dissolve into an echoing silence in which no further contact with it is either necessary or desirable. It is over.

Nothing contributes as conclusively to this conclusion as the material that, paradoxically, makes the least demands on the reader, takes up the least space, occupies the least amount of narrative time and, as a result, is pretty much taken for granted—the material dealing with emigration. While America, site of deliverance and wish fulfillment, is a recurring image, the actuality of the place is left for another day.[28] It is not so much America as such that is significant in *Angela's Ashes* but bringing Ireland as a potential venue for meaningful and productive life to an end. Emigration confirms that *Angela's Ashes* is an album of terminations, deaths, rejections, abandonments, homelessness. But emigration also enables, through *Angela's Ashes,* the recuperation of such losses.

The fact that America is where the emigrant lands clearly contributes to the work of recuperation. America's culture of free speech; its official aspiration to life, liberty, and the pursuit of happiness; its secular gospel of equality before the law; and its embodiment of a usable, pragmatic republican spirit all underwrite the sense of an alternative that persistently, if subconsciously, counterpoints the use of the last word, a use to whom nobody is more entitled than the emigrant, somebody who has endured and overcome. And the use of it is perhaps all the more resonant for coming at a time when not only has old Ireland come to an end—Ireland, the emigrant factory—but when European emigration itself is a thing of the past. Those who participated in the various diasporas are now settled, are now no longer a subject of public misgiving as they previously were and as the participants in non-European diasporas currently are. Perhaps part of the appeal of *Angela's Ashes* is that it marks the end of the psychological journey of all who booked their passage prompted by hunger and the deaths of innocents. More than being true, the book may be a rough-and-ready archetype of what must have been left behind. It places the journey, the upheaval, and the loss at a safe distance and says aloud, at last—and to an Irish public, also striving with its own fraught passage to modernity—"the end."

Notes

1. Frank McCourt, *Angela's Ashes* (New York: Scribner, 1995), 11.

2. Ibid., 364.

3. Ibid., 282.

4. Ibid.

5. Ibid., 363.

6. Ibid., 354.

7. Nuala O'Faolain, *"Angela's Ashes,"* in *Waterstone's Guide to Irish Books*, ed. Cormac Kinsella (n.p., 1998), 35.

8. McCourt, *Angela's Ashes*, 209.

9. Ibid., 132.

10. Ibid., 76.

11. Ibid., 360.

12. Ibid., 11.

13. Ibid., 80.

14. Seamus Deane, "Merciless Ireland," *Guardian,* 12 December 1996, ii, 12.

15. For a corrective view of Angela McCourt, see Margaret O'Brien Steinfels, "I Knew Angela," *Commonweal* 124, no. 19 (7 November 1997): 7. (Thanks to Ellen Skerrett for this reference.) For an alternative view of poverty and community in interwar Limerick, see Críostóir O'Flynn, *There Is an Isle: A Limerick Boyhood* (Cork: Mercier Press, 1998), whose view of the director of the confraternity, "Father Gorey, a zealous and forthright man who, like many another priest or bishop, has been foully caricatured as some sort of tyrannical religious policeman," is an obvious contrast to McCourt's. The author has said that *There Is an Isle* was written long before Frank McCourt was ever heard of.

16. McCourt, *Angela's Ashes*, 46.

17. For the 1904 events, see Dermot Keogh, *Jews in Twentieth-Century Ireland* (Cork: Cork University Press, 1998), 26–53. A briefer account is given in Louis Hyman, *The Jews of Ireland* (Shannon: Irish University Press, 1972), 212–16. For the Limerick soviet, see Liam Cahill, *Forgotten Revolution: Limerick Soviet 1919* (Dublin: O'Brien, 1990).

18. McCourt, *Angela's Ashes*, 340.

19. Clancy was the model for Davin in James Joyce's *A Portrait of the Artist as a Young Man.*

20. Thomas McCarthy, *Gardens of Remembrance* (Dublin: New Island, 1998), 83.

21. McCourt, *Angela's Ashes,* 104.

22. Ibid., 12.

23. Ibid., 52.

24. "The phrase 'cherishing all the children of the nation equally' has been frequently

misread to refer specifically to children. Both from its context here and from the repeated usage in the Proclamation, it is plain that 'all the children of the nation' meant 'all the people of Ireland.'" Liam de Paor, *On the Easter Proclamation and Other Declarations* (Dublin: Four Courts, 1997), 74.

25. McCourt, *Angela's Ashes,* 312.

26. Gerald Griffin, *The Collegians* (Dublin: Appletree, 1992), 72.

27. For more on the varieties and complexities of Irish orality, and the relationships between them and concepts of the national character, see Seamus Deane, *Strange Country: Modernity and Nationhood in Irish Writing since 1790* (Oxford: Clarendon Press, 1997), 41ff.

28. See Frank McCourt, "New in Town," *New Yorker*, 22 February and 1 March, 1999, 50–57; and *'Tis* (New York: Scribner, 1999).

Part Five

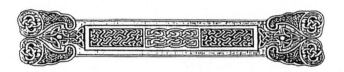

Looking at Fiction of the Diaspora

15

Yank Outsiders: Irish Americans
in Gaelic Fiction and Drama
of the Irish Free State, 1922–1939

Philip O'Leary

In a July 1903 speech, the Gaelic writer Séamus Ó Dubhghaill ("Beirt Fhear") scandalized some of his colleagues in the language movement with his description of Irish Americans who came home to visit:

> Tá dream eile ann, daoine go bhfuil meas mór aca ortha féin, ach ní mór é mo mheassa ortha—na puncánaigh—na Yankees. Buaileann siad anall chughainn annso taréis bheith cúpla bliadhain thall, labharaid go caoch-shrónach, agus badh dhóigh leat agus an fuadar a bhíonn fútha gur leo Ameiricá ar faid agus gur as tóin Ameiricá éirigheann an ghrian—mhaise ní headh, agus dá mb'eadh tá eagla orm-sa ná beadh aghaidh na gréine ro-ghlan.[1]

> [There's another group, people who think a great deal of themselves, but whom I don't have much respect for—the Puncáin—the Yankees. They come over here to us after spending a couple of years over there, they speak through their noses, and you would think with their hustle that they owned all of America and that the sun rose out of America's arse. Indeed it does not, and if it did, I'm afraid the sun's face would be none too clean.]

What troubled his fellow Gaels here was the crudity of his language. In all probability, few would have disagreed with his sentiments otherwise.

Positive images of Irish Americans in the Gaelic literature of the early years of the Gaelic Revival were virtually nonexistent. As is clear from Ó Dubhghaill's diatribe, it was the arrogance and pretentious pomposity of Irish Americans come back to visit that most immediately disgusted many of their countrymen who had stayed home. And so the bombastic and ostentatious Stage "Poncán" or Returned Yank quickly took his (and her) place as a frequently encountered denizen of the world of revival fiction and drama. For many Gaelic activists who gave the question of Irish-American influence on Irish life more sustained and probing thought, the problem was far more serious and threatening. In their analysis, Irish Americans, with their brash self-confidence and conspicuous materialism, were the most

powerful force driving what Patrick Pearse in 1903 called the "Emigration Terror,"[2] the flight from rural Ireland to the supposed wealth and prestige of the New
World, a flight that was at the time decimating those desolate seaboard areas that
were the last enclaves of the language that Gaelic activists were striving to preserve and revive.[3]

Nothing much was to change with independence, as emigration remained an
ongoing crisis challenging both the state and the language movement throughout the 1920s and 1930s. It is, then, hardly surprising that Irish Americans would
continue to figure importantly if ambivalently in the literature of the movement.
For some Gaels, gratitude and tribute were due those who had physically left Ireland but had never forgotten their duties to family, faith, and homeland. The editor of the *Nation* underscored this point in November 1927:

> To our shame, be it said, that were it not for America and the great filial tradition that
> exists between that country and the children of the West there would be no Gaeltacht
> left for us either to save or to lose. The sons and daughters of the old race who are
> forced to cross the Atlantic for a living are never unfaithful to those they leave be-
> hind. . . . How would the remaining Gaels, those priceless assets of an Irish Nation,
> have lived without America?[4]

Nor was American aid merely financial, as the readers of the *Nation* were reminded in a Gaelic editorial in May 1927:

> Is cóir dúinn bheith buidheach d'ár muinntir i Meirice. Do chabhruigheadar go dílis i
> gcomhnuidhe le muinntir an bhaile; níor dhearmhadadar an fód ar tógadh iad. Ní lugha
> ná soin gur chlaoidheadar le n-a dtír dhúthchais i dtroid na saoirse; rinneadar céim ar
> chéim sa chomhrac linn.[5]

> [We should be grateful to our people in America. They always helped the people at
> home loyally; they never forgot the sod on which they were raised. And no less did
> they stand by their native land in the fight for freedom; they matched us step for step in
> the conflict.]

Other Gaels in the Free State were far less impressed with the sacrifices made
by the emigrants. Indeed, in June 1928, one "Faugh-a-Ballagh" all but pronounced
them cowards and traitors in an essay entitled "Love of Country!" in *Honesty:*
"Have we, the sons of such sires, the same love for Ireland to-day? Is the emigrant ship a noble and courageous act towards the memory of such martyred sires
who suffered so much for faith and fatherland? Is there any necessity for emigration? Is there any excuse for such desertion of our country? None whatever."[6]
The same ideas were expressed more succinctly by Father Lawrence Murray in
a December 1928 editorial in *An t-Ultach:*

Is minic a bhíos sé ráidhte gurb iad sgoth na nGaedheal a ghabhas thar sáile. Ní hé sin ar mbaramhail ná brighthin ar sgéil ach gurb iad sgoth na nGaedheal a fhanas sa mbaile le ceart a sheasamh d'Éirinn.[7]

[It is often said that the best of the Irish emigrate. That is not our opinion or understanding of the matter, but rather that the best of the Irish stay home to do their duty for Ireland.]

The motivation behind such an apparently callous attitude to those who were leaving was doubtless concern about the terrible rate of emigration that independence had done nothing to reduce. The editor of the *Dundalk Examiner* faced up to this unpalatable truth in an essay entitled "Emigration from Ireland" ("An Imirce as Éirinn") in October 1930:

Shaoil gach duine ar chuir an cheist buaidhreadh air go mbéadh fuascladh na ceiste seo ar láimh cómh luath géar agus gheobhadh Éireannaigh réim i stiúradh na tíre. Saoileadh, ar ndóighe, nach mbéadh fiachadh ar bith feasta ar Chlannaibh Gaedheal imtheacht thar tuinn le gléas beo a bhaint amach. . . . Mealladh gach duine a rabh an bharamhail sin aige, óir i n-áit laghdú a theacht ar an Imirce as Éirinn isé an rud a mhéaduigh sé le sé nó seacht de bhliadhantaibh.[8]

[Everyone who was troubled by this question thought that the solution would be at hand as soon as the Irish took over the governing of the country. It was thought, of course, that the children of the Gael would no longer have to cross the sea to make a living. . . . Everyone who held that opinion was deceived, for instead of a decrease in emigration from Ireland, it has increased for the past six or seven years.]

This note of angry frustration is evident in editorials and essays throughout the period. For example, in a piece entitled "The Passing of the Language" in *Éire* in June 1924, the editor lamented: "With the emigration of the native speakers that language, with its incommunicable traditions, passes away for ever. Republicans watch in agony and with tied hands the sheer and wanton neglect of the Government in this matter."[9] This Republican agony was only exacerbated by time, as Eithne Ní Chumhaill made clear in *An Phoblacht* in January 1931:

Tá teanga ár sinnsir ag fághail báis gach lá d'á bhfuil ag bánughadh; tá fir agus mná, buachaillí agus cailíní ag éalughadh as Éirinn gach lá do nochtann an grian a geob os cionn uisce na mara.[10]

[The language of our ancestors is dying every day that dawns; men and women, boys and girls are escaping out of Ireland every day the sun peeks over the sea.]

For An tAthair Liam Ó Beirn, writing in 1934, the Irish were not escaping but rather were being expelled by imperial and capitalist interests:

> Tá cuid againn ceart go leór—madraí bhfuil daba acu. B'fheáirrde an domhan (Sasanach) é, agus b'fheárr dúinn féin é, dhá ndéanadh an chuid eile againn soláthar saoghalta ins na hOileáin. Glanamuis amach ar chómhairle lucht na céille![11]

> [Some of us are all right—dogs with a bit to chew on. The world (the English one) would be better off, and we ourselves would be better off, if the rest of us would make our livings in the four corners of the world. Let us clear out on the advice of those who know best.]

Pádraig Ó Gallchobhair expressed a similar anger the same year in an authorial intrusion into his novel *Caoineadh an Choimhighthigh (The Stranger's Lament)*:

> Ba é an saoghal nach rabh rannta cothrom! Buachaillí breághtha ag imtheacht i mbéal a gcinn agus bodaigh, nach salóchadh a mbéal ag caint le daoine bochta, ag gabháil thart ina sáith den tsaoghal![12]

> [Life wasn't divided fairly! Fine lads going off at a headlong pace, and churls, that wouldn't soil their mouths talking to poor people, going around with more than their share!]

The radical weekly *An t-Éireannach,* which saw itself, with justification, as the voice of the Gaeltacht, returned to this theme again and again, stressing that the Gaeltacht people who left their country did so under duress. Thus in a May 1936 editorial in the paper, we read:

> Dhíbir Cromail an Gaedheal go sliabh is go riasg. Ach na Cromailíní beaga atá ar an saoghal anois ní fhágfaidh siad ar shliabh ná ar riasg é: tá siad dá dhíbirt de'n sliabh agus dá dhíbirt anonn thar sáile—anonn go dtig diabhail, áit ar dhiúltaigh a athaireacha roimhe a dhul ach nach bhfuil goir aige-sean a dhiúltú anois.[13]

> [Cromwell banished the Gael to the mountain and the marsh. And now the little Cromwells of the world won't leave him on the mountain and marsh; they are banishing him over the sea—over to the devil's house, where his fathers before him refused to go, but he has no way of refusing now.]

In February of the next year, the paper was more specific in its assignment of blame, printing the entire following excerpt in boldface:

> Sé sgéal na h-imirce an sgéal is boichte agus fós an sgéal is sgannalaighe dá raibh le

cur i leith náisiúin ná riaghaltais go fóill. Sgéal náireach agus sgéal tútach ag Riaghaltas ar bith atá i n-ainm is a bheith ar mhaithe le tír agus le teanga.[14]

[The issue of emigration is the most wretched issue and also the most scandalous issue that a nation or government can be charged with. It is a matter of shame and of ineptitude for any government purporting to be dedicated to the country and to the language.]

Writing in the *Capuchin Annual* in 1938, in the aftermath of the dreadful bothy fire in Scotland in which ten young native speakers from Achill Island, County Mayo, had died, Professor J. B. Whelehan mourned the deaths and indicted his countrymen:

By our neglect they are passing and with them is going the language and spirit of the Gael. And we stand by, we tax ourselves that our children may speak the tongue which these people have conserved for us. We stand by while the Gaeltacht bleeds to death. We fruitlessly tax ourselves for if we do not save the natural custodians of our language, in its stronghold, we might as well try to make Yiddish our mother tongue.[15]

Writers of fiction and drama for the most part approached the issue of America and Americans from a different angle, focusing on the narrative and thematic possibilities of the deceptions and hardships of American life for the Irish emigrant. In Peadar Mac Fhionnlaoich's 1922 story "Pádraig," a man returns home from the United States to a brother who is at first overjoyed to have him back. Soon, however, the returned Yank begins to drink heavily, cursing and otherwise abusing his brother, who then dies of a broken heart. The Yank himself dies penniless and unlamented.[16] Father Patrick Dinneen offered a transposal of these fraternal roles in his 1928 story "An Bheirt Dearbhráthar" ("The Two Brothers"), in which a rich Yank returns home dressed shabbily. His brother rejects him until he learns of his wealth, but by this time the Yank, disgusted, goes back to America, where he leaves his entire fortune to an order of nuns![17] A hardness of heart similar to that of Mac Fhionnlaoich's coarse Yank is implicit in the emigrant children of the protagonists of Seán Ó Dálaigh's 1930 story "Is Giorra Cabhair Dé ná an Doras" ("God's Help Is Closer than the Door") and Criostóir Mac Aonghusa's 1936 story "Cladóir" ("Shore Dweller"). In the former, the children of a poor Corca Dhuibhne couple emigrate, succeed, and then forget their parents altogether.[18] In the latter, an elderly Conamara woman lives in abject poverty at home, almost entirely neglected by her sons and daughters in America. One of those sons is somehow killed in San Francisco,[19] and violent death is also the fate that befalls another emigrant, this one murdered by a barroom gambler and card cheat in the Klondyke, in Mícheál Ó Baoighill's 1930 story "An Choigchríoch" ("The Foreigner").[20]

As had always been true, however, neither stress, poverty, corruption, injustice, nor violence was the greatest danger that the United States held for the Gaelic Catholic emigrant, at least according to a fair number of the writers whose stories appeared in *Timthire Chroidhe Naomhtha Iosa (TCNI)*. The basic premise underlying these stories was outlined by Father P. Doyle in an essay on "The Fate of the Irish Emigrant" in another Catholic periodical, the *Irish Rosary*, in July 1930: "You can save your soul in America. Indeed you can save it anywhere if you are determined to do so. But everywhere and for everyone the work of salvation is not easy, and I think it is safe to say that going to America is not the same as taking a short cut to Heaven."[21] It certainly was not for the emigrant characters in many of these stories in the *Timthire*, such as "Cosamhlacht a Mháthar" ("The Likeness of His Mother") by "T. Ó C." (*TCNI*, December 1923); "Scéal" ("A Story") by Eibhlín Ní Ghairbhfhiaich (*TCNI*, September 1925); "An t-Amhránaidhe" ("The Singer") by Gobnait Ní Líneacháin (*TCNI*, June 1929); "Daille" ("Blindness") by Cáit Ní Éaluighthe (*TCNI*, December 1929); "An Deoraidhe" ("The Exile/Emigrant") by Brighid Ní Cheallacháin (*TCNI*, December 1930); "Cúiteamh na Maighdine" ("The Virgin's Compensation") by "M. Nic A." (*TCNI*, May 1932); "An Filleadh" ("The Return") by S. Ó Curraidhín, S. J. (*TCNI*, January 1935); "Lorg an Fhoirtiúin" ("The Search for Fortune") by Caitlín de Barra (*TCNI*, December 1936); or "Ag Filleadh Abhaile" ("Returning Home") by Brighid Bodhlaeir (*TCNI*, July 1937). The general thematic tone of all of these stories can be summarized with a quote from the earliest of them, "Cosamhlacht a Mháthar," (1922) by "T. Ó C.":

> Ar nós na gcéadta eile níorbh fhada a bhí Pádraig imithe ó aer ghlan diadhanta a bhaile dhúchais go raibh sé ag dul síar diaigh ar ndiaigh ó chleachtadh a chreidimh. Ní raibh sé ag déanamh, dár ndóighe, ach géilleadh do sprid na tíre, sprid na fuaire i neithibh spioradálta.[22]

> [Like the hundreds of others, Pádraig was not long gone from the clean pious air of his native townland until he was retreating bit by bit from the practice of his faith. In this he was, of course, simply yielding to the spirit of the country, the spirit of indifference with regard to spiritual things.]

In this story, it is a vision of his mother's face seen when he is burglarizing a house that brings Pádraig to his senses and inspires him to return to devout Catholic family life at home. Mothers figure prominently in this genre, with the thought of a mother saving a wayward son in Ní Cheallacháin's "An Deoraidhe," and mothers there to welcome their prodigals in Ní Éaluighthe's "Daille" and "Cúiteamh na Maighdine" by "Nic A." In most of these stories, the protagonist makes it home either reformed or susceptible to reformation, although in Brighid

Bodhlaeir's "Ag Filleadh Abhaile" further assistance is needed after the emigrant's return. Having lived rough in the Klondyke, her protagonist has lost his faith and attends church only because everyone else does. One day as he sets out to go fishing, his sister, unbeknownst to him, sews a Sacred Heart medal onto his coat. At sea, his boat is swamped, but he is saved to reform before dying mere days later—in a state of grace, of course.

As had also always been true, however, it was comedy rather than pathos that dominated Gaelic depictions of Americans, whether native born or returned emigrants. The "Stage Yank" continued to flourish throughout the 1920s and 1930s and indeed beyond. In part, these comic treatments were rooted in a real concern about the influence American, and particularly Irish-American, visitors to Ireland could have on Gaeltacht people, a concern made explicit by M. Mac Aodhagáin in a 1932 essay, "An Ghaedhilg agus an Ghaedhealtacht" ("The Irish Language and the Irish-Speaking Districts"), in *Irisleabhar Muighe Nuadhad:*

Dream eile atá ag bascadh Gaedhealachais go mór sa nGaedhealtacht iseadh na Ponncáin. . . . Tagann siad abhaile feistighthe, gallda, neamh-thuilleadh mbuidheach, teann in airgead, mórán meas acu ar Mheiriocá agus beagán tuigsiona agus níos lú ná sin de mheas ar a dtír féin. . . . "Cé'n mhaith a rinne Éire dhom-sa ariamh?" adeir an streabhóg ghléasta agus canamhain oirthí a chuirfeadh fonn múisg ar bhundún leice.[23]

[Another group that is doing much to destroy Gaelicism in the Gaeltacht is the Yanks. . . . They come home dressed up, anglicized, independent, with plenty of money and a very high opinion of America and little understanding and less respect for their own country. . . . "What did Ireland ever do for me?" says the dolled-up lassie with an accent that would make a sea urchin sick.]

Mac Aodhagáin pretty neatly catalogs the characteristics of the Stage Yank in this passage: flashy clothes, conspicuous wealth, ignorance, bombast, and a distressing accent. It was a stereotype Gaelic authors would play for all it was worth, as did Peadar Ó Dubhda in his 1929 story "Gearán an Phuncánaigh" ("The Yank's Complaint"):

Bhí sé bearrtha cíortha go glan. Agus is é a bhí gléasta—gléasta ar nós an phuncánaigh: an bheistín daithte, tá's agat, 's an slabhradh buidhe órdha trasna faoi n-a ucht. . . . An cíor-fhiacal mór cothrom adaí nár phréamuigh annsin ariamh acht a bhogas as a n-ionad uaireannta de bhrigh na cainnte—go mbíonn an t-ór buidhe le feiceál ortha thall 's i bhfus.[24]

[He was clean-shaven and neatly groomed. And he was well-dressed—dressed like a Yank: the colored little vest, you know, and the chain of yellow gold across his breast. . . . That mouthful of big, even teeth that had never been rooted there but that shift out of their places sometimes because of the talking—so that the yellow gold can be seen here and there.]

For some writers, it was American boastfulness that was most distasteful. Thus, in Cormac Mac Cárthaigh's serialized 1932–33 story "Cúrsaí an Bhreithimh" ("The Judge's Career"), we get the following description of the Yank:

Bhí gach aoinne sa chómhursanacht bodhar aige le cuntaisí na tíre thall—an t-slighe in a deintear gach aon rud ann, fiú amháin cabáiste do bheiriú—ní fhéadfadh an tír shuarach so teacht suas leo thall i gceann céad blian. Annsan an méid airgid a bhí le fághail, na postanna breaghtha gan bheith amuigh fé shioc ná fé bháistig, sa phludar ná sa phortach.[25]

[He had everyone in the neighborhood deaf with accounts of the land over yonder—the way everything was done there, even boiling cabbage—this wretched country could never catch up with them over there in a hundred years. Then the amount of money that was to be gotten, the fine jobs, without having to be out in the frost and in the rain, in the muck or in the bog.]

Given this belief that many if not most Yanks were pompous braggarts, it was only natural that Gaelic writers delighted in creating situations in which such characters could get their humiliating comeuppance. For example, in Séamus Mac Confhaola's 1929 story "An t-Éireannach Bhí i Meiriocá" ("The Irishman Who Was in America"), a New Yorker in the window of a tall building being stared at by an Irishman tells the visitor—whom he calls "Paddy"—that these buildings are nothing but stables in comparison to some in the city, only to be answered by the Irishman:

Och . . . bhí a fhios agam go maith nach raibh ionnta acht stáblaí nuair a chonnaic mé ceann an asail amuigh as an bhfuinneóig.[26]

[Och . . . I knew they were only stables when I saw the ass's head out the window.]

In Seán Ó Cearbhaill's "Bhí an t-Éireannach Gasta go Leor Dó" ("The Irishman Was Clever Enough for Him"), a blowhard Yank visiting Dublin, having heard his driver tell him how long it took to build Dublin Castle and the Customs House, says they would have been put up in next to no time in America. When they pass the General Post Office, the driver acts surprised, claiming it hadn't been there earlier that morning![27] A macabre twist on this theme was provided by Séamus Ó Séaghdha in his 1938 radio play *An Taoile Tuile (The Flood Tide)*, in which three men, one a boastful returned Yank, are caught in fog while fishing off the Kerry coast. Their salvation depends on the timing of the turning tide, and the

Yank, with his imposing watch, pontificates on their situation, only to find that he has failed to take daylight savings time into account. All are then apparently drowned.[28]

Other comic tales involve the misadventures of Irish characters in the New World. One of the oddest stories of this sort is Seán Ó Ciarghusa's "An Nathair Nimhe agus an t-Éireannach" ("The Poisonous Snake and the Irishman"), in which a young Irishman whose legs have been amputated in America gets work as a snake charmer in a circus, on the principle that snakes cannot harm people from Ireland. During his show, a snake lunges at him, seems baffled, and slinks away in fear. The young man is made a hero until people find the serpent's tongue in his wooden leg. Despite feeling that they have been duped by him, they pass the hat and send him home.[29] An Irish-speaker's misuse of English provides the humor in León Ó Cinnéide's "A' Solus Aibhléise" ("The Electric Light"), in which two Irishmen in New York gawk at the sights until a streetlight goes on, whereupon one of them asks the other if he sees "an ghealach shuas ar a' mbata" ("the moon up on the stick"). His more sophisticated friend replies: "A ghaosadáin . . . nach bhfeiceann tú fhéin gur ab é an 'neglected light' atá ann?" ("You fool . . . don't you yourself see that it's the 'neglected light'?").[30] Irish provincialism is lightly spoofed in Séamus P. Ó Mórdha's "Citizen de Chuid a' Domhain." Set in "The Franklin Hotel" on fictitious 112th Avenue in New York, the story tells of how the narrator has met a man who claimed to be a true citizen of the world, above national pride and petty politics. When, however, he hears someone insult County Cavan, he pummels the offender and is arrested, prompting the following reflection by the narrator:

Citizen de chuid a' domhain! D'amharc mé síos a' tsráid. Chonnaic mé mo citizen bocht eadar bheirt chonstabla agus iad á' bhreith leó 'na beirice siocair 'a bheith de mhianach ann an fód a sheasamh ar shon onóra Bhreifne.[31]

[A citizen of the world! I looked down the street. I saw my poor citizen between two policemen and they bringing him with them to the barracks because he had the spirit to stand his ground for the honor of Brefny].

There were also a fair number of more serious stories in which emigration to America plays a role. The most famous of these is doubtless Séamus Ó Grianna's 1924 novel *Caisleáin Ó ir (Castles of Gold),* in which, after remaining faithful to his Donegal sweetheart for many years and through many adventures in the American West and the Yukon, the protagonist returns to find her a careworn and overworked old woman on whom he turns his back.[32] Desertion is also the fate of a young woman in Micheul Ó Cinnfhaolaidh's 1922 story "Cuimhne an Fhraoich Bháin" ("The Memory of the White Heather"), whose protagonist, having learned he has inherited money in New York, goes there, gets the money, and decides to spend some time in America. Eventually he receives a letter from his sweetheart, telling him that she wants to marry him. Unsure of what to do, he never responds and is afterwards haunted by thoughts of what might have been.[33] Perhaps the most interesting story of this sort was Seán Mac Maoláin's "An t-Airgead agus an Amaidighe" ("On the Fool's Money," 1936), in which an emigrant who has become wealthy as a bootlegger in New York brings his Québecoise wife to Ireland on their honeymoon. In Glendalough, he meets the young woman he had loved before leaving home but then forgotten. She is in the company of the husband she had met and married in England. Both of these emigrants are now well-off and settled, but the author makes clear they should have stayed home and married each other.[34] The only happy ending to any of these love stories involving Yanks occurs in Annraoi Saidléar's one-act play *Oidhche sa Tabháirne (A Night in the Pub)* performed by An Comhar Drámaidheachta at the Peacock Theatre in November 1937. Saidléar's Yank protagonist returns disguised, in part to test the fiancée to whom he has not written for a good while. After a series of improbable misadventures, the returned emigrant is able to thwart the plans of his fiancée's father to marry her to a fifty-year-old farmer, to restore a farm to its rightful owner, and to marry his longtime love.[35]

It should also be noted that this man is not the only decent returned Yank in the Gaelic literature of this period. Politics provides the point of contrast between the Yank and his Irish neighbors in Seán Ó Dúnaighe's 1923 story "An Pann-cánach," in which a rather arrogant American who had initially fled Ireland after killing a soldier stands up to an Ascendancy woman after a performance of the early revival play *An Dochtúir,* telling her the day of her class is over and the day of the Gael has arrived.[36] Religion forms the bond in Máire Nic Giolla Sheanáin's 1932 story "Mian Shighle" ("Sheila's Wish"), where an aunt home from America brings her niece to the Eucharistic Congress in Dublin, a trip the girl thought she could never make because she had given all her own money to the missions.[37] Another well-off Yank returns to Ireland in "An Deoraidhe" by "T. Ó C." (1931), but he has come back to live gratefully in the homeland he had once scorned.[38] More active cultural service was provided by the returned Yank in Séamus Maguidhir's 1936 piece "An Muirthead." Maguidhir has high praise for this American, who spends much of his time at home in Mayo in search of native lore:

É ina Ghaedheal agus ina Ghaedhilgeoir breagh agus meas thar an gcoitcheann aige ar an Ghaedhilge, a theanga dhúthchais.[39]

[He is a Gael and a fine Irish-speaker, with an extraordinary respect for the Irish language, his native tongue.]

For such a patriotic and cultured Irishman, emigration must indeed have seemed an exile, a banishment from home as the result of the indifference or worse of his own government. A similar sense of injustice is developed in the anonymous 1925 story "An tAthrughadh" ("The Change") in *Fuaim na Mara,* the school journal of Coláiste Mhic Phiarais in Galway. In the story Aranmen have long talked of the change *(athrughadh)* they expect to come after the English are driven out, but even after independence they have to leave the country. For the protagonist, the Free State flag he sees as he emigrates is a bitterly ironic symbol:

> Tháinig an bhratach nuadh faoi n-a shúil arís. Bhris gáire searbhasach ar a bhruasaibh. Sa deireadh bhí an t-Athrughadh Mór chuige.[40]

> [The new flag came into view again. A bitter smile came to his lips. At last the Great Change had come to him.]

From the earliest fiction of the Gaelic revival through the work of writers like Pádhraic Óg Ó Conaire, Máirtín Ó Cadhain and right up to the recent efforts of Colm Ó Ceallaigh, Antoine Ó Flatharta, Maidhc Dainín Ó Sé, Joe Steve Ó Neachtain, Pádraig Ó Siadhail, and John Beag Ó Flatharta, to name just a few, America and its diasporic Irish population have played a disproportionately significant and troubling thematic role in creative writing in the first official language of the home country. If, with a nod to Ó Dubhghaill's memorable image with which we began, America's face has not always been all that clean or appealing, it has never been possible to ignore.

Notes

1. "Oráid Shéamuis Uí Dhubhghaill sa Tuaith" (Seamus Ó Dubhghaill's speech in the country), *An Claidheamh Soluis,* 25 July 1903.
2. "Gleo na gCath" (The tumult of the battles), *An Claidheamh Soluis,* 25 April 1903.
3. I have discussed the treatment of Irish Americans in the literature of the early revival at some length in *The Prose Literature of the Gaelic Revival, 1881–1921: Ideology and Innovation* (University Park: Pennsylvania State University Press, 1994), 141–54.
4. "'To Hell or Connaught,'" editorial, *Nation,* 12 November 1927.
5. "Gaedhealú Éire-thar-Lear" (The Gaelicizing of overseas Ireland), editorial, *Nation,* 21 May 1927.
6. "Faugh-a-Ballagh" (Love of country), *Honesty,* 30 June 1928.
7. "Beannú na Nodlag" (Christmas greeting), editorial, *An t-Ultach* (December 1928): 4. These sentiments were echoed by Father Patrick Dinneen in his essay "Annus Mirabilis—1929" in *The Capuchin Annual* for 1930, 35–41.
8. "An Imirce as Éirinn," editorial, *Dundalk Examiner,* 4 October 1930.

9. "The Passing of the Language," editorial, *Éire/The Irish Nation,* 28 June 1924.

10. Eithne Ní Chumhaill, "Cúis na Saoirse" (The cause of freedom), *An Phoblacht,* 10 January 1931.

11. "An Beirneach," "An Lios" (The fort), in *Seo Siúd* (Gaillimh: Ó Gormáin agus a Chomh., Teach na Clódóireachta, 1934), 62.

12. Pádraig Ó Gallchobhair ("Muirghein"), *Caoineadh an Choimhighthigh,* in *Cáitheamh na dTonn* (Baile Átha Cliath: Oifig Díolta Foillseacháin Rialtais, 1934), 24.

13. "Sinn Féin Amháin a Bhrisfeas Dlighe Chromail/Imirce ó'n nGaedhealtacht" (It is ourselves alone who will break the law of Cromwell/Emigration from the Gaeltacht), editorial, *An t-Éireannach,* 2 May 1936. See also Tom O'Flaherty (brother of Liam), "Coming Home," in *Aranmen All* (Dingle: Brandon, 1991), 164. O'Flaherty was a regular contributor to *An t-Éireannach* before his untimely death in 1936. *Aranmen All* was originally published in 1934.

14. "Gaedhilgeoirí ag Imtheacht le Sruth/Gor dá Thabhairt do'n Bhéarla/Aimsigheadh an Ghaedhealtacht a Deis Anois" (Irish-speakers drifting away/Advantage being given to the English language/Let the Gaeltacht seize its opportunity now), editorial, *An t-Éireannach,* 6 February 1937. Editorials similar in tone appeared in *An t-Éireannach* on 18 January and 16 May 1936.

15. Prof. J. B. Whelehan, "Ten Coffins," *The Capuchin Annual* (1938), 203.

16. "Cú Uladh" (Peadar Mac Fhionnlaoich), "Pádraig," *Fáinne an Lae,* 29 July 1922.

17. Father Patrick Dinneen, "An Bheirt Dearbhráthar" (The two brothers), *Leader,* 14 July 1928.

18. "Common Noun" (Seán Ó Dálaigh), "Is Giorra Cabhair Dé ná an Doras," in *Clocha Sgáil* (Baile Átha Cliath: C. S. Ó Fallamhain i gComhar le hOifig an tSoláthair, 1930), 44–45.

19. Criostóir Mac Aonghusa, "Cladóir," *Irish Press,* 17 February 1936.

20. Micheál Ó Baoighill, "An Choigchríoch," *An t-Ultach* 7, no. 8 (October 1930): 7–8.

21. Rev. P. Doyle, "The Fate of the Irish Emigrant," *Irish Rosary* 34, no. 7 (July 1930): 502.

22. T. Ó C., "Cosamhlacht a Mháthar," *Timthire Chroidhe Naomhtha Iosa* (December 1923): 7. Such stories were not limited to Roman Catholic periodicals. For example, in October 1939, *Ar Aghaidh* published "Sháruigh an Fhoighid an Chinnemahaint" (Patience triumphed over fate) by T. Mac C., a sentimental tale in which an American returns to Ireland just in time for his mother's death.

23. M. Mac Aodhagáin, "An Ghaedhilg agus an Ghaedhealtacht," *Irisleabhar Muighe Nuadhad* 31 (1932): 11.

24. "Cú Chulainn" (Peadar Ó Dubhda), "Gearán an Phuncánaigh," in *Cáith agus Grán* (Baile Átha Cliath: C. S. Ó Fallamhain, Teo. i gComhar le hOifig an tSoláthair, 1929), 71–72.

25. Cormac Mac Cárthaigh, "Cúrsaí an Bhreithimh/Sgéal Leanamhna," *An Muimhneach* 1 (December 1932): 13. For a similar description of the Yank, see Micheál Ó Conaill, *Cinn Lae: Fá Sgáth Shléibh' Eachtgha* (Diary: In the shadow of Slieve Aughty)

(Baile Átha Cliath: Oifig Díolta Foillseacháin Rialtais, 1937), 56, 71, 99, 100–101. Other examples of similarly boastful Yanks are too numerous to mention.

26. Séamus Mac Confhaola, "An t-Éireannach Bhí i Meiriocá," *An Stoc* (November 1929): 2.

27. Seán Ó Cearbhaill, "Bhí an t-Éireannach Gasta go Leor Dó," in *Scéilín is Caogadh le Léigheamh, le Meabhrú agus le hAith-innsint* (Fifty-nine little stories to be read, to be memorized, and to be retold) (Baile Átha Cliath: Comhlucht Oideachais na hÉireann, Teor., 1934), 29.

28. Séamus Ó Séaghdha, "An Taoile Tuile / Dráma don Ráidió," *Bonaventura* 1, no. 4 (spring 1938): 101–9.

29. "Cloch Labhrais" (Seán Ó Ciarghusa), "An Nathair Nimhe agus an t-Éireannach," *Fáinne an Lae,* 2 August 1924. Another Irishman has a run-in with an American snake in Seán Ó Cuill's story "An Nathair Nimhe agus an Gunna Mór" (The snake and the big gun) in *Fáinne an Lae,* 28 June 1924.

30. León Ó Cinnéide, "A' Solus Aibhléise," in *Eithneacha an Ghrinn: Cnuasacht Scéalta* (Kernels of humor: A collection of stories) (Gaillimh: Ó Gormáin Teach Clódóireachta, 1924), 45–48.

31. Séamus P. Ó Mórdha, "Citizen de Chuid a' Domhain," *An t-Ultach* 15, no. 5 (May 1938): 2–3.

32. "Máire" (Séamus Ó Grianna), *Caisleáin Ó ir* (1924; reprint, Corcaigh: Cló Mercier, 1976).

33. Micheul Ó Cinnfhaolaidh, "Cuimhne an Fhraoich Bháin," *Green and Gold: A Magazine of Fiction, etc.* 5 (December 1921–February 1922): 328–32.

34. Seán Mac Maoláin, "An t-Airgead agus an Amaidighe," *An t-Ultach* 12, no. 11 (December 1936): 4, 16.

35. Annraoi Saidléar, *Oidhche sa Tabháirne: Dráma Aon-Mhíre* (Baile Átha Cliath: Oifig an tSoláthair, 1945).

36. Seán Ó Dúnaighe, "An Panncánach," *An Squab,* September 1923, 230–32. He then returns to America, however. A returned Yank is also the voice of advanced nationalism in Seán Mac Maoláin, *Éan Corr* (A strange bird) (Baile Átha Cliath: Oifig an tSoláthair, 1937), 74–78.

37. Máire Nic Giolla Sheanáin, "Mian Shighle," *Timthire Chroidhe Naomhtha Íosa* 1, no. 6 (June 1932): 129–31.

38. T. Ó C., "An Deoraidhe," *The Dundalk Examiner and Louth Advertiser,* 28 November 1931.

39. Séamus Maguidhir, "An Muirthead," in *Fánaidheacht i gConndae Mhuigheo* (Wandering in Mayo) (1944; reprint, Baile Átha Cliath: An Gúm, 1994), 7. This piece originally appeared in *An t-Éireannach* in late 1934.

40. "An tAthrughadh," *Fuaim na Mara: Irisleabhar Choláiste Mhic Phiarais* 1 (1925): 72.

16

Donn Byrne: Bard of Armagh

Ron Ebest

If personality is an unbroken series of successful gestures,
then there was something gorgeous about him.
 —F. Scott Fitzgerald, *The Great Gatsby*

Any study of the life of the Irish-American literary community during the first three decades of the twentieth century begins with Donn Byrne. There are two reasons for this. Because he was the last great "American Celticist," he represents the end of a literary tradition, a fact he recognized and lamented. Perhaps more importantly, despite the fact that his work is now forgotten, Donn Byrne remains one of the most financially, critically, and popularly successful novelists in the Irish-American canon. Among his admirers were Stephen Vincent Benet, James Branch Cabell, Joseph Devlin, Frank Harris, Joyce Kilmer, Amy Lowell, T. P. O'Connor, and John Steinbeck. His short stories were sought by journals across the popular spectrum, from the *Century* to the *Saturday Evening Post;* in 1919, the Hearst publications offered him a standing contract for one short story per month. His writing was translated into Polish, Irish, Swedish, German, Spanish, French, Italian, and Braille. He was the author most frequently read by Admiral Byrd's men during their polar expedition. His work inspired two stage plays, two radio plays, and eleven movies. By the mid-1920s, Donn Byrne was reported to be earning more than thirty thousand dollars per year, a feat his Irish-American compatriot F. Scott Fitzgerald would claim to match a decade later. In 1923, Donn Byrne's writing was taught at Columbia University, on the grounds that his book *Changeling* was the best short story collection in four decades. And Sir Shane Leslie compared W. B. Yeats and James Joyce unfavorably to Byrne.[1]

So who was he? Details of his earliest life are conflicted because, on the one hand, Donn Byrne possessed the romanticist's twin attributes of overimagination and contempt for historical fact, and on the other, it became increasingly important for him, as he grew older, to imagine himself a "true" Irishman. Indeed, on March 31, 1928, he wrote to a publicist to protest a biographical article calling him an American: "That I was born in America," he observed, "is not my fault at all."[2] Nonetheless he *was* born in America, on November 20, 1889, in New York

City. Eleven days later he was baptized a Roman Catholic, an event that in later years would embarrass him and that he would come to suppress.[3] Early stories held that his father, Thomas Fearghail Byrne, was an architect living in the United States while supervising a project. Donn Byrne later claimed that his father was not an architect but "a perfect lunatic on the subject of bridges," who came to the United States to see the Genesee Valley Bridge, and who returned to Ireland with his wife and son three months after the boy's birth.[4] The idea of the elder Byrne taking his wife to the United States to see a bridge seems specious and suggests that Donn Byrne was embroidering in order to make his association with the United States seem that much more incidental. Either way, both architects and bridges figure prominently in many of his later short stories.

Donn Byrne spent his youth in Camlough, near Newry, County Armagh; after the age of fourteen he holidayed at Cushendun in the Glens of Antrim, where he won prizes for his fluency in Irish at festivals organized by Ada McNeill and Sir Roger Casement, and where he heard the popular stories of supernatural events and chivalric romance that would haunt him the rest of his life. "Antrim will ever color my own writing," the autobiographical narrator of one of his novels would later say. "My Fifth Avenue will have something in it of the heather glen. My people will always have a phrase, a thought, a flash of Scots-Irish mysticism. . . . The stories I heard, and I was young, were not of Little Rollo and Sir Walter Scott's, but the horrible tale of the Naked Hangman, who goes through the Valleys on Midsummer's Eve; of Dermot, and Granye of Bright Breasts; of the Cattle Raid of Maeve, Queen of Connacht. . . ."[5] Friends from his youth remembered him as a small boy, "delicate looking and thin, but all brains." Various accounts suggest he manifested nationalistic ideals. Ada McNeill once recalled his publicly singing a lampoon of an unpopular landlord, to the tune of "The Wearing of the Green." Another acquaintance, Bulmer Hobson, remembered taking the young Donn Byrne to numerous political meetings. Donn Byrne, Hobson recalled, "shared all our enthusiasms." To an extent, this was to change.[6]

Impoverished by the death of his father, Donn Byrne financed his education to the university college in Dublin with a modern-language scholarship. There he came to the attention of Douglas Hyde, who admired his fluency in colloquial Irish. (Passages in the Irish language, some untranslated, would punctuate much of Donn Byrne's later fiction.) Some years earlier, Hyde had completed his *Songs of Raftery,*[7] a translation of the work of the balladeer Anthony Raftery (1784–1835). Raftery, blinded by smallpox at the age of nine, had eked out a living as an itinerant minstrel in south Galway. His unflinching heroism in the face of his catastrophe made him a cult figure for Hyde, Yeats, Lady Gregory, and others involved in the Irish Literary Renaissance. There can be little doubt that Hyde communicated his admiration for Raftery to his impressionable student.

The student, meanwhile, helped found a literary journal, the *National Student,* to which he contributed poetry. (Other student authors lampooned his "villain-ous villanelles" in the same pages.) He also won prizes for boxing, which, with horsemanship, would come to symbolize his increasingly overromanticized sense of Irish history as a doomed, noble crusade. A character in one of his later short stories, an Irish-American boxer named "Irish" Mike McCann, prepares for a championship bout while musing that it is "only right that an Irishman—"

> or an Irish-American, which was better still—should hold the middle-weight and heavy-weight championships. Fighting—clean, hard struggle —was the destiny apportioned to them. He knew enough of the history of his race to remember that they had fought under every banner in Europe—the Irish Brigade at Fontenoy, and the men who were in the Pope's Zouaves, and Russia and Germany knew them, and the great regiments the English had, Munsters and Leinsters and Enniskillen Dragoons, and in New York was the beloved Sixty-ninth, the Fighting sixty-ninth.[8]

This passage, in which all of Irish military history is imported into a New York boxing ring, illustrates the point. By seeing war in terms of sport, Donn Byrne domesticates it, redefining combat as a friendly, gentlemanly adventure. The litany of exotic battle sites juxtaposed with even more exotic titles of combat units fur-ther refines warfare. No blood spatters the resulting chivalric image of colorful uniforms, ragged faces, and ghostly, stampeding cavalries. Of course, this habit of seeing war as a species of sport did not begin with Donn Byrne. It was a fairly common metaphor among writers and veterans after 1914.[9] What Donn Byrne added to the equation was what he learned from the laments of his youthful Antrim and from the story of Anthony Raftery: the nobility of honest defeat. Like many other Celtic Twilight writers, Donn Byrne understood that the Irish, boxers as well as soldiers, fought "clean"—and lost. For Celtic Twilight authors, to write about the Irish or Irish Americans in the twentieth century required at least some measure of loss, because each new defeat recalled so many other valiant defeats in Ireland's eight-hundred-year struggle for liberty. "The proper subject of con-versation for an Irishman is Ireland," Donn Byrne explained once. "We knew every man and every engagement in every Irish war. Our legendary heroes are household words with us."[10] Thus, by associating the current "battle," in this case a boxing match, with "legendary" past battles, Donn Byrne turns it into an au-thentic relic of an ongoing Irish tradition. In effect, the clean fight and fated de-feat are what make the battle Irish in the first place.

Additionally, in Donn Byrne at least, the loss affords the Irish or Irish-Ameri-can protagonist the opportunity to rise above the battle by shrugging it off—a sportsmanlike gesture calculated to make the defeat, and indeed the battle itself, appear inconsequential by comparison. The ability to shrug off defeat, like Raftery shrugging off blindness, is the kernel of Irish heroism: the Irish, Donn Byrne once observed, "profit by defeat."[11] It is no coincidence that, immediately upon completing the above reverie, "Irish" Mike goes into the boxing ring and is soundly beaten. Afterward, speaking of the match to his father, Mike "grins" and remarks, "It was a great fight . . . and a good man won."[12] Nor is it a coincidence that the most poignant of all his friends' recollections of Donn Byrne involves boxing. J. J. O'Connell, a lieutenant-general in the Irish Army, remembered attending a match with Donn Byrne in Dublin in 1923. After a "prolonged and passive defence" by one of the boxers, Donn Byrne broke out: "Is our last illusion—that the Irish are a fighting race—about to be dispelled?"[13] The remark could not be taken literally; the years of continual conflict following the uprising in 1916 demonstrated with cruel clarity how willing the Irish were to fight. What embittered Donn Byrne—what he saw disfiguring the Irish character so thoroughly that even a boxing match became unrecognizable—was not an unwillingness to fight. It was the unwillingness to fight like Irishmen. The Anglo-Irish War and the Irish Civil War were inexplicable events because they could not be reconciled with Irish history as Donn Byrne understood it. "I can remember when looking forward we saw revolution as a gallant, chivalrous adventure," he mused unhappily. "Already those great Irish regiments are being forgotten."[14] In their place were a new and strange kind of Irishmen, unsporting, unwilling to fight "clean." Even more bizarre, they were unwilling to lose.

After his graduation in 1910, Donn Byrne went to France and then Germany, intending to earn a doctorate in preparation for a post in the British Foreign Office. He failed. One apocryphal story holds that doctoral candidates at Leipzig were required to take their oral examinations early in the morning, wearing formal evening clothes. Upon learning this, the story goes, Donn Byrne withdrew because, he said, it was beneath the dignity of an Irish gentleman to suffer an examination while dressed like a waiter.[15]

His hopes for foreign service dashed, Donn Byrne returned to New York with the notion of becoming a poet. There he became reacquainted with Dorothea Cadogan, a fellow student from Dublin, whom he married on December 2, 1911. To make extra money, he wrote poetry. At the suggestion of his friend Joyce Kilmer, he submitted a short story, entitled "Battle," to *Smart Set*. *Smart Set* ran the story in February 1914; it paid Donn Byrne fifty dollars. His career was launched.

His success in the lucrative magazine market was so great that by the time of the publication of his first novel in 1919, Byrne had already retired to Connecticut to devote himself to fiction professionally. This first novel, *The Stranger's Banquet*,[16] describes a labor dispute in a Massachusetts shipyard. It is punctuated by the ambivalence prevalent in most Irish-American fictional treatments of labor at the time, the various authors torn between sympathy for the workers on the one hand and the fear of socialism on the other. Donn Byrne's solution to this problem was to imagine both labor and management as honest protagonists duped into conflict by mercenary I.W.W. (Industrial Workers of the World) agitators. Reception for this novel, and his next, *Foolish Matrons,*[17] was mixed; each, however, brought him ten thousand dollars for movie rights. Additionally, *Foolish Matrons* brought him a lawsuit from his agent, Laura Wilck, who claimed he had failed to pay her 10-percent fee.[18]

But it was with the publication of his third novel that Donn Byrne established his reputation in both England and the United States. The novel, *Messer Marco Polo,* created a minor sensation in 1921 among critics who endeavored vainly to explain its allure. The novel is a retelling of the life of Marco Polo, but Donn Byrne's conceit is to put the tale into the mouth of a ninety-year-old Irish balladeer named Malachai Campbell of the Long Glen. In his youth, Donn Byrne had been admired for his ability to mimic balladeers; among his sources for the novel was a folk tale called "Turus Marc O'Polo" he had heard as a boy, in which Marco Polo is confounded with St. Brendan and represented as an Irishman.

The tale itself is a trifle, perhaps fifteen thousand words long. Polo/Brendan, enchanted by a sea captain's stories of the Kubla Khan's daughter and fearing that, should she die, her soul would not enter heaven, travels to China to convert her. Upon seeing her, however, he falls in love and marries her. A brief happy interlude is followed by her untimely death; for the next fourteen years he remains in the service of the Khan. But in time the Khan begins to fear a popular backlash against Polo and asks him to leave. Polo agrees to abandon his beloved's grave only if he receives some sign from heaven. Does he ever. In a shower of golden light his wife literally rises from the dead and bids him to return to Venice. The golden light vanishes, Polo's wife retreats to the tomb, and, the miracle over, Polo turns to a friend and says, "Well . . . that's that," thereby proving himself to be the most pragmatic hero in the history of American literature.[19]

But even the novel's admirers paid scant attention to its story. Instead, its value derives from the unusual effect Donn Byrne achieves by turning Marco Polo's life into a Celtic Twilight romance and putting it in the mouth of an archetypal storyteller. *Messer Marco Polo* is both familiar and alien, simultaneously rich in romance and humor—not all of the humor intentional. In the novel, one of the characters debates the relative merits of Coleridge's "Kubla Khan" versus those of a similar work by an Irish poet, Colquitto Dall McCracken of Skye. He solemnly concludes that the Irish poem is better. A kiss is variously described in terms of soccer, the short game in golf, and salmon fishing. The superbly crafted dialogue suggests that everyone, including the Kubla Khan, is Irish. *Messer Marco Polo* is utterly charming.

His name established, Donn Byrne abruptly sold his Connecticut house in 1922 and moved his family to England. His explanation was characteristically flip: "You know, I can't bear the idea of this radio telephone," he said. "There must be some escape from it. I'm trying Cornwall."[20] The truth was not so amusing. Donn Byrne's ability to earn money was surpassed only by his ability to spend it. They lived, his wife, Dorothea, recalled, "like fighting cocks," squandering a fortune on extravagant travel, a houseboat in Miami, and Donn Byrne's poisonous addiction to gambling. All the proceeds of the sale of Donn Byrne's house, he said, went to creditors.[21]

For several years after 1922, his life was a peripatetic one. He lived variously in rural England, the south of France, the Riviera, and especially Monte Carlo, Dublin, Jerusalem, the United States and, for two summers, at an estate in County Cork called Coolmain Castle. Before his eyes, the world, and particularly Ireland, changed. "It happened that I returned to Ireland after the German War, in a period very unsettling for all countries and for ours particularly so," he recalled. "Many native precious things were gone."[22] These "native precious things"— values of sobriety, gallantry, and community that Donn Byrne associated with feudal Ireland—had been supplanted by an ideology of pervasive, casual cruelty. In the wake of the "German War" and the collapse of Victorian meliorist ideals, life seemed suddenly neither heroic nor tragic. It was merely ironic. (The protagonist of one of Donn Byrne's stories loses the tobacco shop she has owned for thirty-one years. Her sudden poverty drives her mad, provoking her neighbors to observe carelessly that she "must have been bugs.")[23] The Celtic Twilight movement, along with its new world cousin American Celticism, had nourished itself on the Victorian psychology of earnestness. Now both movements starved. Donn Byrne hated this. "Have I heard the last ballad singer, his come-all-you splitting the air?" he asked. "I fear I have."[24] He no longer found a viable market in quality journals like *Scribner's* or the *Century,* and he increasingly sold his work in less "artistic" magazines like the *Pictorial Review.* Colleagues called him a sellout. Critics began to say he was a "synthetic" Irishman and, most insultingly, a "Brooklynite."[25]

Such criticisms were obtuse because they implied that Donn Byrne's rigorous fealty to American Celticism was only mercenary. Donn Byrne liked money, but for him more was at stake. In the waning of the Celtic Twilight movement, he perceived nothing less than the death of Irish literature. "We shall always—please God!—have Irish writers," he noted, "but their models will be Scandinavian or American. Our young men have seen terrible realities, and in the Ireland of the future you must be efficient to live." Against this landscape of "terrible realities," Donn Byrne imagined himself "the last traditional Irish novelist," the final link in a chain he traced back to Goldsmith and Sterne. "And to myself," he asserted, "the work of writing the last traditional Irish novel has fallen."[26] In his imagination, this "traditional Irish novel" derived from the Celtic Twilight: a chivalric romance, its tone, though often humorous, characterized by a Victorian enthusiasm, earnestness, and an uncluttered sense of right and wrong, its purpose to offer an emotional and sensual experience, rather than an intellectual one.

Although it is neither his best nor his most popular work, Donn Byrne's 1924 novel, *Blind Raftery,* comes the closest to demonstrating that ideal. For the hero of this twenty-thousand-word tale, Donn Byrne resurrected the nineteenth-century itinerant Galway poet, but Douglas Hyde's Raftery is merely a scaffolding on which Donn Byrne mounts the accouterments of his "traditional Irish novel." As with *Messer Marco Polo,* the story of *Blind Raftery* is tissue: the poet insults "the Welshman of Claregalway," a landlord who has amassed wealth by taking advantage of Irish bankruptcies. The Welshman takes his revenge by arranging a marriage between his ward, a Spanish noblewoman named Hilaria, and Raftery. Afterward, the Welshman reveals he has already bedded Hilaria. His intention is to render Raftery an outcast because of his allegiance with a "whore," but Raftery responds by insisting boldly that the Irish nobility disregard her stigma and accept her as his wife. They do; meanwhile, the Welshman, himself bankrupt after the collapse of an extravagant investment scheme, is reduced at the novel's end to begging for alms.

It becomes obvious, though, that Donn Byrne is interested in something more than fictionalized biography as early as the novel's first scene. Here we are introduced to Raftery as he supervises the loading of a string of packhorses. Of particular concern is the loading of Raftery's harp. Much later in the novel we are treated to a painstaking description of the harp: upon its front pillar is emblazoned the Latin phrase "Ego sum regina cithararum" ("I am the queen of harps"):

> About it a great tradition hung: that it had been made for Shane O'Neill and that he had played the airs of Ulster on it for Elizabeth the queen. The Red Hand of Ulster was blazoned in crimson and gold beneath the proud Latin proclamation, and under that in Irish: "Donough McShane made me. Gialla Christ Fitz Patrick was my musician and harmonist, and if there were a better, him should I have had: Dermot Ward along with him, two highly accomplished men, whom I had to nurse me; and my God have mercy on them all!" . . . And there was a pathetic signature scrawled with the point of a dagger: "Pierce Ferriter moriturus." "Now Pierce Ferriter dies!"[27]

Shane O'Neill of Ulster led revolts against English rule in the 1560s; about a century later, the poet and revolutionary Pierce Ferriter was executed in Killarney. In effect, the harp is a talisman that carries Irish revolutionary history upon its surface. The tradition of meticulously describing a hero's weaponry and armor dates to *Beowulf,* and by the time of the alliterative poetic revival in England, it had become something of an art in itself. The legend that the hero's weaponry mysteriously carries the burden of his people's history and aspirations has analogues across European and American literatures, from the sword of Roland to

Hawkeye's long rifle. It reaches its apotheosis in Excalibur (and, arguably, its nadir in James Joyce's brilliant satiric description of the Citizen's girdle in the "Cyclops" chapter of *Ulysses*). Like Arthur, who receives the sword Excalibur from the Lady of the Lake, Raftery receives the harp Clanrickarde from his own witch-figure, a 108-year-old woman "who spoke only Latin and the Irish tongue."[28] This peculiar linguistic detail suggests incantation, even as the subordination of Irish to Latin (as on the harp itself) universalizes Raftery's story beyond the confines of Irish history.

What Donn Byrne is doing is creating an epic Irish hero figure, a Cuchulain for the twentieth century. This becomes apparent to us when we realize that Donn Byrne has changed his hero's Christian name: the historic Raftery was named Anthony; Donn Byrne calls his hero "Patrick," thus investing him with the symbolic authority of the Irish patron saint. Donn Byrne makes other associations with heroes and epics as well. Much ink is spilled describing Raftery's athleticism and Herculean physique; we are shown, for example, Raftery swimming "fearlessly" in the Atlantic despite his blindness, "his powerful arms and shoulders sending him through the water like a salmon."[29] On several occasions Raftery demonstrates an intuition that suggests a kind of second sight. Donn Byrne makes it clear that men fear Raftery's wrath, despite his blindness, and although Raftery is a hero to the peasantry, his company is sought by the Irish aristocracy as well. (The frequent descriptions of Irish nobles making speeches, riding horses, and brandishing swords at approximately the historical moment when inequitable land ownership, the pressures of commercialization, and the 1814 depression had conspired to pauperize much of the country's population suggest how far into myth Donn Byrne had penetrated.) And though ostensibly poor, Raftery and his wife travel on horseback, accompanied by a sort of Scottish Sancho Panza who serves as squire and servant.

Finally, and most importantly, Donn Byrne suggests repeatedly that Raftery's ballads, when accompanied by notes from the Clanrickarde harp, have an almost magical power to seduce, influence, or persuade. Indeed, it is the power of one of his ballads that convinces the Irish nobles to accept the legitimacy of his marriage. At the novel's climax, Raftery receives a hero's welcome as he and Hilaria triumphantly enter Dublin; Raftery is called to perform ballads before the Irish houses of commons and lords. The moment of Raftery's appearance in Dublin is a time of joy generally, Donn Byrne tells us, for unwise investments, associated vaguely and anachronistically with the "South Sea" enterprise, have plunged London into "poverty and desolation . . . where Ireland was little affected, if at all. So the sweet Irish ladies went to the theaters and balls, preceded by their small negro pages with torches . . . and the Irish peers rumbled into the capital in their huge coaches. And all, all gave homage to Blind Raftery."[30] This association of

Raftery and his mystical harp with a kind of Irish victory over the English, rendered together as a set piece of a triumphal march through the streets of Dublin, is Donn Byrne's fullest realization of his "traditional Irish novel." Although he had done (and would do) better work, never before or after would he manage to integrate Irish history, Victorian enthusiasm, and chivalric legend into so singular an image. Meager as it was, Donn Byrne had forged his link in the chain that extended to the eighteenth century.

The 1920s wearied Donn Byrne. He hated the trappings of the developing century—democracy, prohibition, machine civilization—because Irish culture as he understood it—feudal, mystical, and pastoral—could not survive them.[31] Plans such as the one to dam the River Shannon so that Connacht could be electrified appalled him. "What a peasant in his cottage wants electric power for I cannot say," he remarked, "and indeed I have not heard any one ask for it."[32] From this new mechanical century he began to retreat. Various offers to lecture in England and the United States were refused. "I am very much afraid I could not possibly give a talk," he answered one. "I have never done such a thing and I fear I should be very much more embarrassed than your young people, so I must beg you to excuse me."[33] He refused to take newspapers or magazines of any kind. "I find that information on world affairs conveyed by word of mouth is always more colorful and interesting than what I am told appears in the press," he explained. "Also I have a slight prejudice in favor of amateur liars as against professionals."[34] Dissatisfied with postwar history, he conceived an alternative, a quasi-Victorian romance featuring himself in the role of the sophisticated gentleman-sportsman. He rode horses, collected sporting dogs, played golf at the Savage Club, and ordered shirts specially made from Fitzgerald and Sons of Cork.[35] He was, he said,

> as much at home playing baccarat at Cannes at the high tables as playing fat tan with a Chinese laundryman in a back street in Panama. The quiet bloke sitting in the Parthenon listening to native guides filling tourists with misinformation is me, the saturnine-looking individual talking to the Sheykd of El Azar is me. . . . The bloke cleaning up after the aeroplane race from the Copenhagen bookies is me, and the bloke cursing mosquitoes that peastum [*sic*] foraging around the Greek Temple is also me.[36]

What makes this self-portrait charming is its sheer, loony audacity. What makes it remarkable is that it carries the full faith and credit of Donn Byrne's conviction. Whatever Donn Byrne imagined he was writing when he composed that description, it was not fiction. In the moments of his finest concentration, he was able simply to will the twentieth century out of existence. The ability astonished even close friends like J. J. O'Connell, who recalled him as early as 1922 living "the life of Ireland . . . in a natural way," that is, as a gentleman and a sportsman, oblivious to the blood spilling almost literally on his doorstep. Donn Byrne himself would later recall that he wrote the novel *Hangman's House* while living at an estate called Montrose, south of Dublin, in 1922. "Much of it was written," he said, "at night behind iron shutters, and many a sentence has been interrupted by the roar of land armies and the rattle of machine guns." But the only memorable action of *Hangman's House* revolves around foxhunting and horse racing, and the gatekeeper of the Montrose lodge remembered that Donn Byrne had come there "for the racin' season." Recalled T. P. O'Connor, "He was able to see in the prosaic and sometimes the squalid surroundings immediately before his eyes the picturesque and moving history that lay behind in the chequered story of his country." Recalled Thurston Macauley, "He talked oceans of nonsense."[37]

But keeping the century at bay was hard work. Occasionally a cog or a bolt of the machine age would pierce the lace curtain of his nineteenth-century domesticity, demonstrating, as a friend put it, that "he was helpless in many ways to deal with the modern world."[38] Complexities of postwar French statutes about rental property, for example, confounded him. In December 1926 he committed some sort of violation that brought a legal action. "The President of the Republic and his assassins and the Pasha of Boulogne have sent the enclosed Stand and Deliver notice which arrived this morning," he complained to an associate in France. "If you could kindly tell the President of the Republic . . . in a perfectly legal way from me that they can all go to blazes, I should be very much obliged."[39] The next year he was involved in three separate automobile accidents. The most serious involved a blown tire, and he asserted afterward that, had he been driving any faster, his car would have overturned.[40]

These incidents, coupled with the rigors of travel and especially the pressures created by work, by fickle literary markets, and by unfriendly critics, overwhelmed him. On 31 May 1928, he informed a friend that he had suffered "a complete breakdown."[41] It was time to rest. Coolmain Castle was for sale. He bought it in 1928, allegedly financing much of its extensive rehabilitation with ten thousand dollars he won playing baccarat at the Cannes Casino. On Friday, June 15, 1928, he took residence there, remarking, "I'm so glad to have a few feet of Irish earth to call my own." The next day, a mirror fell from a wall and smashed to pieces, frightening the superstitious Dorothea.[42]

Two days later, Monday, June 18, Donn Byrne decided to go for a drive. What happened next is not clear; some accounts say the steering on his car failed; others say he lost his way in fog. Either way, his car left the roadway and plunged over a cliff into the Courtmacsherry Bay at high tide. When the waters receded, his body was found under his overturned vehicle. He was thirty-eight.

Obituaries in magazines and newspapers in Europe and the United States celebrated his indefatigable thirst for romantic self-expression, fitting for a man who was born Bernard Byrne of New York, and who in maturity assured acquaintances that his real name was Bryan Oswald Pierre Marie D'Arcy Donn-Byrne O'Byrne, the descendent of wealthy Ulster landowners.[43] But these encomiums to Donn Byrne's wit overlooked the ironic tragedy of his death. The machine age literally killed him: it seemed almost as though he could have predicted it. Indeed, eulogists did not even try to describe Donn Byrne's relationship to the twentieth century. That was unfortunate, because the effort would have proved rewarding. Of course, in much of his fiction Donn Byrne imagined that the modern age did not exist at all, but now and then even he was compelled to give the century his attention. When he did, he found something remarkable. Awful as they were, neither the trenches of Europe nor the manufactories of Detroit offered metaphors grim enough to suggest the horrors of the new century. To find an image as uncivil, awful, and banal as the era it was meant to portray, Donn Byrne had to look to the most notorious scandal in modern Irish political history.

It was the fall of Charles Stewart Parnell that offered Donn Byrne a story with which he could portray his age. Indeed, at some point around 1918, Donn Byrne wrote a scenario for a film biography of Parnell. In the scenario, Donn Byrne envisions a "pathetic hillside" strewn with corpses, the detritus of centuries of unsuccessful Irish military campaigns. But the Irish profit from these defeats: they learn "a newer wisdom." Because emancipation from England cannot be won by force of arms, it must be won by force of intellect. The force of Irish intellect is incarnated in the person of Parnell, an elegant Protestant sportsman—Donn Byrne takes pains to mention his hunting dogs—whose solution to the Irish question is necessarily a gentlemanly one. Donn Byrne intended for the screenplay to loop back to a central image, that of Parnell giving his first speech in Parliament. He imagined that Disraeli, "sitting listlessly on the Treasury bench, suddenly becomes alert, drops his monocle, stares with hard inimical eyes at the new Star. Here is a man to rock the British Empire. . . ."[44]

The scenario is inexpert, even for Donn Byrne—the youthful Parnell is pictured stroking his beard while his mother exhorts him to "invade England with brains"—but in any case it is more valuable as a measure of Donn Byrne's temperament than as a literary artifact. Most important in this regard is its portrait of Parnell as the archetypal Donn Byrne gentleman—a benevolent feudal landlord, aristocratic, sportsmanlike, fond of horses and of hunting dogs, and so charismatic that his mere presence can knock the monocle out of Benjamin Disraeli's eye. That Donn Byrne could articulate this portrait as a model for Irish nationalist decorum two years after Patrick Pearse and James Connolly had occupied the Dublin Post Office shows that by 1918 he had already found among the elegant artifacts of the Victorian age his antidote to the brutal twentieth century. In that sense, at least, the scenario is the seminal Donn Byrne text. Yet he did not finish it. He never explained why; as time passed he may have concluded that the scenario's underlying premise—that physical force would not work—had become obsolete.

But to say he did not finish it is not to say that he abandoned it. On the contrary, the O'Shea scandal haunted Donn Byrne for much of his life. It was his touchstone, a master narrative with which he strove to explain the new century. The dilemma of the gentleman-hero, whose choice between duty and passion threatens his destruction, serves as the most important metaphor in his work. It underlies the novella "An Alley of Flashing Spears," for example, in which a popular American political figure, Nils Riordan, faces ruin because of his affair with a married woman.[45] It animates realistic short stories, such as "Belfasters," in which an Ulster mill owner's dilemma arises after he fathers a child upon one of his employees; fantastical ones, such as "Wisdom Buildeth Her House," an Old Testament tale in which Solomon's throne is usurped by treacherous courtiers because of his illicit love affair with the Sheeban Queen Balkis; and several other fantasies and romances. It is at the core of the novel *O'Malley of Shanganah*, in which a benevolent Ulster landlord is destroyed by his passion for a nun.[46] And it is certainly suggested by the situations faced in *Messer Marco Polo* and *Blind Raftery.*

Parnell's dilemma could serve as Donn Byrne's metaphor for the modern age because of its place upon the cusp of the century. Although he died in 1891, Parnell's is undeniably a modern instance. He was, after all, a popular political figure ruined by a sex scandal. Yet, for Donn Byrne at least, Parnell is not himself a modern person; on the contrary, Parnell (or the various characters based wholly or partly on him) is the archetypal Victorian gentleman. The Parnell hero is, therefore, a nineteenth-century figure trapped in a twentieth-century instance. His dilemma is not that he loves the wrong woman, but that his principles of earnestness and sportsmanship cannot adequately prepare him for the cruelty and irony of his circumstances. His dilemma is the dilemma of Donn Byrne's beloved Irish feudal culture; his destruction is the destruction of "many native precious things." Because Donn Byrne personalized these precious things into the character of a gentleman-sportsman—an identity he labored to make his own—he in effect associated them, and their fate, with himself. He made them emblematic of his own circumstances, of the horseman, boxer, and hunter confounded by French property laws, small-minded critics, and blown automobile tires. The Parnell hero's dilemma could serve as a metaphor for the modern age because it was so perfect a metaphor for Donn Byrne's own life.

But not forever. Toward the end of his life, Donn Byrne modified his thinking, concluding that Parnell was not the last figure of a great age but the first figure of a debauched one, and repudiated him. "As for Parnell," he observed, "for all that is written of him, he was a penniless political adventurer to whom Ireland gave a career and a living, and who let down his country for some woman. Irishmen don't do that."[47] By that time, though, Donn Byrne, embittered by a twentieth century in which he did not feel at home, was repudiating everyone, decrying Dublin as "a city of despair," calling Belfast "as Irish a city as Paisley is," and receiving death threats over his rancorous published contention that Daniel O'Connell was a coward.[48] To the end he maintained pride in his citizenship in the Irish Free State, but, as T. P. O'Connor observed, Donn Byrne's was not "the Ireland that was brought home to me" during the 1910s and 1920s. Of that Ireland, Donn Byrne wanted no part. His relationship to it, and to the rest of the despised modern age, he described with characteristic humor, parodying Synge, in a letter written less than three months before his death. "I have been," he recalled, "the innocent bystander of the Western world."[49]

Notes

1. See Thurston Macauley, *Donn Byrne: Bard of Armagh* (New York: Century, 1929), 66, 87, 97, 166; Andrew E. Malone, "Donn Byrne: An Appreciation," *Dublin Magazine,* October/December 1928, 30; Maureen Russell Modlish, "The Voices of the Past and the Art of American Fiction" (Ph.D. diss., University of Tulsa, 1980), 112; Thomas Kiernan, *The Intricate Music: A Biography of John Steinbeck* (Boston: Little, Brown, 1979), 101, 115; Winthrop Wetherbee, Jr., *Donn Byrne: A Bibliography* (New York: New York Public Library, 1949), 59–60, 63–67, 84. Among the writers who did *not* approve of Donn Byrne was fellow Irish American James T. Farrell. See Charles Fanning, *The Irish Voice in America: Irish-American Fiction from the 1760s to the 1980s* (Lexington: University Press of Kentucky, 1990), 257.

2. Donn Byrne to David Murray, 31 March 1928, Donn Byrne Collection, Boston Public Library.

3. Wetherbee, *Donn Byrne: A Bibliography,* 87.

4. Thurston Macauley, "Passport to Tir Nan Og: The Life, Work and Death of Donn Byrne," *Bookman* 69 (1929): 153; Donn Byrne to David Murray, 31 March 1928, Donn Byrne Collection.

5. Donn Byrne, *Messer Marco Polo* (New York: Century, 1925), 7–8.

6. Macauley, *Donn Byrne: Bard of Armagh,* 7–9, 12.

7. Douglas Hyde, *Songs of Raftery* (1903; reprint, Shannon: Irish University Press, 1979).

8. Donn Byrne, "Irish," *Changeling, and Other Stories* (New York: Century, 1923), 381–82.

9. Paul Fussell, *The Great War and Modern Memory* (London: Oxford University Press, 1975). Fussell's text remains the most comprehensive examination of the phenomenon.

10. Donn Byrne, *Hangman's House* (New York: Century, 1926), vii.

11. Donn Byrne, *Ireland, the Rock Whence I Was Hewn* (Boston: Little, Brown, 1929), 88.

12. Byrne, "Irish," *Changeling*, 393.

13. Macauley, *Donn Byrne: Bard of Armagh*, 113–14.

14. Byrne, *Hangman's House*, xii.

15. Macauley, *Donn Byrne: Bard of Armagh*, 24.

16. Donn Byrne, *The Stranger's Banquet* (New York: Harper, 1919).

17. Donn Byrne, *The Foolish Matrons* (New York: Harper, 1920).

18. "Laura D. Wilck vs. Donn Byrne," 9 March 1923, Appleton-Century Collection, Lilly Library, Indiana University, Bloomington, Indiana.

19. Byrne, *Messer Marco Polo*, 145.

20. "Gossip Shop," *Bookman* 55 (1922): 330.

21. Macauley, *Donn Byrne: Bard of Armagh*, 89.

22. Byrne, *Hangman's House*, x.

23. Byrne, "The Day After Tomorrow," in *The Hound of Ireland and Other Stories* (1935; reprint, Freeport, N.Y.: Books for Libraries Press, 1970), 159.

24. Byrne, *Hangman's House*, xi.

25. Macauley, *Donn Byrne: Bard of Armagh*, 118.

26. Byrne, *Hangman's House*, x.

27. Donn Byrne, *Blind Raftery* (New York: Century, 1924), 128–29.

28. Ibid., 129.

29. Ibid., 9.

30. Ibid., 172.

31. Macauley, *Donn Byrne: Bard of Armagh*, 146.

32. Byrne, *Ireland*, 124.

33. Donn Byrne to Henry C. Dunkey, 26 October 1927, Donn Byrne Collection.

34. Donn Byrne to Rederck Rice, 29 February 1928, Donn Byrne Collection.

35. Donn Byrne to Fitzgerald and Sons, 15 November 1927, Donn Byrne Collection.

36. Donn Byrne to David Murray, 31 March 1928, Donn Byrne Collection.

37. Byrne, *Hangman's House*, x; T. P. O'Connor, foreword to Byrne, *Ireland*, 15; Macauley, *Donn Byrne: Bard of Armagh*, 113, 119–20.

38. Macauley, *Donn Byrne: Bard of Armagh*, 146.

39. Donn Byrne to Bertram Winthrop, 29 November 1927, Donn Byrne Collection.

40. Donn Byrne to Messrs. Dunlop Tyres, 24 November 1927, Donn Byrne Collection.

41. Donn Byrne to Lady Barker, 31 May 1928, Donn Byrne Collection.

42. Macauley, *Donn Byrne: Bard of Armagh*, 202.

43. Donn Byrne changed his first name to "Bryan" (occasionally "Brian") while still a youth. According to his widow, Dorothea, the name "Donn," Irish for "brown," was added "to save one from the million other Byrnes in the telephone book." The name "Oswald," which he adopted as his middle name, belonged to a friend's pet macaw. See Wetherbee, *Donn Byrne: A Bibliography*, 87.

44. "Parnell," unpublished manuscript, Donn Byrne Collection, Boston Public Library.

45. Donn Byrne, "An Alley of Flashing Spears," in *An Alley of Flashing Spears and Other Stories* (New York: Appleton-Century, 1934).

46. Donn Byrne, *O'Malley of Shanganagh* (New York: Century, 1925).

47. Byrne, *Ireland,* 135–36.

48. Ibid., 103, 111; Byrne to L. O'Connell, 23 April 1928, Donn Byrne Collection.

49. Donn Byrne to David Murray, 31 March 1928, Donn Byrne Collection.

17

Winds Blowing from a Million Directions:
Colum McCann's *Songdogs*

Eamonn Wall

Songdogs,[1] Colum McCann's first novel, published in 1995, is a luminous and many-sided series of explorations of places (Mexico, Wyoming, Mayo); of a son's desperate search for a departed mother and for rapprochement with a father; of love gained in youth and lost in middle age; of the primacy of the road over the settled place; of the possibilities offered by American deserts and mountains that allow the human spirit to soar and the contrasting lack of possibility offered by small Irish fields; of the deep bonds that bind women to one another; and of the artist's special duties and responsibilities in relation to his subjects. It is a work of literary and personal hybridity that draws in such influences from American culture as Jack Kerouac, Cormac McCarthy, John Steinbeck, and Woody Guthrie; that contains echoes from the works of other Europeans who have explored the dry and mountainous regions of the United States and Mexico, including Wim Wenders, Graham Greene, and Malcolm Lowry; and that is influenced by such Irish writers as James Joyce, John McGahern, and Dermot Bolger. It is a work that also can be spoken of in relation to other works produced by some of the "New Irish" voices present in America—the poetry of Paul Muldoon, Gerard Donovan, and Sara Berkeley in particular. In terms of the Irish diaspora, *Songdogs* is both relevant and prophetic.

McCann's first book was *Fishing the Sloe-Black River,*[2] a well-received collection of short stories. "Sisters," the first story in the collection, serves as the root from which *Songdogs* emerges. In 1998, he published *This Side of Brightness,*[3] which was described by Mary Morrissy in the *Irish Times* as "a commanding, intricate, achieved novel." She noted that McCann is a writer who "has never been afraid to take risks, and they have richly paid off here."[4] In *This Side of Brightness,* McCann confirms that he is as comfortable writing about urban America as he is in writing about rural Ireland. He believes that "there is a new cartography of thought, a new landscape of desires, among the Irish today. Our mental maps are no longer necessarily located in twenty-six or thirty-two counties. What you have today is young Irish people opening pubs in Manhattan where there's absolutely no romantic reference back to a gone country."[5] Because McCann lives in America, he is engaged with it in his fiction because, as he notes in relation to the current generation of Irish immigrants in the United States and elsewhere, "what they stand for is what they stand on."[6] Such fluidity is also represented in how McCann writes. His is an Irish voice, though one which is intricately modulated by the physical and literary landscapes through which he has traveled.

In *Songdogs,* the characters are bound together by some elemental binary twists and journeys. Both Michael and Conor Lyons, father and son, have been abandoned by their mothers: Michael's mother gave birth to him out of doors (she was unmarried, and her lover had just run away to fight in the Great War), left him "amongst some trampled flowers," and then took off in the direction of the mountains "leaving a trail of her clothes, including the one-sleeved dress."[7] Juanita, Conor's mother, left Mayo after Michael had self-published a book of photographs of her taken in Mexico and America, half-undressed, naked, and full of young love for the photographer. Many of the Mayo locals had gotten their hands on these photos, published without her consent or knowledge, with the result that she had become the subject of both fierce curiosity and derision. Before leaving, she had burned all of her heirlooms and mementos of her married life— and her husband's studio. Neither woman was ever heard from again after her departure. Both Michael and Conor leave Mayo, but return. Conor retraces his father's footsteps in Mexico and America, meeting people in both countries who had known his parents, and he observes closely the places where they had lived in the happy, early years of their marriage. Before returning to Mayo—temporarily, to collect a visa that would allow him to live legally in the United States— he had settled near Jackson Hole, Wyoming, among people connected to his parents. On his brief return to Mayo, Conor seeks to effect a relationship with his father, whom he has hated because of his role in his mother's departure and with whom he has had no contact for years.

In an early scene in *Songdogs,* Conor imagines his mother as a young woman in Mexico, just after she has met his father but before they have married, standing outside her house in the early morning: "Early in the morning she would stand outside her house and hug herself into the weather, the peculiar patterns of clouds that scurried over the Mexican sky, winds that blew from a million directions, carrying strange scents, sounds, squalls of rain, bits of dust. The wind had peculiarities that she made her own."[8] At all times, Juanita seeks communion with the elemental forces of fire, air, earth, and water: such communion is elemental, beyond language, purely part of the instinctual world of desire, and it is at the root of how she loves. In both Mexico and Wyoming, she is able to maintain this dialogue with the natural world, and with her husband, but as she moves eastward—to New York, and finally Mayo—she is torn away from the natural world, which is at her center, and is alienated from her husband. In Ireland, she often enters Conor's room and looks quietly out the window, and he observes that "the thing that got her most was the cold, the more or less constant lack of sun, the way it would seep downward into her marrow."[9] Once, a sandstorm from the Sahara relieved the monotony of the chill weather and delighted Juanita: "She didn't wash the windows for weeks, enthralled by the revisit of red dust to her life. She ran her finger along the window ledge and held it up for me to see, 'Isn't it nice, *m'ijo? A red wind.*'"[10]

The contrast between the climate of the Mexican desert and the wet fields of Mayo is not a simplistic statement of preference. Instead, it is a powerful illustration of the pain of exile felt by Juanita, although it also shows the extent to which the Irish, in their desire to embrace the modern world, have become separated from the natural world and, as a result of this loss, have become incapable of loving. On another level, we are presented with a critique of the settled life: in McCann's vision, people are more content as nomads because the more settled the Lyonses are, the more they are confined and unhappy.

Yet, despite these stark contrasts, so heavily weighted against Ireland, McCann's purpose is not simply to condemn Ireland for its shortcomings but to illustrate Conor's mother's sense of separation from the dry Mexican desert, and to show her son's claiming of her landscape, not his father's. Ireland is merely the place to which fortune has brought her. Ironically, given where she is, Juanita's estrangement from Ireland is resonant, because it touches on emigration, a defining element in Irish history:

> Mam is just about smiling as she looks down at her hands. It is not an unhappy smile, just a little lost on her face. Maybe she's wondering what she's doing here. Wondering what has led her to this. Wondering if life is manufactured by a sense of place, if happiness is dependent on soil, if it is an accident of circumstance that a woman is born in a certain country, and the weather that gives birth to the soil also gives birth to the unfathomable intricacies of the heart.[11]

We are reminded that the Irish are not the only race who emigrate and of how strange Ireland must seem to men and women who are landed there by circumstance. Considering Juanita's predicament in Ireland, one recalls what the Native American poet Wendy Rose notes of her own Hopi culture. She writes that "the worst punishment indigenous societies can inflict, much more than death or imprisonment, is exile or to be stigmatized by your people."[12] Juanita suffers severely from the pain of exile from Mexico, and she is stigmatized when her husband publishes his photographs of her, the latter prompting her to leave her Mayo home.

In *Songdogs,* Ireland is presented as being modern and polluted, whereas Mexico and Wyoming have retained more of the sense of traditional community, or the sort of qualities so often associated with Ireland. Such reversals are illuminating, problematic perhaps in their simplicity, but prophetic. In recent times, as Ireland has become more prosperous, the country has attracted immigrants from less-well-off parts of Europe and Africa who have experienced degrees of estrangement and hostility more often associated with the Irish diaspora. In the future, Ireland will have to develop the moral and psychological wherewithal to amend its view of itself in order to develop the tolerance and structures necessary for it to become a multicultural nation. In McCann's fiction, men and women cross and re-cross national and physical borders. Despite the fact that he believes that men and women inhabit the immediate space where they live, McCann is also aware that much is left behind when people depart their home places. However, McCann also believes that the traveler's primary loss is not the abstract idea of nation but the physical and palpable landscape that is at the root of all human desires. When the natural world is violated by pollution, which is what happens to the river in Mayo, bonds between humans and nature begin the process of breaking, and fissures between wives and husbands and between fathers and sons follow suit. McCann's view of this process of inexorable, but unintentional, alienation has much in common with the views put forward by Cormac McCarthy in his *Border Trilogy.* In *All the Pretty Horses,* the first novel in the trilogy, as the vaqueros sit smoking under the ramada, they are saddened by the news that Rawlins has left Mexico and returned to Texas. However, they understand why he has returned home:

> They were saddened that he was not coming back but they said that a man leaves much when he leaves his own country. They said that it was no accident of circumstance that a man be born in a certain country and not some other and they said that the weathers and seasons that form a land form also the inner fortunes of men in their generations and are passed on to their children and are not so easily come by otherwise.[13]

Ireland has never been a discrete island bounded by an impassable sea: the Irish view of the world has historically been defined by negotiations with travelers from other places and by the experiences of the Irish themselves as travelers. Nowadays, because of economic developments and the relative ease of travel, geographical and national boundaries have begun to disappear, with the result that Ireland has become more of a *frontera,* constantly crossed and re-crossed, than a fixed nation. *Songdogs* is the first great Irish novel to explore this new world and its implications.

At another level, one of McCann's other concerns, or deep questionings, which occupies a prominent place in the novel, is the artist's responsibility to his subjects, especially if these subjects are drawn from immediate family. In the Mexican village, Michael "delighted in the shot of alter boys getting drunk on mass wine" and the photo he took of the priest, "his cassock raised high in the air as he negotiated an open sewer behind one of the bars, exposing some very dark legs and thin ankles, moving delicately over the river of urine, lips pursed, nose scrunched."[14] He was also caught photographing his wife's mother in her underwear, which got him into trouble. Juanita, when she first meets Michael and his camera, "pursed her lips provocatively for his camera, her blouse open flirtatiously, her head thrown sideways like a film actress."[15] However, in both Mexico and Mayo, Michael's photos of Juanita lead to trouble—in the former case when locals break into his studio and steal photos of Juanita naked, which forces Michael and Juanita to leave the village in greater haste than they wanted, and in the latter case, when Michael self-publishes a book of photos of Juanita—taken over their years together—without either her permission or her knowledge. The end result of this action is Juanita's burning of Michael's studio and her sudden departure from Mayo, Ireland, Conor, and Michael. Michael's publication of these photos indicates a deep sense of bitterness—with his failure as a photographer, with the loss of youth—and his compulsion is to destroy all that was once important by making what should remain private open to the world. It is an act of exploitation and revenge. And it could also be read as an act of colonization by an Irish photographer.

Furthermore, McCann reminds us of the relative unimportance of the artist's self-indulgent vision. The great visionary figure in the novel is not Michael, the Irish photographer, but Juanita, the uneducated Mexican woman, who so magnificently tends her chickens, cares for her friends, and paints the walls of her kitchen pink. She, like the mother in Alice Walker's *In Search of Our Mother's Gardens,*[16] is the genuine artist, whereas Michael is the fraud. Her son, Conor, understands this, and this is why he has gone off in search of her and why he has settled outside of Jackson Hole, Wyoming. It is an open space associated with his mother's genius in contrast to an enclosed Mayo, which reflects his father's bitterness and failure.

It is true in *Songdogs* that the ways of women are creative ways, whereas the ways of men generally are not. For the man to be creative, he must go the way of his mother, as Conor does. Men are more powerful: Michael is the photographer, so the narrative of the marriage that villagers learn in Mexico and Ireland is his, not hers, and it is his bitterness, his withdrawal, his landscape that undermine the marriage, not hers. The narrative is weighted against Michael. Juanita, for example, by giving her chickens the names of local people, is able to bring theater to work and vice-versa with a dexterity Michael is incapable of, although she too is destroyed by time, by the ebbing of love, by what McCann calls the "lethargy of the present that terrifies us all. The slowness, the mundanity, the sheer plod of each day."[17] In Mayo, the wall she builds outside is a folly, as symbolic and as useless as Michael's hopes of catching a great salmon of knowledge in the depleted and polluted river. The relationship between Michael and Juanita toward the end is similar to that which exists between Moran and Rose in John McGahern's *Amongst Women*,[18] although the former marriage was at one time deeply passionate, something that can hardly be said of the Moran union. In fact, the Mayo part of *Songdogs* is very McGahernesque in tone and settings. Both writers—McGahern through his illustration of the deep relationships that have developed between Rose and her stepdaughters, and McCann through examination of the deep relationship between Juanita and Alice O'Leary—show that women seek deep social bonds with one another, which both writers contrast with the surly solitude of men.

Colum McCann is one of many young Irish writers who have settled in America in recent years. These writers are different from other generations of Irish writers—Thomas Kinsella and Seamus Heaney most prominently—because they have come to America as young immigrants and not as fully fledged, mature writers. They have been formed, to a large extent at least, in, and by, America. In fact, they have come to America, a country learned through books, music, and films, to complete their apprenticeships. Unlike immigrants of earlier generations, they have grown up on American culture, so they are entering an arena they feel they know. These writers have not shown much interest in the more traditional and predominantly urban worlds of Irish-American writing exemplified in the works of James T. Farrell, William Kennedy, and Mary Gordon, but have, instead, gravitated toward a more visionary, Whitmanesque view of America, one that the realist modes of expression traditionally used by Irish-American writers could not accommodate. This is not to suggest that Irish-American writing is a monolith: as Charles Fanning has made clear in his work, Irish-American writing is multifaceted.[19] But what these new writers are interested in about America is worth noting: the West, Native America, African American culture, multicultural America, being on the road rather than being centered in an urban neighborhood. Their legendary hero is more likely to be Martin Luther King, Jr., than J.F.K. In this regard, it is notable that the best-known recent tribute to Dr. King is "Pride," written and performed by Ireland's U2.[20] These interests are exemplified in the poetry of Gerard Donovan, who writes of Christopher Columbus:

> After many years of ruminating
> we've sent Columbus back
> because he keeps hanging around
> the basketball courts, drinking whiskey
> and dreaming of buffalo.[21]

It is also clear from Donovan's and McCann's work that America is no longer solely represented by the United States but encompasses the regions north and south of the borders as well as the islands. And, as a consequence of this expansion and these authors' attraction to multicultural America, the language that is heard is not just English. What one finds in McCann's and Donovan's writing is echoed in the more recent work written by Sara Berkeley,[22] in Greg Delanty's Florida poems,[23] and in Paul Muldoon's "Yarrow," which loops splendidly across times, spaces, and cultures:

> To the time I hunkered with Wyatt Earp and Wild Bill Hickok
> on the ramparts of Troy
> as Wild Bill tried to explain to Priam
> how 'saboteur' derives from *sabot*, a clog:
> to the time we drove ten thousand head from U-Cross
> to Laramie with Jimi and Eric riding point.[24]

The movements from country to country, and the backward and forward motions of the search for parents' places, are featured prominently in *Songdogs*. In this novel, it is a consequence of the facts of Michael Lyons's journey from Mayo across Central and North America and his return to Ireland. For his son, Conor, born and raised in County Mayo, the motherland is not Ireland but the western desert of Mexico and the Rocky Mountains in Wyoming: the first, because it is where Juanita was born and met Michael, and the latter, because it was a location associated with their youthful happiness and love, which has not survived their movement into middle age and their removal to County Mayo, to a landscape that could not sustain them. For McCann as a writer, these are regions explored by Gary Snyder and Jack Kerouac, two writers whose works have been important in shaping his vision. For the Irish, it is redundant to mention Ireland when we talk of going home. However, in a world where people are mobile, where Ireland is becoming a place into which people with no connection to it immigrate, it is increasingly likely in the future that Irish men and women, like Conor Lyons, will have to venture forth from Ireland in search of an "old country" heard about after dinner over cups of tea. Ireland will no longer have exclusive claim on this designation. One of many strengths of *Songdogs* is McCann's brilliant illumination of the past and present, and the prophetic, Whitmanesque eye he casts toward the future. It is certainly a fact that McCann understands that "there is a new cartography of thought, a new landscape of desires, among the Irish today," and this is certainly true of *Songdogs*, a novel that, among other things, reaches out widely to explore the Irish diaspora by turning it inside out and upside down.[25]

Notes

1. Colum McCann, *Songdogs* (New York: Picador USA, 1995).

2. Colum McCann, *Fishing the Sloe-Black River* (New York: Holt, 1996).

3. Colum McCann, *This Side of Brightness* (New York: Metropolitan Books, 1998).

4. Mary Morrissy, review of *Songdogs,* by Colum McCann, *Irish Times,* Online, Internet (26 January 1998): 3.

5. Colum McCann, "The International Bastards," *Irish Echo Supplement* (March 1998): 38.

6. Ibid.

7. McCann, *Songdogs,* 6.

8. Ibid., 38.

9. Ibid., 167.

10. Ibid., 168.

11. Ibid., 138.

12. Wendy Rose, "The Great Pretenders: Further Reflections On Whiteshamanism," in *The State of Native America: Genocide, Colonization and Resistance,* ed. M. Annette Jaimes (Boston: South End Press, 1992), 411.

13. Cormac McCarthy, *All the Pretty Horses* (New York: Vintage, 1992), 226.

14. McCann, *Songdogs,* 44–45.

15. Ibid., 36.

16. Alice Walker, *In Search of Our Mother's Gardens* (San Diego: Harcourt, Brace, Jovanovich, 1983).

17. McCann, *Songdogs,* 73.

18. John McGahern, *Amongst Women* (New York: Penguin, 1990).

19. Charles Fanning, *The Irish Voice in America* (Lexington: University Press of Kentucky, 1999).

20. U2, "Pride," *Rattle and Hum,* Island Records, 1988.

21. Gerard Donovan, *Columbus Rides Again* (Galway: Salmon Publishing, 1992), 16.

22. Sara Berkeley, *Facts about Water: New and Selected Poems* (Dublin: New Island Books, 1994).

23. Greg Delanty, *American Wake* (Belfast: Blackstaff, 1995); *Southward* (Baton Rouge: Louisiana State University Press, 1992).

24. Paul Muldoon, "Yarrow," in *The Annals of Chile* (New York: Farrar, Straus, and Giroux., 1994), 71.

25. McCann, "The International Bastards," 38.

18

Ireland as Source-Country in New Zealand Fiction: Dan Davin and Maurice Duggan

Charles Fanning

On the opening page of *The Irish in Australia* (1986), his at once pioneering and magisterial study, Patrick O'Farrell urged his subject's "comparative dimension" as follows: "The American Irish experience has been traditionally the measure of all Irish emigrant things. Recent research has revealed a unique and contrasting Canadian Irish dimension. It needed a very brief sojourn in Irish America to convince my wife and myself that the atmosphere of Irish Australia was very different and that much might be learnt from historical exercises in comparison. . . . [There is] much to be done, much to be begun."[1] Happily, the usefulness of comparative historical study of different immigrant destinations is now well established, thanks to the work of Donald Akenson and Malcolm Campbell, among others.[2] Moreover, it is safe to assume that similar benefits will accrue from the application of comparative techniques to immigrant and ethnic literatures.

Indeed, what has been to me a fruitful way of looking at recent Irish-American fiction grew from a preliminary exploration of Irish Antipodean literature, one that this essay extends. Much in evidence in Irish-American writing since the 1960s, this is a view of ethnic otherness not as destructive self-estrangement but as creative expansion of possibility—ethnicity not as crippling but as what I call "liberating doubleness." When it operates thematically in fiction, this constructive, functional, balanced perspective presents the doubleness of ethnic consciousness as enriching and clarifying. Stylistically, this liberating doubleness manifests itself as an Irish license to use the English language experimentally, creatively, in flights and gripes of tours de force, as in the works of Jonathan Swift, William Carleton, James Joyce, and Flann O'Brien; or, in Irish-American writing, the work of Finley Peter Dunne, who unabashedly appropriated Irish dialect with his "Mr. Dooley" pieces, both for a realistic rendering of the common life of working-class Irish Americans and for inspired riffs of linguistic fancy.[3]

Now, in the overall history of ethnic American literature, including Irish, such confident, positive voices as Dunne's, while persistent, have not been the only voices. There has always been a strain of ethnic writing spurred by anger and bitterness at the perceived distortions and limitations of the author's own cultural lineage. Such frustrations are often visible in the first novels of young writers who feel the need to exorcise the disturbing or embarrassing ghosts of their own upbringings and family lives. Sometimes these books are funny, sometimes merely abrasive, but, because of their skewed perspective, their personal ax-grinding agendas, they almost never last. This is the kind of novel that the immature Danny O'Neill thinks about writing when, in the middle of James T. Farrell's *Studs Lonigan* trilogy, he vows that "some day, he would drive this neighborhood and all his memories of it out of his consciousness with a book."[4] I hasten to add that Farrell himself never wrote such a book.

The Antipodean Irish and their literature provide useful contrast to this pattern. For the Irish in Australia, the key historical difference, writes Oliver MacDonagh, "is that the Irish were a founding people in Australia and maintained their position in the new society, more or less, for almost a century and a half," whereas in America, "the Catholic Irish at least entered a firmly stratified society, an already elaborated class structure and an established economy," and "were doomed to slotting into the bottom layers, or even layer, of the hierarchy of occupations."[5] Moreover, in Irish-Australian writing, the sense of ethnicity as liberating doubleness is consistently observable all along the way—from the extensive Irish contribution to the beginnings of Australian literature in the 1890s by Christopher Brennan, Victor Daley, Bernard O'Dowd, and Roderick Quinn; to the first fictional masters, Joseph Furphy (*Such Is Life,* 1903) and "Henry Handel Richardson" (the pseudonym of Ethel Florence Richardson), author of the trilogy *The Fortunes of Richard Mahony* (1917–29); to the richness and assurance of such contemporary writers as Thomas Keneally and Peter Carey. Probably the most popular Australian versifier has been "John O'Brien" (the Irish Catholic priest, Father Patrick Hartigan), whose collection *Around the Boree Log* has been in print since its appearance in 1921. There is much to be done here as well.[6]

Similar characteristics obtain in the culture and literature of the Irish in New Zealand. Donald Akenson has determined that the Irish immigration to New Zealand was a "fairly representative slice" of the diaspora—mostly young and unskilled, and three-quarters of them Catholic—but atypical in that the great majority came after the Famine. Immigrant and ethnic Irish constituted a significant minority—between one-fifth and one-sixth of non-Maori (white, or *pakeha* in Maori) New Zealanders—from the mid-nineteenth to the mid-twentieth century, with the peak time for Irish-born inhabitants in the last quarter of the nineteenth century. The numbers were never large, but then New Zealand has well under four million people now. From 1871 to 1920, 2,000 to 3,000 came per year, with blips of 9,000 in 1874 and 6,500 in 1875. Using his own formula, Akenson has computed that the population of Irish immigrants and identifiable ethnics went from 7,300 (or 12.3 percent of the total *pakeha* population) in 1858 to 53,800 (18 percent) in 1874, and that the numbers held steady at roughly 18 percent of New Zealanders through the turn of the twentieth century and up to 1945, when the numbers were 272,000, 17.1 percent.[7] They came first for gold. As many as one-fourth of the 1867 goldfields population on the west coast of the South Island were Irish born. Also, after the Maori Wars of the 1860s, many Irish in the British army were given land grants around Auckland.[8] Both of these groups look more like voluntary adventurers than fugitives from famine and deprivation.

A significant minority presence in New Zealand, the Irish have thus been, not surprisingly, a significant literary presence as well. In his seminal essay, "Irish Elements in New Zealand Literature, 1890–1990," Richard Corballis argues forcibly for the primacy of Irish models at the outset of New Zealand literary self-consciousness in the 1890s, and for the important contributions of New Zealand writers of Irish background ever since. In the earliest days of New Zealand literary culture, there was an Irish presence in the dialect satire of Thomas Bracken, an Irish immigrant journalist for the Wellington *Saturday Advertiser.* The columns of this Kiwi "Mr. Dooley" were collected as *Paddy Murphy's Budget* (1880) and *Musings in Maoriland* (1890). It is also clear from the work of New Zealand's first poets that W. B. Yeats and other Irish Renaissance writers were models for the beginnings of New Zealand literary self-awareness. Notable here is Eileen Duggan, the daughter of Irish Catholic immigrants and the first new Zealand poet to achieve an international reputation. Her first collection, *Poems* (1921), was full of Irish nationalist and immigration themes.[9]

Subsequently, there have been many New Zealand writers for whom Irish background provides a shaping perspective, both for understanding their own works and for illuminating comparison with other Irish ethnic literatures, including American. Valuable for setting the nineteenth-century context is Helen Wilson's *Moonshine* (1944), which describes a South Island Irish settlement in the 1880s and 1890s. David Ballantyne's *The Cunninghams* (1948, a novel much admired by James T. Farrell) and Bill Pearson's *Coal Flat* (1963) use social realism to depict working-class Irish life in New Zealand small towns. In *The God-Boy* (1958), Ian Cross convincingly renders the precocious wrestling with God and fate of eleven-year-old Jimmy Sullivan, a Catholic boy in a North Island coastal town. Perhaps the most accomplished all-around man of letters in New Zealand today is Vincent O'Sullivan, who has edited Katherine Mansfield's letters for Oxford University Press, published many volumes of poetry, and written fiction, an important theme of which is New Zealand ethnic experience, including Greek and Eastern European as well as Irish and Catholic.[10]

To reinforce the concept of liberating doubleness, I want to introduce here another idea that is similarly clarifying for the comparative context, one that also applies to both Irish-American and Irish-Antipodean writing. This is the concept of a "source-country," as explained in a brilliant essay, "Imagination's Home," by Australian poet Vincent Buckley, himself the grandson of Irish immigrants. For Buckley, a "source-country" is the genius loci of "a knowledge which goes very deep into the psyche, and . . . has an almost superstitious integrity. The country is a source in the sense that the psyche grows from and in it, and remains profoundly attuned to it." Such a place "already potential to poetry" gives us all manner of gifts: habits of perception, images, natural objects and events, places, place-names, genealogical systems, historical events, language, patterns of family life, myths and legends, folklore, customs and special days, and "an accent, a pace, a pitch, a rhythm of speech." As "most of these things could not be brought to Australia" in the nineteenth century, "what remained was the ache of their absence." Buckley locates this sense of loss in the founding generation of Irish-Australian writers—notably novelist Joseph Furphy and poet Christopher Brennan. But he also includes himself, declaring that, "after repeated stays there, I experience Ireland as a source-country in a way in which I experience no other place." Although born and raised in Melbourne, "for feelings of source, Ireland is primary, and Australia secondary." Given this displacement, Buckley asks, "Where's home then?" and his answer is that wherever he lives, for Vincent Buckley as writer, Ireland is "imagination's home."[11]

Moreover, this artist's self-conscious identification is only one part of the story. Buckley cites his father, the son of Irish immigrants:

Irish to the marrow-bone, he professed non-Irishness; he resisted all talk of being "Irish." . . . He retained (or was told) not one single anecdote to do with Ireland. However, he was full of tales, yarns, jokes, near-legends, nicknames, all voiced in a vivacious ongoing Irish fashion; of songs, emotional attitudes and gestures, a desire for musical instruments, an instinct or respect for poetry. All of these were Australian in content, Irish in mode (a judgement my father would not have understood or acknowledged). The source had been rejected as rejecting. It was like disowning the memory of a cruel mother. . . . He was Australian, and that was that. Yet some of the most chilling sentences I have ever heard about death or mortality were spoken by him, in an Irish mode adopted so naturally you'd have thought he brooded on nothing else.

Thus, for Buckley's father, Ireland was, by turns resisted and unconscious, but nonetheless inescapably, a source-country in terms of "mode," by which I take him to mean "style" in the deepest sense—as understood, say, by W. B. Yeats, who equated it with "personality" (the term and obsession of his father, John Butler Yeats) and "character."[12]

Buckley's concept is not pseudomystical chauvinism. He is getting at the ways people understand and map their worlds, and it is especially useful to see Antipodean Irish writing in this way. All diasporic writers have the problem of having been uprooted, of having lost their indigenous spirit of place and place-lore.

This loss must have been especially acute for the Irish, who have had a highly developed sense of place, reflected imaginatively all the way back to the early tradition of *Dinnsenchas,* poetry of place-lore. The problem, however, is different in different immigrant destinations. For the Irish in America, although there was topographical unfamiliarity, the greater problem was social dislocation and distraction—the unfamiliar urgency of polyglot urban life for a previously rural population. In Australia and New Zealand, on the other hand, it was more a problem of profoundly alien geography—of vacancy, distances, and wildly exotic flora and fauna—the outback stretching west interminably from Botany Bay, or the rain-forest-framed glaciers of New Zealand's South Island. Thus, the need—and not only for artists—to keep an imagined and imaginative connection with a source-country such as Ireland.

For tracing literary echoes in particular, it is useful to separate the two ways in which Vincent Buckley explains that a source-country can be "imagination's home" for an artist living elsewhere: thematically by virtue of certain explicit images, places, names, historical events, legends, folklore, and patterns and customs both familial and cultural; and stylistically by virtue of an implicit "mode" that is expressed by certain habits of perception, by language retained or remembered, or by "an accent, a pace, a pitch, a rhythm of speech." Both can help us understand the nature, quality, and persistence of Irish immigrant and ethnic fiction throughout the world.

This essay considers the two New Zealand Irish writers whose fiction, I believe, best exemplifies the concepts of ethnicity as liberating doubleness and Ireland as artistic source-country: Dan Davin, a realist chronicler of Antipodean rural life for whom Ireland is a dominant thematic source, and Maurice Duggan, in whose stories of the urban and suburban middle class the connection is emphatically stylistic.

Dan Davin (1913–1990) was a native of Irish Catholic Southland, the towns of Gore and Invercargill and the surrounding farms at the bottom of the world on New Zealand's South Island. Educated there in Catholic schools, at the University of Otago in Dunedin, and then as a Rhodes scholar at Oxford, he served in the New Zealand Division during World War II and went on to publish his first story collection and his first three novels, all in four years. Subsequently, he settled in Oxford as an editor and eventually became director of the academic division at Oxford University Press.

The persistent power of Ireland as a source-country in New Zealand is obvious in Davin's recollections of his immigrant and ethnic generation. Born "in Southland's transplanted Galway," he describes having been "brought up a Catholic by Irish parents from Galway and Cork—people for whom the North meant, not our New Zealand north (a hot, soft place), but the Black North Ulster, full of Black Protestants and bigoted Orangemen."[13] Davin locates a kinship with his friend Dylan Thomas, who "also realized that whatever the form of Christianity in a Celtic countryside—Welsh or Irish—it has a primitiveness in common, a kind of provincial puritanism. We were alike, also, in that we had each lost his father's language."[14] Davin further emphasizes the Irish context of New Zealand's South Island in the 1920s and 1930s by recalling conversations with another friend, Itzik Manger, a Yiddish writer and refugee from the Warsaw Ghetto:

> We talked about fathers and I told him about my own father, so much more fortunate than his, an immigrant to New Zealand and a man who had also lived by hard work and his hands, an Irish speaker who like Itzik had lost the background in which his first language made sense. I told him also of Larry Hynes, another immigrant to New Zealand and an Irish speaker, a wandering story-teller like Itzik, a *seanachai,* one of the last of his Irish kind, who had travelled on his bicycle round the Irish farms of Southland and on winter nights, in front of fires made of totara or Black Diamond coal, not turf, had made us shiver with his tales of ghosts and shape-changers, and fairies stealing little children to leave changelings in their place, and magic warriors battling in the evening clouds, and revenants from fairyland who had lived a hundred years in the course of a day and a night of fairy love, coming back to cold ashes, cottages of fallen stone, and new unremembering generations.[15]

Davin's early stories of Southland's Connolly family begin his detailed chronicling of the rural New Zealand Irish between the two World Wars. Mostly published in his first collection, *The Gorse Blooms Pale* (1947), these are well crafted coming-of-age pieces, in the tradition of the adolescent initiation narratives of Joyce and Frank O'Connor.[16] Indeed, Davin acknowledges *Dubliners* in the first two stories of his first collection. Like the narrator of Joyce's first story, "The Sisters," Davin's young protagonist worries about "that word in the catechism, simony." He then reads in "the Catholic weekly" an indictment of *Ulysses*: "The editor kept talking about Liffey mud and the disgrace to the glorious literary tradition of Ireland."[17]

In the opening story, "The Apostate," Davin has his nine-year-old narrator, Mick Connolly, work through this train of thought: "Green was the colour of God. It was the colour of the grass and of the trees and of the sea and of all the best things, of God's things. Green was the colour of Ireland. In Ireland, his father said, everything was green. Even the fairies. Green was Ireland's National Colour. And the Irish were the best people. Even here in New Zealand you knew that."[18] At story's end, the loss of a prized new pencil causes Mick to swing from faith to doubt, but the strong sense of positive Irish identity remains. The second story, "The Vigil," finds young Mick exiled to watching the cows in the back paddock, where he imagines his own death among sorrowing friends and family and thinks about becoming a writer. In "Milk Round," Mick delivers milk around Invercargill, and his emotional world expands to include feelings of sympathy for his family's poorer customers and puzzled hurt after experiencing anti-Catholic prejudice from the Protestant bank manager's wife. Revelations of intellect and emotion continue in "Late Snow," where Mick's imagination is fired by "The Rime of the Ancient Mariner," and he shares moments of wonder and grief when his father takes him to see baby rabbits who subsequently drown in the small floods of an untimely spring snow.

Other stories feature similar rural experiences of initiation—the deaths of a favorite dog gone bad ("Death of a Dog") and of a bull calf ("Growing Up"), after which "Mick felt the layers of feeling inside his father, the indifference— almost callousness—forced by life which held these necessities, under this the gentleness that puzzled at the necessity, the strength and weakness of man forced by life to give life and take it."[19] In "The Tree," the Connolly boys chop down the only tree that their father had spared years before when clearing a section of land, "and Mick saw that what had added to his own past was taken from his father's."[20] Throughout these fine, clear sketches, Davin creates a strong sense of place, for Mick Connolly grows up surrounded by named, familiar landmarks— streets, houses, shops, churches, farms, rivers, and special trees. In Davin's collections, these Southland Irish stories are followed by other autobiographical stories of initiation into the wider world of a young New Zealander who goes to Oxford in the late 1930s and then endures World War II combat experience in Crete and Italy.

In his best novel, *Roads from Home* (1949), Davin chronicles the lives of the Hogans of Invercargill, especially the coming of age of young Ned Hogan. Here the Southland Irish are presented as strong, proud, and connected to both Ireland and New Zealand. The death of their community's last traditional storyteller, old Larry O'Daly from Galway, prompts Ned's observations about the "roads from home" of his immigrant forebears and himself. He recalls his own childhood experience as a spellbound listener to the old man, who is modeled on Davin's friend Larry Hynes: "'That is my story,' he used to say while they all sat round him on the half-filled potato sacks, gaping, or if it was winter round the big fire of redpine in the dining room. 'Sin é mo sgeál-sa' [That is my story]. If there's no life in it then let there be." Ned concludes that when his neighbors had listened to Larry's stories, they became "aware of themselves for the time heroically, as people whose past had not suddenly begun from a broken link but went back unending; the children wide-eyed and feeling in themselves a stirring strength that surely would never be subdued to the plough." The told tales reinforce the "pride" that these Southland farmers feel "at seeing a harvest saved and stacked, a cow brought safely to calf."[21]

Later, Ned muses more generally about the Irish diaspora, again with a positive perspective:

These were men. They had taken their choice, sailing out of Galway Bay all those years ago with their few saved sovereigns knotted in their singlets when they slept at night in the crowded steerage, their only assets their strong hands, their endurance, their well-conned memories of the famine and the bailiff they were leaving behind, memories which would drive them and their like to plough a furrow across their future as straight as any furrow on their farms.

Ned sees that his father and twelve brothers and sisters "grew up to the strength that had scattered them now to Australia, America, Canada and New Zealand," and further states that

> hardship [in Ireland] had made it easy for them. . . . And remembering that and the rent that had gone up whenever a tenant dug a garden, his father had had easy aims: to work hard until he had a house he owned, to marry a wife like the mother dead in Galway not long after his going, and to bring up children who would not have to learn their letters under a hedge or walk barefoot in winter between stone walls scaring crows. They had had the advantage of such aims as these and of being too busy trying to bring them about to question them.

There is no sense that these aims are in danger of being thwarted by outside forces of xenophobia. Ned's is a wholly positive sense of ethnic doubleness. For him, the contrast between the Old World and the New is a tool with which to build. As Ned summarizes:

> They admired the primitive virtues and they had their strength, stubbornness, endurance, loyalty. Conventional, yes. But by conventions that were good for the life they wanted, were made for it and by it. . . . And if you had questioned these things they would not have understood you. For, the good with the bad, this was the epic pattern of their lives. And they asked for no other. . . . A bargain was a bargain.[22]

Very different from the American, urban experience, the continuity of a rural culture between the old country and the new is crucial for the Southland Irish. However, Ned recognizes as well that in this respect his is a transitional generation:

> The Church, too, was primitive, its value epic also. It, too, failed to understand this transition to industrial prose, to a generation whose feet were on asphalt and whose heads among neon lights, not among the stars, a generation which, defying the angel with the sword, saw no reason why they should not battle their way back to Paradise, and, unwilling to deputise their understanding as their fathers had done, groped once more at the Knowledge-tree.[23]

Davin's is a balanced presentation of the Southland Irish, expressed as the healthy sense of doubleness that carries over to Ned Hogan's generation, to the more complex set of challenges that he faces. Ned's is the familiar struggle to fly by the nets of family and religion. However, it is important to note that he breaks away from the constraints of his background with understanding, not bitterness, and that his family's immigrant experience is a model, a precedent, for his own striking out on new "roads from home." The book is a prototype of ethnic awareness as liberating. On the way to Larry O'Daly's funeral,

> Ned looked down at the road again. A plurality of worlds. And only by abstraction do we see the same things. This road, like other roads, was for him a road by which you traveled forwards, carrying with you ineluctably the self from which you were trying to escape and which for every twist and turn you or the road made came with you still, gripping its identity under every disguise and waiting to smile at you whenever you were most unlike yourself, after anguished prayer or laughter.[24]

Thus, the "roads from home" of Davin's Irish New Zealanders look both ways at once—ahead to possibility and potential and back to a still usable, not yet obliterated, past. This novel ends with a combined blessing and release. Ned Hogan emerges from mass, "the wet touch of the holy water . . . drying on his forehead," realizing first that "he was free now like others to believe at some times and at other times not to believe, to come and go with God," and knowing further "that there was something you could never give to others: your right to lose your soul in your own way." So poised, Ned resolves "to go North, free. There was no wall to keep him."[25]

In *No Remittance* (1959), a much less successful novel but still of interest for its historical background, Davin backs up a generation to tell a story set between the Boer War and the great influenza epidemic of 1918. Here is further evidence of the close connections between late-nineteenth-century Ireland and New Zealand. Davin documents vivid folk memories of Cromwellian massacres, the Great Hunger, and the rise and fall of Charles Stewart Parnell, in a community characterized by public boisterousness and private puritanism—declamatory speeches and pub fights about Irish nationalism by New Zealanders who are afraid to kiss their wives in public.[26] In Davin's middle years, another tie with Ireland was a book of essays, never completed, *The Character of Ireland,* which he conceived and worked on with his Irish friends, the poets W. R. Rodgers and Louis MacNeice.[27]

Maurice Duggan (1922–1974), a wonderfully talented writer of short fiction, moved with authority in a life cut short by cancer, from early, conventional stories in the realist tradition to late stories characterized by fragmentary internal monologue and prose-poetic beauty. These later works are trailblazing for New

Zealand writing, and in them Duggan is a masterful, challenging stylist in an identifiably Irish mode. Vincent O'Sullivan has placed him as "this country's writer
who stands most surely in that strong European tradition in which style is also a
moral touchstone; where the stamp of a writer's engagement is found primarily
in a language which is self-conscious, elaborate, closer to the intricate grain of
living than more subdued styles usually permit."[28]

Duggan's life was grimly challenging and heroically accomplished, and both
aspects get into his fiction. He was born to Irish immigrant parents in Auckland
in 1922. Like Vincent Buckley, he had a father, born in Ireland in 1886 and a
draper by trade, whose relationship to his own Irishness was emphatically rejecting: "'I'm no bloody immigrant, boyo: I paid for my own freighting,'" and "'You
can have the lovely priest-ridden land and its lights and loomings, proud mists,'
was what I understood him to say. And Joyce? And Synge? And Wilde? And
Shaw? Bloody word-mongers and traitors, the lot. Parnell? Casement? (That patriotic bugger.) And Yeats? Who? And de Valera." Indeed, Duggan has located
himself mordantly as "a first-generation New Zealander," a product of "the sad
Irish bravura; the drear Irish Catholicism; the Irish syndrome—booze, melancholy
and guilt; the pointless loud pride—for what had they to be proud of, each man a
Joseph in his coat of bright verbs?; the intolerance; the low superstition; the peculiarly Irish deceit. (What in God's name would it be like to be a Scot?)."[29] And
yet, in his late stories that same "coat of bright verbs" carries Duggan's great
literary gift and conveys rewarding connectedness with his ethnicity. As well,
Duggan's own ambivalent image of his forebears combines fear, respect, and admiration: "Only four generations back, there he sits, disowned, my dark ances-
tor, stitching a boot in the doorway of a sod hut, hating the stranger, spitting upon
Ireland, this damned land, aching in every bone from the rotten damp, a sullen,
moody, violent man feared by his family, too fierce for friendliness, his life packed
down like black explosive powder in a hole."[30]

Duggan left Catholic boarding school at age thirteen and spent hours and years
passionately committed to rugby teams: "There seemed no end to the running."
At seventeen, osteomyelitis and infection caused the amputation of a leg, after
which it was "up the hill to night school, across the slope to the public library."
At nineteen came a bout of tuberculosis: "But happily I was losing my self-pity—
you can't keep that for long in the public wards of hospitals—though the intense
social embarrassment never abated."[31] At this point, Duggan started to write in
earnest. Ultimately, he became an advertising copywriter and seriously alcoholic.
His friend Ken Arvidson told me that as Duggan got better at advertising he hated
it more and drank more, and then got better at advertising. Still, he seemed to
have licked the drinking just before he was diagnosed with inoperable lung cancer, at which point, as his friend put it, he stopped drinking entirely so as to be

conscious of what was happening to him.[32] He died in December 1974 at age fifty-two.

Duggan published thirty stories in thirty years, from the first at age twenty-two in 1945 to the last, published posthumously in 1975. His lovely essay "Beginnings" ends with this self-judging hymn to the creative process:

> I look in vain for big books, the decent output. I work too slowly, and too irregularly. (There is no substitute for will.) The output has been small, and I must take what confidence I can from what seem to me small successful things. And still there remains, at least, a sense of mystery, when I do not abuse it with whisky and rant (Joyce's "flushpots of Euston and the hanging garments of Marylebone"). And sometimes the light invades through green bars and there, inexplicably, beginnings lie; if I will be diffident before the page; if I will wait and in whatever unease allow the flooding of the senses, allow the daemon to enter; and set to work.[33]

One group of early Duggan stories constitutes realistic sketches set in New Zealand Catholic boarding schools, in which the perspective is often that of Brother Ignatius, an aging, tired monk and dormitory prefect, who finds himself increasingly unable to meet the challenges of his energetic, irreverent charges. The educational milieu of the Irish Christian Brothers documented here could as easily be in Dublin as in Auckland, a similarity that explains a crucial way in which Ireland has remained a source-country for the Antipodes.[34] Another fine rendering of middle-aged loneliness is "Blues for Miss Laverty," Duggan's bleak yet compassionate portrait of a threadbare, spinster piano teacher who tries to counter her desperate, humiliating encounters with strangers by drinking "gin and angostura and lemonade, pink as a varnished nail."[35]

A second group of stories traces the unfortunate, lackluster life of Patrick "Paddy" Lenihan, a dour, middle-aged Irish immigrant struggling to keep from drowning in Kiwi bourgeois respectability. In "The Deposition," Lenihan is a department store manager with two young children and a profoundly depressed wife. He begins an affair with an employee, Grace Malloy, who sweeps in, takes over the household, and bullies Lenihan into marrying her a scant month after his wife's death.[36] In "A Small Story," the newly married couple return to tell the Lenihan kids their news, establishing a tone of obliquity and unease for this ill-fated family. In "Race Day," a day of fun at the track is ruined by the humorless Grace, and "The Departure" describes the now trapped Lenihan moving houses and jobs to another town in a last-ditch effort to rejuvenate his marriage and himself.[37] The final Sunday dinner in the old place is a "long, unenjoyable and ill-tempered meal," with Lenihan carving the inevitable roast and "stabbing out the potatoes." Grace's sister Sylvia, a guest at this grim table, is left wondering what could have justified "their having undertaken this life of bitterness and reproach which could promise no possible coincidence of mood or pleasure. Poor kids, she said to herself, looking at the empty sky."[38]

"Six Place Names and a Girl" was Duggan's tenth published story (in *Landfall,* 1949) but the earliest one that he included in his first collection, *Immanuel's Land* (1956). This breakthrough piece of only three pages was described by Duggan as "perhaps less a story than a prose celebration of a topography and a time that, in rediscovery and re-creation, moved me strongly enough to force me away from what had become a habit of rhetoric. If it was to be strong, it had to be simple; the language must be a focusing glass and not, as had up to now been the case, a sort of bejewelled and empty casket."[39] The story is a lyrical essay in *Dinnsenchas* describing six Maori place-names, each evoking youthful memories: swimming in a creek, duck hunting in a swamp, playing polo "on short slow stockmen's ponies," digging up a Maori skull and "chipped greenstone *mere* [a ceremonial club head]," running away from home to a night out in the cold, exploring a ghost town from the 1860s gold-mining boom ("An old post-office with *Victoria Regina* on a plaque. Summer and the sun shining and a breeze coming through the funnel of the gorge"). The girl of the title is "Pelly," the unnamed narrator's first love, one of the Maori family with whom he lives "all summer . . . , eating enormously and drinking home-brewed beer and singing on the wide verandah with the maori voices all singing in harmony, the lyrics toned down with the maori sound, so that if you were not lucky enough to be a maori you stopped singing and just listened a long time in the light summer night."[40]

The sketch of "Pelly" blossomed into a beautiful long story in Duggan's late, lyrical style—"Along Rideout Road That Summer,"—which fills out the adolescent summer idyll of "bookish" Buster O'Leary, in flight from his fiercely respectable middle-class Irish–New Zealand parents, and Fanny Hohepa, the "reputedly wild" daughter of the Maori whose farmhand Buster becomes. There is here a provocative reversal of the typical adversarial hierarchy that has fueled so many Irish diasporic experiences, in fiction as in life. "It pains me, gentlemen," says Buster, "to confess that she was too good for me by far. Far. Anything so spontaneous and natural could be guaranteed to be beyond me: granted, I mean, my impeccable upbringing under the white-hot lash of respectability. . . . How then could I deem Fanny's conduct proper when I carried such weals and scars, top-marks in the lesson on the wickedness of following the heart."[41] Buster is the self-described "sun-burnt scion of an ignorant, insensitive, puritan and therefore prurient, Irishman," a banker obsessed with appearances, "a pillar of our decent, law-abiding community, masonic in his methodism, brother, total abstainer, rotarian, and non-smoker, addicted to long volleys of handball." Moreover, his mother is a driven advocate of "causes," always "off somewhere moving . . . that this meeting make public its whole-hearted support for the introduction of flogging and public castration for all sex offenders and hanging, drawing and quartering, for almost everyone else." Buster perceives clearly "a certain discrepancy between the real and the written"—between the relaxed mores of his Maori hosts and his parents' uptight, bourgeois ways. His image for "this profound, cultural problem affecting dramatically the very nature of my inheritance" is "watching mum with a shoehorn wedging nines into sevens and suffering merry hell. . . . nines into sevens in this lovely smiling land."[42]

Against this are contrasted the Hohepas, stolid, "loamy," silent—probably to a fault in the long run, were there to be one, but Fanny and Buster wordlessly agree that theirs is "no more than a summer's dalliance, a season's thoughtless sweetness." Buster measures the gulf between the two New Zealand cultures in domestic terms. At Hohepa's, they "were always silent, through all meals. It made a change from home where all hell lay between soup and sweet, everyone taking advantage of the twenty minutes of enforced attendance to shoot the bile, bicker and accuse, rant and wrangle through the grey disgusting mutton and the two veg." When Buster's father visits Hohepa's farm in his black banker's suit, he discovers his son and Fanny in bed together and explodes, "the fire in his heart . . . fed by such rank fuel, skeezing envy, malice, revenge, hate, and parental power." On the Maoris' front porch, the cultures clash in person: "Puti Hohepa and his lass in sunlight on the steps, smoking together, untroubled, natural and patient; and me and daddy glaring at each other in the shades like a couple of evangelists at cross-pitch." Finding only silence and mistaking it for contempt, Buster's father charges off: "The mad figure of him went black as a bug out over the lawn, out over the loamy furrows where the tongue of ploughed field invaded the home paddock."

Abruptly, his son is surprised by feeling: "And for a moment I was caught in a passion of sympathy for him, something as solid as grief and love, an impossible pairing of devotion and despair. The landscape flooded with sadness as I watched the scuttling, black, ignominious figure hurdling the fresh earth, the waving arms, seemingly scattering broadcast the white and shying gulls, his head bobbing on his shoulders, as he narrowed into distance." In the end, Buster leaves too. "Discrepancy" includes the gap between "dulcimer and ukelele," for he has been reading and declaiming Coleridge's "Kubla Khan" all summer, and ultimately he leaves "old STC in the tractor tool box along with the spanner that wouldn't fit any nut I'd ever tried it on and the grease gun without grease and the last letter from mum, hot as radium."[43] This is a fine story, a rich, lyrical, and authoritative juxtaposition of driven ethnic respectability and relaxed, indigenous self-possession.

Elsewhere in New Zealand fiction, relationships between Irish–New Zealand and Maori characters are often presented as more sympathetic to one another than mainstream British New Zealanders are to the native Polynesians. True, both Irish and Maoris are outsiders; but, again, the resulting positive mutual feelings illus-

trate ethnic doubleness as liberating rather than constricting. Akenson notes that
the rate of marriage between Maoris and Irish Catholic New Zealanders has been
proportionately large, and he cites the similar cultures of the extended rural communities of the Maori *marae* and the Irish *clachan*.[44] In any case, the familiar
American pattern of animosity among competing minorities is much less in evidence in New Zealand–Irish writing. Dan Davin's story "Bluff Retrospect," for
example, recalls a picnic outing at the port town just south of Invercargill, during which an old woman orders the narrator's family to leave the unmarked site
of a Maori cemetery. At first he is embarrassed that "it should have been his family,
Irish people who were in this country because life in their own had been made
impossible, their priests proscribed, their chiefs dispersed and their graves forgotten, who had even innocently violated the soil of another conquered race, especially that part of it which was sacred to the dead." In a moment of enlightenment, however, he rejects this idea as a facile, sentimental connection of Irish
and Maori colonial exploitation:

> For there was something false in it. Maori and *pakeha* had been driven to what they did
> and were by forces beyond the mastery of any individual. It was life that had been at
> work. It was all very well to be "enlightened." What was he going to do about it other
> than indulge the sort of regret that had lain behind their own dreams of being chief-
> tains long ago? There was nothing he would do about it. Nothing whatever. King Arthur
> never came back.[45]

The refusal to take easy solace in the view of oneself and one's ancestors as victims, and the related sense that surrogate identification through history with currently exploited minorities can be uselessly self-indulgent—these exemplify the
healthy perspective on ethnicity that characterizes much Antipodean fiction: it is
a doubleness that leads more often to enlarged understanding than to nostalgia
or alienation.[46]

Two accomplished earlier Duggan stories also show the thematic importance
of both the migratory impulse and the limitations of its efficacy for change. "Chapter" (*Landfall,* 1955) is a brilliantly concise triangulated fix upon New Zealand
patterns of landscape and life. In flight from the city and a puzzling personal relationship, the unnamed narrator crosses the parched, barren, austerely beautiful
central plain in midsummer: "The lion-colored hot country stretched away slightly
rolling to the foothills and the mountains. The far off rising ground hung in a
haze, broken away from the plain, and nearby on the dry brown hillocks the grass
was chased with shadows. The veins of clay lay dry and open under the sun."
Then comes a bus ride to the seaside, which highlights the country's two cultures as the narrator observes a prim, disapproving *pakeha* school teacher, "Miss
Mackintosh," and a group of ebullient young Maoris singing and drinking beer

on their way to a dance. "Perhaps it was beginning now," a real escape from the complexities of commitment, thinks the narrator, only to be brought up short by a last reminder that he's "running away."[47]

"Voyage" (its first part appeared in *Landfall* in 1951) extends the theme of leaving home and romantic trouble to its typical Antipodean extreme, as the narrator travels by boat from Wellington to Europe. Based on Duggan's own trip from 1950 to 1952, the story consists of lovely, fragmentary perceptions of landscape—Pitcairn Island, the Panama Canal, Curaçao; then Venice, the Pyrenees, Barcelona, and Mallorca. Again, the urge for going is sharpened by the open-ended unease of a woman left behind in New Zealand. At the end, the narrator finds "tucked among the magazines on the seat in the great Mallorquin fireplace" a cache of love letters that brings him back from the tourist's flight to a revelation of promise for both life and art:

The last page was a poem by Thomas Wyatt.

> *They flee from me that sometime did me seek,*
> *With naked foot stalking in my chamber . . .*

A breath of empty tenderness; torture most exquisitely contrived. I didn't doubt my right to read [the letters], alone and mildly feverish in the empty house. Whose they were I couldn't say: there was nothing to be gained in asking. I took them with me and went away, up the scrubbed stairs. Here too, in these painful pages, without suspect generalization, was the hope of the miracle.[48]

Maurice Duggan's last completed work includes three extraordinary fictional pieces, all of which indicate Ireland as liberating source-country for both theme and style. Two are novellas, "O'Leary's Orchard" and "Riley's Handbook." Published in Duggan's third and last collection, their juxtaposition creates a meaningful dialectic on the joys and limits of language. Both stories feature middle-age protagonists in full retreat from societal and personal commitments. Both have changed their names without changing ethnicity: "From 'O'Brien' to 'O'Leary'— you didn't change far. Is one to detect a national loyalty?" To which O'Leary replies: "A national disease."[49] And, in changing from his given name of Fowler, Riley declares: "I chose my mother's name for the disgrace I hope to bring upon it before I die. . . . Riley then; christian name optional, and lower case intentional."[50]

"O'Leary's Orchard," first published in 1967, embodies the Irish virtuoso love of language, especially in the exaggerated, histrionic wordplay that holds emotion and self-exposure at bay. The answer is "no" when the eponymous O'Leary is asked "Don't you ever think something and not say it?"[51] Also, there's a good deal of drinking,to comic rather than to destructive effect, and a pervasive sense of loss, as in the story's postcoital leitmotif, "All animals are sad at such a time." Mr. Gerald Aloysius Martin ("Gambo") O'Leary is a semireclusive fruit farmer whose isolated self-sufficiency is threatened by the reciprocated love of an impetuous young woman half his age: "O'Leary, preferring autumn and its pyres and palls, embraced summer: her flesh was almost too hot to hold."[52] And yet, he maintains his equilibrium in ending the impossibly problematic affair (and the story) with selflessness and grace. Throughout, Duggan's tone balances wryness and lyricism, as here in the final paragraphs:

> He had lied. He would miss her more than that. His life had been a preparation for a sense of loss. He had missed her often enough already, over the years. It would continue, an indulgence of himself, O'Leary's O of regret, unvoiced. It was what his life was fashioned to contain, this gentle fabrication, this bright figment. . . .
>
> O'Leary re-entered his oasis slowly, closing the wicket behind him and standing in the dark of the barn. Oasis flooded with smells—lingering, acrid, inexpungeable smells: rotted fruit long dried, sawn boxwood, packing straw, oil, petrol, fertilizer. And overriding all, the natural, full-bodied smell of blood and bone, dominant, pervasive, as pungent as loving.[53]

Duggan strikes the same familiarly Irish notes of loquacity, drinking, and fatalism in "Riley's Handbook," the earlier and longer piece, published first in 1961. In this story, however, language is not a defensive weapon with which to parry feeling, but the relentless, probing tool for unblinkered self-examination and moral dead reckoning. Here, an indignant exposure of delusion, Swiftian in its savagery, reaches to sustained vituperative urgency—for Riley is a one-eyed painter dying of tuberculosis and facing daily the frustrations of his failed artistic career. He uses language to build his ship of death, and the result is a bravura performance in which the story-as-written constitutes the minimal, barely sufficient, hard-won victory over hopelessness of the artist's endeavor: "No not for me this yodelling despair despair despair. If anything I'm a prodder."[54] Riley rages against the dying of the light from his perch on a pub stool at Tunny's Reach, a seedy hotel based roughly on the Captain Cook Hotel in Dunedin, where Maurice Duggan lived for some months in 1960. A cross between Beckett and Berryman's *Dream Songs,* "Riley's Handbook" has been a much admired, inspiring piece of fiction among younger New Zealand writers for its "extravagance of genius on the brink of the abyss."[55]

Among many notable entries in "Riley's Handbook" is an eloquent composition of place for colonial New Zealand:

> What was it? What dream of a fading glory and aristocratic demise prompted the siting of this pisgah pub, in the good old days when hope was dead and stinking, here,

on the clay hillroad as it must have been. Spanned and straining the drayhorses drag-
ging foot by foot from the dark, the flowerspiced dark, the torch, the carriagelamp, the
gleam of brasswork, the Monday Wednesday Saturday news. Stovepipe hats in the
stovepipe dark, hup, hupatit, over and on to new settlings over impossible roads. And
doubtless, christ, the crying of the child waking neglected to the rumble and the
horsesmell, the spice of darkened flowers and the dark like a coffining.[56]

Another is an ongoing, fierce struggle with the ghosts of the protagonist's dead
parents, especially his mother, Pegeen:

Fathered on clay mother one hot mowing afternoon, premaritally, under the pines at
dusk of an outing when the walking distance had chafed him into a semblance of goatish
desire. . . . No; it is unlikely, knowing them, that they used each other with anything
more than the usual restrained enthusiasm. She was too moody a bitch to be cracking
sexual jokes with. And my relationship as close to them then as is now the arc of this
falling piss to the gone Pegeen's unmarked grave. Forgive the spice of the unabsorbed
residuum of alcohol, orally ingested, the quantity thus expressed as waste negligible in
terms of the quantity careering in the blood. My father is beyond my range, which
rather piques me.[57]

A third is Duggan's penultimate, salutary meditation on his craft and sullen art:

Get on then. Let me say it, straight, and have done. I'm no aesthetic technician, art
as craft or artycrafty, nor no technical aesthete neither. I'll be my own man if I can,
dream and dreamer, penman and reader, poet and sufferer, in a host of one. I'm doing
the thing for the sake of the thing and what's wrong with that could you tell me? Riley.
To hell with pseudobeing; this is no private matter for all the fucking rape of a mind in
the matter of producing. If it's anything, and you may opt out for all I care, it's the
process of civilization coming to a head. Well expressed.[58]

And again, a few pages further on: "I've nothing to do with an audience. I dig
the pit to my own dimension. It's no use coming to Tunny's hospice expecting
entertainment or ritual or magic. It's the proper job we're after, here. It's enough,
all said, to be sweating over making something out of nothing. I'm not in the
amusement racket. Mind the slope, that's all, if you've come to watch."[59]
    Duggan's last, trenchant word on the artist's life is "The Magsman Miscel-
lany," the piece he was closest to finishing at the time of his death. A thoroughly
satisfying coda, this is a story of the peaceful coexistence of everyday and imaginative lives. Ben McGoldrick is a happily married man with both an office job
and a writing vocation. In a taped reading, Duggan explained that "magsman" is
"a piece of nineteenth-century slang used by Ben McGoldrick at once to confess
himself to himself and also to conceal himself from others; it may be thought of
as a euphemism, a code or an evasion."[60] In the story we are privy to the thoughts

of Ben and his wife, Rosie. During one quiet evening at home, a piece of writing gets done—a proposal that a husband and wife, called Ben and Rosie McGoldrick, separate; and the next morning, as is his habit, Ben leaves the piece by his breakfast plate for Rosie to read. With Beckett-like inversions, Rosie dissects and establishes the work as fiction: "At no time had the McGoldricks received presents of a tandem bicycle or a moustache-cup; Rose's mother had not been alive at the time of their marriage and, in fact, Ben had never met her. Ben and Rose were not considering separation. Neither had she ever given him weak tea in a mug."[61] Ben's thoughts include articulated aesthetic principles of selectivity and clarity reminiscent of Joyce's Stephen Dedalus: "In the process of trying to see what we wish to see we are involved in selecting from that which we do not wish to see; and the latter may influence us more than the former. . . . Nothing is, perhaps, more filled with secrets than the obvious: we know this and have forgotten it: we look elsewhere, always."[62] He then quotes Aristotle's *Poetics*: "'The perfection of style is to be clear without being mean. The clearest style is that which uses only current or proper words; at the same time it is mean—witness the poetry of Cleophon and Sthenelus.' And so on. So speaks the Greek from Stavrotown."[63] In adding a further connotation to "magsman," Ben also advances the greater value of imagination over reality as guide to life:

> Only imagination can take us through the mirror, through the looking glass. Magus the magician does not report upon the surface tensions. He hears the clamour of the fallen leaf, sees the fracture and refractions of the image, is involved in the reverberations of noise and of light. . . .
>
> . . . Reports upon reality merely beguile us, offer us the "planted" evidence of a choice of the many ways of losing our way in what we can scarcely call the world: reports locate the magsman and the villain some distance from where we stand, and read. But such reports return us little profit, no benefit, in our search to find ourselves; our search to be ourselves; our search for the materials or elements with which we may fashion or refashion ourselves. . . .

This meditation leads to a statement of faith. The moments "through the looking glass, through the superficial fascinations of the mirror-image, past the deceitful gaze to the concentration of the puzzle" to which imagination leads us,

> such moments, reflected upon, may offer illuminations of possible directions. The reverberation of the plucked string, whilst not the clamour of the brazen gong, may teach us in its ordinary cry the truth of incidental things. Once through the looking glass we shall ask our usual questions of a different ambience and receive, if we listen and if we ponder upon what we hear, the unusual replies.[64]

"The Magsman Miscellany" is a subtly crafted embodiment of the interwoven mystery and mundaneness of art. In it, Duggan once more forges an Irish connection both in stylistic mode and in thematic allusions. One lovely touch is his acknowledging of the ancient origins of Irish literature. The lyric poems found in the margins of manuscript copies of the gospels made by Irish monks in the seventh century are the oldest vernacular literature in Western Europe; and Duggan's last story opens with Ben McGoldrick's sense of the artist's "presumption to think of one's marginalia as being possessed of any special interest: they exist. A greater presumption might be to embark upon a central text. . . . Marginalia seems appropriate; some have traced the beginnings of literature even to the margins of Holy Writ."[65]

Appropriately for a writer with palpable ties to ethnic doubleness and a source-country separate from his homeland, Duggan's stories are of place and displacement and the effects of migration on identity. His fiction charts a pilgrimage: from the promise of moving on, to the achieved or illusory perspective of arrival someplace else, to the ultimate understanding that a true fresh start is both impossible and not to be desired. The title and epigraph, from *Pilgrim's Progress,* of Duggan's first collection of stories present the prototype of the farthest off, most exotic, and spiritual locus of that pilgrimage:

> When the morning was up they had him to the top of the house and bid him look south. So he did and behold at a great distance he saw a most pleasant mountainous country beautified with woods vineyards fruits of all sorts flowers also with springs and fountains very delectable to behold. Then he asked the name of the country. They said it was Immanuel's Land.

But of course, this is not Immanuel's Land; it is New Zealand. And the difference is the whole point. Migration carries the poignant hope of salvation for Duggan's troubled protagonists—the narrators of "Chapter" and "Voyage," Paddy Lenihan, Buster O'Leary along Rideout Road, Gerald Aloysius O'Brien/O'Leary in his orchard, Paddy Fowler/Riley on his pub stool, the magsman Ben McGoldrick. What they achieve, though, is both harder and more valuable: enlightening affiliation with persisting echoes of style and theme from Irish origins that remain useful in shaping experience toward understanding, ethnic trace elements both indispensable and malleable, distant and vital at once. In this, Duggan's characters and Duggan himself corroborate Stephen Dedalus's revelation in the Dublin National Library: "Every life is many days, day after day. We walk through ourselves, meeting robbers, ghosts, giants, old men, young men, wives, widows, brothers-in-love. But always meeting ourselves."[66]

Notes

1. Patrick O'Farrell, *The Irish in Australia* (Kensington: New South Wales University Press, 1986), 1.

2. Donald Harman Akenson, *Small Differences: Irish Catholics and Protestants, 1815–1922, An International Perspective* (Kingston, Ont.: McGill-Queens University Press, 1988); and Akenson, *The Irish Diaspora: A Primer* (Toronto: Meany, 1993). Malcolm Campbell, "The Other Immigrants: Comparing the Irish in Australia and the United States," *Journal of American Ethnic History* 14, no. 3 (spring 1995): 3–22; Campbell, "Irish Nationalism and Immigrant Assimilation: Comparing the United States and Australia," *Australasian Journal of American Studies* 16, no. 2 (December 1996): 24–43; and Campbell, "Immigrants on the Land: Irish Rural Settlement in Minnesota and New South Wales, 1830–1890," *New Hibernia Review* 2, no. 1 (spring 1998): 43–61.

3. This concept was introduced in Charles Fanning, "The Heart's Speech No Longer Stifled: New York Irish Writing Since the 1960s," in *The New York Irish,* ed. Ronald H. Bayor and Timothy J. Meagher (Baltimore: Johns Hopkins University Press, 1996), 508–31.

4. James T. Farrell, *Studs Lonigan: A Trilogy* (1935; reprint, Urbana: University of Illinois Press, 1993), 453.

5. Oliver MacDonagh, "Emigration from Ireland to Australia: An Overview, in *Australia and Ireland 1788–1988, Bicentenary Essays,* ed. Colm Kiernan (Dublin: Gill & Macmillan, 1986), 133–34. For many extremely useful perspectives on Irish-Australian historical and literary relations, see this seminal book.

6. Since the pioneering fiction of Furphy and Richardson, there have been many Australian books in which Irish ethnic doubleness figures largely. Eleanor Dark (the daughter of story writer and poet Dowell O'Reilly) writes of the Australian Irish around 1800 in *The Timeless Land* (1941) and two other novels forming a trilogy. Ruth Park describes a slum-suburb of Sydney in *The Harp in the South* (1948) and *Poor Man's Orange* (1949). Gavin Casey chronicles Irish-Australian working-class lives, especially those of miners, in the story collections *It's Harder for Girls* (1942) and *Birds of a Feather* (1943). Xavier Herbert brings stylistic verve and thematic focus to the interaction between Australian Irish and the exploited Aborigines in two fine novels published nearly forty years apart, *Capricornia* (1938), a successful combination of comic vision and social protest, and *Poor Fellow My Country* (1975), an angry and eloquent epic. The Australian *Last Hurrah* is Frank Hardy's *Power without Glory* (1962), a saga of Melbourne politics between 1890 and 1950. In the 1960s and 1970s, several novels of Irish Australian coming of age appeared, including Barry Oakley's *A Wild Ass of a Man* (1967) and *The Feet of Daniel Mannix* (1975), Desmond O'Grady's *Deschooling Kevin Carew* (1974), Laurie Clancy's *A Collapsible Man* (1975), D'Arcy Niland's *Dead Men Running* (1969), Gerald Murnane's *Tamarisk Row* (1974) and *A Lifetime on Clouds* (1976), Peter Kenna's *A Hard God* (1974), and Ron Blair's *The Christian Brother* (1976).

There are also the strange and various Adelaide novels of Barbara Hanrahan, who has a second successful career as a printmaker, among them *Sea-Green* (1974), and *Where the Queens All Strayed* (1978), *The Peach Groves* (1979), and *The Frangipani Gardens*

(1980), a trilogy of historical novels set, respectively, in 1906, 1884, and 1927. A late Australian contribution to the vein of violent, blackly humorous, satiric fiction is the work of David Ireland, whose bleak fables of alienated rebels and dispossessed castaways include *The Chantic Bird* (1968), *The Unknown Industrial Prisoner* (1971), *The Flesheaters* (1972), *The Glass Canoe* (1977), and *A Woman of the Future* (1980).

Finally, contributions to the strains of Irish ethnic stylistic and thematic liberating doubleness have also been made by two contemporary Australian writers of undisputed major status in world literature: Peter Carey and Thomas Keneally. Carey began with bizarre and often grotesque stories, collected as *The Fat Man in History* (1974) and *War Crimes* (1979), but his remarkable large-scale novels, *Illywhacker* (1985) and *Oscar and Lucinda* (1988, winner of the Booker Prize), are gorgeous, vibrant, picaresque narratives that take all of Australia as their province. Especially in *Illywhacker*, there are many memorable encounters with ethnic Australians, Irish and otherwise, who leaven the story and the landscape. Keneally's writing career began with three Irish Catholic coming-of-age novels, *The Place at Whitton* (1964), *The Fear* (1965), and *Three Cheers for the Paraclete* (1968), as well as a stunning evocation of early Australian convict life, *Bring Larks and Heroes* (1967). From there he has expanded his fictional scope dramatically and has produced a wonderfully various body of work, including novels of Antarctic exploration (*The Survivor*, 1969, and *Victim of the Aurora*, 1977), Joan of Arc's campaigns (*Blood Red, Sister Rose*, 1974), studies of wartime uprootings set in Europe during World War I (*Gossip from the Forest*, 1975), and World War II (*Schindler's List*, 1982, winner of the Booker Prize), and during the American Civil War in Virginia (*Confederates*, 1980). More recent Keneally novels with Irish ethnic themes include *The Playmaker* (1987) and *A River Town* (1995). There is no more adventurous novelist in contemporary fiction today than Thomas Keneally, and a unifying concern of his body of work is the experience of migration, displacement, ethnic struggle, and attempted assimilation. Indeed, Keneally's novels dramatically enforce the value of making connections among the various migrations and ethnicities.

7. Akenson, *Irish Diaspora*, 59–69. See also Donald Harman Akenson, *Half the World from Home: Perspectives on the Irish in New Zealand, 1860–1950* (Wellington: Victoria University Press, 1990), which adds valuable detail to the pattern established in the other book.

8. Patrick O'Farrell, "The Irish in Australia and New Zealand, 1791–1870," in *A New History of Ireland, V: Ireland Under the Union I, 1801–1870* (Oxford: Oxford University Press, 1989), 671–77. See also Patrick O'Farrell, *Vanished Kingdoms: Irish in Australia and New Zealand* (Kensington: New South Wales University Press, 1990); Philip Ross May, *The West Coast Gold Rushes*, 2nd ed. (Christchurch: Pegasus, 1967); and Richard P. Davis, *Irish Issues in New Zealand Politics, 1868–1922* (Dunedin, N.Z.: University of Otago Press, 1974).

9. Richard Corballis, "'It's a Long, Long Way to Tipperary, But My Heart's Right There': Irish Elements in New Zealand Literature, 1890–1990," in *Anglistentag 1990, Marburg, Proceedings,* ed. Claus Uhlig and Rüdiger Zimmermann (Tübingen: Max Niemeyer, 1991), 398–412. Eileen Duggan's first book was reviewed favorably by W. B. Yeats's friend George Russell ("A.E.") in his *Irish Homestead*. See F. M. McKay, *Eileen*

Duggan (Wellington: Oxford University Press, 1977), 6–13. Useful general studies of New Zealand literature include E. H. McCormick, *New Zealand Literature, A Survey* (London: Oxford University Press, 1959); Heather Roberts, *Where Did She Come From? New Zealand Woman Novelists 1862–1987* (Wellington: Allen & Unwin, 1989); and Terry Sturm, ed., *The Oxford History of New Zealand Literature in English* (New York: Oxford University Press, 1991).

10. These are among O'Sullivan's best stories. His Greek story is "Mavvy Phoenix," in *New Zealand Short Stories: Third Series,* ed. Vincent O'Sullivan (Wellington: Oxford University Press, 1975). His Eastern European story is "The Boy, The Bridge, The River," in *The Boy, The Bridge, The River* (Dunedin, N.Z.: John McIndoe, 1978). Two of his Irish and Catholic stories are "Vocations" and "Survivals," both in *Survivals* (Wellington: Allen & Unwin, 1985). "Dandy Edison for Lunch" is a fine, subtle study of New Zealand ethnic and class insecurities in which an Irish council-flat upbringing is contrasted to the declining but still formidable Anglocentric elite. O'Sullivan chose it as his own contribution to the comprehensive anthology he edited, *The Oxford Book of New Zealand Short Stories* (Auckland: Oxford University Press, 1992).

11. Vincent Buckley, "Imagination's Home," *Quadrant* 140 (March 1979): 24–29.

12. Richard Ellmann declares that from the 1890s, W. B. Yeats "considered [style] to be the element which in literature corresponded to the moral element in life; that is, by its emphases it determined delicate gradations of value and was a direct indication of the writer's personality. For style was a question of the vigor with which positions were taken and of the honesty with which qualifications were made; it had to do with the degree of emotion to be expressed, and with the degree of contemporaneity in the expression." *The Identity of Yeats* (New York: Oxford University Press, 1954), 116–17.

13. Dan Davin, *Closing Times* (London: Oxford University Press, 1975), 48, 25.

14. Ibid., 130.

15. Ibid., 173. Similarly emphatic is Irish-Australian novelist Thomas Keneally's sense of the persistence of Ireland as a source-country in Australia in the 1940s and 1950s:

Yes, it did shape us because in many ways Australia was the most Irish of all the New World countries, so there was a heavy Irish component from convict times forward. With it came an attempt to live a monolithic Catholic life in the midst of a protestant and non-conformist plurality. That attempt ultimately broke down and Australia turned us all into what it would, which generally has been strange subtropic paranoid hedonists. Until after my childhood, Australia was much like Ulster translated to the Western South Pacific. To be a Catholic and to be Irish was a political identity as well as a cultural and religious one.

An interview with Thomas Keneally, in Ray Willbanks, *Australian Voices, Writers and Their Work* (Austin: University of Texas Press, 1991), 131.

16. Dan Davin, *The Gorse Blooms Pale* (London: Nicholson & Watson, 1947). Connoting loss of religious certainty, the title is from "Perspective," a poem of Davin's, which is the book's epigraph. Here are the first two stanzas:

God blazed in every gorsebush
When I was a child.
Forbidden fruits were orchards,
And flowers grew wild.

God is a shadow now.
The gorse blooms pale.
Branches in the orchard bow
With fruits grown stale.

17. Ibid., 11, 16.

18. Ibid., 9.

19. Ibid., 54.

20. This early story was collected much later in *Breathing Spaces* (London: Robert Hale, 1975), 40.

21. Dan Davin, *Roads from Home* (1949; Auckland: Auckland University Press, 1976), 146. This edition has an excellent introduction by Lawrence Jones. See also Lawrence Jones, "The Persistence of Realism: Dan Davin, Noel Hilliard, and Recent New Zealand Short Stories," *Islands* 6 (December 1977): 182–200; James Bertram, "Dan Davin: Novelist of Exile," *Meanjin Quarterly* 32 (June 1973): 148–56; James Bertram, *Dan Davin* (Auckland: Oxford University Press, 1983); and Donald Harman Akenson, "Dan Davin, Irish Catholic Historian," in *Half the World from Home*, 89–122.

22. Davin, *Roads from Home*, 179–80.

23. Ibid., 180.

24. Ibid., 142.

25. Ibid., 249–50.

26. Dan Davin, *No Remittance* (London: Michael Joseph, 1959).

27. The frustrations of this unfinished project are explained in Davin's essays about his friends Rodgers and MacNeice in his fascinating memoir, *Closing Times*.

28. Vincent O'Sullivan, "Introduction," in *New Zealand Short Stories: Third Series*, iii. All of Duggan's fiction has been collected with a very fine introduction in *Maurice Duggan, Collected Stories*, ed. C. K. Stead (Auckland: Auckland University Press/Oxford University Press, 1981). See also Peter Simpson, "Maurice Duggan's Magsman Miscellany," *SPAN* (Brisbane) 13 (October 1981): 28–31; and Lachlan Murray, "'Riley's Handbook': A Dictionary of Dugganisms," *Commonwealth* 12, no. 2 (spring 1990): 7–16.

29. Maurice Duggan, "Beginnings," *Landfall* 80 (20: 4 December 1966), 337.

30. Ibid., 337–38. Compare one of Stephen Dedalus's diary entries at the end of Joyce's *A Portrait of the Artist as a Young Man*:

14 *April:* John Alphonsus Mulrennan has just returned from the west of Ireland. (European and Asiatic papers please copy.) He told us he met an old man there in a mountain cabin. Old man had red eyes and short pipe. Old man spoke Irish. Mulrennan spoke Irish. Then old man and Mulrennan spoke English. Mulrennan spoke to him about universe and stars. Old man sat, listened, smoked, spat. Then said:

—Ah, there must be terrible queer creatures at the latter end of the world.

I fear him. I fear his redrimmed horny eyes. It is with him I must struggle all through this night till day come, till he or I lie dead, gripping him by the sinewy throat till . . . Till what? Till he yield to me? No. I mean him no harm.

James Joyce, *A Portrait of the Artist as a Young Man,* in *The Portable James Joyce,* ed. Harry Levin (New York: Viking, 1968), 524–25.

31. Duggan, "Beginnings," 332.

32. Conversation with Ken Arvidson in Wellington, New Zealand, May 1979. Molly Macalister, another good friend of Duggan's, has said

I think he really triumphed in this last year of his life, and I think that all his friends felt closer to him than they had ever felt before. As to what I remember of him over the last twenty-eight years—a brilliant, tender, prickly soul, dazzling in his wit, suffering from amongst other things what he called "the Irish syndrome", looking at life with too much intelligence to allow himself illusions. A person who fended off only because of a type and depth of understanding that I think he found nearly intolerable. A shining man with too few skins.

"Maurice Duggan 1922–74," *Islands* 10 (summer 1974): 342.

33. Duggan, "Beginnings," 338–39.

34. See especially "Guardian," "Salvation Sunday," and "In Youth Is Pleasure," all in Duggan's first collection, *Immanuel's Land* (Auckland: Pilgrim, 1956).

35. Maurice Duggan, *Summer in the Gravel Pit* (Auckland: Longwood Paul, 1965), 17.

36. "The Deposition," in *Summer in the Gravel Pit,* 75–99.

37. "A Small Story" and "Race Day" are collected in *Immanuel's Land.* "The Departure" is collected in *Summer in the Gravel Pit.*

38. "The Departure," in *Summer in the Gravel Pit,* 107, 112, 110.

39. Duggan, "Beginnings," 335.

40. "Six Place Names and a Girl," in *Immanuel's Land,* 14–17.

41. "Along Rideout Road That Summer," in *Summer in the Gravel Pit,* 59.

42. Ibid., 61, 55, 56.

43. Ibid., 65, 68, 64, 66, 72.

44. Akenson, *Half the World from Home,* 201.

45. Davin, "Bluff Retrospect," in *New Zealand Short Stories: Third Series,* 14–15.

46. Australian Thomas Keneally has explored the ethnic-indigenous relationship in several novels, most memorably in *The Chant of Jimmy Blacksmith* (1972), which describes the tragic walkabout of a half-Aboriginal boy whose attempts at assimilation end in berserk violence. This book was made into an excellent film. New Zealand's Maurice Shadbolt is an accomplished novelist whose partial Irish ancestry figures in his thematic engagement with the imposition of European colonial dreams on the real life of Pacific islanders. In *Strangers and Journeys* (1972), set in New Zealand in the 1950s, he develops the theme of this cultural collision. A further analysis of complex ethnic layers oc-

curs in Shadbolt's *Season of the Jew* (1987), a historical novel about the revolt in 1868 against British rule by a Maori convert to Judaism.

47. Duggan, "Chapter," in *Immanuel's Land,* 48, 67, 68.

48. Duggan, "Voyage," in *Immanuel's Land,* 93.

49. Duggan, "O'Leary's Orchard," in *O'Leary's Orchard and Other Stories* (Christchurch: Caxton, 1970), 66.

50. Duggan, "Riley's Handbook," in *O'Leary's Orchard,* 112–13.

51. Duggan, "O'Leary's Orchard," 48.

52. Ibid., 70.

53. Ibid., 73–74.

54. Duggan, "Riley's Handbook," 136.

55. Stead, *Collected Stories,* 18.

56. Duggan, "Riley's Handbook," 143.

57. Ibid., 124–25.

58. Ibid., 152.

59. Ibid., 157.

60. Duggan, "The Magsman Miscellany," *Islands* 12 (winter 1975): 133.

61. Ibid., 132.

62. Ibid., 122.

63. Ibid., 124.

64. Ibid., 124.

65. Ibid., 119.

66. James Joyce, *Ulysses* (1922; reprint, New York: Vintage, 1966), 213.

Contributors

Index

Contributors

Andrew Carpenter is an associate professor of English at University College Dublin, where he received his doctorate in 1970. He is the former associate editor of the *Field Day Anthology of Irish Writing*. His most recent book is *Verse in English from Eighteenth-Century Ireland*.

Ron Ebest is completing a doctoral dissertation at Southern Illinois University Carbondale that analyzes Irish-American literature composed between 1900 and 1935. His publications include essays in *Eire-Ireland* as well as forthcoming essays in *MELUS* and *The Encyclopedia of the Irish in America*.

Charles Fanning teaches English and history and is the director of Irish and Irish Immigration Studies at Southern Illinois University Carbondale. His recent books include *The Exiles of Erin: Nineteenth-Century Irish-American Fiction*, an edition of *Chicago Stories of James T. Farrell*, and *The Irish Voice in America: 250 Years of Irish-American Fiction*.

Patricia J. Fanning is an assistant professor in the Sociology and Anthropology Department at Bridgewater State College in Massachusetts. She earned her doctorate in sociology from Boston College. Her publications include several essays on connections between the arts, primarily photography and literature, and the wider American culture.

Lawrence W. McBride is a professor of history at Illinois State University in Normal. He has published several articles and is editing a book on the theme of images, icons, and the Irish nationalist imagination. His most recent publication is *The Reynolds Letters: An Irish Emigrant Family in Manchester, England, 1878–1904*.

Lawrence J. McCaffrey is a professor of history emeritus at Loyola University of Chicago. He received his doctorate from the University of Iowa. A cofounder of the American Conference for Irish Studies, he has published several articles and books on Irish and Irish-American subjects. His books include *The Irish*

Question: Two Centuries of Conflict, *The Irish Catholic Diaspora in America*, and *Textures of Irish America*.

Kerby A. Miller is a former senior fellow at the Institute of Irish Studies at the Queen's University of Belfast and currently a professor of Irish and Irish-American history at the University of Missouri–Columbia. His publications include *Emigrants and Exiles: Ireland and the Irish Exodus to North America*, which won the Merle Curti and Theodore Saloutos awards in social and immigration history, respectively, and *Irish Popular Culture, 1650–1850*, coedited with James S. Donnelly Jr.

Maureen Murphy is a professor of secondary education and English at Hofstra University and the project director of the New York State Great Irish Famine Curriculum. She edited Asenath Nicholson's *Annals of the Famine* and a forthcoming edition of Nicholson's *Ireland's Welcome to the Stranger*.

Grace Neville is a statutory/senior lecturer in French at University College, Cork. She studied at University College, Cork, and at universities in Lille and Caen, France. Her area of specialization is the interface between French and Irish literature and culture from the medieval period onward.

George O'Brien is a professor of English at Georgetown University. He is the author of three volumes of memoirs—*The Village of Longing*, *Dancehall Days*, and *Out of Our Minds*—and of *Brian Friel* and *Brian Friel: A Research Guide*. He contributed the notes and introduction to *The Ireland Anthology*.

Edward J. O'Day is an associate professor of history emeritus at Southern Illinois University Carbondale, where he won several awards for teaching excellence in modern European history. He is the former president of the Illinois State Genealogical Society (1989–1991) and a longtime member of the executive board of the Genealogical Society of Southern Illinois.

Philip O'Leary teaches Irish literature and the Irish language in the Irish Studies Program at Boston College. He is the author of numerous essays and reviews on Irish culture and literature in Irish both early and contemporary. He also wrote the award-winning study of modern literature in Irish, *The Prose Literature of the Gaelic Revival (1881–1921): Ideology and Innovation*.

Richard F. Peterson is a professor of English at Southern Illinois University Carbondale. He is the author of many essays on modern literature and of books about James Joyce, William Butler Yeats, and the Irish short-story writer Mary Lavin. The founder and editor of *Crab Orchard Review*, he also edits the Writing Baseball Series at Southern Illinois University Press.

James Silas Rogers is the managing editor of *New Hibernia Review*, a journal of Irish Studies published by the University of St. Thomas in Minnesota. He has published several articles on Irish-American sports figures, coauthored (with Norman Sims) the entry on Joseph Mitchell for the *Dictionary of Literary Biography*, and contributed articles on regional Irish history to *The Encyclopedia of the Irish in America*.

Ellen Skerrett is an independent scholar, the editor of *At the Crossroads: Old Saint Patrick's and the Chicago Irish*, and the coauthor of *Catholicism, Chicago Style*; *The Irish in Chicago*; and *Chicago: City of Neighborhoods*. She did graduate work with the Committee on Social Thought at the University of Chicago.

Eamonn Wall is an associate professor of English at Creighton University in Omaha, Nebraska. He has published two collections of poetry—*Dyckman-200th St* and *Iron Mountain Road*—and numerous essays and reviews on contemporary Irish and Irish-American writing.

Terence Winch has published two books of poems, *Irish Musicians/American Friends*, which won an American Book Award, and *The Great Indoors*, which won the Columbia Book Award. He has also published a book of short stories titled *Contenders* and numerous chapbooks. His work has appeared in many anthologies, including *Best American Poetry 1997*, and he has received an NEA Fellowship in poetry.

Index

Abbott, Edith, 2
Adams, William Forbes, 2, 94, 109
Addams, Jane, 189–92, 212–16
African Americans, 3, 21–22, 60, 73, 83–
   87, 172, 177–78
Akenson, Donald, 5, 15–20, 289–90, 302
Alexander, Charles, 181
Alias Grace (Atwood), 129
Alien and Sedition Acts, 79
All the Pretty Horses (C. McCarthy), 284
American Revolution, 75, 77, 80, 82–83,
   88, 169
America's National Game (Spalding),
   177, 179
Amongst Women (McGahern), 286
Angela's Ashes (McCourt), 236–49
"Annie Laurie" (song), 123
An Taoile Tuile (Ó Séaghdha), 260
Appel, John J., 154
Argentina, 16
Aristotle, 306
Around the Boree Log (Hartigan), 290
Arthur, King, 273, 302
athleticism, 16, 178, 273
Atwood, Margaret, 129
Australia, 15, 16, 19–21, 120, 289–90,
   292–93, 296

Ballantyne, David, 291
Baltimore (Md.), 23, 67, 73, 82, 176,
   180–81, 183, 197
Barnett, Rev. Samuel A., 190
baseball, 176–85
Bayor, Ronald H., 6
Beckett, Samuel, 304, 306

Beecher, Catherine, 158
Beecher, Rev. Lyman, 196
Belfast, 25, 88, 96, 99, 106, 238, 278
Benet, Stephen Vincent, 266
Beowulf, 272
Bergen, Marty, 179
Berkeley, Sara, 281, 287
Berryman, John, 304
Birch, Thomas Ledlie, 79
Bisbee, E. S., 155
Blair, Hugh, 66–67
Blessing, Patrick, 6
Blind Raftery (Byrne), 272, 277
Bodhlaeir, Brighid, 258–59
Bodnar, John, 4
Bolger, Dermot, 281
Border Trilogy (C. McCarthy), 284
Boston, 23, 77, 96–99, 107–8, 133, 143–
   46, 150, 168, 176, 180, 183, 198
Bottom of the Harbour, The (Mitchell),
   52, 58, 60
Bourke, Angela, 34
Bracken, Thomas, 291
Brennan, Christopher, 290, 292
Brewer, Eileen, 4
Britain, 15–21, 77, 94, 118, 272, 274
British, 73, 76, 80, 82, 86, 93–94, 103,
   153, 171, 176, 242–43, 263, 268, 272,
   301
Brown, Thomas N., 3
Buckley, Vincent, 292–93, 298
Buffalo (N.Y.), 19, 21, 23
Burke, Ædanus, 82
Burke, T. H., 171
Burns, Ken, 180–81
Buscher, Anthony, 195–96

Butler, Pierce, 82
Byrne, Donn, 266–80

Cabell, James Branch, 266
Caisleáin Ó ir (Ó Grianna), 261
Campbell, Malcolm, 16, 289
Canada, 15–16, 19–21, 24, 93–94, 96, 107, 120, 170, 289, 296
canals, 93, 102
Caoineadh an Choimhighthigh (Ó Gallchobhair), 256
Carey, Hugh, 50
Carey, Peter, 290
Carleton, William, 60, 289
Carse, Robert, 194
Casement, Roger, 267, 298
Catholicism, 16–18, 20–21, 23–24, 35, 42–43, 76–83, 117–18, 135–36, 140–41, 144, 145–46, 147, 149, 169, 189–222, 224, 236–37, 242, 246, 258–59, 267, 293–94, 296–97, 298, 299, 307
Cavendish, Lord Frederick, 171
Celtic Twilight, 268, 270–71
census, 15, 52, 84, 109, 212
Chicago, 131–37, 140, 142–43, 145–48, 150–51, 176, 180, 182, 189–222, 238; Great Fire of 1871, 210–11
Churchill, Winston, 40
civil war: American, 84, 183; Irish, 269
Clark, Dennis, 4
Clarke, Sister Mary Frances, 198
Clinton, President Bill, 20
Coal Flat (Pearson), 291
Coleridge, Samuel Taylor, 270, 301
Collegians, The (Griffin), 246
Collins, Michael, 145
Columbus, Christopher, 286
Comiskey, Charles A., 182
Comiskey, John, 195
Concanen, Matthew, 65
Connacht (Ireland), 103, 106–9, 267, 274
Connolly, James, 276
Corballis, Richard, 291
Corrigan, Archbishop Michael, 23–24

County Antrim, 66–67, 76–77, 83–84, 106, 267
County Armagh, 267
County Cavan, 106, 261
County Clare, 47, 98, 156, 198
County Cork, 83, 93, 97–98, 107–10, 197–98, 271, 274, 293
County Derry, 93, 106
County Donegal, 65, 79, 103, 106, 109, 261
County Down, 98, 106
County Galway, 47, 49–50, 82, 93, 102–3, 107–8, 110, 263, 267, 272, 293, 295–96
County Kerry, 65, 107–9, 260
County Kilkenny, 107, 109
County Leitrim, 131–32
County Limerick, 93, 108, 236–38, 240–44, 246
County Mayo, 98, 257, 262, 281–87
County Monaghan, 106
County Offaly, 98
County Roscommon, 103, 107–8
County Tipperary, 107, 211
County Tyrone, 56, 98, 102
County Waterford, 102, 107
County Westmeath, 108
County Wexford, 29, 36, 108
County Wicklow, 98, 108
Crane, Hart, 28
Crimean War, 86
Croker, T. Crofton, 117
Cromwell, Oliver, 256, 297
Crosby, Alfred, 229
Cross, Ian, 291
Cullen, Paul Cardinal, 22
Cunninghams, The (Ballantyne), 291
Curran, Joseph M., 6, 18
Curtis, L. Perry, 153, 154

Daley, Victor, 290
Dalrymple, Louis, 156, 158, 167
Damen, Rev. Arnold, SJ, 192–98, 211–12
dancing, 46, 121, 123–25, 127, 136

Davin, Dan, 293–97, 302
de Barra, Caitlín, 258
Delanty, Greg, 287
Deserted Village, The (Goldsmith), 66, 69
Detroit, 22, 276
de Valera, Eamon, 298
Devlin, Jim, 179
Devlin, Joseph, 266
Devotional Revolution, 22, 172, 194
DiMaggio, Joe, 177
Diner, Hasia, 4, 24
Dinneen, Rev. Patrick, 257
Dinnsenchas tradition, 293, 300
Disraeli, Benjamin, 276
Donovan, Gerard, 281, 286–87
Doyle, David Noel, 21, 94, 109–10
Doyle, Rev. P., 258
Dream Songs (Berryman), 304
Dublin, 25, 39, 51, 57, 65, 77, 86, 93, 96,
    98, 108, 118, 171, 198, 226, 238, 260,
    262, 269, 271, 273–76, 278, 299, 307
Dubliners (Joyce), 294
Dudden, Faye, 158
Duggan, Eileen, 291
Duggan, Maurice, 293, 297–307
Dunne, Finley Peter, 5, 215, 225, 289

Easter 1916 Proclamation, 245
education, 24–25, 83, 147–48, 190, 193–
    94, 197–209, 210, 213
Ehrhart, Samuel, 157, 160
Eisenhower, President Dwight, 42
Elliott, Bruce, 107
Ellis Island, 127
Emmet, Robert, 86
Engels, Friedrich, 134
England, Bishop John, 82

Famine, Great, 20, 22, 78–79, 82, 86, 88,
    93–94, 96, 99, 102–3, 106, 108–10,
    118, 131–32, 140, 183, 194, 209, 213,
    242, 246, 290, 296–97
Fanning, Charles, 5–6, 129, 286
Farrell, James T., 138, 189, 286, 290

Feehan, Archbishop Patrick A., 212, 214
Fenians, 56, 153, 170, 214
Ferriter, Pierce, 272
Finnegans Wake (Joyce), 52, 59
Fischer, Roger, 172
Fishing the Sloe-Black River (McCann),
    281
Fitzgerald, F. Scott, 266
Fitzgerald, Rev. Thomas S., SJ, 213–14
Fitzpatrick, David, 5, 94, 96, 109
Foolish Matrons (Byrne), 270
Fortunes of Richard Mahoney
    (Richardson), 290
Foster, Roy, 88, 153
Freemasons, 146, 300
French Revolution, 78
Furphy, Joseph, 290, 292

Gaelic culture, 15–16, 48, 76–77, 81,
    253–60, 262
Gaelic Revival, 253, 263
Gaeltacht, 254, 256–57, 259
Galicia, 31
Gallup Poll, 15
Galwey, Mother Margaret, RSCJ, 197
"Garden Where the Praties Grow, The"
    (song), 54
Geertz, Clifford, 1
German Americans, 20, 23, 47, 54, 144,
    176–77, 190, 192, 195, 223
Gibbons, James Cardinal, 23–24
Gilley, Sheridan, 5
Ginsberg, Allen, 38
Girl's Reading Book, 158, 168
Glazier, Michael, 6
God-Boy, The (Cross), 291
Gold Rush: American, 97; New Zealand,
    291
Goldsmith, Oliver, 66, 69, 271
Gombrich, E. H., 154
Gordon, Mary, 286
Gorse Blooms Pale, The (Davin), 294
Grace, William R., 168
Graetz, F., 166

Great Gatsby, The (Fitzgerald), 266
Greeley, Rev. Andrew, 4
Greenberg, Hank, 177
Greene, Graham, 28
Gregory, Augusta, 267
Griffin, Gerald, 246
Griffin, Syd B., 157, 167
Guinane, Timothy W., 19
Guthrie, Woody, 281

Handlin, Oscar, 2–3
Hangman's House (Byrne), 275
Hansen, Marcus Lee, 2, 93–94, 106
Harrigan and Hart, 56
Harris, Frank, 266
Hartigan, Rev. Patrick (pseud. John
    O'Brien), 290
Heaney, Joe, 46
Heaney, Seamus, 88, 286
Helms, Jesse, 88
Hemans, Felicia Dorothea, 168
Hibernians, Ancient Order of, 143–44
Hoggart, Richard, 2, 8
Houston, Cecil J., 5
Howarth, F. M., 155
Hurley, Sister Mary Agatha, 198
Hyde, Douglas, 267, 272

identity, 15, 17–18, 21, 23, 75, 79, 81–83,
    86, 88, 127, 171, 216, 294, 307
Immanuel's Land (Duggan), 300
influenza epidemic, 223–35
In Search of Our Mother's Gardens
    (Walker), 285
Ireland, Archbishop John, 19, 23–24
Irish language, 30, 65, 76, 83, 117–30,
    253–65
Irish Literary Renaissance, 267, 291
Irish Rebellion (1798), 67, 77, 84
Irish Revolution (1916–21), 147, 245, 269
Irish Sisters of Mercy, 197
Irish Volunteers, 81, 144
Isenberg, Michael T., 6

Italian Americans, 177, 191, 213–15, 223,
    266

James, Bill, 170–82
James Joyce Society, 52
Jay's Treaty, 78, 82
Jefferson, Thomas, 78, 79, 81
Jesuits, 191–93, 196–97, 209–10, 212–13
Jews, 40, 172, 177, 210, 211, 214, 243
Joe Gould's Secret (Mitchell), 58, 59–60
Johnson, Samuel, 67
Jones, Bob, 88
Jones, Thomas Alfred, 152
journalism, 52–54, 56, 59–61
Joyce, James, 52, 247, 266, 273, 281, 289,
    294, 298–99, 306, 307

Kane, Sister Mary Isabella, 198, 209
Kelleher, John V., 1, 3
Kelly, "Honest John," 169
Kelly, Mike "King," 176, 180
Keneally, Thomas, 290
Kennedy, John F., 3, 286
Kennedy, Lucy, 177–78
Kennedy, William, 286
Kenny, Kevin, 6
Kerouac, Jack, 281, 287
Kilmer, Joyce, 266
King, Martin Luther, Jr., 286
King of the Beggars (O'Faolain), 17
Kinsella, Thomas, 286
Knights of Columbus, 144, 146
Knights of Labor, 23
Know-Nothing Party, 87
Korean War, 223
Kraut, Alan, 223–24

labor, 16–19, 21, 23–25, 75, 97–99, 102–
    3, 135, 152–75, 177, 184, 193–94,
    212, 213, 226, 269–70
Ladies' Home Journal, 216
Larkin, Emmet, 22
"Last Rose of Summer, The" (song), 53
Lees, Lynn Hollen, 5

Leinster (Ireland), 98, 106, 108, 268
Lennon, John, 38–39
Leslie, Shane, 266
Levine, Edward M., 3
Leyburn, James, 3, 77
Lincoln, Abraham, 38
Lindbergh, Charles, 42
Little Sisters of the Poor, 212–13
Liverpool (England), 96, 147, 238
London, 60, 141, 149, 189–90, 213, 273
Londonderry (N.H.), 77–80
Lowell, Amy, 266
Lowell (Mass.), 93
Lowry, Malcolm, 281
Lyrical Ballads (Wordsworth), 67

Mac Aodhagáin, M., 259
Mac Aonghusa, Criostóir, 257
Mac Cárthaigh, Cormac, 260
Mac Confhaola, Séamus, 260
MacCurtain, Margaret, 152
MacDonagh, Martin, 129
MacDonagh, Oliver, 290
Mac Fhionnlaoich, Peadar, 257
MacGregor, Rev. James, 77
Mack, Connie, 182
Mac Maoláin, Seán, 262
MacNeice, Louis, 297
Maguidhir, Séamus, 262
"Maid of Coolmore, The" (song), 123
"Maid of Galway Town, The" (song), 123
Malamud, Bernard, 34
Manchester (England), 131–37, 140, 142–43, 145, 147–51
Mansfield, Katherine, 291
Maori of New Zealand, 290–91, 300–302
Marco Polo, 270
Massachusetts Bay Colony, 77
McCaffrey, Lawrence, 4, 53, 178
McCann, Colum, 281–88
McCarthy, Cormac, 281, 284
McCarthy, Mary, 228
McCloskey, John Cardinal, 169

McCourt, Frank, 236–49
McGahern, John, 281, 286
McGuinness, Peter J., 54–56
McMillan, John, 79
McNeill, Ada, 267
McNulty, John, 54
McQuaid, Bishop Bernard, 23–24
"McSorley's Inflation" (Harrigan and Hart), 56
McSorley's Wonderful Saloon (Mitchell), 56–58
Meagher, Timothy J., 6
Memories of a Catholic Girlhood (M. McCarthy), 228
Messer Marco Polo (Byrne), 270, 272, 277
Methodism, 83
Mexico, 281–85, 287
Midwest (USA), 19, 21–24, 136, 193, 209
Miller, David W., 18–19
Miller, Kerby A., 4, 15–16, 118–19, 122
Mitchell, Joseph, 52–61
Modest Proposal, A (Swift), 237
Moonshine (H. Wilson), 291
Moore, Thomas, 67
Morris, William, 189
Mozart, Wolfgang Amadeus, 210
Mozeen, Thomas, 65
Muldoon, Paul, 281, 287
Mulvihill, Brendan, 51
Munroe, George, 167
Munster (Ireland), 106–9, 268
Murnane, Tim, 183
Murray, Rev. Lawrence, 254
music, 18, 33, 40, 44–46, 50–51, 53–54, 65, 68, 118, 120–25, 127, 163, 166, 167, 176, 196, 210, 214, 216, 239, 272–74, 286
Musings in Maoriland (Bracken), 291
"My Charming Kate O'Neill" (song), 122
My Ears Are Bent (Mitchell), 54
"My Lovely Irish Rose" (song), 123
"My Wild Irish Rose" (song), 54

"Nancy, Lovely Nancy, Ten Thousand Times Adieu" (song), 123
Napoleonic Wars, 94
Nast, Thomas, 153
National Catholic Welfare Conference, 24
nationalism, Irish and Irish-American, 15–17, 19–25, 76–77, 80, 82–83, 86, 88, 145, 153–55, 165, 170–72, 210, 243–46, 276–78, 291, 297
nativism, 15, 18, 20–21, 79, 87, 93, 155, 169, 178, 184, 223
Natural, The (Malamud), 177
naturalization, 98–99, 102–3, 106, 109
New Deal, the, 24
New England, 21, 78, 93–114, 177, 223, 225
Newfoundland, 68, 72
New York, 23, 31, 38, 45–47, 49–50, 52–56, 59–61, 83, 96–97, 118, 143–44, 156–57, 168–69, 176–78, 182–83, 195, 211, 239–40, 242, 261–62, 266, 268–69, 275, 283
New Zealand, 15–16, 19–21, 289–313
Ní Cheallacháin, Brighid, 258
Ní Chumhaill, Eithne, 255
Ní Dhomhnaill, Nuala, 30
Ní Éaluighthe, Cáit, 258
Ní Ghairbhfhiaich, Eibhlín, 258
Ní Líneacháin, Gobnait, 258
"Nora McShane" (song), 123
"Noreen Bawn" (song), 121
No Remittance (Davin), 297
Norwood (Mass.), 223–35
nursing, 24–25

Ó Baoighill, Mícheál, 257
Ó Beirn, Liam, 256
O'Brien, Flann, 289
O'Brien, Hugh, 168
O'Brien, John. *See* Hartigan, Rev. Patrick
O'Brien, Michael J., 76
Ó Cadhain, Máirtín, 263
Ó Ceallaigh, Colm, 263
Ó Cearbhaill, Seán, 260

Ó Ciarghusa, Seán, 261
Ó Cinnéide, León, 261
Ó Cinnfhaolaidh, Micheul, 261
Ó Conaire, Pádhraic Óg, 263
O'Connell, Daniel, 18, 23, 78, 86, 93, 278
O'Connor, Murrough, 65
O'Connor, Patrick, 194
O'Connor, T. P., 266, 278
Ó Curraidhín, S., 258
Ó Dálaigh, Seán, 257
O'Dowd, Bernard, 290
O'Driscoll, Robert, 5
Ó Dubhda, Peadar, 259–60
Ó Dubhghaill, Séamus, 253, 263
Ó Dúnaighe, Seán, 262
O'Faolain, Sean, 17
O'Farrell, Patrick, 5, 289
Ó Flatharta, Antoine, 263
Ó Flatharta, John Beag, 263
Ó Gallchobhair, Pádraig, 256
Ó Grianna, Séamus, 261
O'Hara, John, 223, 225
Oidhche sa Tabháirne (Saidléar), 262
"Old Bog Road, The" (song), 45
Old Mr. Flood (Mitchell), 59
Ó Mórdha, Séamus P., 261
Ó Neachtain, Joe Steve, 263
O'Neill, Shane, 272
Opper, Frederick, 153–72
Orangeism, 20, 77–78, 86, 293
O'Regan, Bishop Anthony, 193
O'Rourke, Orator Jim, 182
Orr, James, 65–74
Ó Sé, Maidhc Dainín, 263
Ó Séaghdha, Séamus, 260–61
Ó Siadhail, Pádraig, 263
Ó Súilleabháin, Seán, 117
O'Sullivan, Patrick, 6
O'Sullivan, Vincent, 291, 298
O'Toole, Fintan, 17
Ó Tuathaigh, M. A. G., 5

Paddy Murphy's Budget (Bracken), 291
Paisley, Ian, 88

Parnell, Charles Stewart, 151, 276–78, 297–98
Pearse, Patrick, 254, 276
Pearson, Bill, 291
penal laws, Irish, 81
Perrin, Noel, 58
Pilgrim's Progress (Bunyan), 307
Poetics (Aristotle), 306
poetry, 59, 65–68, 120, 128, 153, 168, 196, 229, 268–70, 272, 281, 283, 286, 291–93, 297, 303
politics, 16, 54–56, 78–82, 87, 143–44, 167, 168–70, 195, 215–16, 225–26
Poor Law Unions, Irish, 107–9
popes: John Paul II, 24; Leo XIII, 24, 168–69, 190; Pius X, 24; Pius XI, 24
Potter, George, 3
Powderly, Terence V., 23
Powers, "Johnny," 215–16
Presbyterianism, 15, 18, 59, 66, 75–80, 82–83, 85–86, 88, 196
Protestantism, 16, 18–21, 23, 47, 76–83, 85, 87–88, 145, 176, 189, 193–95, 211, 242, 276, 293–95
Puck, 152–75

Quadragesimo Anno (Pope Pius XI), 24
Quakers, 86
Québec, 262
Quinn, Peter, 56
Quinn, Roderick, 290

Rader, Benjamin, 179
Rafferty, Patrick, 195
Raftery, Anthony, 267–68, 272–74
Randolph, Rev. Warren, 198
Repeal Association, Irish, 93
Rerum Novarum (Pope Leo XIII), 24
Reynolds, Lorna, 5
Rich, Adrienne, 38
Richardson, Ethel Florence (pseud. Henry Handel Richardson), 290
Riess, Steven A., 179–80, 183
Roads from Home (Davin), 295

"Road to Rasheen, The" (song), 239
Robinson, Jackie, 177
Robinson, Lennox, 129
Roman Catholic Mutual Relief Society, 98
Rome, 23–24, 42, 146–48, 169, 172, 190–91, 196, 198, 267
Roosevelt, Franklin D., 24
Roosevelt, Theodore, 144
Rose, Wendy, 283
Rosenberg, Charles, 224
Rossa, Jeremiah O'Donovan, 170–72
Rush, Dr. Benjamin, 223
Ruskin, John, 189
Ryan, Monsignor John A., 24

Sacred Heart, Religious of the, 197, 198, 213
Saidléar, Annraoi, 262
Scanlan, John F., 214
Schrier, Arnold, 3
Scotch-Irish, 18, 59, 67, 75–84, 87–88, 267
Scots, 52, 66, 176, 273
Scott, Walter, 267
Seminole War, 85
servants, 24, 117, 152–54, 156–58, 166–68, 170–72, 184, 193
Seymour, Harold, 181
Shakespeare, William, 237, 239
Shannon, William V., 3
Shaw, George Bernard, 170
Sheanáin, Máire Nic Giolla, 262
Sheridan, Mother Elizabeth, 213
Shultz, A. B., 158
Singer, Isaac Bashevis, 29–30
Sisters of Charity of the Blessed Virgin Mary, 213
Skerrett, Ellen, 6
slavery (American), 84–87
"Slide, Kelly, Slide" (song), 176
Sloan, John, 57
Smyth, William J., 5
Snyder, Gary, 287

Songdogs (McCann), 281–82, 284–86
Songs of Raftery (Hyde), 267
South Africa, 15
South Dakota, 38–39
Spalding, A. G., 176, 177, 179, 183
Spink, Alfred H., 182
Starr, Ellen Gates, 189–90, 212, 215–16
Steinbeck, John, 266, 281
Stephenson, George M., 2
stereotypes, 17, 53, 126, 152–75, 178,
    181, 183–84, 259
Sterling, James, 65
Sterne, Laurence, 271
St. Louis, 82, 197
St. Paul, 19, 23–24
Stranger's Banquet, The (Byrne), 269–70
"Strawberry Fields Forever" (Lennon), 38
Studs Lonigan (Farrell), 138, 290
Such Is Life (Furphy), 290
Sullivan, John L., 6
Sunlit Field, The (L. Kennedy), 177–78
Sweeney, Charlie, 179
Swenson, Robert, 229
Swift, Jonathan, 289, 304
Swift, Roger, 5
Synge, John M., 278, 298

Takaki, Ronald, 4
Tammany Hall, 169
Taylor, John, 18
Tenants, The (Malamud), 34
Tenniel, John, 153
"That's How I Spell Ireland" (song), 53
theater, 16, 17–18, 46, 253, 259, 273
Thernstrom, Stephan, 3, 21
Third Avenue, New York (McNulty), 54
This Side of Brightness (McCann), 281
Thomas, Dylan, 294
Thomas, W. I., 224
Thomson, Samuel, 66
"Tiddly-Aye-Aye for the One-Eyed
    Reilly" (song), 54
Tiernan, Silent Mike, 182
Timon, Bishop John, 19

Tone, Wolfe, 246
Trillin, Calvin, 52
Truman, Harry, 40

Ulster, 15, 17–18, 20, 65–68, 75–83, 86–
    87, 98, 103, 106, 109, 272, 276–77,
    293
Ulysses (Joyce), 52, 273, 294
United Irishmen, 67, 78–79, 81, 86
United Irish Societies, 153
Up in the Old Hotel (Mitchell), 59
U2, 286

van Gennep, Arnold, 120
Van Osdel, John, 194, 197
Vietnam War, 223
Vinyard, Jo Ellen, 22

wakes: Irish, 117–18, 120–21, 125–29,
    227; American, 106, 117–30
Wales, J. A., 156, 169
Walker, Alice, 285
Wallace, R. S., 78
war, 20, 147, 184, 226, 268
War of 1812, 84
Washington, George, 38
Wellington, Duke of, 18
Wenders, Wim, 281
West (USA), 22, 67–68, 129, 193, 261,
    286
Whelan, Kevin, 79
Whelehan, J. B., 257
Whiskey Insurrection (1794), 79
"Whiskey, You're the Divil" (song), 54
White, Ryan, 38
Whitman, Walt, 28, 286, 287
Whyte, Laurence, 65–66
"Widow McGinnis's Pig" (song), 54
Wilde, Oscar, 298
Williams, William H. A., 6
Wilson, Helen, 291
Wilson, Woodrow, 82
Wittke, Carl, 2
Wolfe, Thomas, 28

Woolf, Michael Angelo, 155
Wordsworth, William, 67
World War I, 147, 223, 294
World War II, 53, 223, 293–95
Wyatt, Thomas, 303
Wyndham Act (1903), 172

Yeats, John Butler, 292
Yeats, William Butler, 60, 266, 267, 291,
    292, 298

DATE DUE

MY 27 '04			
OC 25 '06			
		WITHDRAWN	